Key Writii

Some titles are not available in North America.

Key Writings

Henri Bergson

Edited by
Keith Ansell Pearson and John Ó Maoilearca

Mélanges translated by
Melissa McMahon

BLOOMSBURY ACADEMIC
LONDON • NEW YORK • OXFORD • NEW DELHI • SYDNEY

BLOOMSBURY ACADEMIC
Bloomsbury Publishing Plc
50 Bedford Square, London, WC1B 3DP, UK

BLOOMSBURY, BLOOMSBURY ACADEMIC and the Diana logo
are trademarks of Bloomsbury Publishing Plc

English translation first published in 2002 by the Continuum
International Publishing Group Ltd
This Bloomsbury Revelations edition first published in 2014 by Bloomsbury Academic
Reprinted 2014 (twice), 2016 (twice), 2018, 2019

Bloomsbury Publishing Plc does not have any control over, or responsibility
for, any third-party websites referred to or in this book. All internet addresses
given in this book were correct at the time of going to press. The author
and publisher regret any inconvenience caused if addresses have changed or
sites have ceased to exist, but can accept no responsibility for any such changes.

A catalogue record for this book is available from the British Library.

Library of Congress Cataloging-in-Publication Data
Bergson, Henri, 1859-1941.
[Works. Selections. English. 2014]
Key writings / Henri Bergson; edited by Keith Ansell Pearson and John Ó Maoilearca;
translated by Melissa Mcmahon.
pages cm
Includes bibliographical references and index.
ISBN 978-1-4725-2801-8 (pbk. : alk. paper) – ISBN 978-1-4725-2178-1 (epub) –
ISBN 978-1-4725-3114-8 (epdf : alk) 1. Philosophy. I. Ansell-Pearson, Keith, 1960-
editor of compilation. II. Mcmahon, Melissa, editor of compilation. III. Title.
B2430.B381A57 2014
194–dc23
2013050018

ISBN: PB: 978-1-4725-2801-8

Series: Bloomsbury Revelations

Typeset by Newgen Knowledge Works (P) Ltd., Chennai, India
Printed and bound in Great Britain

To find out more about our authors and books visit www.bloomsbury.com
and sign up for our newsletters.

Contents

Abbreviations

Chronology of Life and Works

1859 18 October: Henri-Louis Bergson born, 18 rue Lamartine, Paris, the second son of four boys and three girls to Polish father, Michael Bergson (originally Berek-son) and English mother, from Doncaster in Yorkshire, Katherine Levison.

1869 Bergson family move to London (21 Shirland Road), Bergson remains in Paris and educated at lycée Fontaine (lycée Condorcet).

1877 Bergson wins first prize in mathematics for the Concours Général, and the 'plane solution of Pascal' is published the following year in the *Nouvelles Annates de Mathématiques*. Bergson's teacher, Desboves, would recount the solution in his *Etude sur Pascal et les géomètres contemporains.* At the time Bergson's future is seen to lie in geometry as he viewed things spatially. Bergson also distinguishes himself in philosophy, winning first prize with the essay 'Perceptions réelles et perceptions acquises'. Bergson expected to enter the Ecole Normale to study mathematics and his decision to study philosophy instead disappoints Desboves, who wrote to him, 'you will only be a philosopher and have missed your vocation'.

1878 Enters the Ecole Normale, in the same class as Jean Jaures, and Emile Durkheim is a fellow student. Bergson reads John Stuart Mill and Herbert Spencer, studying carefully the latter's *First Principles*, and initially attracted to materialism and mechanism. Bergson studying under the influence of his tutor, Emile Boutroux (author of works on the contingency of nature and the idea of natural law) and also Félix Ravaisson and Jules Lachelier.

1881 Leaves the Ecole Normale with an *agrégé de philosophie*. Begins a teaching post in Angers and enrols for a doctorate at the University of Paris.

1882 Takes up teaching post at the lycée Blaise-Pascal, Clermont-Ferrand.

1883 While at the lycée Blaise-Pascal publishes an edition of Lucretius' *De Rerum Natura* under the title of *Extraits de Lucrèce* with a commentary and notes.

In a letter to William James of 9 May 1908, Bergson singles out the years 1881–3 as a decisive period in his intellectual development: 'Until that point I had remained completely steeped in the mechanistic theories to which I had been introduced very early on by reading Herbert Spencer, the philosopher to whom I adhered more or less unreservedly'.[1] He tells James that he was awoken from his dogmatic mechanistic slumbers by the realization that 'scientific time has no *duration*'.

1886 Bergson publishes his first essay, 'De la simulation inconsciente dans l'état d'hypnotisme', in *Revue Philosophique*.

1888 Returns to Paris to teach, first at the Collège Rollin, then at the lycée Henri-Quatre as Professor of Rhetoric, where he remains until 1897. Submits two theses to the University of Paris: *Quid Aristoteles de loca sensorit?* (*What is Aristotle's Conception of Place?*) *and Essai sur les données immédiates de la conscience* (*Time and Free Will*).

1889 Bergson marries Louise Neuburger, aged 19, and cousin of Marcel Proust, who was a page-boy at the wedding. Later, on the publication of *Swann's Way*, the first volume of *A la recherche du temps perdu*, Proust would resist attempts to describe him as a Bergsonian novelist.

1896 Publishes *Matter and Memory*. William James wrote to Bergson that the work makes a Copernican Revolution and compares it to Berkeley's *Principles of Human Knowledge* and Kant's *Critique of Pure Reason*.

1897 Applies unsuccessfully, and second time round, for a post at the Sorbonne. Assumes position of *maître de conférences* at the Ecole Normale.

1900 Appointed Chair of Ancient Philosophy at the Collège de France, having been rejected the previous year, in favour of Gabriel Tarde, for the Chair of Modern Philosophy.

Publication of *Laughter: An Essay on the Meaning of the Comic*.

1901 Made a member of the *Académie des sciences morales et politiques*. 20 March: Presents a lecture on 'Dreams' at the Institut Psychologique, Paris.

1903 Publishes 'Introduction to metaphysics' in *Revue de métaphysique et de morale*.

1904 Transfers to Chair of Modern Philosophy at the Collège de France on the death of Gabriel Tarde.

1907 Publishes *Creative Evolution*. William James described the book as 'a real wonder in the history of philosophy'.

1908 William James lectures on Bergson as part of his 'Hibbert Lectures' delivered at Manchester College, Oxford, attacking Oxford idealism and calling for a 'radical empiricism' (published as *A Pluralistic Universe* in 1909).

1911 English translation of *Creative Evolution* appears, and in France a translation of James's *Pragmatism* is published with an Introduction, 'Verité et realité', by Bergson.

Delivers a paper on 'Philosophical intuition' at the Fourth International Congress of Philosophy, held in Bologna. Papers also delivered by Hans Driesch, Paul Langevin and Henri Poincaré. The same year he visits England and gives lectures at Oxford, Birmingham and London. On 26–7 May speaks at Oxford, in French, on the 'Perception of change', and receives an honorary doctorate. On 29 May gives the 'Huxley Lecture' on 'Life and consciousness' at Birmingham. October: lectures at University College London. Newspaper reports on the lectures speak of 'The new French philosophy' (*Glasgow Herald*), and of 'The Bergson cult' (*South African News*, *Daily Mail*).

1912 On leave from the Collège de France.

Bertrand Russell's article 'The philosophy of Bergson' is published in *The Monist*. Russell notes that as Bergson's philosophy cuts across all recognized divisions, whether empiricist, realist or idealist, any attempt to classify it will not meet with much success.

1913 January, makes the first of three visits to the United States, sailing to New York to gives lectures at Columbia University. Bergson is met on his arrival at Columbia by its librarian, who presents him with a pamphlet entitled 'A contribution to the bibliography of Henri Bergson' that lists hundreds of books and articles. Bergson also speaks at Princeton and Harvard in February.

    28 May: gives the Presidential Address to the Society for Psychical Research, London, with a paper entitled ' "Phantasms of the living" and psychical research'.

1914 Bergson elected a member of the *Académie française*, and resumes teaching duties at the Collège de France with courses on modern philosophy and the philosophy of Spinoza.

    April and May: delivers the Gifford Lectures on 'The problem of personality' at Edinburgh University.

    June: Bergson's philosophy is condemned by the Roman Catholic Church and his books are placed on the Index.

1917 January to May, Bergson returns to the USA as a special envoy of the French government, and meets President Wilson and his special aide, urging the American government to enter the war.

1918 Bergson visits the USA once again as an envoy from May to September.

1919 Publication of *Mind-Energy*.

1920 Bergson retires from the Collège de France (his Chair given to Edouard Le Roy). Receives honorary doctorate from Cambridge University.

1922 Meets Einstein at the Collège de France and publishes *Duration and Simultaneity*.

    Appointed President of the 'International Commission of Intellectual Co-operation' set up by the League of Nations.

1925 Severe arthritis forces Bergson to retire from public life.

1928 Awarded the Nobel Prize for Literature, though Bergson is unable to travel to Stockholm to receive it.

1932 Publishes his last major work, *The Two Sources of Morality and Religion*.

1933 A collection of essays, *La Pensée et le Mouvant* (*The Creative Mind*), published.

1937 February: Bergson prepares a will that prohibits the posthumous publication of any unedited papers.

1940 Bergson offered exemption from anti-Semitic regulations promulgated by the Nazis, but refuses and registers in Paris as a Jew.

1941 3 January: Bergson dies from a severe cold and is buried in the cemetery of Garches on the outskirts of Paris.

Introduction

This selection of key writings is designed to contribute to the task of reinstating Bergson as a major figure in modern European thought.[1] Bergson makes a number of important contributions to the staging of philosophical problems, problems concerning the nature of time, of consciousness, perception, representation and memory, of life and evolution. These problems continue to inform thinking to this day, and the fact that Bergson's contribution to them remains a vitally important one means he can also be regarded as our contemporary. Some of the innovations his thinking makes include the following:

1　To conceive of time in terms of duration and to insist that time not be confused with space.

2　To forge a distinction between two kinds of multiplicity, the continuous (virtual) and the discrete (actual).

3　To approach questions of metaphysics in terms of diverse planes of experience and different fields of knowledge.

4　To demonstrate the need to situate the theory of knowledge in the wider context of a theory of life.

In what follows we shall endeavour to illuminate something of the nature of these innovations and to do so by focusing largely on the material we have selected from the complete writings.[2]

Duration and the two multiplicities

Duration cannot be made the subject of a logical or mathematical treatment. This is owing to its character as a virtual multiplicity. Towards the end of part three of *Creative Evolution* Bergson turns to address the status of his construal of life in terms of an 'impetus' (the notorious if poorly understood *élan vital*). He explicitly conceives it in terms of a 'virtual multiplicity' (*virtuellement multiple*). He acknowledges that describing life in terms of an impetus is to offer little more than an image, an 'image of thought' as it were. The image, however, is intended to disclose something about the essential character of life, namely, that it is not of a mathematical or logical order but a psychological one. The term psychological might appear to be a troubling one to use in this context. But Bergson uses it for a specific reason, as the following reveals: 'In reality, life is of the psychological order, and it is of the essence of the psychical to enfold a confused plurality of interpenetrating terms' (*CE*, p. 257). The contrast he is making is with space, in which the multiplicity posited or found therein will be of a distinct kind, that is, one made up of discrete elements or components that are related to one another in specific terms, namely, relations of juxtaposition and exteriority. Bergson argues that 'abstract unity' and 'abstract multiplicity' are determinations of space *and* categories of the understanding (that is, they are schemas imposed upon the real in order to make it something uniform, regular, and calculable *for us*). He then goes on to argue that what is psychical in nature cannot entirely correspond with space or fit neatly into categories of the understanding (take, for example, the question: is a person at any moment one or manifold?).

In his first published work *Time and Free Will* (*TFW*) Bergson had sought to show that the actuality of our psychic states presupposes a virtual multiplicity of duration. The different degrees of a mental state correspond to qualitative changes, changes that do not admit of simple measure or number. When we ordinarily speak of time we think of a homogeneous medium in which our conscious states are placed alongside one another as in space, and so form a discrete multiplicity. The question is whether the multiplicity of our psychic states resembles the multiplicity of the units of number and whether duration has anything to do with space. If time is simply a medium in which our conscious states are strung out as a discrete series that can be counted, then time would indeed be space. The question Bergson poses is whether time can legitimately be treared as such a medium.

It is in chapter 2 of *TFW* that Bergson will make central to his argument the distinction between two kinds of multiplicity. This material has been extracted from the book and is presented here in full. The distinction Bergson draws between the discrete and the continuous represents a reworking of a distinction initially introduced by the mathematician G. B. Riemann, who had utilized the distinction in his 1854 *Habilitationsschrift* entitled 'On the hypotheses which provide the grounds for geometry'. Riemann forged a distinction between a discrete multiplicity or manifoldness that contains the principle of its metrical division (the measure of one part is given by the number of elements in a multiplicity) and a continuous multiplicity in which the metrical principle is located in the binding forces which act upon it. Definite or distinct portions of a multiplicity are distinguished by a mark or a boundary. In the case of both multiplicities, therefore, we are dealing with an issue of 'Quanta'. In the case of a discrete magnitude we make the comparison with quantity by counting, and in the case of a continuous one by measuring. The measure consists either in the superposition of the magnitudes to be compared (which requires a means of using one magnitude to act as the standard for another) or, where this is not possible, comparing two magnitudes when one is a part of the other (in this case it is possible only to determine the more or less and not the how much). This makes for an interesting case of magnitudes since it refers us to ones that cannot be treated independently of position or as ever expressible in terms of a unit, but rather as 'regions in a manifoldness'.

Gilles Deleuze has argued that Bergson was well aware of the contribution of Riemann and that an indirect engagement with him informs the treatment of Relativity in *Duration and Simultaneity* (*DS*) (Deleuze 1991, p. 39). Bergson's contribution is to transform the nature of the distinction between the two multiplicities by linking the continuous with the realm of duration. Deleuze's claim is that:

> for Bergson, duration was not simply the indivisible, nor was it the nonmeasurable. Rather, it was that which divided only by changing in kind, that which was susceptible to measurement only by varying

its metrical principle at each stage of the division. Bergson did not confine himself to opposing a philosophical vision of duration to a scientific conception of space but took the problem into the sphere of two kinds of multiplicity. He thought that the multiplicity proper to duration had, for its part, a 'precision' as great as that of science; moreover, that it should react upon science and open up a path for it that was not necessarily the same as that of Riemann and Einstein. (ibid., p. 40)

Deleuze maintains that Bergson's usage of multiplicity is not part of the traditional vocabulary, especially when thought in relation to a continuum. And as Robin Durie astutely points out, Bergson 'does not begin with a predetermined concept of time', from which could then be derived the nature of temporal relations. Instead, the procedure is to discover 'the formally determinate relations which determine the "objects" comprising differing provinces' and from this discovery the two concepts of time (duration and spatial time) are articulated on the basis of the relations determining the multiplicities.[3] With a non-numerical multiplicity we can speak of 'indivisibles' at each stage of the division: a multiplicity like a qualitative duration divides but each time it does it changes in kind. In this way there '*is other* without there being *several*'; number exists only potentially (Deleuze 1991, p. 42). There is more than is actually present at any single moment and a change will always be qualitative. In a non-numerical multiplicity not everything is actual. In contrast, in a numerical multiplicity everything is actual although it may not be realized. Thus, when something does get realized it simply has existence added to it, it does not change its nature.

Is time space?

Are states of consciousness external to one another and spread out in time as a spatial medium? Looked at from the perspective of pure duration our states can be seen to permeate and melt into one another without precise outlines and without any affiliation with number, in which past and present states form a whole, 'as happens when we recall the notes of a tune, melting, so to speak, into one another' (*TFW*, p. 100; see below, p. 72). These are involved in qualitative changes that disclose a 'pure heterogeneity'. When we interrupt the rhythm of a tune by perhaps dwelling longer than is customary on one note, it is not the exaggerated length that signals the mistake to us but rather the qualitative change caused in the whole of the piece of music.

> We can thus conceive of succession without distinction, and think of it as a mutual penetration, an interconnexion and organization of elements, each one of which represents the whole, and cannot be distinguished or isolated from it except by abstract thought. (*TFW*, p. 101; see below, p. 73)

Duration is non-representational, and as soon as we think it we necessarily spatialize it (which clearly presents a major, if not insuperable, problem for any thinking of duration). It could be called an intensive magnitude 'if intensities can be called magnitudes' (*TFW*, p. 106; see below, p. 76). Bergson hesitates on this point because he does not wish to treat duration as a quantity. Because we have the idea of space we set our states side by side so as to perceive them simultaneously: we project time into space, express duration in terms of extensity, and succession assumes the form of a continuous chain. A decisive movement or shift takes place in our thinking, albeit one we are ordinarily not aware of:

> Note that the mental image thus shaped implies the perception, no longer successive, but simultaneous, of a *before* and *after*, and that it would be a contradiction to suppose a succession which was only a succession, and which nevertheless was contained in one and the same instant. (*TFW*; see below, p. 73)

The important point is this: we could not introduce order into terms without first distinguishing them and then comparing the places they occupy. As Bergson writes, 'if we introduce an order in what is successive, the reason is that succession is converted into simultaneity and is projected into space' (p. 102; see below, p. 73). Moreover, since the idea of a reversible series in duration, even of a certain *order* of succession in time, itself implies the representation of space, it cannot be used to define it.

Reducing time to simple movement of position is to confuse time with space. It is this confusion between motion and the space traversed which explains the paradoxes of Zeno. The interval between two points is infinitely divisible, and if motion is said to consist of parts like those of the interval itself, then the interval can never be crossed. But the truth of the matter is different:

> each of Achilles' steps is a simple indivisible act . . . after a given number of these acts, Achilles will have passed the tortoise. The mistake of the Eleatics arises from their identification of this series of acts, each of which is *of a definite kind and indivisible*, with the homogeneous space which underlies them. (p. 113; see below, p. 79)

Because this space can be divided and put together again according to any kind of abstract law, the illusion arises that it is possible to reconstruct the movement of Achilles not with his step but with that of the tortoise. In truth, we have only two tortoises that agree to make the same kind of steps or simultaneous acts so never to catch one another. Let us now take the paradox of the flying arrow which at any point is not in flight. If the arrow is always at a point, when is it ever in flight or mobile? Instead, we might ask, what is it in this example that leads us to saying that the arrow *is* at any point in its course? (admittedly, it might be, but only in the sense of it passing and stopping at a particular point, at which point it would come to rest and its flight would cease). Within any posited motionless trajectory it is possible to count as many immobilities as we like. What we fail to see is that 'the trajectory is created in one stroke, although a certain time is required for it; and that although we can divide at will the trajectory once created, we cannot divide its creation, which is an act in progress and not a thing' (*CE*, p. 309).

The key insight concerns the difference between extensity and intensity: the space traversed is a matter of extension and quantity (it is divisible), but the movement is an intensive act and a quality. Bergson is insistent that it is 'through the quality of quantity that we form the idea of quantity without quality', not the other way round. Qualitative operations are even at work in the formation of numbers (the addition of a third unit to two others alters the nature, the rhythm, of the whole, even though our spatial habits lead us to disregard the significance of these qualitative aspects) (*TFW*, p. 123; see below, p. 85).

Bergson contrasts psychic time with clock time. It is the latter that treats time as a magnitude (pp. 107–8; see below, p. 77). Motion, however, in so far as it is a passage from one point to another, 'is a mental synthesis, a psychic and therefore unextended process . . . If consciousness is aware of anything more than positions, the reason is that it keeps the successive positions in mind and synthesizes them' (p. 111; see below, p. 78). The conclusion is reached in *TFW* that 'the interval of duration exists only for us and on account of the interpenetration of our conscious states'. Outside ourselves we find only space, and consequently nothing but simultaneities, 'of which we could not even say that they are objectively successive, since succession can only be thought through *comparing* the present with the past' (p. 116; see below, p. 81). The qualitative impression of change cannot, therefore, be felt outside consciousness. Duration and motion are not objects but 'mental syntheses' (p. 120; see below, p. 83). In our consciousness, states permeate one another, imperceptibly organize themselves into a whole, and bind the past to the present. Conceived as a virtual, qualitative multiplicity, this duration 'contains number only potentially, as Aristotle would have said' (p. 121; see below, p. 84). Does this mean that duration, conceived as a pure heterogeneity, is simply an aspect of consciousness, that is, is it something solely phenomenological or psychological and peculiar to the way in which we experience the world?

This restriction of duration to consciousness is one that Bergson will seek to overcome in subsequent texts. This requires breaking down the form/matter opposition that structures his account of mind and the world in *TFW*. Even in this work Bergson is already aware of the problems connected with any account which construes the relation between mind and world in terms of a form simply being imposed upon matter: 'assuming that the forms alluded to, into which we fit matter, come entirely from the mind, it seems difficult to apply them constantly to objects without the latter soon leaving their mark on them . . . forms applicable to things cannot be entirely our own work . . . if we give much to matter we probably receive something from it . . .' (p. 223). It is in *Matter and Memory* (*MM*) that Bergson will provide a very different account of matter and perception. He now seeks to show that the real is made up of *both* extensity and duration, but this 'extent' is not that of some infinite and infinitely divisible space, the space of a receptacle, that the intellect posits as the place in which and from which everything is built. It is necessary, then, to separate a concrete extension, diversified and organized at the same time, from 'the amorphous and inert space which subtends it' (*MM*, p. 187). This is the space that we divide indefinitely and within which we conceive movement as a multiplicity of instantaneous positions. Homogeneous space is not, then, logically anterior to material things but posterior to them.

Bergson and Russell on continuity

There have been a number of criticisms of Bergson's account of duration. Often these centre on privileging a mathematical treatment of continuity over a philosophical one. In Lecture V of his *Our Knowledge of the External World* on 'The theory of continuity', Bertrand Russell, for example, proclaims that continuity is a purely mathematical subject and not, strictly speaking, part of philosophy. A notion of change must fit into a logical framework, with the result that logical necessity compels us to a conception of 'instants without duration' (Russell 1922, p. 158).

It needs to be made clear: in privileging a mathematical treatment of continuity Russell is not contesting Bergson's stress on continuity and falling back on discontinuous states; rather, the difference is over how continuity is to be thought and mapped out. This explains why he is able to appreciate the force of Bergson's exposition of Zeno's paradoxes while at the same time insisting on the need to think the continuity of motion in a different way to the 'interpenetrarion' argument of Bergson. For Russell, however, the force of Bergson's exposition only holds if we accept the initial force of Zeno's paradoxes, and he doesn't: 'A cinematograph in which there are an infinite number of films, and in which there is never a *next* film because an infinite number come between any two, will perfectly represent a continuous motion. Wherein, then, lies the force of Zeno's argument?' (1922, p. 339).[4] Before we explore this further by looking at the lecture on the theory of continuity, let us just pause to note the paradoxical nature of Russell's own position (he has answered Zeno by substituting one paradox for another). In evincing the argument that motion can be shown to be continuous because there is never anything that comes next, Russell has deprived the movement of time itself, as a movement of virtual time (the coexistence or immanence of past and present), of any efficacy and replaced this movement with an infinite number of discrete motions. In short, he is seeking to construct continuity out of discreteness. Russell has replaced a philosophical treatment of time (a virtual multiplicity) with a mathematical one (a numerical multiplicity).

In this lecture Russell is concerned to reconcile the philosophical and the logical: how can the mathematical treatment of time in terms of points and instants be squared with our feeling, intimated at by many philosophers, that time is a continuity? His response is to say that while it is wrong to divide time into a *finite* number of points and instants, the correct way forward, one that will stop us from falling back into Bergson's confused response to Zeno, is to appeal to an *infinite* number of these points and instants. But surely won't infinitely numerous points and instants simply provide us with a jerky motion and a succession of different immobilities? Russell raises this question himself and answers it by saying that to assume this to be the case is to fail to realize, both imaginatively and abstractly, the nature of a continuous series as understood in mathematics. In short, we lack the *intuition* to conceive of such a continuity and we need to learn how, says Russell, to *feel* its complete adequacy and validity (1922, p. 136).

Russell seeks to show that when mathematics thinks continuity it does so in terms of it being a property of a series of terms, which is to suppose an 'order' or arrangement of time, in which something comes before something else (though this is not required, he notes, in the theory of cardinal number). Thus, continuity does not belong to a set of terms themselves but to a set in a certain order (in this case we can say that in the example of continuity the relations established are always external to their terms). Russell then introduces his idea of 'compactness' as a way of accounting for the lowest degree of continuity within the arrangement of any series: 'A series is called "compact" when no two terms are consecutive, but between any two there are others' (p. 138), and he gives the simple example of a series of fractions in order of magnitude. Between any two fractions, however small the difference, there can be posited an infinite number of other fractions. Now while mathematical space and time have the property of compactness, it is not clear that we can extend this to actual space and time. It seems as if mathematics reaches an empirical limit at this point. But this is not enough to stop Russell from persisting with this logicizing of space and time.

In short, Russell reaches the view that there are no discontinuous leaps in something changing from one state or position to another; rather, continuity is to be thought in terms of an infinite number of positions. This explains why it is illegitimate, he argues, to say what something will be at the next instant or where it will be in its next position – there are no such 'nexts'. The movement of time is to be conceived then not in terms of *consecutive* points and instants but rather in terms of a *continuous series* of infinite points and instants. It is important we get Russell right on this point and not commit a logical blunder. It would be mistaken to suppose that he is arguing with this model that between the positions and states of things there are infinitesimal distances in space or periods of time, and that it is this which allows us to multiply indefinitely the points and instants. This is clearly not the case. His argument is rather that in a continuous motion the interval between any two positions and instants is always finite; the continuity lies solely in the fact that, however near together the two positions or instants are taken to be, 'there are an infinite number of positions still nearer together, which are occupied at instants that are also still nearer together' (p. 142). This means that a moving body 'never jumps from one position to another, but always passes by a gradual transition through an infinite number of intermediaries' (ibid.). No instant, therefore, can be said to last for a finite time and neither can it be said that an instant has a beginning and an end. The conclusion is reached that although the facts or logic itself do not necessitate this model of continuous motion in terms of a particular conception of points and instants, it is at least 'consistent' with the facts and with logic. Whether this defence rests on a vicious circle will not be discussed here; we simply wish to note that time has been thought away on this mathematical model, which, in spite of its criticism of the consecutive, is still a model of points and instants in accordance with a discrete or an actual multiplicity.

We might now ask, what is the relation between this mathematical treatment of continuity and *actual* space and time? This is an issue that is raised by Russell himself. He adopts the position that while points and instants cannot be taken to be actual physically existing entities we can posit an analogy between the continuity of actual space and time and the continuity that mathematics works with. However, he also wishes to stress that the theory of mathematical continuity is an abstract logical theory, the validity of which is *not* dependent upon any properties of actual space and time (Russell 1922, pp. 135–58, p. 137). But this is not the whole of Russell's position, for he also argues that the logical theory has more empirical purchase than any other theory, including what he takes to be its major rival, that of Bergson. He speaks of translating the propositions of physics into propositions about objects given to us in sensation 'by a sort of dictionary' (p. 147). Although he has no such basis upon which to make the claim, he argues that within the sphere of immediate sense-data it is both necessary and more consonant with the facts than any other view to distinguish states of objects as instantaneous ones which form a compact series. What he will not allow is that Bergson's conception of time as a virtual multiplicity has any empirical purchase whatsoever; it is rather to be understood solely in terms of an illusion of experience and a mistaken inference from available sense-data. Now, this is clear evidence of an outright dogmatism on the part of Russell's logicism. This is so because he has clearly stated that we know very little from the evidence of our sense-data about the empirical character of space and time, and yet he is insistent that the choice to be made is not between a philosophical thinking of time and a mathematical one, but rather choosing between various mathematical alternatives. For Russell the empirical data can be read in all sorts of ways, and this means that we are simply dealing with certain *logical* difficulties, such as our failure of imagination and abstraction when it comes to appreciating how a continuous series can be thought in terms of infinite numbers within mathematics. This means, in effect, that while the mathematical account of continuity is not dependent for its validity upon any properties of actual space and time, it arrogates to itself the right to dictate what should be the proper *philosophical* account of space and time.

Towards an ontology of duration

Bergson's thinking of time undergoes some major and quite dramatic shifts after *TFW*. In the first work he is clearly adhering to the view that the experience of duration requires an act of mental synthesis and thus time is a phenomenon of consciousness and something solely inner or psychological (external reality is simply space). The innovation of this work lies not in any new cosmology or theory of evolution but in its conception of time as a non-spatial and continuous multiplicity. In *MM* he speculates whether non-spatial time or duration can be extended to external things – do they endure in their own way? – and although he ends producing a vision of matter that he believes will fatigue our intellect, he remains undecided on the issue. By the time of *CE* he has reached the view that duration is 'immanent to the universe', and aims to show that duration is the key notion for understanding the creative character of evolution. He seeks to show that physics deals with closed and artificial systems in which time has been left out of the picture. Once we apply ourselves to the movement of the 'whole' then duration has to be admitted into our account of the evolution of life.

Deleuze has argued that in Bergson duration comes to be seen less and less as reducible to a psychological experience and becomes instead the 'variable essence of things'; in short, it becomes an ontology (Deleuze 1991, p. 34). The question 'Do external things endure?' can only remain indeterminate from the standpoint of psychological experience. If external things do not endure and duration is a phenomenon of consciousness only, then the danger arises of it being readily treated as a subjective determination (that of a mere appearance). Deleuze cites Bergson himself on the issue: 'Although things do not endure as we do, nevertheless there must be some incomprehensible reason why phenomena are seen to *succeed* one another instead of being set out all at once' (ibid., p. 48; quoting from *TFW*, p. 227). If it can be demonstrated that movement belongs to things as much as to consciousness then movement will not be confused with psychological duration; rather, as Deleuze put it in his *Bergsonism*, 'Psychological duration should be only a clearly determined case, an opening onto *ontological* duration' (ibid., pp. 48–9).

The articulation of duration as immanent to the whole of the universe informs Bergson's stress in *CE* on the study of life or living systems over the claims of physics and chemistry, which, he contends, deal only with closed or isolated systems. Evolution has a history and an irreversibility to it. Whereas in the first book, *TFW*, he had seen only psychic states as non-mechanical and non-determined, contesting in the process the application of the law of the conservation of energy to the domain of psychology, in *CE* he now wants to extend this to claims about the evolution of life. 'The universe *endures*' is the key opening claim of the book. Bergson then writes: 'The more we study the nature of time, the more we shall comprehend that duration means invention, the creation of forms, the continual elaboration of the absolutely new' (that is, it is not a mere rearrangement of parts) (*CE*, p. 11; see below, p. 216 Just as key is this claim: 'There is no reason, therefore, why a duration, and so a form of existence like our own, should not be attributed to the systems that science isolates, provided such systems are reintegrated into the Whole' (p. 177). Consider the way in which our perception construes an object in terms of distinct outlines. This distinct individuality of an object is no more than the design of a certain kind of influence we exert on a certain point of space. The universal interaction between things is halted (this provides us with an insight into what Bergson means by the 'whole'). Science does the same in constituting isolable systems, that is it extracts them from the movement of the whole that they are implicated in: 'let me say I am perfectly willing to admit that the future states of a closed system of material points are calculable and hence visible in its present state. But . . . this system is extracted, or abstracted, from a whole which, in addition to inert and unorganised matter, comprises organization' (*CM*, p. 103; see below, p. 281). Now, Bergson does not deny that the material world is made up of individuated bodies (organisms) or that nature itself has carved out relatively closed systems, but this is not the whole of the picture and conforms in large part to our mental habits and evolutionary needs, in short, to our diagrammatic designs upon reality. The categories of the understanding – categories that also inform science to a large degree – provide us with access to one line of the real but it also blocks off access to other lines, which are treated as merely 'metaphysical' and in need of a critique.

What needs to be overcome, then, are certain ingrained habits of the mind, habits which also inform how science approaches the real, such as:

1   the view that change is reducible to an arrangement or rearrangement of parts or that change merely involves a change of position regarding unchangeable things;

2   that the irreversibility of time is only an appearance relative to our ignorance and that the impossibility of turning back is only a

human inability to put things in place again (consider the illusion of time travel);

3   that time has only as much reality for a living system as an hour-glass. We are fixated on reducing time to instants (mathematical points). This is to deny time any positive reality and to think it spatially. In Einsteinian Relativity, for example, what is measured is the abstract and quantitative simultaneity of two clock readings according to a convention for determining under which circumstances they should be called simultaneous.

With regard to our treatment of evolution the dominant conception we have is one where duration and invention are lacking; there are merely pre-formed possibilities which are then brought into being by being realized. Of course Bergson appreciates the important contribution Darwinism makes to a theory of evolution, but argues that every generation of form is bound up with a unique history that reflects specific durational conditions of existence. In other words, the Darwinian conditions of life, such as adaptation, are built into the evolving life-form, 'they are peculiar to that phase of its history in which life finds itself at the moment of producing the form' (*CE*, p. 28; see below, p. 225). Let us suppose that life is indeed mechanism. This still leaves the question of what kind of mechanism: 'is it the mechanism of parts artificially isolated within the whole of the universe, or is it the mechanism of the real whole?' What does Bergson mean? If we posit the 'real whole' as an indivisible continuity then the systems we cut out within it would not, strictly speaking, be parts but rather '*partial* views of the whole' (p. 31; see below, p. 227).

Bergson's thought is first and foremost a pluralism and an empiricism.[5] Its complicated character as a practice of philosophy stems from the fact that it also makes use of typically idealist categories like the 'whole' and the 'image'. Such notions, however, are really part of an attempted 'superior' empiricism. The 'whole', for example, cannot be approached in terms of ready-made criteria of an organic totality. The pluralist and the empiricist will thus invoke and appeal to a whole that is only ever the whole of an acentred mobile continuity, a continuity of moving parts and wholes in which the 'whole' that they are implicated in does not denote an organic unity. Even when we think the whole on the level of life it is not necessary that we posit either a logical development or approach evolution with a set of organicist prejudices.

Matter, perception and memory

MM is a book that has perplexed and beguiled its readers since it was first published in 1896. William James compared its effect to a Copernican Revolution, making it a philosophical work to be ranked with Berkeley's *Principles of Human Knowledge* and Kant's *Critique of Pure Reason.* Unlike the revolutions of Berkeley and Kant, however, that effected by Bergson in *MM* consists in neither reducing the world to our perception or idea of it nor restricting knowledge of it to our *a priori* sensible and cognitive forms. It is not until the final part of the book that the true nature of Bergson's revolution becomes clear when he insists that nature goes beyond our representation of it and aims to present a vision of matter that is fatiguing for the intellect. Indeed, the opening part of the book gives the impression that Bergson is a kind of idealist or empiricist in the Berkeleyean sense. The book cannot, then, be read without due regard for its complex movements of thought. *MM* is a text that anticipates many of the recent moves made in the philosophy of mind, such as the stress on approaching perception not in terms representational but rather as bound up with the action and movement of a body, and on consciousness as an emergent property of a network or assemblage of components; it is only abstractly that we can separate brain, body and world.[6]

Chapter 1, reproduced here in full, unfolds the argument that perception is not an interior subjective vision, or some mysterious manifestation of matter. The perception of a consciousness has its basis in an impersonal perception that is common to matter in its simplest mode. To demonstrate this Bergson uses the notion of a 'pure perception', a perception without memory. It is also in the opening chapter that Bergson will approach the question of matter and its perception in terms of the notion of image. He uses this notion extensively: chapter 1 of the book is devoted to the 'selection of images', chapter 2 to the 'recognition of images', chapter 3 to the 'survival of images' (parts of which we have included in this reader) and chapter 4 to the 'delimiting and fixing of images'. All becomes image on his model, including the body, nerve centres, the brain, etc. (in the essay on 'Brain and thought' in *Mind-Energy*, which we have included here, these get described as 'ideas'). The notion has more than one sense in Bergson, and the tensions within his usage reflect its complex application in the history of philosophy.

The difficulty in determining the precise character of Bergson's philosophical position in *MM* is compounded by the fact that he makes concessions to idealism – for example, in his very usage of the term image – and sees it an inevitable component in our thinking about the world. He ultimately wants to move beyond idealism, whether in its Berkeleyean or Kantian presentation, and he aims to show how this is possible (Kant is depicted as both an idealist and a realist in the book so as not to equate his position with Berkeley's). One of the novel aspects of the book is how it aims to show that realism also ends up in an idealist trap. Briefly: for the idealist the world is the product of our ideas and cannot exist independently of them. For the realist (sometimes called a materialist) the mental is reduced to the cerebral and in this way the brain is made into the progenitor of our representations of the world. Bergson will take both to task for reducing the relation of the body to the world into one of speculative knowledge as opposed to vital activity. Realism becomes an idealism when it locates perception and consciousness in a centre or some detached isolated object, which has the effect of divorcing embodied cognition from its conditions of action in the world.[7] Both idealism and realism err in making the presentation of the part – the mind or the brain – equivalent to the presentation of the whole (the real).

Bergson is not committed to a strong Berkeleyean position (images exist only when perceived), for he will go on to argue that images exist when unperceived. By describing the objects of matter and of the world as images Bergson is suggesting that they have the potential to be perceived.[8] A key question guides Bergson's analysis in chapter 1. He poses it as follows: What is the relation between the image I term my body, which is an image that occupies a centre, and the image I call the universe? Moreover, how is it possible for the same images to belong at one and the same time to two different systems, to one in which each image varies for itself and another in which images change for a single image that occupies a privileged centre? To see why Bergson should raise this question about the existence of these two systems of images we have to jump ahead a little in the unfolding of the argument and appreciate that Bergson gives primacy to a continuity of material extensity. In its aspects this continuity changes from moment to moment and can be conceived in terms of a whole that changes like a kaleidoscope: there is no centre since everything is bound together in relations. Indeed, Bergson argues that empiricism has only a vague conception of the artificial character of the relations uniting the terms, but it holds to these terms and neglects the relations (*MM*, p. 183). Once we have artificially broken up the moving continuity of the whole we seek to re-establish the unions and bonds that exist between things, but we do so by replacing a 'living unity' with an empty diagram that is as 'lifeless as the parts which it holds together' in which relations are being conceived in logical and spatial terms. In addition to the moving whole of this material extensity we also speak of bodies with clearly defined outlines – they have their own substance and individuality – and which move in terms of their relations with each other. Bergson begins from the perspective of the continuity of a moving whole since he thinks this offers us the best chance of explaining the formation of individuated bodies (they first emerge from it as 'zones of indetermination'). At the same time, however, he is concerned to expose the illusions that the intellect generates for itself in its neglect of the whole: generating, for example, the illusion of bodies changing in homogeneous space, a space which is then extended to time itself.

My body is unique in that I do not simply know it 'from without' in terms of perception but also 'from within', as it were, in terms of 'affections', which interpose themselves between the excitations a body receives from the outside and the movements it executes in response. My body exists, then, amidst the aggregate of images that makes up the material world, and, as such, it can only be regarded as one image amongst many which, like other images, receives movement and gives it back. It is at this point that Bergson begins to describe everything as image: afferent and efferent nerves, the brain, my body, and so on. If the brain is an image existing in the material world among other images, then it cannot be reified into the condition upon which the *whole* image of the world depends (that is, its part cannot be made equivalent to the whole): 'Neither nerves nor nerve centres can, then, condition the image of the universe' (*MM*, p. 19; see below, p. 104). Moreover, in claiming that the brain is part of the material world, and resisting the view that the material world is somehow contained in the physical entity we call the bounded brain, Bergson is aiming to show that if the image that is the material world is eliminated then we at the same time destroy the brain and its cerebral disturbances: the brain cannot exist in the absence of the images of the material world. This leads him to exposing what he calls 'the fiction of an isolated material object', which results in an absurd position, namely, that such an object as the nervous system, in its physical properties, can exist independently of its relations with the rest of the universe, such as the organism which nourishes it, the body that houses it and the atmosphere of the earth that envelops the organism, and so on. If we keep hold of the relations then it makes no sense to reduce perceptions to the molecular movements of the cerebral mass, simply because these movements remain bound up with the rest of the material world. In addition, Bergson advances the argument that on the model he has constructed it can be seen that the body, as a living centre, is first and foremost a centre of action and not a house of representation. It is not abstracted from the world, simply contemplative in relation to it; rather it is intimately bound up with it and with its movements, with actions and reactions. Replacing the self-transparency of the Cartesian *cogito* with the isolated brain divorced from the images that inform it leads to the illusion that if we could penetrate into the inside of the brain it would be possible to understand the phenomenon of consciousness simply by observing the dance of the atoms of the cortex. This is to commit the error of positing a simple, linear or automatic account of the relation between the cerebral and the mental. Bergson does not deny that there is a relation, only that it is one of either parallelism or epipheno-menalism. Psychic life can be said to be highly varied, varying in accordance with the 'attention to life' and made up of diverse tones and rhythms.

It is important to appreciate the unorthodox character of Bergson's utilization of the notion of image. His usage does not conform to certain patterns that have established themselves within our thinking, such as the classic divisions of subject and object, mind and matter. He neither construes the problem of perception or consciousness in representational terms nor does he hold that images are simply in our heads.[9] The person who might wish to claim that although the world is not dependent on our consciousness – it would still exist should the consciousness that reflects on the being of its being disappear – the images our minds produce of it are dependent on our consciousness, is not even entitled to say this on Bergson's model. But, we might ask, why construe the brain as an image or idea? Is this not already to concede too much to idealism (all that I know of the brain is what I perceive of it or what is available to me as an idea)? What sense does it make to describe nerve centres as images? Perhaps it is useful to bear in mind that in the opening chapter of the book Bergson is thinking in terms of common sense and has not yet, at this point in the book, developed an engagement with the realism of science. On an initial phenomenological level, therefore, matter is how it appears, simply as image. But this is not an adequate way to characterize Bergson's position, simply because his approach is not one which privileges an intentional consciousness. In the essay of 1904 on 'Brain and thought' Bergson picks up this conception again and speaks of nerve centres as images in the sense of 'moving pictures' that contain 'movable parts', taking in movements from the outside and producing in response internal movements. On this level, therefore, all that the brain is doing is receiving the influences from the movements of other images and responding to them. It exists only as a part in relation to the whole, it is not identical with this whole (the moving-images that compose the material universe). It is clear that Bergson has deployed an idealist category in an unconventional sense. For Bergson if the world is approached as an aggregate of images then it makes little sense to ask whether the world is within or without us. This is because 'interiority and exteriority are only relations among images'. Thus, 'to ask whether the universe exists only in our thought, or outside of our thought, is to put the problem in terms that are insoluble, even if we suppose them to be intelligible' (p. 25; see below, p. 109).

It is in the context of this insistence upon matter as image that Bergson begins to develop his claim that perception operates in a subtractive fashion. Although such a conception of perception is often held to be one of the distinctive features of Bergson's thought, it can already be found articulated in strikingly similar terms in earlier thinkers, such as Schopenhauer and Nietzsche, for example. Bergson invites us to think about the difference between 'presence' and 'representation', a difference that seems to explain the 'interval' between matter and its conscious perception. He argues that if we were to move from the one to the other in terms of adding something – the representation of matter being greater than its simple presence – then the passage from matter to perception becomes mysterious. If we make the less obvious move and construe perception as involving a narrowing or subtracting of the real then the passage to perception can be rendered intelligible.

Bergson does not deny that there is a relation between the cerebral and the mental, only that the two are completely identical. It is a category mistake to infer from an analysis of the brain that motor activity functions autonomously and can assume the role of some miraculous generator of our perception of the world. The character of movement differs in accordance with the differences between visual, auditory and tactile impressions. Perceptions do not spring from automatic sensory vibrations but rather from the kind of questions posed to motor activity. A great deal of neuroscience, and what passes for the philosophy of mind, inadvertently produces an idealism of the cerebral substance by severing motor activity from the processes of perception, localizing perception in the sensory nervous elements. But this is an error in thinking: 'the truth is that perception is no more in the sensory centres than in the motor centres; it measures the complexity of their relations, and is, in fact, where it appears to be' (p. 46; see below, p. 25). The view that Bergson wishes to combat most is that which would, in treating sensations merely as signals in which the office of each sense is to translate homogeneous and mechanical movements into its language, posit on the one hand homogeneous movements in space and, on the other, extended sensations in consciousness (a quantitative outside and a qualitative inside). In contrast with this view Bergson wishes to argue that the identity resides not between the cerebral and the mental or spiritual, but rather between the real action of sensory elements and the *virtual* action of perception (including the motor diagrams).[10] Thus, perception is a part of things (it is not an interior, subjective vision), just as an affective sensation (such as the capacity to experience pain or pleasure) does not spring from the depths of inner consciousness by extending itself into an outer realm (affection is not a simple movement from an inner intensive state to an outer extensity), simply because it is intimately bound up with the modifications which inform the movement of one body with other bodies.

In chapters 2 and 3 of the book Bergson shifts his attention to memory and develops his well-known claim that memory-images are not stored in the brain and unfolds his distinction between psychological memory, the memory of habit-formation (a bodily memory), and an ontological memory (the memory of pure recollection). The movement of his thought here is subtle and can easily mislead, for there are two phases to the presentation of his theory. On the one hand, Bergson gives us an explanation of *recollection* that espouses a dualism between psychological-recollection and habit-recollection (chapter 2); on the other, he gives us a three-part theory of *memory* involving these two types of recollection and one form of unrecollected pure memory (chapter 3). This last memory, he tells us, is pure because of its unrecollected or virtual state, whereas any form of recollected or actual memory is one simplification or another of this virtuality. Even a hostile critic such as Russell could bring himself to credit Bergson with making a major contribution to our understanding of types of memory (Russell 1912, p. 328).[11] Moreover, the work of Gilles Deleuze makes extensive use of the uncovering of a pure past/memory, locating within it a new image of time (see Deleuze 1989).

In *MM* Bergson lays great stress on the importance of approaching consciousness in terms of a plurality of planes of existence (a plane of action, a plane of recollection, a plane of dreams, etc.).[12] His thinking on memory can only be adequately understood when it is viewed in terms of the presentation of these different planes. Bergson's theory of memory argues that the past is preserved under two distinct forms, namely, motor mechanisms and independent recollections. This means that the usefulness of memory can manifest itself in different ways, sometimes through action, which will involve an automatic setting in motion of an adaptive mechanism, and sometimes through an intellectual effort when we place ourselves directly in the past and contract elements of it to suit a present requirement. A lived body is one embedded in a flux of time, but one in which it is the praxial requirements of the present that inform its constant movement within the dimension of the past and horizon of the future. If the link with the 'real' is severed, in this case the field of action in which a lived body is immersed, then it is not so much the past images that are destroyed but the possibility of their actualization, since they can no longer act on the real: 'It is in this sense, and in this sense only, that an injury to the brain can abolish any part of memory' (*MM*, p. 79).

As Patrick McNamara shows in his recent study of mental Darwinism, for Bergson the contraction of the past takes place as a way of addressing the present. However, when a level of the past gets contracted the contraction is experienced by present consciousness as an expansion, simply because its repertoire of images and moments of duration are increased and intensified (McNamara 1999, p. 37). That Bergson's theory of memory rests on understanding these contractions and relaxations (memory in relation to the synthesis of past and present) is crucial to his argument and it is only when they are cast aside that we end up in confusion with respect to his thinking on time-memory. Bergson's realism about the pure past – a realism that is required in order to mark an ontological difference between perception and memory – leads one to wonder, however, how the present, being in part the actualized image of the past, can be anything more than the realization of some stored-away memory (see Maoilearca 1999a, p. 53). However, the argument that Bergson has, in effect, negated or obliterated the present by folding it back within a virtual memory, in which it then becomes indistinguishable from a rearrangement of something *pre-existent*, could be seen to neglect what he says about the movement of time-memory, viz., contractions, expansions and relaxations, a movement that determines that the junction of 'past' and 'present' happens in terms of an intersection of planes (planes of contemplation, of action, of dream-images, states of reverie, etc.). However, the crucial issue would remain whether these contractions and expansions are themselves truly qualitative changes or simply quantitative ones (rearrangements). This is, admittedly, one of the most difficult aspects of Bergson's theory to comprehend.

When we learn something a kind of natural division takes place between the contractions of habit and the independent recollection of events that involve dating. If I wish to learn a poem by heart I have to repeat it again and again through an effort of learning, in which I decompose and recompose a whole. In the case of specific bodily actions and movements habitual learning is stored in a mechanism that is set in motion by some initial impulse and that involves releasing automatic movements within a closed system of succession and duration. The operations of independent recollection, however, are altogether different. In the formation of memory-images the events of our daily life are recorded as they take place in a unique time and provide each gesture with a place and a date. This past is retained regardless of its utility and practical application. As beings of action and creatures of habit we are always remounting the slope of our past. The past is preserved in itself, providing a specific region of the becoming of being, and, *at the same time*, contracted in various states of virtuality by the needs of action that are always seated in a present. This repetition of memory-images through action merits the ascription of the word memory nor because it is involved in the conservation of past images but rather because it prolongs their utility into a present moment. The task of this kind of memory is to ensure that the storage of memory-images is rendered subservient to praxis, making sure that only those past images come into operation that can be coordinated with a present perception and so enabling a useful combination to emerge between past and present images: 'Thus is ensured the appropriate reaction, the correspondence to environment – adaptation, in a word – which is the general aim of life' (*MM*, p. 84). An *actual* consciousness is one which simply reflects the adaptation of the nervous system to the present situation. Without this coordination of memory-images by the adaptive consciousness the practical character of life would be distorted and the plane of dreams would mingle with the plane of action (in fact, as Bergson fully concedes, the planes do communicate and cannot be treated as isolable dimensions of consciousness and unconsciousness; the issue is rather to be approached in terms of different tensions, different stresses and strains of time). Viewed as a virtual whole there is nothing that is mechanical or simply automatic about the interplay between the different planes. The pure past – by which is simply meant the preservation of the past in and for itself, that is, independent of its actualization in a present – is inhibited from freely expressing itself by the practical bent of our bodily comportment, 'by the sensori-motor equilibrium of a nervous system connecting perception with action' (p. 95). Not only is there more than one kind of memory, but memory-images enjoy more than the one kind of existence, being actualized in multiple ways in accordance with their virtual plane of existence: 'Memory thus creates anew the present perception, or rather it doubles this perception by reflecting upon it either its own image or some other memory-image of the same kind' (p. 101). Our life moves – contracts, expands and relaxes – in terms of circuits, and it is the whole of memory that passes over into each of these circuits but always in a specific form or state of contraction.

In chapter 3 of *MM* Bergson penetrates further into the internal mechanism of psychical and psycho-physical actions in order to show how the past actualizes itself and thus 'reconquers the influence it had lost' (p. 131). He has posited a unity made up of three processes: pure memory, memory-images and perception. The last is never simply a contact of the mind with a present object but is impregnated with memory-images; in turn these images partake of a pure memory that they materialize or actualize and are bound up with the perception that provides it with an actual embodiment. Pure memory is, like pure perception, a theoretical hypothesis designed to enable a superior empiricism to pursue various lines of enquiry into questions of matter and mind and to overcome the limits of associationism. Pure memory shows us that there is a movement at work in the actualization of memory-images, we do not just pass from one isolated perception or memory to another. Bergson is thus proposing a truly innovative theory of the mind in which there are different planes and in which its operations and movements are approached in terms of virtual-actual circuits and processes. In this respect the movement of the mind is akin to the movement of life itself, involving a passage from the less realized to the more realized, from the intensive to the extensive, and from a reciprocal implication of parts and elements to their juxtaposition (*ME*, p. 230; see also p. 203).

In order to develop this conception of the movement of mind and memory it is necessary to dispel a number of illusions, a key one being that memory only comes into being once an actual perception has taken place. This illusion is generated by the requirements of perception itself, which is always focused on the needs of a present. While the mind or consciousness is attending to things themselves it has no need of pure memory which it holds to be useless. Moreover, although each new perception requires the powers afforded by memory, a reanimated memory appears to us as the effect of perception. This leads us to suppose that the difference between perception and memory is simply one of intensity and degree, in which the remembrance of a perception is held to be nothing other than the same perception in a weakened state, resulting in the illegitimate inference that the remembrance of a perception cannot be created while the perception itself is being created or be developed at the same time (pp. 160–1; see below, p. 125). It is, in fact, by recognizing the virtual character of pure memory and its images that we can begin to appreciate that the difference between perception and memory is one of kind and not merely degree; in short, memory has to be credited with its own specific and peculiar modality of being. Memory is made up of memory-images, but the recollection of an image is not itself an image (it is closer to a concentrated act of intellectual effort). Bergson insists that 'To *picture* is not to *remember*' (*MM*, p. 135; see below, p. 153). As a recollection becomes actual it comes to live in an image, but 'the converse is not true, and the image, pure and simple, will not be referred to the past unless, indeed, it was in the past that I sought it' (ibid.; see below, p. 153). The progress of memory consists in a process of materialization.

The relation between memory and perception can be compared to that between an image reflected in a mirror and the actual object in front of the mirror. Such an object can be touched and it allows itself to be acted upon and it acts upon us. In this regard it can be said to be 'pregnant with possible actions'. But although it is pregnant with possibility such an object is always *actual*. The image, by contrast, is necessarily *virtual*, in that while it obviously resembles the object it is also fundamentally different from it since it is not capable of doing what the object does. Far from being chimerical or hallucinatory the virtual image is fully real, though clearly it can be assigned a specific mode of the real. This division between the actual object and the virtual image is what leads Bergson to claim that at every moment of our lives we are presented with two aspects, even though the virtual aspect may be imperceptible owing to the very nature of the operations of perception:

> Our actual existence then, whilst it is unrolled in time, duplicates itself all along with a virtual existence, a mirror-image. Every moment of our life presents two aspects, it is actual and virtual, perception on the one side and memory on the other. Each moment is split up as and when it is posited. Or rather, it consists in this very splitting, for the present moment, always going forward, fleeting limit between the immediate past which is now no more and the immediate future which is not yet, would be a mere abstraction were it not the moving mirror which continually reflects perception as a memory. (*ME*, p. 165; see below, p. 181)

It is because the past does not simply follow the present but coexists with it that we can develop an explanation of paramnesia or the illusion of false recognition, often named '*déjà-vu*'. As Deleuze notes, 'there is a recollection of the present, contemporaneous with the present itself, as closely coupled as a role to an actor' (1989, p. 79). Furthermore, it is from this simple idea of a splitting of time that we get the paradoxes of time. These paradoxes result from the limit of the present and the need to implicate it in the movement of a virtual past, with the result that the passing of time can only be conceived as a virtual co-existence of past and present and not simply in terms of a straightforward succession (chronological time).

Bergson insists that what is being duplicated at each moment in our lives into perception and memory is not simply the actual past of particular dates, times and places, but rather a totality. This is a totality, however, that only ever exists in states of contraction and expansion. There is always a virtual whole that is being actualized, but such a whole exists only in a confused intensive form. In life we never simply relive the past, that is, it is not a question of rendering actual what is simply virtual and making the two identical. Being is always of the order of difference, which explains why Bergson insists that our memory is always, in the element or dimension of its virtuality, and on the plane of action, a memory of the present. Memory, qua the virtual, is a movement of differences.

Life as a virtual multiplicity

Bergson's *CE* is one of the first great books on systems (open and closed, natural and artificial), and it is a stress on the 'open' that informs his approach to the matter of a *creative* evolution. It is also in this text that Bergson will once again utilize the notion of a virtual multiplicity, and with novel results.

A conception of the evolution of life in terms of a virtual multiplicity is opposed to the idea that we are only ever dealing with an actual kind. If we approach evolution in terms of an actual or spatial multiplicity then time becomes little more than the process of mechanically bringing about the realization of pre-existent possibilities. The notion of the virtual, then, is opposed to that of possibility. An application of the notion of possibility is to be delimited to closed systems; however, in the case of an open system, such as the evolution of life, the notion of a virtual multiplicity is required in order to bring to light its characteristic features. Bergson's conception of a creative evolution can still be put to work today since a great deal of evolutionary thinking remains in the grip of spatialized habits and unknowingly operates on the level of actual multiplicities.

Why is a thinking of evolution that focuses on the realization of the possible so inadequate? The simple answer to this is that it deprives evolution of any inventiveness or creativity. If the products of evolution are given in advance, in the form of pre-existent possibles, then the actual process of evolution is being treated as a pure mechanism which simply adds existence to something that already had being in the form of a possible. In effect, there is no difference between the possible and the real since the real is simply an image of the possible and indistinguishable from it. If the real merely resembles the possible then we are providing ourselves with a real that is ready-made (preformed) and that comes into existence by a series of successive limitations. In the case of the virtual, however, the situation is quite different, for here the process of differentiation does not proceed in terms of resemblance or limitation but rather in terms of divergent lines that require a process of invention. But there is another aspect to our construction of the possible and the real which plays a crucial role in Bergson's attempt to expose the operations involved when we think events in terms of space and not time (duration): it is not simply the case that the real comes to resemble or mirror the possible but rather the other way round (the possible resembles the real). This is because our notion of the possible is arrived at by abstracting from the real once it has been made and then projected backwards.

To what extent can we produce a coherent conception of *evolution* if we construe it solely and strictly in terms of a set or series of discrete mechanisms (including discrete informational units), ones, it is alleged, that will automatically produce successful adaptations solely through the exogenous workings of natural selection? (let us note that it is selection that is doing all the work of finality in the theory). Can a thinking of evolution be sustained on the basis of this privileging of actual or discrete multiplicities? Some key points are perhaps worth stressing:

1   The claim is not that the scientist has no right to deal with closed systems. Bergson's concern is with what happens when this focus on closed systems, systems from which duration has been artificially extracted, is extended to an explanation

of life. His contention is that the focus on closed systems
is itself the result of certain intellectual tendencies that have
become dominant in the history of our evolution, leading to
the ironic result that the human intellect, on account of its
spatial habits, which are highly useful for manipulating and
regulating matter, is unable adequately to understand its own
conditions of existence, that is, unable to comprehend its own
creative evolution. Bergson does not deny that there are closed
systems. Rather he wishes to point out that isolable systems
that can be treated geometrically are the result of a certain
tendency of matter itself but that this tendency never is fully
actualized or reaches a point of completion. If science does
isolate a system completely this is for convenience of study;
it must still be recognized that a so-called isolated system
remains subject to external influences.

2　There is a role for calculation and computability (aspects of the
present can be calculable as functions of the past), such as in
the realm of organic destruction, but this cannot be extended
uncritically to all domains, such as organic creation and other
evolutionary phenomena which elude mathematical treatment.

3　It is necessary to distinguish between artificial and natural
systems, or between the dead and the living. In the case of
the living body of an organism the present moment cannot
be explained by a preceding moment since the whole past of
an organism needs referring to. An artificial system is one in
which time is reduced to a series of discrete instants. But the
idea of the immediately preceding instant is a fiction and an
abstraction. In effect it denotes that which is connected with a
present instant by the interval dt: 'All that you mean to say . . . is
that the present state of the system is defined by the equations
into which differential coefficients enter, such as $ds\backslash dt$, $dv\backslash$
dt, that is to say, at bottom, *present* velocities and present
accelerations' (*CE*, p. 22; see below, pp. 223–4). In short, in
such systems we are only ever dealing with an instantaneous
present, one that carries with it a tendency but which it treats as
a number (in Bergson a tendency has number *only potentially*):
'In short, *the world the mathematician deals with is a world that*

dies and is reborn at every instant – the world which Descartes was thinking of when he spoke of continued creation' (ibid.; see below, p. 224).

4   A coherent conception of evolution requires the notion of duration in which there is a persistence and prolongation of the past in the present. In a natural system the interval denotes a concrete duration and not simply an extremity. However, duration is implicated in original situations. The novelty of evolution – the events of evolution, if one likes – is to be explained in terms of the interplay between 'organic memory' and new conditions or situations (this is in contrast to the research paradigm of neo-Darwinism, which conceives evolution taking place in terms of the mechanical sum of discrete genetic codes and the algorithmic process of natural selection). For Bergson the variation of evolution is being produced continuously and insensibly at every moment, although, of course, it is only within specific conditions and under specific circumstances that it gives rise to a new species. No amount of knowledge of elementary causes will suffice to foretell the evolution of a new life form.

5   Contrary to widespread misconception which has persisted from Gaston Bachelard onwards, Bergson's thinking of creative evolution places a notion of contingency at the centre of its concerns and conceives duration precisely in terms of an interruption and discontinuity: duration involves 'incommensurability between what goes before and what follows' (*CE*, p. 29; see below, p. 489). Indeed, it is only by thinking of time as duration that the features of rupture and discontinuity can be rendered intelligible. There is a common prejudice running from Bachelard to Badiou that Bergson cannot think discontinuity. Such an assumption fails to recognize that Bergsonism provides an account of continuity *and* discontinuity.

Mechanism is not wholly illegitimate or simply false in Bergson's view. It is a reflection of our evolved habits of representation rather than an adequate reflection of nature itself. These are habits that conform in large measure to certain tendencies of matter. Mechanism gives us only a partial view of reality and neglects other crucial aspects such as duration. Mechanism is often blind to its own mechanisms and ignorant of the fact that it is the product of a certain kind of impulse, namely, one towards utility. In conforming to the necessities of language and the symbolism of science most philosophy has been unable to identify positive attributes in time. Instead it has rested content with mechanism. The difference to be thought is between an 'evolution' in which continuous phases interpenetrate, and an 'unfurling' in which distinct parts are juxtaposed with each other. In the former case rhythm and tempo are constitutive of the kind of movement in play, so that a retardation or an acceleration are internal modifications in which content and duration are one and the same thing. Throughout his writings Bergson is insistent that states of consciousness and material systems can both be treated in this way. If we say that time merely 'glides over' these systems then we are speaking of simple systems that have been constituted as such only artificially through the operations of our own intellect. Such systems can be calculated ahead of time since they are being posited as existing prior to their realization in the form of possibles (when a possible is realized it simply gets existence added to it, its fundamental nature has not changed). The successive states of this kind of system can be conceived as moving at any speed, rather like the unrolling of a film: it does not matter at what speed the shots run, an 'evolution' is not being depicted. The reality here is more complex, however, but the complexity is concealed. An unrolling film, for example, remains attached to consciousness that has its own duration and which regulates its movement. If we pay attention to any closed system, such as a glass of sugared water where one has to wait for the sugar to dissolve, we discover that when we cut out from the universe systems for which time is an abstraction, a relation or a number, the universe itself continues to evolve as an open system.

From the disposition of the intellect emerge the specific conceptions of matter that have characterized a great deal of Western metaphysics and science. Intelligence, for example, conceives the origin and evolution of the universe as an arrangement and rearrangement of parts which simply shift from one place to another. This is what Bergson calls the Laplacean dogma that has informed a great deal of modern enquiry, leading to a determinism and a mechanism in which, by positing a definite number of stable elements, all possible combinations can be deduced without regard for the reality of duration (*CE*, p. 38; see below, p. 229).

The study of life needs to be approached in terms of problems that are *immanent* to an evolutionary process or movement. The directionality and movement of life are not, however, to be understood in terms of a simple mechanical realization of pre-existing goals. Rather, the problems of life are general ones, evolving within a virtual field that is responded to in terms of specific solutions (an example to illustrate this would be cases of convergent evolution, such as the eye, representing solutions to general problems that are common to different phylogenetic lineages, in this case that of light and the tendency 'to see', or vision, and which involve a heterogeneity in the mechanisms actually involved). Bergson is struck by the fact that evolution has taken place in terms of a *dissociation* of tendencies and through divergent lines that have not ceased to radiate new paths. The evolution of life becomes intelligible when it is viewed in terms of the *continuation* of this impetus that has split up into *divergent* lines. On Bergson's model no dominant tendency within evolution can be identified, and neither can the different forms of life be construed in terms of the development of one and the same tendency.

The aim is one not of simply attacking mechanism but rather trying to determine the precise character of the mechanisms of life and the nature of adaptation. What is the notion of mechanism we are thinking with? For Bergson evolution can be thought in terms of a 'single indivisible history' (1983, p. 37; see below, p. 229). Mechanism errs in focusing attention only on those isolable systems that it has detached from the whole. A mechanical explanation is only possible through such an artificial extraction. Evolution cannot simply be made explicable in terms of a mechanical adjustment to external conditions or circumstances. Bergson argues, for example, that the theory of mechanism cannot adequately explain a crucial element in the evolution of the eye, namely, 'correlation'. On the one hand we have a complex organ, and on the other we have a unity and simplicity of function. It is this contrast, says Bergson, which should make us pause for thought. If vision is 'one simple fact' how is it possible to account for its organization and operation in purely exogenous terms and in terms of chance modifications (1983, p. 88; see below, p. 242)? If we are to take seriously the idea that a complex organ like the eye was the result of a gradual formation, as well as of a process of highly complex correlation (which Bergson does believe), then it becomes necessary to attribute to organized matter the power of constructing complicated machines able to utilize the excitations that it undergoes (p. 72). Bergson makes it clear, in responding to a critical point on utility which would argue that the eye is not made to see but creatures see because they have eyes, that he is not simply referring to an eye that has the capacity to see when speaking of an eye that 'makes use of' light. Rather, he is saying that what needs paying attention to are the precise relations existing between the organ and the apparatus of locomotion. In other words, the problem is not that of a discrete organ, such as the eye, but the complexity of its evolution in relation to other systems of an organism.

Bergson and relativity

A meeting between Bergson and Einstein actually took place at the Collège de France in Paris in April 1922, where the physicist and the philosopher attempted to exchange views on time. Einstein concluded the exchange by stating that there was an unbridgeable gulf between the time of the physicist and the time of the philosopher, the latter being a complete mystery to him. The gulf that divided them continues to inform the relation between philosophy and physics on the question of time. Relativity dealt a fatal blow to any theory that presupposed a definite present instant in which all matter is simultaneously real (an absolute present). The idea of a huge, instantaneous 'Now' spread transversally across the universe is well-entrenched in the human mind. But although Einstein did not believe in the reality of time, or the flow of time, he adhered to the fiction of the instant: the simultaneity of instants is what is relative. The question continues to persist and linger: did Einstein, along with much of the tradition, spatialize time? At the end of his book called *About Time* Paul Davies argues that the 'greatest outstanding riddle concerns the glaring mismatch between physical time and subjective or psychological time' (Davies 1995, p. 283). And he asks, in his determinism and denial of the flux of time, how different was Einstein from Newton and Laplace? Although these are valid and important questions it would be myopic on our part to suppose that the conflict between physics and philosophy simply or solely turns around the competing claims of phenomenology and cosmology. If the philosopher maintains, contra the physicist, that time flows then it can legitimately be asked: for whom does time flow? Is the experience of the flowing of time possible outside the domain of transcendental (subjective) conditions of experience? Or might the delimitation of time to such conditions of possibility rest on a disavowal of time's reality? The physicist will rightly suspect that a philosophical thinking of *durée* has turned the 'observer' into a phenomenologist (which is pretty much what Bergson does in *DS*). But then the philosopher can come back to the physicist and ask: If time does not flow does this mean that its experience is merely the result of a psychological illusion? What conception of time are we left with once we have shown that time does not flow? Are we thinking time at all in physics?

Bergson's response to Relativity is best seen in the wider context of his ontology of becoming, in which he seeks to show that our perception and understanding must presuppose as their basis a 'fluid' and moving 'continuity of the real'. Everything that lives perceives, from simple beings that vibrate to complex beings that are able to contract trillions of vibrations and oscillations within a single perception. Indeed, for Bergson the primary and primal function of perception is to grasp a series of elementary changes (movements in the environment) under the form of a quality or a single state and to do this through a work of condensation. Within the moving continuity of the real we can posit and locate the boundaries of bodies that exist in varying degrees of individuation (again, from the contractions of a simple protoplasm to living systems with highly developed nervous systems). All these bodies change 'at every moment', resolving themselves into groups of qualities consisting of a succession of elementary movements (*CE*, p. 302). The stability of a body lies in its instability – it never ceases changing and it changes qualities without ceasing to be or become what it is. It is such a body, conceived as a relatively closed system, that we are entitled to isolate within the continuity of matter. What is 'real' are two things: the moving continuity of the whole and the continual change of form within a living body. We need to note here that 'form' as such is only 'a snapshot view of a transition'. And what our perception does is to solidify the fluid continuity of the real or the open whole into discontinuous or discrete images. It does this *necessarily* as a condition of its evolution and adaptation. The changes taking place in the whole, however, are received by perceptual living systems as if on a surface. A system like ours, with its evolved habits of representation, either turns away from the movement of life or becomes interested only in the unmoveable part and plan of the movement rather than the movement itself. All kinds of acts are reduced to the image of simple movement or movement in general, and knowledge comes to bear on a state rather than a change. In short, we develop three kinds of representations that correspond to three categories of words: qualities (adjectives), forms of essences (substantives) and acts (verbs). While the first two are designed to capture states, the latter is related to movement but expresses something we find it hard to think.

Bergson argues that 'becoming' is infinitely varied and yet we have fostered the habit of extracting from these variations in order to provide ourselves with an image of 'becoming *in general*'. He writes:

> An infinite multiplicity of becomings variously coloured . . . passes before our eyes: we manage so that we see only differences of colour, that is to say, differences of state, beneath which there is supposed to flow, hidden from our view, a becoming always and everywhere the same, invariably colourless. (p. 304)

In short, as a way of facilitating the exigencies of social life and linguistic communication, we have produced a 'cinematographic' model of the real: which is to say, we reconstitute and compose the mobility of the real in terms of a series of juxtaposed and successive immobilities, and so generate for ourselves the illusion of continuity. The real moving continuity of the whole is concealed from us, therefore, by our very habits of representation, which are largely spatial. For us movement is something impersonal, mechanical, abstract and simple. There is a good reason for the congruence between our knowledge of the operations of nature and its practical effectiveness. This is because the 'cinematographical character of our knowledge of things is due to the kaleidoscopic character of our adaptation to them' (p. 306). If our body is related to other bodies in terms of an arrangement that is like the pieces of glass in a kaleidoscope, we can say that each time the kaleidoscope is given a shake what we detect or decode is not the shake in and for itself but rather only the new picture that has emerged from the transformation. In short, it is owing to the practical character of our understanding and intellect that there is generated the illusion that change is an illusion. For us change is decomposable, almost at will, into states, and out of this decomposition we produce a movement from out of a series of immobilities.

For Bergson modern science is the daughter of astronomy. Its prime concern is with calculating the positions of the objects or forces (planets, for example) of any material system and in which all moments are treated equally. Now, the key point for Bergson is that modern science aspires to treat *time* as an independent variable in its calculation of a system and to relate all other magnitudes to the magnitude of time. But, the question is, what is this 'time' of modern science? For Bergson it cannot be the time of duration, of a virtual qualitative multiplicity, which is characterized by a 'continuity of inter-penetration' and not discreteness (p. 341), simply because modern science treats all moments equally as 'virtual stopping-places' (p. 336), that is, as immobilities, in effect. Time can be divided at any moment and sliced or cut up as science pleases. What does not interest science is either the flux of time or the effect of this flux on a consciousness. Instead of intuiting or mapping out the flux, science deals with the counting of *simultaneities*. And for science the 'object' is always the simultaneity of *instants*, not that of fluxes (pp. 337–8). Modern physics deals with isolated systems, that is, with events and systems of events that have been detached from the whole, so that it counts 'simultaneities between the events that make up this time and the positions of the mobile T on its trajectory' (p. 342). So while modern physics differs from ancient science in considering any moment of time, it still rests on a substitution of 'time-length' for 'time-invention'.

Contra modern science, then, Bergson wishes to claim that there is an actual succession within things and that this succession is more than a number and not equivalent to space. Moreover, he wishes to point out that the time that is given all at once, or that can run at any speed, is not real duration. As he asks, why is not the life of the universe given at once as on the film of the cinematograph? Why do things take (their) time and why do we, as beings of duration implicated in other durations, have to *learn* time? Now, if time is not given, if the future of living systems and forms cannot be read off from the present state of the material universe, then there has to be a time of 'invention' or 'creative evolution'. Bergson, it should be noted, does not deny the validity of modern science with respect to its calculation of time; rather, he wants to show how its 'image' of time still rests on a cinematographic model and to ask whether there can be any conciliation between the time of the physicist and the time of the philosopher.

Bergson tells us that he is convinced that Einstein has provided not only a new physics but new ways of thinking. He wishes to find out the extent to which the concept of duration is compatible with Einstein's views on time. Bergson, however, presents the encounter badly and confusedly. This is because he places the emphasis on the 'direct and immediate experience' of duration, rather than emphasizing what he has shown in texts such as *MM* and *CE*, namely, that time qua duration is not simply an 'immediate data of consciousness' or experience but equally a condition of the becoming of matter and of evolutionary life. In *DS* Bergson appears to be drawing mainly on arguments presented in his first book, *TFW*: that succession presupposes a consciousness able to synthesize the qualitative aspects of a duration (a 'before' and an 'after'). Because of this it is quite easy for critics of Bergson to argue that in his engagement with Relativity he has misconceived the 'observer' issue by turning the observer (which, as we have already noted, could be a machine or a device) into a phenomenological consciousness.

There is, we believe, a specific reason as to why Bergson presents his own case – the fact that he is posing more than a phenomenological challenge to science – so poorly in *DS*. This is owing to his placing on his own thought and on modern physics a restrictive empiricism. This empiricism consists, in short, in the argument that any time we can conceive has to be perceived and lived, or capable of being so (so we get the equation: conceived time = perceived time = lived time). This means that any time which we cannot perceive, that does not have the potential of being perceptible, is unreal and phantasmatic (such as the multiple times of Relativity). Appearances are real, says Bergson, until they have been proven to rest on illusions. In the essay 'The perception of change' (1911), however, he declares that philosophy is born from out of the *insufficiency* of our faculties of perception and insists that our experience and knowledge of the universe cannot be based on the claims of a natural perception (*CM*, pp. 132, 135; see below, p. 308). Philosophy, he says, must learn how to think 'beyond the human condition'. With the position he adopts in *DS*, however, Bergson not only places severe and unwarranted limits on the praxis of science, he also places unnecessary limits on his own thinking.

Bergson has no desire to resurrect pre-Relativistic physics. There is much in the theories of Relativity that he accepts and that he finds compatible with his own thinking: he accepts the mathematical expression of the constancy of the speed or velocity of light; he too rejects the idea of there being any absolute frame of reference and appreciates the need to jettison the idea of a motionless ether (as a kind of carrier of motion within which the speed of light would be relative and not absolute). He brings to bear on Relativity the notion of a virtual multiplicity. The puzzling aspect of *DS*, however, resides in Bergson's claim that there is a 'single time' common to all times, including the multiple times of Relativity. How do we make sense of this notion of a single time? Is this not a simple refusal on his part to take seriously the claims of Relativity? The task is one of showing that the notion of a single time does not mean that everything that exists beats according to the same rhythm of time (in *MM* Bergson had argued that there are multiple tensions of duration and that our duration is simply one among many). Once we have understood how a virtual multiplicity can be a single time, the answer to the second question swiftly comes into view. It is important to get this right simply because Bergson argues in *DS* that Relativity itself shows us that the positing of a plurality of times supposes a single time. The error to be avoided – one that Bergson himself does not avoid in *DS* – is that of confusing single time with the claim that in the universe there is only a single tension of duration. This would take us back to the 'universal now' of pre-Einsteinian physics, or to one possible rendition of it.

Deleuze points out that the confrontation Bergson stages with Relativity is, in part, necessitated by the fact that the theory invokes similar concepts, such as expansion, contraction, tension and dilation in relation to space and time. Moreover, the confrontation does not come about abstractly or arbitrarily but is prepared by the notion of multiplicity. Bergson reworked Riemann's distinction between the two multiplicities in *TFW*, and Einstein drew heavily on Riemann's new geometries (see Einstein 1999, pp. 86, 108, 111, 154). Bergson's essential challenge emerges out of this common source: is time to be treated as a virtual and continuous multiplicity or an actual and discrete one? Moreover, does Relativity confuse the one with the other, namely, the virtual and the actual? Deleuze insists that the proper question to pose is not, 'is duration one or many?', but rather, 'what is the multiplicity that is specific and peculiar to it?' Duration does not have to be construed as simply multiple; it can be a One but 'in conformity with *its* type of multiplicity' (Deleuze 1991, p. 85). Bergson's principal argument is that the fourth dimension of space–time serves the role of a 'supplementary dimension' in which the relativity of simultaneous instants can be fixed and placed. It is this which informs his criticism, not of Relativity's preoccupation with spatialization as such (he acknowledges that this is the domain in which modern physics moves and makes its contribution), but with the specific spatialization of time that the theory effects. Relativity knows and recognizes no other time than that of spatialization.

Science, Bergson argues, works exclusively with measurements, and the measuring of time consists in counting simultaneities (*DS*, p. 40; see below, p. 261). In dealing with time the concern of physics is with the extremities of time, and the illusion is generated that the extremities of an interval are identical with the interval itself. What takes place in the interval – an actual duration – is neglected and lost sight of, and this means that the counting of simultaneities can only take the form of a counting of *instants*. Bergson goes further: it does not matter at what speed time runs, if the number of extremities is indefinitely increased, or if the intervals are indefinitely narrowed, these changes would have no great impact on the calculations of time carried out by the physicist:

> The speed of unfolding of this external, mathematical time might become infinite; all the past, present, and future states of the universe might be found experienced at a stroke; in place of the unfolding there might be only the unfolded. The motion representative of time would then have become a line; to each of the divisions of this line there would correspond the same portion of the unfolded universe that corresponded to it before in the unfolding universe; nothing would have changed in the eyes of science. (*DS*, p. 41; see below, p. 262)

But everything would have changed in terms of a qualitative duration that does not admit of measurement, such as that belonging to a living system whose duration, or spatio-temporal dynamics, are bound up with the flow of things in nature and its environment. Our question is this: is such a duration merely to be judged an illusion by physics, and is such an experience of duration no more than an appearance belonging to a phenomenological subject? Against the former, Bergson contends that its simultaneities are instantaneities that have been artificially abstracted from a concrete duration and, moreover, are purely mental views and habits (2000, p. 42; see below, p. 263). Furthermore, he argues that the simultaneity of instants measured by the physicist is dependent upon a simultaneity of fluxes which it neglects as its condition (p. 37; see below, p. 259). The simultaneity of the instant is needed in order to fix the simultaneity with a clock moment. However, Bergson contends that unless the simultaneity of two motions outside us which are taken to measure time are connected to the moments of an 'inner duration', we would not even be able to formulate an actual measurement of time. This leads Bergson to ask whether the 'real' of Relativity exists anywhere else than in the equations of the physicist.

It could be argued that Bergson is not, in fact, advocating the view that the time actually lived in a system has to be the same for every system. Rather, his point is that each system treats, and can only treat, its system as an absolute one. As he points out: 'if all motion is relative and if there is no absolute point of reference, no privileged system, the observer inside a system will obviously have no way of knowing whether his system is in motion or at rest' (p. 24). In other words, we are always inside a system, bounded by a specific perspective or horizon of space–time, and cannot freely move around different systems. As Robin Durie notes, Bergson is not suggesting that from the perspective of one observer the time lived by another is not real because it is different to that observer's lived time. His argument is rather that any time projected by one observer to another observer's system of reference is an imaginary time since it is not a time lived by any observer.[13] But is this not a platitude? Does it not completely miss the challenge of Relativity? For surely Relativity is not positing multiple times from the perspective of 'projection' (it is clear from the text that Bergson refuses in the example of the twins to climb the ascent to the viewpoint of the physicist).[14] If we take Bergson's perspectivism seriously it means there is only a single time that can be lived, simply because there can only be the single system at any one time. Is Bergson suggesting we cannot step outside our own system?

The single time cannot name the fact that each system only lives its own time and acts as if its relative perspective were an absolute one. If this is the case then the single time simply collapses back into an empty multiplicity of times (each one is relative but treats itself as absolute). Now, although the single time does not necessitate the idea that the same actual time is lived by all systems (in terms of its tension, rhythm, tempo, etc.), it does mean that the duration of any system – the system of nature or matter, the system of a life form such as ourselves – will have the features of a virtual multiplicity. So, whether the times of Relativity are declared to be real or phantasmatic is not the most relevant issue for negotiating the nature of Bergson's challenge. Again we think that a great deal of the most important work being done in Bergson's philosophy rests on the notion of a virtual multiplicity.

Intuition beyond Kant

Scattered throughout Bergson's writings one finds an engagement with the legacy of Kant's Copernican Revolution. His response to Kant is as sophisticated as that we find in say Hegel or Schelling, and it deserves to be more widely known. It also provides us with one more context in which to comprehend the nature of his own project.

In a letter to Christian Garve of September 1798 Kant discloses that the origins of his critique lay in his consideration of the antinomies of pure reason, antinomies that arise when reason oversteps the bounds of sense and understanding and freely speculates on issues it is not equipped to adequately deal with and that generate so many contradictions, such as: 'The world has a beginning in time. The world does not have a beginning in time,' or 'Man has complete freedom' pitted against the opposite and rival claim that 'There is no freedom since everything operates in accordance with natural necessity.' Bergson holds that Kant's philosophy 'lives and dies' by these antinomies.[15] His claim is that it is possible to think outside of their terms but to do this requires opening up the possibilities of thinking. Once we are able to think in terms of duration the antinomies dissolve since they only ensnare the mind when it thinks time in terms of space. The thesis and antithesis of an antinomy suppose the 'perfect coincidence of matter with geometrical space', and they vanish once 'we cease to extend to matter what is true only of pure space', that is, when we think matter in terms other than parts that are absolutely external to one another (*CE*, p. 205; see below, p. 352).

Bergson goes much further than this in refusing to accept the terms under which the *Critique* has been laid down and put forward. He does not accept the thesis that knowledge is relative to our faculties of knowing, and he does not accept that metaphysics is impossible on the grounds that there can be no knowledge outside of science or that science has correctly determined the bounds of metaphysics. In short, Bergson does not accept Kant's delimitation of metaphysics, bounded as it is by the privileging of Newtonian mechanism. A new relation between philosophy and science is called for and knowledge of the absolute is to be restored (*CM*, p. 65). Bergson makes two major claims contra Kant: first, that the mind cannot be restricted to the intellect since it 'overflows' it; and second, that duration has to be granted an 'absolute existence', which requires thinking time on a different plane to space. A 'theory of knowledge' and a 'theory of life' are to be viewed as inseparable since if our thinking of life is not accompanied by a critique of knowledge it will blindly accept the concepts – of matter, of life, of time, etc. – which the understanding has placed at our disposal. We will not generate a thinking of life but simply enclose the facts within a set of pre-existing frames. Thus, in order to think beyond the human condition it is necessary to provide a generative account of that condition. Once the understanding is situated within the evolutionary conditions of life it is possible to show how the frames of knowledge have been constructed and how they can be enlarged and gone beyond.

Instead of resting content with this critique of the dogmatic tendency of metaphysics, and uncritically privileging Newtonian mechanism, the effort should be made to recover the mind's contact with the real. This requires providing a generative account of the understanding (the abstract intellect), which would serve to show that homogeneous space and time are neither properties of things *nor* essential conditions of our faculty of knowing these things; rather their homogeneous character expresses 'the double work of solidification and division which we effect on the moving continuity of the real in order to obtain there a fulcrum for our action, in order to fix within it starting points for our operation, in short, to introduce into it real changes' (*MM*, p. 211). In other words, Kant's conception of space and time as forms of sensibility is shown to have an 'interest', one that is 'vital' and not merely 'speculative'. Instead of ending up with a split between appearance and reality, or between phenomenon and noumenon, we approach epistemological issues in terms of the relation between parts (our partial perspective on the real in accordance with our vital needs of adaptation) and a mobile whole (the moving continuity of the real). The sensible intuition of a homogeneous time and space presupposes for Bergson a 'real duration' and a 'real extensity': the former are stretched out beneath the latter in order that the moving continuity can be divided and a becoming can be fixed. There arises at this point the need for another way of thinking, another kind of intuition.

Kant himself entertained the possibility of such an intuition but famously denies we, as human beings, can have access to it. Our mode of intuition can only be of a derivative kind and not an original one. We have no access to an *intellectual* intuition. Kant allows for the fact that the way the human being intuits time and space may not be peculiar to it alone but may be something to be found among all finite beings that have a capacity of self-representation. But what he will not allow for is the possibility that we could overstep the bounds of our finitude and attain a higher intuition such as an intellectual one. This can only belong to the 'primordial being' (*Critique of Pure Reason*, B 72). The most we can do is to posit a 'transcendental object' (*Objekt*) which may be the ground of the appearance we call matter, but this is an object without quantity or substance, it is 'a mere something of which we should not understand what it is, even if someone were in a position to tell us' (A277/B333). To be able to intuit things without the aid of our senses would mean that we could have knowledge 'altogether different from the human, and this not only in degree but as regards intuition likewise in kind' (A278/B 334). But of such non-human beings we do not know them to be possible or how they would be constituted. Kant does not deny that through observation and analysis it is possible that we can penetrate into 'nature's recesses', but he insists that this is nature conceived only in the aspect or dimension of its *appearance*: 'with all this knowledge, and even if the whole of nature were revealed to us, we should still never be able to answer those transcendental questions which go beyond nature', that is, beyond nature qua appearance (ibid.). Admittedly, it is strange that Kant should in this passage speak of the recesses of nature if all we can ever develop knowledge of is of nature as appearance (this whole issue is bound up with his preference for laying out the field of experience and knowledge in terms of the image of a sphere and not a plane, A762/B790). Ultimately, Kant is led to positing a *problematic* noumenon, which is not the concept of any determinate object but rather bound up with the limitation of human sensibility. This provides a 'place' for speculation with regard to there being objects outside of our specific field of intuition, objects 'other and different' to what we are able to intuit through our particular a *priori* intuitions of time and space, but of their existence nothing can be either denied or asserted (A288/B 344).

The possibility of a supra-sensuous intuition is treated again by Kant in the critique of teleological judgement. Its importance for an appreciation of Bergson is perhaps self-evident. Given the centrality of intuition to his thinking of duration it is imperative that he wrestles with Kant in order to demonstrate precisely how it is possible to think 'beyond the human condition'. Now, this does not mean turning ourselves into God or the primordial being, but it does entail beginning at a different place and showing that the possibilities of thinking are not limited to, or determined by, subjective conditions. If Bergson were to accept the territory on which Kant has established his *Critique* then the ambition of thinking beyond the human condition would be a vain and hopeless one.

The abstract intellect, which has evolved as an organ of utility and calculability, proceeds by beginning with the immobile and simply reconstructs movement with juxtaposed immobilities. By contrast, intuition, as he conceives it, starts from movement and sees in immobility only a snapshot taken by our mind (*CM*, pp. 34–5). He argues that in order to reach this intuition it is not necessary, as Kant supposed, to transport ourselves outside the domain of the senses: 'After having proved by decisive arguments that no dialectical effort will ever introduce us into the beyond and that an effective metaphysics would necessarily be an intuitive metaphysics, he added that we lack this intuition and that this metaphysics is impossible. It would in fact be so *if there were no other time or change* than those which Kant perceived' (p. 128; see below, p. 302, our emphasis). So while Kant acknowledges the 'peculiar' character of 'our (human) understanding relative to our power of judgement in reflecting on things in nature', and concedes that this peculiarity implies the idea 'of a possible understanding different from the human' (he mentions a similar implication in the first *Critique* regarding its allowing for 'another possible form of intuition', Kant 1952, section 77, p. 61), it is this route intimated at but blocked off by Kant that is pursued by Bergson. By recovering intuition Bergson hopes to save science from the charge of producing a relativity of knowledge (it is rather to be regarded as 'approximative') and metaphysics from the charge of indulging in empty and idle speculation.

Bergson conceives intuition as a form of mental attentiveness, it is a special kind of 'attention that the mind gives to itself, over and above, while it is fixed upon matter, its object' (p. 79). It is an attention that can be 'methodically cultivated and developed', forming the basis of a new science of the mind and a veritable metaphysics. Metaphysics will no longer be the activity of a pure intelligence, an intelligence that defined the mind by a set of negations. It is a gross error, Bergson wishes to point out, to confuse his method of intuition with instinct or feeling (p. 88).[16] This metaphysics will operate via 'differentiations and qualitative integrations', and in an effort to reverse the normal directions of the workings of thought it will have a rapport with modern mathematics, notably the infinitesimal calculus:

> Modern mathematics is precisely an effort to substitute for the *ready-made* what is in process of *becoming*, to follow the growth of magnitudes, to seize movement no longer from outside and in its manifest result, but from within and in its tendency towards change, in short, to adopt the mobile continuity of the pattern of things. (p. 190; see below, p. 339).[17]

Metaphysics differs from modern mathematics (the science of magnitudes), however, in that it has no need to make the move from intuition to symbol. Its understanding of the real is potentially boundless because of this: 'Exempt from the obligation of arriving at results useful from a practical standpoint, it will indefinitely enlarge the domain of its investigations' (p. 191; see below, p. 339). Metaphysics can adopt the 'generative idea' of mathematics and seek to extend it to all qualities, 'to reality in general' (ibid.). The aim is not to effect another Platonism of the real, as in Kant's system, he contends, but rather to enable thought to re-establish contact with continuity and mobility.[18] A form of knowledge can be said to be relative when, through an act of forgetting, it ignores the basis of symbolic knowledge in intuition, and is forced to rely on pre-existing concepts and to proceed from the fixed to the mobile.

Absolute knowledge by contrast refuses to accept what is pre-formed and instead cultivates 'fluid concepts', seeking to place itself in a mobile reality from the start and so adopting *the life itself of things*' (p. 192; see below, p. 340) and to follow 'the real in all its sinuosities' (1983, p. 363; see below, p. 358). To achieve this requires relinquishing the method of construction that leads only to higher and higher generalities and thinking in terms of a concrete duration 'in which a radical recasting of the whole is always going on' (ibid.).

Bergson argues that science operates with an 'unconscious metaphysics', while Kantianism rests on an uncritical acceptance of the diagrams for modelling reality that are specific to the tasks of science. In short, neither is able to produce a genesis of the intellect that would account for the relativity of our knowledge. Bergson cognizes the specific achievement of Kant's transcendental aesthetic: extension cannot be regarded as a material attribute of the same kind as others, simply because, while we cannot determine the modalities of heat, colour and weight without recourse to actual experiences of these things, it is quite different with the notion of space. Even if it is given empirically by sight and touch, this does not rule out the ability of the mind to cut out in it *a priori* figures, whose properties we also determine *a priori*. It is this transcendental ideality of space that infuses the whole of Kant's enterprise, including the antinomies. But this means not simply that intelligence bathes in an atmosphere of spatiality but that this atmosphere closes down the possibilities of thinking. If our perceptions are 'impregnated by our geometry' we should not be surprised when thinking finds in matter the mathematical properties which the faculty of perception has already deposed there. Matter yields itself to the docility of our reasonings. Because any other knowledge of matter and the real has been denied, such as that offered by the intuition of mobility, we should also not be surprised if the result is a set of antinomies in which one affirmation immediately gives rise to a contrary affirmation equally plausible and equally demonstrable.

Morality and sociobiology

The Two Sources of Morality and Religion (*TSMR*) has been described as an attempt to temper the primacy given to the 'group mind' in modern sociology by drawing greater attention to the role of the individual.[19] As such, what *TSMR* takes as two symptoms of this group mind, closed society and static religion, 'were the last entries', it has been said, 'in a column of partial negatives, beginning with mathematics and science generally'.[20]

The first noteworthy feature of *TSMR* is that it is primarily a work in sociobiology rather than metaphysics; indeed, as regards its analysis of religion, it is *the* sociobiological study, according to Charles Hartshorne.[21] Bergson's main claim is that the nature of social relations is not fixed, but an ongoing creation.[22] This is not to argue that it is a by-product of intrinsically individual human endeavour – at all times in this book Bergson tries to balance the claims of methodological and theoretical individualism with those of collectivism – but rather that society and culture are evolutionary rather than self-explanatory.[23] We must seek their origins or 'sources' in the biological exigencies of life, as a creator both of the species and of individuals: 'all we have to do is to consider man again in his place among living things, and psychology as a part of biology'. Having done so, we will have replaced sociability back within the 'general evolution of life'.[24]

Two caveats must be added to this rather bare manifesto: first, that Bergson's is certainly not a reductive sociobiology; there is no hint here that he wishes to deflate culture to 'merely' animal, biological or genetic forces. In tandem with his redemptive and anti-reductionist views in biology, his is, if anything, an inflationary discourse; biological influence merits much more worth than we give it: 'let us then give to the word biology the very wide meaning it should have, and will perhaps have one day'. Second, this will be a truly evolutionary sociobiology. Bergson's complaint against similar analyses of that time and earlier (one thinks of Herbert Spencer) was that they 'take society for granted', and end up using biology to aggrandize and consolidate a particular status quo: they are conformist rather than evolutionist.[25] It is irrelevant whether the analysis is liberal or conservative in political orientation: the error of false sociobiology is its search for legitimizing natural essences, when in truth the 'sources' of society only provide us with natural tendencies, one of which will actually be the tendency to renounce all notions of natural essence in favour of the continual creation of new social forms – what Bergson will dub 'open morality'. Hence, Bergson sidesteps the frozen essentialism of reductive naturalists as well as the liquid relativism of culturalists: society is indeed moulded by nature, but by a creative nature which in part tries to break its own moulds!

Irrespective of what form sociobiology takes, its main struggle will be with those who reject its premise altogether and seek to explain society and morality wholly in terms of the instruments of human intelligence. A part of the first chapter, which we have included in our selection, consists of two attacks Bergson makes on this intellectualist view. One of them rests on his earlier work in *CE* that shows that intelligence itself is the offspring of biology and so must 'correspond to vital needs'; this evolutionary epistemology shows that rationality cannot be the direct agency behind culture and ethics but acts at best by proxy for vital forces. Of course, Bergson is careful not to reduce reason to a parody of itself when rejecting its efficacy; it would be too simplistic to say that passion rules wholesale over rationality. He accepts that moral decisions must be channelled through reason in any particular situation. It is also true that the more 'economical' a society becomes (in the literal sense of that term), the more the dictates of its operative morality are logically integrated, giving succour to the intellectualists' conviction as to their ultimate origin.[26] The sources Bergson is invoking do not bear down transparently on our every decision; indeed, it would be impossible to act if we did have to refer to them explicitly. The two sources are both varieties of proto-morality, as the term 'source' implies. They represent the conditions of possibility, so to speak, for making moral judgements at all and for having a moral sensibility. But neither fits an intellectualized model of ethics, for, as we will see, they are infra-rational and supra-rational. *TSMR* does not set out an alternative system of ethics or '*morale*'.[27]

By an 'intellectualized model of ethics' Bergson does not mean a specifically rationalist ethics such as Kantianism, so much as any ethical model which systematically derives a set of codes from some initial premise or premises on the assumption that coherence is a facet of morality: 'general interest, personal interest, self-love, sympathy, pity, logical consistency, etc., there is no principle of action from which it is not possible to deduce more or less the morality that is generally accepted'. In each case, morality is deemed deducible from and reducible to an evidential base, whatever it may be. But the essential is thereby omitted. In other words, what is moral in morality, that is, what is 'moving' (in every sense), remains unexplained by intellectualism. This point relates to Bergson's second line of attack: the old idea that the virtue of coherence or consistency lacks any real impetus to practical action: 'reason can only put forward reasons, which we are apparently always at liberty to counter with other reasons'.[28]

We should take care not to think that Bergson's meta-ethics is emotivist. At least in respect to sympathy, Bergson clearly argues against its adequacy as a starting point for ethics.[29] But something more complex again distances Bergson from any possible identification with emotivist theory: his conception of emotion itself. One comprehends only one side of the affective realm by thinking of emotion in terms of sensations, hormonal processes or, less physiologically, simple blind impulses. Alongside such desiccated, spatialized feelings, Bergson will argue for the primacy of 'creative emotion' in ethics, emotions that are opposed to neither reason nor representation but incubate a certain form of intentionality. At this level too, Bergson tries to reconcile (or reverse) the dichotomy of emotivism and rationalism in ethics by means of an inflationary or redemptive picture of emotion itself:

> alongside of the emotion which is a result of the representation and which is added to it, there is the emotion which precedes the image, which virtually contains it, and is to a certain extent its cause . . . an emotion capable of crystallising into representations and even into an ethical doctrine.[30]

There are, of course, 'natural', easily recognized emotions, ones which are inspired by thought, social convention and even nature itself; but a genuinely new, creative emotion is not caused by a representation or inspiration; it is 'pregnant' with its own representations: it is supra-rational.

The metaphysics of Bergson's theory of life must always be kept in mind when discussing his sociobiological examination of ethics and religion. That said, the first manifestation of this is the dualism evident in this work from the very beginning. There are *two* sources of morality and religion, and both are biological. They can both be biological because there are two major facets to Bergson's theory of evolution, what he describes as a virtual type of organization on the one hand and the expression of that order in actual organic forms on the other: evolution itself and fragments of the evolved. Two facets of time, in other words, time flowing and time flown.

In *TSMR*, these biological influences appear in morality as two types of motivation: moral obligation and moral aspiration, each corresponding to the evolved and the evolving respectively. The first acts as a type of pressure, a centripetal movement of closure, fostering a closed model of society (or association) and a static form of religion. The second is an outward, dissociative and centrifugal movement, bearing within it the seeds of open sociability and dynamic spirituality. As neither source of the two is 'strictly and exclusively moral' it would be foolish, Bergson writes, to try to explain either in terms of moral or religious theory.[31] Our sociobiology must be biological.

Bergson compares the first type of movement, that of moral obligation, to the integrative pressure that maintains the unity of cells within an organism, only in society it is habit that plays the role of the binding force. We must note that there is no causal agency implied going from the biological substratum to the sociological superstratum here: rather, both realms evince a type of movement which is not modelled on one or the other but on a third principle we might call 'transcendental'. The force maintaining the unity of animal societies bound by instinct is another parallel given, though again instinct *per se* is not meant to be the 'cause' of our sense of obligation but simply another manifestation of this type of movement.[32]

As regards these social obligations, Bergson argues that no particular one has any superior value over the next in terms of its being closer to a biological origin; the only social form which is significant to Bergson is the very general one that there are obligations as such, the 'totality of obligation' that plays the role of an infra-rational social adhesive. However, we never feel the action of this totality except when we depart from it: rarely is it that obligations or duties do not harmonize with our own habitual tendencies. It is only when we make a transgression that we become conscious of them, for consciousness is the very 'hesitation' (in the language of *TFW*) or 'disruption of movement' (as *MM* would say) evinced when we struggle between social and personal motives. Deviating from accepted moral convention causes an internal resistance within ourselves which, 'if we resist this resistance', leads to a 'state of tension or contraction'. From this abnormal, limit case stems the mistaken notion that obligation is an independent self-explanatory principle of ethics. Generalizing from the particular brings about the erroneous idea of the self-sufficiency of duty, set (at least potentially) within a rationalistic ethics. But at heart, this view confuses a perceived pressure to restore an obligation with the origin of the obligation. Intelligence only supplies the hesitation, the resistance to a resistance, not the obligation itself.[33]

Arising from this obligation is a type of conscience that we properly call 'social' in that it indicates the desire for socialization and the preservation of our social identity. One trait of social obligation is that it immediately installs a 'closed society, however large'. It is in its nature to form social groupings like the family, the nation, the race and so on, each of which acts as an intermediary reinforcement of habitual social mores. Society in general occupies the broadest and most abstract of these concentric circles surrounding the self. Within each circle, all are regarded in an equal light and all are allowed the same rights and freedoms. What is essential about such bounded domains, however, is that they are more or less closed to the outside. A social formation may be very broad and even continue to grow broader by incorporating previously ostracized minority groups; no matter, they remain closed in the type of movement they instantiate: 'their essential characteristic is nonetheless to include at any moment a certain number of individuals, and exclude others'. Every in-group requires an out-group or 'enemy' (as Bergson puts it) such that our bonds of social equality and tolerance are purchased through an act of exclusion 'against all other men'.[34] It would not be going too far to say that closed morality barely deserves the name of morality at all if we mean by that some wholly un-self-interested altruism.

Whatever feelings we have for the group, writes Bergson, 'imply a choice, therefore an exclusion; they may act as incentives to strife, they do not exclude hatred'. This is closed morality: a set of rules and balances, pressures and obligations bearing down on the individual, homogenizing him or her by removing his or her evolutionary alterity. In terms of religion, the closed society tends towards a static form of faith, a codified, institutionalized spirituality that expresses above all the interests of the group rather than a supposedly universal divinity. Static religion is not the same as closed morality, however, for the former can often demand acts of superstitious barbarism deemed immoral by the latter: yet it remains that the two serve the same form of social order and are often found together.[35]

But alongside social obligation, social conscience and the closed societies they sustain, there is another type of conscience which responds, not to the need to be kept within the closed fold of society, but to the desire for openness, specifically the desire to be open towards openness: a welcome owed to those who are themselves 'opening'. Behind the command to 'love all' lies this other morality – biological too, but in another sense than 'merely' naturalistic. Bergson talks now of a 'complete morality' or 'absolute morality' and describes the 'extreme limit' of its movement as follows.[36]

> The other attitude is that of the open soul. What, in that case, is allowed in? Suppose we say that it embraces all humanity: we should not be going too far, we should hardly be going far enough, since its love may extend to animals, to plants, to all nature. And yet no one of these things which would thus fill it would suffice to define the attitude taken by the soul, for it could, strictly speaking, do without all of them. Its form is not dependent on its content. We have just filled it; we could as easily empty it again. 'Charity' would persist in him who possesses 'charity', though there be no other living creature on earth.[37]

Pure openness sympathizes 'with the whole of nature', but it is also a contact with a principle of nature which expresses itself in quite a different attachment to life than that found in a sympathy for the other members of one's group. It is described as an objectless emotion that loves who or what it does only 'by passing through' rather than aiming for them.[38]

Now it must be added that both these moralities, closed and open, are only 'extreme limits', and are never found in any actual society in their pure form. The forces of openness and closure are present in varying degrees in every society and are intermixed in actual morality. Such actual morality encompasses what Bergson describes as a 'system of orders dictated by impersonal social requirements', as well as a 'series of appeals made to the conscience of each of us by persons who represent the best there is in humanity'.[39] Nonetheless, the two remain distinct while being united in their difference, for they represent 'two complementary manifestations of life'.[40] There never has been nor could be either a truly open society or a fully closed one. These are ideal limits.[41]

We've seen that open morality finds its inspiration in a personal appeal rather than through the impersonal pressure which regulates the morality of a closed society. Some form of direct or indirect interpersonal relationship is required. Where closed morality lies in obedience before the law, open morality lies in an 'appeal', 'attraction' or 'call'. But the call does not come from just any one: it requires a privileged personality. What is best in our society is bequeathed to us by individuals Bergson calls heroes, and each hero – living or dead – 'exerts on us a virtual attraction'. Bergson certainly is not asserting a hard and fast dimorphism between leaders and their followers here – every individual possesses within him or herself 'a leader with the instinct to command and a subject ready to obey' – it is simply that our closed societies are configured to ensure a herd-mentality in the majority.[42]

The heroism Bergson describes is of a religious variety, though one that is dynamic and wholly active rather than institutional and reified.[43] Bergson also calls these heroes 'mystics', though, again, the notion of some ascetic contemplative is far from what he has in mind. These mystics are creators, transgressing the boundaries of life, mind and society in their inspirational morality. As an earlier essay puts it, their moral existence is nearest to life itself: such 'inventive and simple heroism' is 'the great success of life', being at once its 'culminating point' and most primitive 'source'.[44] In crossing all frontiers, mysticism goes 'beyond the limits of intelligence', the ultimate end of mysticism being to establish a partial coincidence with the creative effort which life manifests. Such inherent creativity can appear as mental pathology, and Bergson takes time to spell out the differences between the symptoms of genuine mental transcendence and those of simple insanity.[45] Mental imbalance is frequently regarded by Bergson as an excess of mental power rather than a deficiency: the usual restrictive role of the brain has been weakened to allow a greater degree of consciousness to flood the subject. The weakness of such disorder lies in the inability to restore equilibrium between this new surplus and the surrounding environment.[46] The mystic has that ability to restore the equilibrium. He or she has travelled the same route as the madman but has also discovered the way back.[47]

So, what is moral action? Oddly enough, what allows the hero to act as a model for others is described as a type of passivity before life. It entails 'the complete and mysterious gift of self'.[48] What is termed 'complete mysticism' is wholly for the other rather than self-absorbed: 'true, complete, active mysticism aspires to radiate, by virtue of the charity which is its essence'.[49] How it actually radiates is through the contagious properties of a genuinely creative emotion: 'for heroism itself is a return to movement, and emanates from an emotion – infectious like all emotions – akin to the creative act'.[50] But again, the etymology of emotion should be taken into account: Bergson is not endorsing some private ecstasy but a type of movement rich in meaning, a movement of openness. In one very interesting analysis, Bergson describes Socrates as a mystic and religious hero before being a philosophical model. When philosophers constructively engage with society, they do not follow the Socratic archetype so much as actualize the Socratic movement and thereby make him live again.[51]

Mélanges

Our first selection from *Mélanges* – the collection of letters and rarer essays published in French in 1972 – is his 1895 lecture on 'good sense' or '*le bon sens*', which has both an ethical and an intellectual function. In this respect we are dealing with a crucial harbinger of Bergson's later moral philosophy. While the other senses place us in relation with things, *le bon sens*, he observes, governs our relations with people, orienting our attention 'in the direction of life'. It is the principle of social justice, though it is a justice 'living and acting' rather than 'theoretical and abstract'. *Le bon sens* is first and foremost a 'strength of feeling' of which theoretical justice is a derivative form. It is also described as an attention to life, though this attention is neither an extended experience, nor a more exact deduction, nor a more rigorous logic: it remains a spirit of justice. Nevertheless, *le bon sens* also has an intellectual role, demanding the sacrifice of our firmest convictions and best explanations in order to preserve us from 'intellectual automatism'.[52] Such beliefs must be made provisional if we are to remain open to the opinions and solutions of others. As one critic describes it: 'good sense demands both flexibility and perpetual readaptation of means to ends: in a word, it demands openness'.[53]

It is when *le bon sens* is addressed under the alternative designation of 'common sense' that this notion enters the foreground of Bergson's thought. Now it is no longer only an attention to the sensibilities of human beings which depicts it accurately; it is an attention to otherness as such before the bifurcation between the enduring and the inert has been performed. Common sense becomes a trap when it is no longer a good sense, but is instead what only emphasizes the common. By this we mean that the good common sense, *le bon sens* directed towards otherness as such, seems to retain the proportionality required to temper its own perspective with that of the other, whereas the bad common sense enforces the sacrifice of its own alterity to the communal view: self-homogenization. *Le bon sens* is thereby the sense that equally demands that we adopt a position that will always and necessarily be ours alone.[54]

Our other selections from this 'mix' of Bergson's lesser-known texts is mostly composed of his correspondence, in particular with William James. The intellectual harmony and tension between the philosophies of James and Bergson is worthy of a book in itself: their joint 'discovery' of the stream or duration of consciousness, their pragmatist theory of knowledge and their treatment of 'abnormal mental states' as modes of knowledge with genuine '*noetic* value'[55] are all hallmarks of their strong philosophical kinship. What is also worth taking away from reading their correspondence is their divergence (at least in Bergson's eyes), especially as regards the notion of truth, as can be seen from the following from Bergson's letter to James in June 1907:

> Would I go so far as to affirm with you that '*truth is mutable*'? I believe in the mutability of *reality* rather than that of *truth*. If we can make our intuition accord with the mobility of the real, would not this accord be something stable, and would not truth – which can only be this accord itself – participate in this stability?[56]

No less interesting than the distinction Bergson asserts here between himself and James's theory of truth is the inconsistency it creates with his own claim elsewhere that all thought, even 'erroneous' thought, stands for something: 'Error itself', Bergson writes, 'is a source of truth':

'*yes* and *no* are sterile in philosophy. What is interesting . . . is *in what measured*?'[57] What starts out as merely a 'refractory' representation can become a given truth, clear and intelligible, simply in virtue of our historical acquaintance with the concept. A true affirmation can thus have a 'retroactive' or 'retrograde' movement: 'the paradox of today is often only the truth of tomorrow'.[58] Truth *grows* on us. If we give up on truth, it is only because we have a false conception of what truth should be, 'in virtue of the principle deep-rooted in our intellect, that all truth is eternal. If the judgement is true now, it seems to us it must always have been so.'[59] But it is truth which is multiple for Bergson because it is an emergent process: 'the true growth of truth'.

The other letters from *Mélanges* reproduced here – to Lechalas, Höffding and Delattre – throw extra light on the intrinsic meaning and overall philosophical position of the key Bergsonian concepts of the body and perception, intuition and duration, and the *élan vital* respectively. These texts will reward close study while also helping to offset some of the myriad misconceptions surrounding Bergson's work. But we complete this particular selection and this volume of key writings with Bergson's message to the Descartes Congress of 1937. It is perhaps ironic that our last text should focus on Descartes (who Bergson cites here as the spiritual founder of modern metaphysics), for one can read Bergson as the one philosopher who, straddling the nineteenth and twentieth centuries, did more than any other to subvert so many of the dogmas of modern Cartesian philosophy: the spatiality of time, the speculative nature of reason, the mechanism of life – all of these philosophical tenets, fundamental to all thought for the last four hundred years, were devastingly critiqued by Bergson first, and with such success that to oppose them today is almost an intellectual platitude. He transcended a great deal of the axioms and methodology of classicism and rationalism (though he also retained a number of their assumptions). Perhaps his style was too personal and at times too clear for his doctrine to transcend his own exposition of it. He did not leave a 'scientific' method as Husserl did upon which his followers might base a school. A philosopher of his own time, he was attacked by both the emerging Analytic tradition and the Thomist one. In many ways, he stands at a crossroads in philosophy: he reset the agenda of what our philosophical questions should be and how they should be put. He was neither a classical philosopher, for he rejected its world-view, nor a full-blown 'postmodernist', for he still retained a modern approach to the possibility and importance of metaphysics. Many lost sight of this and criticized Bergsonism only for what it lacked, to the exclusion of what it gave to our whole postmodern tradition as such.

In a letter of 7 March 1914 to the editor of *Le Figaro* Bergson wrote (from London) of what he himself thought about Bergsonism. He says that the spread of what has become known as 'Bergsonism' is due to people seeing that they have here to do with a

> metaphysic moulded on experience (whether exterior or interior); with an unpretentious philosophy determined to base itself on solid ground; with a doctrine that is in no sense systematic, that is not provided with an answer to every question, and that distinguishes different problems to examine one by one – a philosophy capable, like science, of indefinite progress and advance. . . .

He then adds: 'Each of my books has cost me several years of scientific research; and each of them issues in no vague generalities but in conclusions which are able to throw light on some one aspect of very special problems.' Perhaps it is despite the early popularity of his work rather than because of it that we should return to his writings and rediscover the immense effort that went into creating each of his philosophical concepts, giving back to them the intellectual effort and close attention they deserve. His was a philosophy whose ideological effect, being so all-pervasive that by name it became invisible, should not because of that be deemed any less important in fact. We hope that presenting the key texts from his writings in this collection will alert the contemporary reader of philosophy to the enormous – but often unacknowledged – significance of his arguments as well as the ongoing productivity of his ideas.

Time and Free Will[1]

The Idea of Duration[2]

Number may be defined in general as a collection of units, or, speaking more exactly, as the synthesis of the one and the many. Every number is one, since it is brought before the mind by a simple intuition and is given a name; but the unity which attaches to it is that of a sum, it covers a multiplicity of parts which can be considered separately. Without attempting for the present any thorough examination of these conceptions of unity and multiplicity, let us inquire whether the idea of number does not imply the representation of something else as well.

It is not enough to say that number is a collection of units; we must add that these units are identical with one another, or at least that they are assumed to be identical when they are counted. No doubt we can count the sheep in a flock and say that there are fifty, although they are all different from one another and are easily recognized by the shepherd: but the reason is that we agree in that case to neglect their individual differences and to take into account only what they have in common. On the other hand, as soon as we fix our attention on the particular features of objects or individuals, we can of course make an enumeration of them, but not a total. We place ourselves at these two very different points of view when we count the soldiers in a battalion and when we call the roll. Hence we may conclude that the idea of number implies the simple intuition of a multiplicity of parts or units, which are absolutely alike.[3]

And yet they must be somehow distinct from one another, since otherwise they would merge into a single unit. Let us assume that all the sheep in the flock are identical; they differ at least by the position which they occupy in space, otherwise they would not form a flock. But now let us even set aside the fifty sheep themselves and retain only the idea of them. Either we include them all in the same image, and it follows as a necessary consequence that we place them side by side in an ideal space, or else we repeat fifty times in succession the image of a single one, and in that case it does seem, indeed, that the series lies in duration rather than in space. But we shall soon find out that it cannot be so. For if we picture to ourselves each of the sheep in the flock in succession and separately, we shall never have to do with more than a single sheep. In order that the number should go on increasing in proportion as we advance, we must retain the successive images and set them alongside each of the new units which we picture to ourselves: now, it is in space that such a juxtaposition takes place and not in pure duration. In fact, it will be easily granted that counting material objects means thinking all these objects together, thereby leaving them in space. But does this intuition of space accompany every idea of number, even of an abstract number?

Any one can answer this question by reviewing the various forms which the idea of number has assumed for him since his childhood. It will be seen that we began by imagining e.g. a row of balls, that these balls afterwards became points, and, finally, this image itself disappeared, leaving behind it, as we say, nothing but *abstract* number. But at this very moment we ceased to have an image or even an idea of it; we kept only the symbol which is necessary for reckoning and which is the conventional way of *expressing* number. For we can confidently assert that 12 is half of 24 without thinking either the number 12 or the number 24: indeed, as far as quick calculation is concerned, we have everything to gain by not doing so. But as soon as we wish to picture *number* to ourselves, and not merely figures or words, we are compelled to have recourse to an extended image. What leads to misunderstanding on this point seems to be the habit we have fallen into of counting in time rather than in space. In order to imagine the number 50, for example, we repeat all the numbers starting from unity, and when we have arrived at the fiftieth, we believe we have built up the number in duration and in duration only. And there is no doubt that in this way we have counted moments of duration rather than points in space; but the question is whether we have not counted the moments of duration by means of points in space. It is certainly possible to perceive in time, and in time only, a succession which is nothing but a succession, but not an addition, i.e. a succession which culminates in a sum. For though we reach a sum by taking into account a succession of different terms, yet it is necessary that each of these terms should remain when we pass to the following, and should wait, so to speak, to be added to the others: how could it wait, if it were nothing but an instant of duration? And where could it wait if we did not localize it in space? We involuntarily fix at a point in space each of the moments which we count, and it is only on this condition that the abstract units come to form a sum. No doubt it is possible, as we shall show later, to conceive the successive moments of time independently of space; but when we add to the present moment those which have preceded it, as is the case when we are adding up units, we are not dealing with these moments themselves, since they have vanished for ever, but with the lasting traces which they seem to have left in space on their passage through it. It is true that we generally dispense with this mental image, and that, after having used it for the first two or three numbers, it is enough to know that it would serve just as well for the mental picturing of the others, if we needed it. But every clear idea of number implies a visual image in space; and the direct study of the units which go to form a discrete multiplicity will lead us to the same conclusion on this point as the examination of number itself.

Every number is a collection of units, as we have said, and on the other hand every number is itself a unit, in so far as it is a synthesis of the units which compose it. But is the word *unit* taken in the same sense in both cases? When we assert that number is a unit, we understand by this that we master the whole of it by a simple and indivisible intuition of the mind; this unity thus includes a multiplicity, since it is the unity of a whole. But when we speak of the units which go to form number, we no longer think of these units as sums, but as pure, simple, irreducible units, intended to yield the natural series of numbers by an indefinitely continued process of accumulation. It seems, then, that there are two kinds of units, the one ultimate, out of which a number is formed by a process of addition, and the other provisional, the number so formed, which is multiple in itself, and owes its unity to the simplicity of the act by which the mind perceives it. And there is no doubt that, when we picture the units which make up number, we believe that we are thinking of indivisible components: this belief has a great deal to do with the idea that it is possible to conceive number independently of space.

Nevertheless, by looking more closely into the matter, we shall see that all unity is the unity of a simple act of the mind, and that, as this is an act of unification, there must be some multiplicity for it to unify. No doubt, at the moment at which I think each of these units separately, I look upon it as indivisible, since I am determined to think of its unity alone. But as soon as I put it aside in order to pass to the next, I objectify it, and by that very deed I make it a thing, that is to say, a multiplicity. To convince oneself of this, it is enough to notice that the units by means of which arithmetic forms numbers are *provisional* units, which can be subdivided without limit, and that each of them is the sum of fractional quantities as small and as numerous as we like to imagine. How could we divide the unit, if it were here that ultimate unity which characterizes a simple act of the mind? How could we split it up into fractions whilst affirming its unity, if we did not regard it implicitly as an extended object, one in intuition but multiple in space? You will never get out of an idea which you have formed anything which you have not put into it; and if the unity by means of which you make up your number is the unity of an act and not of an object, no effort of analysis will bring out of it anything but unity pure and simple. No doubt, when you equate the number 3 to the sum of $1 + 1 + 1$, nothing prevents you from regarding the units which compose it as indivisible: but the reason is that you do not choose to make use of the multiplicity which is enclosed within each of these units. Indeed, it is probable that the number 3 first assumes to our mind this simpler shape, because we think rather of the way in which we have obtained it than of the use which we might make of it. But we soon perceive that, while all multiplication implies the possibility of treating any number whatever as a provisional unit which can be added to itself, inversely the units in their turn are true numbers which are as big as we like, but are regarded as provisionally indivisible for the purpose of compounding them with one another. Now, the very admission that it is possible to divide the unit into as many parts as we like, shows that we regard it as extended.

For we must understand what is meant by the *discontinuity* of number. It cannot be denied that the formation or construction of a number implies discontinuity. In other words, as we remarked above, each of the units with which we form the number 3 seems to be indivisible while we are dealing with it, and we pass abruptly from one to the other. Again, if we form the same number with halves, with quarters, with any units whatever, these units, in so far as they serve to form the said number, will still constitute elements which are provisionally indivisible, and it is always by jerks, by sudden jumps, so to speak, that we advance from one to the other. And the reason is that, in order to get a number, we are compelled to fix our attention successively on each of the units of which it is compounded. The indivisibility of the act by which we conceive any one of them is then represented under the form of a mathematical point which is separated from the following point by an interval of space. But, while a series of mathematical points arranged in empty space expresses fairly well the process by which we form the idea of number, these mathematical points have a tendency to develop into lines in proportion as our attention is diverted from them, as if they were trying to reunite with one another. And when we look at number in its finished state, this union is an accomplished fact: the points have become lines, the divisions have been blotted out, the whole displays all the characteristics of continuity. This is why number, although we have formed it according to a definite law, can be split up on any system we please. In a word, we must distinguish between the unity which we think of and the unity which we set up as an object after having thought of it, as also between number in process of formation and number once formed. The unit is irreducible while we are thinking it and number is discontinuous while we are building it up: but, as soon as we consider number in its finished state, we objectify it, and it then appears to be divisible to an unlimited extent. In fact, we apply the term *subjective* to what seems to be completely and adequately known, and the term *objective* to what is known in such a way that a constantly increasing number of new impressions could be substituted for the idea which we actually have of it. Thus, a complex feeling will contain a fairly large number of simple elements; but, as long as these elements do not stand out with perfect clearness, we cannot say that they were completely realized, and, as soon as consciousness has a distinct perception of them, the psychic state which results from their synthesis will have changed for this very reason. But there is no change in the general appearance of a body, however it is analysed by thought, because these different analyses, and an infinity of others, are already visible in the mental image which we form of the body, though they are not realized: this actual and not merely virtual perception of subdivisions in what is undivided is just what we call objectivity. It then becomes easy to determine the exact part played by the subjective and the objective in the idea of number. What properly belongs to the mind is the indivisible process by which it concentrates attention successively on the different parts of a given space; but the parts which have thus been isolated remain in order to join with the others, and, once the addition is made, they may be broken up in any way whatever. They are therefore parts of space, and space is, accordingly, the material with which the mind builds up number, the medium in which the mind places it.

Properly speaking, it is arithmetic which teaches us to split up without limit the units of which number consists. Common sense is very much inclined to build up number with indivisibles. And this is easily understood, since the provisional simplicity of the component units is just what they owe to the mind, and the latter pays more attention to its own acts than to the material on which it works. Science confines itself, here, to drawing our attention to this material: if we did not already localize number in space, science would certainly not succeed in making us transfer it thither. From the beginning, therefore, we must have thought of number as of a juxtaposition in space. This is the conclusion which we reached at first, basing ourselves on the fact that all addition implies a multiplicity of parts simultaneously perceived.

Now, if this conception of number is granted, it will be seen that everything is not counted in the same way, and that there are two very different kinds of multiplicity. When we speak of material objects, we refer to the possibility of seeing and touching them; we localize them in space. In that case, no effort of the inventive faculty or of symbolical representation is necessary in order to count them; we have only to think them, at first separately, and then simultaneously, within the very medium in which they come under our observation. The case is no longer the same when we consider purely affective psychic states, or even mental images other than those built up by means of sight and touch. Here, the terms being no longer given in space, it seems, *a priori*, that we can hardly count them except by some process of symbolical representation. In fact, we are well aware of a representation of this kind when we are dealing with sensations the cause of which is obviously situated in space. Thus, when we hear a noise of steps in the street, we have a confused vision of somebody walking along: each of the successive sounds is then localized at a point in space where the passer-by might tread: we count our sensations in the very space in which their tangible causes are ranged. Perhaps some people count the successive strokes of a distant bell in a similar way, their imagination pictures the bell coming and going; this spatial sort of image is sufficient for the first two units, and the others follow naturally. But most people's minds do not proceed in this way. They range the successive sounds in an ideal space and then fancy that they are counting them in pure duration. Yet we must be clear on this point. The sounds of the bell certainly reach me one after the other; but one of two alternatives must be true. Either I retain each of these successive sensations in order to combine it with the others and form a group which reminds me of an air or rhythm which I know: in that case I do not *count* the sounds, I limit myself to gathering, so to speak, the qualitative impression produced by the whole series. Or else I intend explicitly to count them, and then I shall have to *separate* them, and this separation must take place within some homogeneous medium in which the sounds, stripped of their qualities, and in a manner emptied, leave traces of their presence which are absolutely alike.[4] The question now is, whether this medium is time or space. But a moment of time, we repeat, cannot persist in order to be added to others. If the sounds are separated, they must leave empty intervals between them. If we count them, the intervals must remain though the sounds disappear: how could these intervals remain, if they were pure duration and not space? It is in space, therefore, that the operation takes place. It becomes, indeed, more and more difficult as we penetrate further into the depths of consciousness. Here we find ourselves confronted by a confused multiplicity of sensations and feelings which analysis alone can distinguish. Their number is identical with the number of the moments which we take up when we count them; but these moments, as they can be added to one another, are again points in space. Our final conclusion, therefore, is that there are two kinds of multiplicity: that of material objects, to which the conception of number is immediately applicable; and the multiplicity of states of consciousness, which cannot be regarded as numerical without the help of some symbolical representation, in which a necessary element is *space*.

As a matter of fact, each of us makes a distinction between these two kinds of multiplicity whenever he speaks of the impenetrability of matter. We sometimes set up impenetrability as a fundamental property of bodies, known in the same way and put on the same level as e.g.

weight or resistance. But a purely negative property of this kind cannot be revealed by our senses; indeed, certain experiments in mixing and combining things might lead us to call it in question if our minds were not already made up on the point. Try to picture one body penetrating another: you will at once assume that there are empty spaces in the one which will be occupied by the particles of the other; these particles in their turn cannot penetrate one another unless one of them divides in order to fill up the interstices of the other; and our thought will prolong this operation indefinitely in preference to picturing two bodies in the same place. Now, if impenetrability were really a quality of matter which was known by the senses, it is not at all clear why we should experience more difficulty in conceiving two bodies merging into one another than a surface devoid of resistance or a weightless fluid. In reality, it is not a physical but a logical necessity which attaches to the proposition: 'Two bodies cannot occupy the same place at the same time.' The contrary assertion involves an absurdity which no conceivable experience could succeed in dispelling. In a word, it implies a contradiction. But does not this amount to recognizing that the very idea of the number 2, or, more generally, of any number whatever, involves the idea of juxtaposition in space? If impenetrability is generally regarded as a quality of matter, the reason is that the idea of number is thought to be independent of the idea of space. We thus believe that we are adding something to the idea of two or more objects by saying that they cannot occupy the same place: as if the idea of the number 2, even the abstract number, were not already, as we have shown, that of two different positions in space! Hence to assert the impenetrability of matter is simply to recognize the inter-connexion between the notions of number and space, it is to state a property of number rather than of matter. – Yet, it will be said, do we not count feelings, sensations, ideas, all of which permeate one another, and each of which, for its part, takes up the whole of the soul? – Yes, undoubtedly; but, just because they permeate one another, we cannot count them unless we represent them by homogeneous units which occupy separate positions in space and consequently no longer permeate one another. Impenetrability thus makes its appearance at the same time as number; and when we attribute this quality to matter in order to distinguish it from everything which is not matter, we simply state under another form the distinction established above between extended objects, to which the conception of number is immediately applicable, and states of consciousness, which have first of all to be represented symbolically in space.

It is advisable to dwell on the last point. If in order to count states of consciousness, we have to represent them symbolically in space, is it not likely that this symbolical representation will alter the normal conditions of inner perception? Let us recall what we said a short time ago about the intensity of certain psychic states. Representative sensation, looked at in itself, is pure quality; but, seen through the medium of extensity, this quality becomes in a certain sense quantity, and is called intensity. In the same way, our projection of our psychic states into space in order to form a discrete multiplicity is likely to influence these states themselves and to give them in reflective consciousness a new form, which immediate perception did not attribute to them. Now, let us notice that when we speak of *time*, we generally think of a homogeneous medium in which our conscious states are ranged alongside one another as in space, so as to form a discrete multiplicity. Would not time, thus understood, be to the multiplicity of our psychic states what intensity is to certain of them, – a sign, a symbol, absolutely distinct from true duration? Let us ask consciousness to isolate itself from the external world, and, by a vigorous effort of abstraction, to become itself again. We shall then put this question to it: does the multiplicity of our conscious states bear the slightest resemblance to the multiplicity of the units of a number? Has true duration anything to do with space? Certainly, our analysis of the idea of number could not but make us doubt this analogy, to say no more. For if time, as the reflective consciousness represents it, is a medium in which our conscious states form a discrete series so as to admit of being counted, and if on the other hand our conception of number ends in spreading out in space everything which can be directly counted, it is to be presumed that time, understood in the sense of a medium in which we make distinctions and count, is nothing but space. That which goes to confirm this opinion is that we are compelled to borrow from space the images by which we describe what the reflective consciousness feels about time and even about succession; it follows that pure duration must be something different. Such are the questions which we have been led to ask by the very analysis of the notion of discrete multiplicity. But we cannot throw any light upon them except by a direct study of the ideas of space and time in their mutual relations.

We shall not lay too much stress on the question of the absolute reality of space: perhaps we might as well ask whether space is or is not in space. In short, our senses perceive the qualities of bodies and space along with them: the great difficulty seems to have been to discover whether extensity is an aspect of these physical qualities – a quality of quality – or whether these qualities are essentially unextended, space coming in as a later addition, but being self-sufficient and existing without them. On the first hypothesis, space would be reduced to an abstraction, or, speaking more correctly, an extract; it would express the common element possessed by certain sensations called representative. In the second case, space would be a reality as solid as the sensations themselves, although of a different order. We owe the exact formulation of this latter conception to Kant: the theory which he works out in the Transcendental Aesthetic consists in endowing space with an existence independent of its content, in laying down as *de jure* separable what each of us separates *de facto*, and in refusing to regard extensity as an abstraction like the others. In this respect the Kantian conception of space differs less than is usually imagined from the popular belief. Far from shaking our faith in the reality of space, Kant has shown what it actually means and has even justified it.

Moreover, the solution given by Kant does not seem to have been seriously disputed since his time: indeed, it has forced itself, sometimes without their knowledge, on the majority of those who have approached the problem anew, whether nativists or empiricists. Psychologists agree in assigning a Kantian origin to the nativistic explanation of Johann Müller; but Lotze's hypothesis of local signs, Bain's theory, and the more comprehensive explanation suggested by Wundt, may seem at first sight quite independent of the Transcendental Aesthetic. The authors of these theories seem indeed to have put aside the problem of the nature of space, in order to investigate simply by what process our sensations come to be situated in space and to be set, so to speak, alongside one another: but this very question shows that they regard sensations as inextensive and make a radical distinction, just as Kant did, between the matter of representation and its form. The conclusion to be drawn from the theories of Lotze and Bain, and from Wundt's attempt to reconcile them, is that the sensations by means of which we come to form the notion of space are themselves unextended and simply qualitative: extensity is supposed to result from their synthesis, as water from the combination of two gases. The empirical or genetic explanations have thus taken up the problem of space at the very point where Kant left it: Kant separated space from its contents: the empiricists ask how these contents, which are taken out of space by our thought, manage to get back again. It is true that they have apparently disregarded the activity of the mind, and that they are obviously inclined to regard the extensive form under which we represent things as produced by a kind of alliance of the sensations with one another: space, without being extracted from the sensations, is supposed to result from their co-existence. But how can we explain such an origination without the active intervention of the mind? The extensive differs by hypothesis from the inextensive: and even if we assume that extension is nothing but a relation between inextensive terms, this relation must still be established by a mind capable of thus associating several terms. It is no use quoting the example of chemical combinations, in which the whole seems to assume, of its own accord, a form and qualities which did not belong to any of the elementary atoms. This form and these qualities owe their origin just to the fact that we gather up the multiplicity of atoms in a single perception: get rid of the mind which carries out this synthesis and you will at once do away with the qualities, that is to say, the aspect under which the synthesis of elementary parts is presented to our consciousness. Thus inextensive sensations will remain what they are, viz., inextensive sensations, if nothing be added to them. For their co-existence to give rise to space, there must be an act of the mind which takes them in all at the same time and sets them in juxtaposition: this unique act is very like what Kant calls an *a priori* form of sensibility.

If we now seek to characterize this act, we see that it consists essentially in the intuition, or rather the conception, of an empty homogeneous medium. For it is scarcely possible to give any other definition of space: space is what enables us to distinguish a number of identical and simultaneous sensations from one another; it is thus a principle of differentiation other than that of qualitative differentiation, and consequently it is a reality with no quality. Someone may say, with the believers in the theory of local signs, that simultaneous sensations are never identical, and that, in consequence of the diversity of the organic elements which they affect, there are no two points of a homogeneous surface which make the same impression on the sight or the touch. We are quite ready to grant it, for if these two points affected us in the same way, there would be no reason for placing one of them on the right rather than on the left. But, just because we afterwards interpret this difference of quality in the sense of a difference of situation, it follows that we must have a clear idea of a homogeneous medium, i.e. of a simultaneity of terms which, although identical in quality, are yet distinct from one another. The more you insist on the difference between the impressions made on our retina by two points of a homogeneous surface, the more do you thereby make room for the activity of the mind, which perceives under the form of extensive homogeneity what is given it as qualitative heterogeneity. No doubt, though the representation of a homogeneous space grows out of an effort of the mind, there must be within the qualities themselves which differentiate two sensations some reason why they occupy this or that definite position in space. We must thus distinguish between the perception of extensity and the conception of space: they are no doubt implied in one another, but, the higher we rise in the scale of intelligent beings, the more clearly do we meet with the independent idea of a homogeneous space. It is therefore doubtful whether animals perceive the external world quite as we do, and especially whether they represent externality in the same way as ourselves. Naturalists have pointed out, as a remarkable fact, the surprising ease with which many vertebrates, and even some insects, manage to find their way through space. Animals have been seen to return almost in a straight line to their old home, pursuing a path which was hitherto unknown to them over a distance which may amount to several hundreds of miles. Attempts have been made to explain this feeling of direction by sight or smell, and, more recently, by the perception of magnetic currents which would enable the animal to take its bearings like a living compass. This amounts to saying that space is not so homogeneous for the animal as for us, and that determinations of space, or directions, do not assume for it a purely geometrical form. Each of these directions might appear to it with its own shade, its peculiar quality. We shall understand how a perception of this kind is possible if we remember that we ourselves distinguish our right from our left by a natural feeling, and that these two parts of our own extensity do then appear to us as if they bore a different *quality*; in fact, this is the very reason why we cannot give a proper definition of right and left. In truth, qualitative differences exist everywhere in nature, and I do not see why two concrete directions should not be as marked in immediate perception as two colours. But the conception of an empty homogeneous medium is something far more extraordinary, being a kind of reaction against that heterogeneity which is the very ground of our experience. Therefore, instead of saying that animals have a special sense of direction, we may as well say that men have a special faculty of perceiving or conceiving a space without quality. This faculty is not the faculty of abstraction: indeed, if we notice that abstraction assumes clean-cut distinctions and a kind of externality of the concepts or their symbols with regard to one another, we shall find that the faculty of abstraction already implies the intuition of a homogeneous medium. What we must say is that we have to do with two different kinds of reality, the one heterogeneous, that of sensible qualities, the other homogeneous, namely space. This latter, clearly conceived by the human intellect, enables us to use clean-cut distinctions, to count, to abstract, and perhaps also to speak.

Now, if space is to be defined as the homogeneous, it seems that inversely every homogeneous and unbounded medium will be space. For, homogeneity here consisting in the absence of every quality, it is hard to see how two forms of the homogeneous could be distinguished from one another. Nevertheless it is generally agreed to regard time as an unbounded medium, different from space but homogeneous like the latter: the homogeneous is thus supposed to take two forms, according as its contents co-exist or follow one another. It is true that, when we make time a homogeneous medium in which conscious states unfold themselves, we take it to be given all at once, which amounts to saying that we abstract it from duration. This simple consideration ought to warn us that we are thus unwittingly falling back upon space, and really giving up time. Moreover, we can understand that material objects, being exterior to one another and to ourselves, derive both exteriorities from the homogeneity of a medium which inserts intervals between them and sets off their outlines: but states of consciousness, even when successive, permeate one another, and in the simplest of them the whole soul can be reflected. We may therefore surmise that time, conceived under the form of a homogeneous medium, is some spurious concept, due to the trespassing of the idea of space upon the field of pure consciousness. At any rate we cannot finally admit two forms of the homogeneous, time and space, without first seeking whether one of them cannot be reduced to the other. Now, externality is the distinguishing mark of things which occupy space, while states of consciousness are not essentially external to one another, and become so only by being spread out in time, regarded as a homogeneous medium. If, then, one of these two supposed forms of the homogeneous, namely time and space, is derived from the other, we can surmise *a priori* that the idea of space is the fundamental datum. But, misled by the apparent simplicity of the idea of time, the philosophers who have tried to reduce one of these ideas to the other have thought that they could make extensity out of duration. While showing how they have been misled, we shall see that time, conceived under the form of an unbounded and homogeneous medium, is nothing but the ghost of space haunting the reflective consciousness.

The English school tries, in fact, to reduce relations of extensity to more or less complex relations of succession in time. When, with our eyes shut, we run our hands along a surface, the rubbing of our fingers against the surface, and especially the varied play of our joints, provide a series of sensations, which differ only by their *qualities* and which exhibit a certain order in time. Moreover, experience teaches us that this series can be reversed, that we can, by an effort of a different kind (or, as we shall call it later, *in an opposite direction*), obtain the same sensations over again in an inverse order: relations of position in space might then be defined as reversible relations of succession in time. But such a definition involves a vicious circle, or at least a very superficial idea of time. There are, indeed, as we shall show a little later, two possible conceptions of time, the one free from all alloy, the other surreptitiously bringing in the idea of space. Pure duration is the form which the succession of our conscious states assumes when our ego lets itself *live*, when it refrains from separating its present state from its former states. For this purpose it need not be entirely absorbed in the passing sensation or idea; for then, on the contrary, it would no longer *endure*. Nor need it forget its former states: it is enough that, in recalling these states, it does not set them alongside its actual state as one point alongside another, but forms both the past and the present states into an organic whole, as happens when we recall the notes of a tune, melting, so to speak, into one another. Might it not be said that, even if these notes succeed one another, yet we perceive them in one another, and that their totality may be compared to a living being whose parts, although distinct, permeate one another just because they are so closely connected? The proof is that, if we interrupt the rhythm by dwelling longer than is right on one note of the tune, it is not its exaggerated length, as length, which will warn us of our mistake, but the qualitative change thereby caused in the whole of the musical phrase. We can thus conceive of succession without distinction, and think of it as a mutual penetration, an interconnexion and organization of elements, each one of which represents the whole, and cannot be distinguished or isolated from it except by abstract thought. Such is the account of duration which would be given by a being who was ever the same and ever changing, and who had no idea of space. But, familiar with the latter idea and indeed beset by it, we introduce it unwittingly into our feeling of pure succession; we set our states of consciousness side by side in such a way as to perceive them simultaneously, no longer in one another, but alongside one another; in a word, we project time into space, we express duration in terms of extensity, and succession thus takes the form of a continuous line or a chain, the parts of which touch without penetrating one another. Note that the mental image thus shaped implies the perception, no longer successive, but simultaneous, of a *before* and *after*, and that it would be a contradiction to suppose a succession which was only a succession, and which nevertheless was contained in one and the same instant. Now, when we speak of an *order* of succession in duration, and of the reversibility of this order, is the succession we are dealing with pure succession, such as we have just defined it, without any admixture of extensity, or is it succession developing in space, in such a way that we can take in at once a number of elements which are both distinct and set side by side? There is no doubt about the answer: we could not introduce *order* among terms without first distinguishing them and then comparing the places which they occupy; hence we must perceive them as multiple, simultaneous and distinct; in a word, we set them side by side, and if we introduce an order in what is successive, the reason is that succession is converted into simultaneity and is projected into space. In short, when the movement of my finger along a surface or a line provides me with a series of sensations of different qualities, one of two things happens: either I picture these sensations to myself as in duration only, and in that case they succeed one another in such a way that I cannot at a given moment perceive a number of them as simultaneous and yet distinct; or else I make out an order of succession, but in that case I display the faculty not only of perceiving a succession of elements, but also of setting them out in line after having distinguished them: in a word, I already possess the idea of space. Hence the idea of a reversible series in duration, or even simply of a certain *order* of succession in time, itself implies the representation of space, and cannot be used to define it.

To give this argument a stricter form, let us imagine a straight line of unlimited length, and on this line a material point A, which moves. If this point were conscious of itself, it would feel itself change, since it moves: it would perceive a succession; but would this succession assume for it the form of a line? No doubt it would, if it could rise, so to speak, above the line which it traverses, and perceive simultaneously several points of it in juxtaposition: but by doing so it would form the idea of space, and it is in space and not in pure duration that it would see displayed the changes which it undergoes. We here put our finger on the mistake of those who regard pure duration as something similar to space, but of a simpler nature. They are fond of setting psychic states side by side, of forming a chain or a line of them, and do not imagine that they are introducing into this operation the idea of space properly so called, the idea of space in its totality, because space is a medium of three dimensions. But how can they fail to notice that, in order to perceive a line as a line, it is necessary to take up a position outside it, to take account of the void which surrounds it, and consequently to think a space of three dimensions? If our conscious point A does not yet possess the idea of space – and this is the hypothesis which we have agreed to adopt – the succession of states through which it passes cannot assume for it the form of a line; but its sensations will add themselves dynamically to one another and will organize themselves, like the successive notes of a tune by which we allow ourselves to be lulled and soothed. In a word, pure duration might well be nothing but a succession of qualitative changes, which melt into and permeate one another, without precise outlines, without any tendency to externalise themselves in relation to one another, without any affiliation with number: it would be pure heterogeneity. But for the present we shall not insist upon this point; it is enough for us to have shown that, from the moment when you attribute the least homogeneity to duration, you surreptitiously introduce space.

It is true that we count successive moments of duration, and that, because of its relations with number, time at first seems to us to be a measurable magnitude, just like space. But there is here an important distinction to be made. I say, e.g., that a minute has just elapsed, and I mean by this that a pendulum, beating the seconds, has completed sixty oscillations. If I picture these sixty oscillations to myself all at once by a single mental perception, I exclude by hypothesis the idea of a succession. I do not think of sixty strokes which succeed one another, but of sixty points on a fixed line, each one of which symbolizes, so to speak, an oscillation of the pendulum. If, on the other hand, I wish to picture these sixty oscillations in succession, but without altering the way they are produced in space, I shall be compelled to think of each oscillation to the exclusion of the recollection of the preceding one, for space has preserved no trace of it; but by doing so I shall condemn myself to remain for ever in the present; I shall give up the attempt to think a succession or a duration. Now if, finally, I retain the recollection of the preceding oscillation together with the image of the present oscillation, one of two things will happen. Either I shall set the two images side by side, and we then fall back on our first hypothesis, or I shall perceive one in the other, each permeating the other and organizing themselves like the notes of a tune, so as to form what we shall call a continuous or qualitative multiplicity with no resemblance to number. I shall thus get the image of pure duration; but I shall have entirely got rid of the idea of a homogeneous medium or a measurable quantity. By carefully examining our consciousness we shall recognize that it proceeds in this way whenever it refrains from representing duration symbolically. When the regular oscillations of the pendulum make us sleepy, is it the last sound heard, the last movement perceived, which produces this effect? No, undoubtedly not, for why then should not the first have done the same? Is it the recollection of the preceding sounds or movements, set in juxtaposition to the last one? But this same recollection, if it is later on set in juxtaposition to a single sound or movement, will remain without effect. Hence we must admit that the sounds combined with one another and acted, not by their quantity as quantity, but by the quality which their quantity exhibited, i.e. by the rhythmic organization of the whole. Could the effect of a slight but continuous stimulation be understood in any other way? If the sensation remained always the same, it would continue to be indefinitely slight and indefinitely bearable. But the fact is that each increase of stimulation is taken up into the preceding stimulations, and that the whole produces on us the effect of a musical phrase which is constantly on the point of ending and constantly altered in its totality by the addition of some new note. If we assert that it is always the *same* sensation, the reason is that we are thinking, not of the sensation itself, but of its objective cause situated in space. We then set it out in space in its turn, and in place of an organism which develops, in place of changes which permeate one another, we perceive one and the same sensation stretching itself out lengthwise, so to speak, and setting itself in juxtaposition to itself without limit. Pure duration, that which consciousness perceives, must thus be reckoned among the so-called intensive magnitudes, if intensities can be called magnitudes: strictly speaking, however, it is not a quantity, and as soon as we try to measure it, we unwittingly replace it by space.

But we find it extraordinarily difficult to think of duration in its original purity; this is due, no doubt, to the fact that we do not *endure* alone; external objects, it seems, *endure* as we do, and time, regarded from this point of view, has every appearance of a homogeneous medium. Not only do the moments of this duration seem to be external to one another, like bodies in space, but the movement perceived by our senses is, so to speak, the palpable sign of a homogeneous and measurable duration. Nay more, time enters into the formulae of mechanics, into the calculations of the astronomer, and even of the physicist, under the form of a quantity. We measure the velocity of a movement, implying that time itself is a magnitude. Indeed, the analysis which we have just attempted requires to be completed, for if duration properly so-called cannot be measured, what is it that is measured by the oscillations of the pendulum? Granted that inner duration, perceived by consciousness, is nothing else but the melting of states of consciousness into one another, and the gradual growth of the ego, it will be said, notwithstanding, that the time which the astronomer introduces into his formulae, the time which our clocks divide into equal portions, this time, at least, is something different: it must be a measurable and therefore homogeneous magnitude. – It is nothing of the sort, however, and a close examination will dispel this last illusion.

When I follow with my eyes on the dial of a clock the movement of the hand which corresponds to the oscillations of the pendulum, I do not measure duration, as seems to be thought; I merely count simultaneities, which is very different. Outside of me, in space, there is never more than a single position of the hand and the pendulum, for nothing is left of the past positions. Within myself a process of organization or interpenetration of conscious states is going on, which constitutes true duration. It is because I *endure* in this way that I picture to myself what I call the past oscillations of the pendulum at the same time as I perceive the present oscillation. Now, let us withdraw for a moment the ego which thinks these so-called successive oscillations: there will never be more than a single oscillation, and indeed only a single position, of the pendulum, and hence no duration. Withdraw, on the other hand, the pendulum and its oscillations; there will no longer be anything but the heterogeneous duration of the ego, without moments external to one another, without relation to number. Thus, within our ego, there is succession without mutual externality; outside the ego, in pure space, mutual externality without succession: mutual externality, since the present oscillation is radically distinct from the previous oscillation, which no longer exists; but no succession, since succession exists solely for a conscious spectator who keeps the past in mind and sets the two oscillations or their symbols side by side in an auxiliary space. Now, between this succession without externality and this externality without succession, a kind of exchange takes place, very similar to what physicists call the phenomenon of endosmosis. As the successive phases of our conscious life, although interpenetrating, correspond individually to an oscillation of the pendulum which occurs at the same time, and as, moreover, these oscillations are sharply distinguished from one another, we get into the habit of setting up the same distinction between the successive moments of our conscious life: the oscillations of the pendulum break it up, so to speak, into parts external to one another: hence the mistaken idea of a homogeneous inner duration, similar to space, the moments of which are identical and follow, without penetrating, one another. But, on the other hand, the oscillations of the pendulum, which are distinct only because one has disappeared when the other appears on the scene, profit, as it were, from the influence which they have thus exercised over our conscious life. Owing to the fact that our consciousness has organized them as a whole in memory, they are first preserved and afterwards disposed in a series: in a word, we create for them a fourth dimension of space, which we call homogeneous time, and which enables the movement of the pendulum, although taking place at one spot, to be continually set in juxtaposition to itself. Now, if we try to determine the exact part played by the real and the imaginary in this very complex process, this is what we find. There is a real space, without duration, in which phenomena appear and disappear simultaneously with our states of consciousness. There is a real duration, the heterogeneous moments of which permeate one another; each moment, however, can be brought into relation with a state of the external world which is contemporaneous with it, and can be separated from the other moments in consequence of this very process. The comparison of these two realities gives rise to a symbolical representation of duration, derived from space. Duration thus assumes the illusory form of a homogeneous medium, and the connecting link between these two terms, space and duration, is simultaneity, which might be defined as the intersection of time and space.

If we analyse in the same way the concept of motion, the living symbol of this seemingly homogeneous duration, we shall be led to make a distinction of the same kind. We generally say that a movement takes place *in* space, and when we assert that motion is homogeneous and divisible, it is of the space traversed that we are thinking, as if it were interchangeable with the motion itself. Now, if we reflect further, we shall see that the successive positions of the moving body really do occupy space, but that the process by which it passes from one position to the other, a process which occupies duration and which has no reality except for a conscious spectator, eludes space. We have to do here not with an *object* but with a *progress*: motion, in so far as it is a passage from one point to another, is a mental synthesis, a psychic and therefore unextended process. Space contains only parts of space, and at whatever point of space we consider the moving body, we shall get only a position. If consciousness is aware of anything more than positions, the reason is that it keeps the successive positions in mind and synthesizes them. But how does it carry out a synthesis of this kind? It cannot be by a fresh setting out of these same positions in a homogeneous medium, for a fresh synthesis would be necessary to connect the positions with one another, and so on indefinitely. We are thus compelled to admit that we have here to do with a synthesis which is, so to speak, qualitative, a gradual organization of our successive sensations, a unity resembling that of a phrase in a melody. This is just the idea of motion which we form when we think of it by itself, when, so to speak, from motion we extract mobility. Think of what you experience on suddenly perceiving a shooting star: in this extremely rapid motion there is a natural and instinctive separation between the space traversed, which appears to you under the form of a line of fire, and the absolutely indivisible sensation of motion or mobility. A rapid gesture, made with one's eyes shut, will assume for consciousness the form of a purely qualitative sensation as long as there is no thought of the space traversed. In a word, there are two elements to be distinguished in motion, the space traversed and the act by which we traverse it, the successive positions and the synthesis of these positions. The first of these elements is a homogeneous quantity: the second has no reality except in a consciousness: it is a quality or an intensity, whichever you prefer. But here again we meet with a case of endosmosis, an intermingling of the purely intensive sensation of mobility with the extensive representation of the space traversed. On the one hand we attribute to the motion the divisibility of the space which it traverses, forgetting that it is quite possible to divide an *object*, but not an *act*: and on the other hand we accustom ourselves to projecting this act itself into space, to applying it to the whole of the line which the moving body traverses, in a word, to solidifying it: as if this localizing of a *progress* in space did not amount to asserting that, even outside consciousness, the past co-exists along with the present!

It is to this confusion between motion and the space traversed that the paradoxes of the Eleatics are due; for the interval which separates two points is infinitely divisible, and if motion consisted of parts like those of the interval itself, the interval would never be crossed. But the truth is that each of Achilles' steps is a simple indivisible act, and that, after a given number of these acts, Achilles will have passed the tortoise. The mistake of the Eleatics arises from their identification of this series of acts, each of which is of *a definite kind* and *indivisible*, with the homogeneous space which underlies them. As this space can be divided and put together again according to any law whatever, they think they are justified in reconstructing Achilles' whole movement, not with Achilles' kind of step, but with the tortoise's kind: in place of Achilles pursuing the tortoise they really put two tortoises, regulated by each other, two tortoises which agree to make the same kind of steps or simultaneous acts, so as never to catch one another. Why does Achilles outstrip the tortoise? Because each of Achilles' steps and each of the tortoise's steps are indivisible acts in so far as they are movements, and are different magnitudes in so far as they are space: so that addition will soon give a greater length for the space traversed by Achilles than is obtained by adding together the space traversed by the tortoise and the handicap with which it started. This is what Zeno leaves out of account when he reconstructs the movement of Achilles according to the same law as the movement of the tortoise, forgetting that space alone can be divided and put together again in any way we like, and thus confusing space with motion. Hence we do not think it necessary to admit, even after the acute and profound analysis of a contemporary thinker,[5] that the meeting of the two moving bodies implies a discrepancy between real and imaginary motion, between *space in itself* and indefinitely divisible space, between concrete time and abstract time. Why resort to a metaphysical hypothesis, however ingenious, about the nature of space, time, and motion, when immediate intuition shows us motion within duration, and duration outside space? There is no need to assume a limit to the divisibility of concrete space; we can admit that it is infinitely divisible, provided that we make a distinction between the simultaneous positions of the two moving bodies, which are in fact in space, and their movements, which cannot occupy space, being duration rather than extent, quality and not quantity. To measure the velocity of a movement, as we shall see, is simply to ascertain a simultaneity; to introduce this velocity into calculations is simply to use a convenient means of anticipating a simultaneity. Thus mathematics confines itself to its own province as long as it is occupied with determining the simultaneous positions of Achilles and the tortoise at a given moment, or when it admits *a priori* that the two moving bodies meet at a point X – a meeting which is itself a simultaneity. But it goes beyond its province when it claims to reconstruct what takes place in the interval between two simultaneities; or rather it is inevitably led, even then, to consider simultaneities once more, fresh simultaneities, the indefinitely increasing number of which ought to be a warning that we cannot make movement out of immobilities, nor time out of space. In short, just as nothing will be found homogeneous in duration except a symbolical medium with no duration at all, namely space, in which simultaneities are set out in line, in the same way no homogeneous element will be found in motion except that which least belongs to it, the traversed space, which is motionless.

Now, just for this reason, science cannot deal with time and motion except on condition of first eliminating the essential and qualitative element – of time, duration, and of motion, mobility. We may easily convince ourselves of this by examining the part played in astronomy and mechanics by considerations of time, motion, and velocity.

Treatises on mechanics are careful to announce that they do not intend to define duration itself but only the equality of two durations. 'Two intervals of time are equal when two identical bodies, in identical conditions at the beginning of each of these intervals and subject to the same actions and influences of every kind, have traversed the same space at the end of these intervals.' In other words, we are to note the exact moment at which the motion begins, i.e. the coincidence of an external change with one of our psychic states: we are to note the moment at which the motion ends, that is to say, another simultaneity; finally we are to measure the space traversed, the only thing, in fact, which is really measurable. Hence there is no question here of duration, but only of space and simultaneities. To announce that something will take place at the end of a time *t* is to declare that consciousness will note between now and then a number *t* of simultaneities of a certain kind. And we must not be led astray by the words 'between now and then,' for the interval of duration exists only for us and on account of the interpenetration of our conscious states. Outside ourselves we should find only space, and consequently nothing but simultaneities, of which we could not even say that they are objectively successive, since succession can only be thought through *comparing* the present with the past. – That the interval of duration itself cannot be taken into account by science is proved by the fact that, if all the motions of the universe took place twice or thrice as quickly, there would be nothing to alter either in our formulae or in the figures which are to be found in them. Consciousness would have an indefinable and as it were qualitative impression of the change, but the change would not make itself felt outside consciousness, since the same number of simultaneities would go on taking place in space. We shall see, later on, that when the astronomer predicts, e.g., an eclipse, he does something of this kind: he shortens infinitely the intervals of duration, as these do not count for science, and thus perceives in a very short time – a few seconds at the most – a succession of simultaneities which may take up several centuries for the concrete consciousness, compelled to live through the intervals instead of merely counting their extremities.

A direct analysis of the notion of velocity will bring us to the same conclusion. Mechanics gets this notion through a series of ideas, the connexion of which it is easy enough to trace. It first builds up the idea of uniform motion by picturing, on the one hand, the path AB of a certain moving body, and, on the other, a physical phenomenon which is repeated indefinitely under the same conditions, e.g., a stone always falling from the same height on to the same spot. If we mark on the path AB the points M, N, P . . . reached by the moving body at each of the moments when the stone touches the ground, and if the intervals AM, MN and NP are found to be equal to one another, the motion will be said to be uniform: and any one of these intervals will be called the velocity of the moving body, provided that it is agreed to adopt as unit of duration the physical phenomenon which has been chosen as the term of comparison. Thus, the velocity of a uniform motion is defined by mechanics without appealing to any other notions than those of space and simultaneity. Now let us turn to the case of a variable motion, that is, to the case when the elements AM, MN, NP . . . are found to be unequal. In order to define the velocity of the moving body A at the point M, we shall only have to imagine an unlimited number of moving bodies A_1, A_2, A_3 . . . all moving uniformly with velocities V_1, V_2, V_3 . . . which are arranged, e.g., in an ascending scale and which correspond to all possible magnitudes. Let us then consider on the path of the moving body A two points M' and M", situated on either side of the point M but very near it. At the same time as this moving body reaches the points M', M, M", the other moving bodies reach points $M_1'M_1M_1"$, $M_2'M_2M_2"$ . . . on their respective paths; and there must be two moving bodies A_h and A_p such that we have on the one hand M'M = $M_h'M_h$ and on the other hand MM" =$M_pM_p"$. *We shall then agree to say that the velocity of the moving* body A at the point M lies between V_h and V_p. But nothing prevents our assuming that the points M' and M" are still nearer the point M, and it will then be necessary to replace V_h and V_p by two fresh velocities V_f and V_n, the one greater than V_h and the other less than V_p. And in proportion as we reduce the two intervals M'M and MM", we shall lessen the difference between the velocities of the uniform corresponding movements. Now, the two intervals being capable of decreasing right down to zero, there evidently exists between V_f and V_n a certain velocity V_m, such that the difference between this velocity and V_h, V_f . . . on the one hand, and V_p, V_n, . . . on the other, can become smaller than any given quantity. It is this common limit V_m which we shall call the velocity of the moving body A at the point M. – Now, in this analysis of variable motion, as in that of uniform motion, it is a question only of spaces once traversed and of simultaneous positions once reached. We were thus justified in saying that, while all that mechanics retains of time is simultaneity, all that it retains of motion itself – restricted, as it is, to a *measurement* of motion – is immobility.

This result might have been foreseen by noticing that mechanics necessarily deals with equations, and that an algebraic equation always expresses something already done. Now, it is of the very essence of duration and motion, as they appear to our consciousness, to be something that is unceasingly being done; thus algebra can represent the results gained at a certain moment of duration and the positions occupied by a certain moving body in space, but not duration and motion themselves. Mathematics may, indeed, increase the number of simultaneities and positions which it takes into consideration by making the intervals very small; it may even, by using the differential instead of the difference, show that it is possible to increase without limit the number of these intervals of duration. Nevertheless, however small the interval is supposed to be, it is the extremity of the interval at which mathematics always places itself. As for the interval itself, as for the duration and the motion, they are necessarily left out of the equation. The reason is that duration and motion are mental syntheses, and not objects; that, although the moving body occupies, one after the other, points on a line, motion itself has nothing to do with a line; and finally that, although the positions occupied by the moving body vary with the different moments of duration, though it even creates distinct moments by the mere fact of occupying different positions, duration properly so called has no moments which are identical or external to one another, being essentially heterogeneous, continuous, and with no analogy to number.

It follows from this analysis that space alone is homogeneous, that objects in space form a discrete multiplicity, and that every discrete multiplicity is got by a process of unfolding in space. It also follows that there is neither duration nor even succession in space, if we give to these words the meaning in which consciousness takes them: each of the so-called successive states of the external world exists alone; their multiplicity is real only for a consciousness that can first retain them and then set them side by side by externalising them in relation to one another. If it retains them, it is because these distinct states of the external world give rise to states of consciousness which permeate one another, imperceptibly organize themselves into a whole, and bind the past to the present by this very process of connexion. If it externalises them in relation to one another, the reason is that, thinking of their radical distinctness (the one having ceased to be when the other appears on the scene), it perceives them under the form of a discrete multiplicity, which amounts to setting them out in line, in the space in which each of them existed separately. The space employed for this purpose is just that which is called homogeneous time.

But another conclusion results from this analysis, namely, that the multiplicity of conscious states, regarded in its original purity, is not at all like the discrete multiplicity which goes to form a number. In such a case there is, as we said, a qualitative multiplicity. In short, we must admit two kinds of multiplicity, two possible senses of the word 'distinguish,' two conceptions, the one qualitative and the other quantitative, of the difference between *same* and *other*. Sometimes this multiplicity, this distinctness, this heterogeneity contains number only potentially, as Aristotle would have said. Consciousness, then, makes a qualitative discrimination without any further thought of counting the qualities or even of distinguishing them as *several*. In such a case we have multiplicity without quantity. Sometimes, on the other hand, it is a question of a multiplicity of terms which are counted or which are conceived as capable of being counted; but we think then of the possibility of externalising them in relation to one another, we set them out in space. Unfortunately, we are so accustomed to illustrate one of these two meanings of the same word by the other, and even to perceive the one in the other, that we find it extraordinarily difficult to distinguish between them or at least to express this distinction in words. Thus I said that several conscious states are organized into a whole, permeate one another, gradually gain a richer content, and might thus give any one ignorant of space the feeling of pure duration; but the very use of the word 'several' shows that I had already isolated these states, externalised them in relation to one another, and, in a word, set them side by side; thus, by the very language which I was compelled to use, I betrayed the deeply ingrained habit of setting out time in space. From this spatial setting out, already accomplished, we are compelled to borrow the terms which we use to describe the state of a mind which has not yet accomplished it: these terms are thus misleading from the very beginning, and the idea of a multiplicity without relation to number or space, although clear for pure reflective thought, cannot be translated into the language of common sense. And yet we cannot even form the idea of discrete multiplicity without considering at the same time a qualitative multiplicity. When we explicitly count units by stringing them along a spatial line, is it not the case that, alongside this addition of identical terms standing out from a homogeneous background, an organization of these units is going on in the depths of the soul, a wholly dynamic process, not unlike the purely qualitative way in which an anvil, if it could feel, would realize a series of blows from a hammer? In this sense we might almost say that the numbers in daily use have each their emotional equivalent. Tradesmen are well aware of it, and instead of indicating the price of an object by a round number of shillings, they will mark the next smaller number, leaving themselves to insert afterwards a sufficient number of pence and farthings. In a word, the process by which we count units and make them into a discrete multiplicity has two sides; on the one hand we assume that they are identical, which is conceivable only on condition that these units are ranged alongside each other in a homogeneous medium; but on the other hand the third unit, for example, when added to the other two, alters the nature, the appearance and, as it were, the rhythm of the whole; without this interpenetration and this, so to speak, qualitative progress, no addition would be possible. Hence it is through the quality of quantity that we form the idea of quantity without quality.

It is therefore obvious that if it did not betake itself to a symbolical substitute, our consciousness would never regard time as a homogeneous medium, in which the terms of a succession remain outside one another. But we naturally reach this symbolical representation by the mere fact that, in a series of identical terms, each term assumes a double aspect for our consciousness: one aspect which is the same for all of them, since we are thinking then of the sameness of the external object, and another aspect which is characteristic of each of them, because the supervening of each term brings about a new organization of the whole. Hence the possibility of setting out in space, under the form of numerical multiplicity, what we have called a qualitative multiplicity, and of regarding the one as the equivalent of the other. Now, this twofold process is nowhere accomplished so easily as in the perception of the external phenomenon which takes for us the form of motion. Here we certainly have series of identical terms, since it is always the same moving body; but, on the other hand, the synthesis carried out by our consciousness between the actual position and what our memory calls the former positions, causes these images to permeate, complete, and, so to speak, continue one another. Hence, it is principally by the help of motion that duration assumes the form of a homogeneous medium, and that time is projected into space. But, even if we leave out motion, any repetition of a well-marked external phenomenon would suggest to consciousness the same mode of representation. Thus, when we hear a series of blows of a hammer, the sounds form an indivisible melody in so far as they are pure sensations, and, here again, give rise to a dynamic progress; but, knowing that the same objective cause is at work, we cut up this progress into phases which we then regard as identical; and this multiplicity of elements no longer being conceivable except by being set out in space, since they have now become identical, we are necessarily led to the idea of a homogeneous time, the symbolical image of real duration. In a word, our ego comes in contact with the external world at its surface; our successive sensations, although dissolving into one another, retain something of the mutual externality which belongs to their objective causes; and thus our superficial psychic life comes to be pictured without any great effort as set out in a homogeneous medium. But the symbolical character of such a picture becomes more striking as we advance further into the depths of consciousness: the deep-seated self which ponders and decides, which heats and blazes up, is a self whose states and changes permeate one another and undergo a deep alteration as soon as we separate them from one another in order to set them out in space. But as this deeper self forms one and the same person with the superficial ego, the two seem to *endure* in the same way. And as the repeated picture of one identical objective phenomenon, ever recurring, cuts up our superficial psychic life into parts external to one another, the moments which are thus determined determine in their turn distinct segments in the dynamic and undivided progress of our more personal conscious states. Thus the mutual externality which material objects gain from their juxtaposition in homogeneous space reverberates and spreads into the depths of consciousness: little by little our sensations are distinguished from one another like the external causes which gave rise to them, and our feelings or ideas come to be separated like the sensations with which they are contemporaneous.

That our ordinary conception of duration depends on a gradual incursion of space into the domain of pure consciousness is proved by the fact that, in order to deprive the ego of the faculty of perceiving a homogeneous time, it is enough to take away from it this outer circle of psychic states which it uses as a balance-wheel. These conditions are realized when we dream; for sleep, by relaxing the play of the organic functions, alters the communicating surface between the ego and external objects. Here we no longer measure duration, but we feel it; from quantity it returns to the state of quality; we no longer estimate past time mathematically: the mathematical estimate gives place to a confused instinct, capable, like all instincts, of committing gross errors, but also of acting at times with extraordinary skill. Even in the waking state, daily experience ought to teach us to distinguish between duration as quality, that which consciousness reaches immediately and which is probably what animals perceive, and time so to speak materialized, time that has become quantity by being set out in space. Whilst I am writing these lines, the hour strikes on a neighbouring clock, but my inattentive ear does not perceive it until several strokes have made themselves heard. Hence I have not counted them; and yet I only have to turn my attention backwards to count up the four strokes which have already sounded and add them to those which I hear. If, then, I question myself carefully on what has just taken place, I perceive that the first four sounds had struck my ear and even affected my consciousness, but that the sensations produced by each one of them, instead of being set side by side, had melted into one another in such a way as to give the whole a peculiar quality, to make a kind of musical phrase out of it. In order, then, to estimate retrospectively the number of strokes sounded, I tried to reconstruct this phrase in thought: my imagination made one stroke, then two, then three, and as long as it did not reach the exact number four, my feeling, when consulted, answered that the total effect was qualitatively different. It had thus ascertained in its own way the succession of four strokes, but quite otherwise than by a process of addition, and without bringing in the image of a juxtaposition of distinct terms. In a word, the number of strokes was perceived as a quality and not as a quantity: it is thus that duration is presented to immediate consciousness, and it retains this form so long as it does not give place to a symbolical representation derived from extensity.

We should therefore distinguish two forms of multiplicity, two very different ways of regarding duration, two aspects of conscious life. Below homogeneous duration, which is the extensive symbol of true duration, a close psychological analysis distinguishes a duration whose heterogeneous moments permeate one another; below the numerical multiplicity of conscious states, a qualitative multiplicity; below the self with well-defined states, a self in which *succeeding each other means melting into one another* and forming an organic whole. But we are generally content with the first, i.e. with the shadow of the self projected into homogeneous space. Consciousness, goaded by an insatiable desire to separate, substitutes the symbol for the reality, or perceives the reality only through the symbol. As the self thus refracted, and thereby broken to pieces, is much better adapted to the requirements of social life in general and language in particular, consciousness prefers it, and gradually loses sight of the fundamental self.

In order to recover this fundamental self, as the unsophisticated consciousness would perceive it, a vigorous effort of analysis is necessary, which will isolate the fluid inner states from their image, first refracted, then solidified in homogeneous space. In other words, our perceptions, sensations, emotions and ideas occur under two aspects: the one clear and precise, but impersonal; the other confused, ever changing, and inexpressible, because language cannot get hold of it without arresting its mobility or fit it into its common-place forms without making it into public property. If we have been led to distinguish two forms of multiplicity, two forms of duration, we must expect each conscious state, taken by itself, to assume a different aspect according as we consider it within a discrete multiplicity or a confused multiplicity, in the time as quality, in which it is produced, or in the time as quantity, into which it is projected.

When e.g. I take my first walk in a town in which I am going to live, my environment produces on me two impressions at the same time, one of which is destined to last while the other will constantly change. Every day I perceive the same houses, and as I know that they are the same objects, I always call them by the same name and I also fancy that they always look the same to me. But if I recur, at the end of a sufficiently long period, to the impression which I experienced during the first few years, I am surprised at the remarkable, inexplicable, and indeed inexpressible change which has taken place. It seems that these objects, continually perceived by me and constantly impressing themselves on my mind, have ended by borrowing from me something of my own conscious existence; like myself they have lived, and like myself they have grown old. This is not a mere illusion; for if today's impression were absolutely identical with that of yesterday, what difference would there be between perceiving and recognizing, between learning and remembering? Yet this difference escapes the attention of most of us; we shall hardly perceive it, unless we are warned of it and then carefully look into ourselves. The reason is that our outer and, so to speak, social life is more practically important to us than our inner and individual existence. We instinctively tend to solidify our impressions in order to express them in language. Hence we confuse the feeling itself, which is in a perpetual state of becoming, with its permanent external object, and especially with the word which expresses this object. In the same way as the fleeting duration of our ego is fixed by its projection in homogeneous space, our constantly changing impressions, wrapping themselves round the external object which is their cause, take on its definite outlines and its immobility.

Our simple sensations, taken in their natural state, are still more fleeting. Such and such a flavour, such and such a scent, pleased me when I was a child though I dislike them today. Yet I still give the same name to the sensation experienced, and I speak as if only my taste had changed, whilst the scent and the flavour have remained the same. Thus I again solidify the sensation; and when its changeableness becomes so obvious that I cannot help recognizing it, I abstract this changeableness to give it a name of its own and solidify it in the shape of a *taste*. But in reality there are neither identical sensations nor multiple tastes: for sensations and tastes seem to me to be *objects* as soon as I isolate and name them, and in the human soul there are only *processes*. What I ought to say is that every sensation is altered by repetition, and that if it does not seem to me to change from day to day, it is because I perceive it through the object which is its cause, through the word which translates it. This influence of language on sensation is deeper than is usually thought. Not only does language make us believe in the unchangeableness of our sensations, but it will sometimes deceive us as to the nature of the sensation felt. Thus, when I partake of a dish that is supposed to be exquisite, the name which it bears, suggestive of the approval given to it, comes between my sensation and my consciousness; I may believe that the flavour pleases me when a slight effort of attention would prove the contrary. In short, the word with well-defined outlines, the rough and ready word, which stores up the stable, common, and consequently impersonal element in the impressions of mankind, overwhelms or at least covers over the delicate and fugitive impressions of our individual consciousness. To maintain the struggle on equal terms, the latter ought to express themselves in precise words; but these words, as soon as they were formed, would turn against the sensation which gave birth to them, and, invented to show that the sensation is unstable, they would impose on it their own stability.

This overwhelming of the immediate consciousness is nowhere so striking as in the case of our feelings. A violent love or a deep melancholy takes possession of our soul: here we feel a thousand different elements which dissolve into and permeate one another without any precise outlines, without the least tendency to externalise themselves in relation to one another; hence their originality. We distort them as soon as we distinguish a numerical multiplicity in their confused mass: what will it be, then, when we set them out, isolated from one another, in this homogeneous medium which may be called either time or space, whichever you prefer? A moment ago each of them was borrowing an indefinable colour from its surroundings: now we have it colourless, and ready to accept a name. The feeling itself is a being which lives and develops and is therefore constantly changing; otherwise how could it gradually lead us to form a resolution? Our resolution would be immediately taken. But it lives because the duration in which it develops is a duration whose moments permeate one another. By separating these moments from each other, by spreading out time in space, we have caused this feeling to lose its life and its colour. Hence, we are now standing before our own shadow: we believe that we have analysed our feeling, while we have really replaced it by a juxtaposition of lifeless states which can be translated into words, and each of which constitutes the common element, the impersonal residue, of the impressions felt in a given case by the whole of society. And this is why we reason about these states and apply our simple logic to them: having set them up as genera by the mere fact of having isolated them from one another, we have prepared them for use in some future deduction. Now, if some bold novelist, tearing aside the cleverly woven curtain of our conventional ego, shows us under this appearance of logic a fundamental absurdity, under this juxtaposition of simple states an infinite permeation of a thousand different impressions which have already ceased to exist the instant they are named, we commend him for having known us better than we knew ourselves. This is not the case, however, and the very fact that he spreads out our feeling in a homogeneous time, and expresses its elements by words, shows that he in his turn is only offering us its shadow: but he has arranged this shadow in such a way as to make us suspect the extraordinary and illogical nature of the object which projects it; he has made us reflect by giving outward expression to something of that contradiction, that interpenetration, which is the very essence of the elements expressed. Encouraged by him, we have put aside for an instant the veil which we interposed between our consciousness and ourselves. He has brought us back into our own presence.

We should experience the same sort of surprise if we strove to seize our ideas themselves in their natural state, as our consciousness would perceive them if it were no longer beset by space. This breaking up of the constituent elements of an idea, which issues in abstraction, is too convenient for us to do without it in ordinary life and even in philosophical discussion. But when we fancy that the parts thus artificially separated are the genuine threads with which the concrete idea was woven, when, substituting for the interpenetration of the real terms the juxtaposition of their symbols, we claim to make duration out of space, we unavoidably fall into the mistakes of associationism. We shall not insist on the latter point, which will be the subject of a thorough examination in the next chapter. Let it be enough to say that the impulsive zeal with which we take sides on certain questions shows how our intellect has its instincts – and what can an instinct of this kind be if not an impetus common to all our ideas, i.e. their very interpenetration? The beliefs to which we most strongly adhere are those of which we should find it most difficult to give an account, and the reasons by which we justify them are seldom those which have led us to adopt them. In a certain sense we have adopted them without any reason, for what makes them valuable in our eyes is that they match the colour of all our other ideas, and that from the very first we have seen in them something of ourselves. Hence they do not take in our minds that common-looking form which they will assume as soon as we try to give expression to them in words; and, although they bear the same name in other minds, they are by no means the same thing. The fact is that each of them has the same kind of life as a cell in an organism: everything which affects the general state of the self affects it also. But while the cell occupies a definite point in the organism, an idea which is truly ours fills the whole of our self. Not all our ideas, however, are thus incorporated in the fluid mass of our conscious states. Many float on the surface, like dead leaves on the water of a pond: the mind, when it thinks them over and over again, finds them ever the same, as if they were external to it. Among these are the ideas which we receive ready made, and which remain in us without ever being properly assimilated, or again the ideas which we have omitted to cherish and which have withered in neglect. If, in proportion as we get away from the deeper strata of the self, our conscious states tend more and more to assume the form of a numerical multiplicity, and to spread out in a homogeneous space, it is just because these conscious states tend to become more and more lifeless, more and more impersonal. Hence we need not be surprised if only those ideas which least belong to us can be adequately expressed in words: only to these, as we shall see, does the associationist theory apply. External to one another, they keep up relations among themselves in which the inmost nature of each of them counts for nothing, relations which can therefore be classified. It may thus be said that they are associated by contiguity or for some logical reason. But if, digging below the surface of contact between the self and external objects, we penetrate into the depths of the organized and living intelligence, we shall witness the joining together or rather the blending of many ideas which, when once dissociated, seem to exclude one another as logically contradictory terms. The strangest dreams, in which two images overlie one another and show us at the same time two different persons, who yet make only one, will hardly give us an idea of the interweaving of concepts which goes on when we are awake. The imagination of the dreamer, cut off from the external world, imitates with mere images, and parodies in its own way, the process which constantly goes on with regard to ideas in the deeper regions of the intellectual life.

Thus may be verified, thus, too, will be illustrated by a further study of deep-seated psychic phenomena, the principle from which we started: conscious life displays two aspects according as we perceive it directly or by refraction through space. Considered in themselves, the deep-seated conscious states have no relation to quantity, they are pure quality; they intermingle in such a way that we cannot tell whether they are one or several, nor even examine them from this point of view without at once altering their nature. The duration which they thus create is a duration whose moments do not constitute a numerical multiplicity: to characterize these moments by saying that they encroach on one another would still be to distinguish them. If each of us lived a purely individual life, if there were neither society nor language, would our consciousness grasp the series of inner states in this unbroken form? Undoubtedly it would not quite succeed, because we should still retain the idea of a homogeneous space in which objects are sharply distinguished from one another, and because it is too convenient to set out in such a medium the somewhat cloudy states which first attract the attention of consciousness, in order to resolve them into simpler terms. But mark that the intuition of a homogeneous space is already a step towards social life. Probably animals do not picture to themselves, beside their sensations, as we do, an external world quite distinct from themselves, which is the common property of all conscious beings. Our tendency to form a clear picture of this externality of things and the homogeneity of their medium is the same as the impulse which leads us to live in common and to speak. But, in proportion as the conditions of social life are more completely realized, the current which carries our conscious states from within outwards is strengthened; little by little these states are made into objects or things; they break off not only from one another, but from ourselves. Henceforth we no longer perceive them except in the homogeneous medium in which we have set their image, and through the word which lends them its commonplace colour. Thus a second self is formed which obscures the first, a self whose existence is made up of distinct moments, whose states are separated from one another and easily expressed in words. I do not mean, here, to split up the personality, nor to bring back in another form the numerical multiplicity which I shut out at the beginning. It is the same self which perceives distinct states at first, and which, by afterwards concentrating its attention, will see these states melt into one another like the crystals of a snow-flake when touched for some time with the finger. And, in truth, for the sake of language, the self has everything to gain by not bringing back confusion where order reigns, and in not upsetting this ingenious arrangement of almost impersonal states by which it has ceased to form 'a kingdom within a kingdom.' An inner life with well-distinguished moments and with clearly characterized states will answer better the requirements of social life. Indeed, a superficial psychology may be content with describing it without thereby falling into error, on condition, however, that it restricts itself to the study of what has taken place and leaves out what is going on. But if, passing from statics to dynamics, this psychology claims to reason about things in the making as it reasoned about things made, if it offers us the concrete and living self as an association of terms which are distinct from one another and are set side by side in a homogeneous medium, it will see difficulty after difficulty rising in its path. And these difficulties will multiply the greater the efforts it makes to overcome them, for all its efforts will only bring into clearer light the absurdity of the fundamental hypothesis by which it spreads out time in space and puts succession at the very centre of simultaneity. We shall see that the contradictions implied in the problems of causality, freedom, personality, spring from no other source, and that, if we wish to get rid of them, we have only to go back to the real and concrete self and give up its symbolical substitute.

Matter and Memory

Introduction¹

This book affirms the reality of spirit and the reality of matter, and tries to determine the relation of the one to the other by the study of a definite example, that of memory. It is, then, frankly dualistic. But, on the other hand, it deals with body and mind in such a way as, we hope, to lessen greatly, if not to overcome, the theoretical difficulties which have always beset dualism, and which cause it, though suggested by the immediate verdict of consciousness and adopted by common sense, to be held in small honour among philosophers.

These difficulties are due, for the most part, to the conception, now realistic, now idealistic, which philosophers have of matter. The aim of our first chapter is to show that realism and idealism both go too far, that it is a mistake to reduce matter to the perception which we have of it, a mistake also to make of it a thing able to produce in us perceptions, but in itself of another nature than they. Matter, in our view, is an aggregate of 'images'. And by 'image' we mean a certain existence which is more than that which the idealist calls a *representation*, but less than that which the realist calls a thing – an existence placed halfway between the 'thing' and the 'representation'. This conception of matter is simply that of common sense. It would greatly astonish a man unaware of the speculations of philosophy if we told him that the object before him, which he sees and touches, exists only in his mind and for his mind or even, more generally, exists only for mind, as Berkeley held. Such a man would always maintain that the object exists independently of the consciousness which perceives it. But, on the other hand, we should astonish him quite as much by telling him that the object is entirely different from that which is perceived in it, that it has neither the colour ascribed to it by the eye nor the resistance found in it by the hand. The colour, the resistance, are, for him, in the object: they are not states of our mind; they are part and parcel of an existence really independent of our own. For common sense, then, the object exists in itself, and, on the other hand, the object is, in itself, pictorial, as we perceive it: image it is, but a self-existing image.

This is just the sense in which we use the word image in our first chapter. We place ourselves at the point of view of a mind unaware of the disputes between philosophers. Such a mind would naturally believe that matter exists just as it is perceived; and, since it is perceived as an image, the mind would make of it, in itself, an image. In a word, we consider matter before the dissociation which idealism and realism have brought about between its existence and its appearance. No doubt it has become difficult to avoid this dissociation now that philosophers have made it. To forget it, however, is what we ask of the reader. If, in the course of this first chapter, objections arise in his mind against any of the views that we put forward, let him ask himself whether these objections do not imply his return to one or the other of the two points of view above which we urge him to rise.

Philosophy made a great step forward on the day when Berkeley proved, as against the 'mechanical philosophers,' that the secondary qualities of matter have at least as much reality as the primary qualities. His mistake lay in believing that, for this, it was necessary to place matter within the mind and make it into a pure idea. Descartes, no doubt, had put matter too far from us when he made it one with geometrical extensity. But, in order to bring it nearer to us, there was no need to go to the point of making it one with our own mind. Because he did go as far as this, Berkeley was unable to account for the success of physics, and, whereas Descartes had set up the mathematical relations between phenomena as their very essence, he was obliged to regard the mathematical order of the universe as a mere accident. So the Kantian criticism became necessary, to show the reason of this mathematical order and to give back to our physics a solid foundation – a task in which, however, it succeeded only by limiting the range and value of our senses and of our understanding. The criticism of Kant, on this point at least, would have been unnecessary; the human mind, in this direction at least, would not have been led to limit its own range;

metaphysics would not have been sacrificed to physics, if philosophy had been content to leave matter half way between the place to which Descartes had driven it and that to which Berkeley drew it back – to leave it, in fact, where it is seen by common sense.

There we shall try to see it ourselves. Our first chapter defines this way of looking at matter; the last sets forth the consequences of such a view. But, as we said before, we treat of matter only in so far as it concerns the problem dealt with in our second and third chapters, that which is the subject of this essay: the problem of the relation between soul and body.

This relation, though it has been a favourite theme throughout the history of philosophy, has really been very little studied. If we leave on one side the theories which are content to state the 'union of soul and body' as an irreducible and inexplicable fact, and those which speak vaguely of the body as an instrument of the soul, there remains hardly any other conception of the psychophysiological relation than the hypothesis of 'epiphenomenalism' or that of 'parallelism', which in practice – I mean in the interpretation of particular facts – both end in the same conclusions. For whether, indeed, thought is regarded as a mere function of the brain and the state of consciousness as an epiphenomenon of the state of the brain, or whether mental states and brain states are held to be two versions, in two different languages, of one and the same original, in either case it is laid down that, could we penetrate into the inside of a brain at work and behold the dance of the atoms which make up the cortex, and if, on the other hand, we possessed the key to psychophysiology, we should know every detail of what is going on in the corresponding consciousness.

This, indeed, is what is most commonly maintained by philosophers as well as by men of science. Yet it would be well to ask whether the facts, when examined without any preconceived idea, really suggest an hypothesis of this kind. That there is a close connection between a state of consciousness and the brain we do not dispute. But there is also a close connection between a coat and the nail on which it hangs, for, if the nail is pulled out, the coat falls to the ground. Shall we say, then, that the shape of the nail gives us the shape of the coat, or in any way corresponds to it? No more are we entitled to conclude, because the psychical fact is hung onto a cerebral state, that there is any parallelism between the two series psychical and physiological.

When philosophy pleads that the theory of parallelism is borne out by the results of positive science, it enters upon an unmistakably vicious circle; for, if science interprets connection, which is a fact, as signifying parallelism, which is an hypothesis (and an hypothesis to which it is difficult to attach an intelligible meaning[2]), it does so, consciously or unconsciously, for reasons of a philosophic order: it is because science has been accustomed by a certain type of philosophy to believe that there is no hypothesis more probable, more in accordance with the interests of scientific inquiry.

Now, as soon as we do, indeed, apply to positive facts for such information as may help us to solve the problem, we find it is with memory that we have to deal. This was to be expected, because memory – we shall try to prove it in the course of this work – is just the intersection of mind and matter. But we may leave out the reason here: no one, at any rate, will deny that, among all the facts capable of throwing light on the psychophysiological relation, those which concern memory, whether in the normal or in the pathological state, hold a privileged position. Not only is the evidence here extremely abundant (consider the enormous mass of observations collected in regard to the various kinds of aphasia), but nowhere else have anatomy, physiology and psychology been able to lend each other such valuable aid. Anyone who approaches, without preconceived ideas and on the firm ground of facts, the classical problem of the relations of soul and body, will soon see this problem as centring upon the subject of memory, and, even more particularly, upon the memory of words: it is from this quarter, undoubtedly, that will come the light which will illumine the obscurer parts of the problem.

The reader will see how we try to solve it. Speaking generally, the psychical state seems to us to be, in most cases, immensely wider than the cerebral state. I mean that the brain state indicates only a very small part of the mental state, that part which is capable of translating itself into movements of locomotion. Take a complex thought which unrolls itself in a chain of abstract reasoning. This thought is accompanied by images, that are at least nascent. And these images themselves are not pictured in consciousness without some foreshadowing, in the form of a sketch or a tendency, of the movements by which these images would be acted or played in space – would, that is to say, impress particular attitudes upon the body, and set free all that they implicitly contain of spatial movement. Now, of all the thought which is unrolling, this, in our view, is what the cerebral state indicates at every moment. He who could penetrate into the interior of a brain and see what happens there, would probably obtain full details of these sketched-out, or prepared, movements; there is no proof that he would learn anything else. Were he endowed with a superhuman intellect, did he possess the key to psychophysiology, he would know no more of what is going on in the corresponding consciousness than we should know of a play from the comings and goings of the actors upon the stage.

That is to say, the relation of the mental to the cerebral is not a constant, any more than it is a simple, relation. According to the nature of the play that is being acted, the movements of the players tell us more or less about it: nearly everything, if it is a pantomime; next to nothing, if it is a delicate comedy. Thus our cerebral state contains more or less of our mental state in the measure that we reel off our psychic life into action or wind it up into pure knowledge.

There are then, in short, divers *tones* of mental life, or, in other words, our psychic life may be lived at different heights, now nearer to action, now further removed from it, according to the degree of our *attention to life*. Here we have one of the ruling ideas of this book – the idea, indeed, which served as the starting point of our inquiry. That which is usually held to be a greater complexity of the psychical state appears to us, from our point of view, to be a greater dilatation of the whole personality, which, normally narrowed down by action, expands with the unscrewing of the vice in which it has allowed itself to be squeezed, and, always whole and undivided, spreads itself over a wider and wider surface. That which is commonly held to be a disturbance of the psychic life itself, an inward disorder, a disease of the personality, appears to us, from our point of view, to be an unloosing or a breaking of the tie which binds this psychic life to its motor accompaniment, a weakening or an impairing of our attention to outward life. This opinion, as also that which denies the localization of the memory-images of words and explains aphasia quite otherwise than by such localization, was considered paradoxical at the date of the first publication of the present work (1896). It will appear much less so now. The conception of aphasia then classical, universally admitted, believed to be unshakeable, has been considerably shaken in the last few years, chiefly by reasons of an anatomical order, but partly also by reasons of the same kind as those which we then advanced.[3]

And the profound and original study of neuroses made by Professor Pierre Janet has led him, of late years, to explain all *psychasthenic* forms of disease by these same considerations of psychic 'tension' and of attention to reality which were then presumed to be metaphysical.[4]

In truth, it was not altogether a mistake to call them by that name. Without denying to psychology, any more than to metaphysics, the right to make itself into an independent science, we believe that each of these two sciences should set problems to the other and can, in a measure, help it to solve them. How should it be otherwise, if psychology has for its object the study of the human mind working for practical utility, and if metaphysics is but this same mind striving to transcend the conditions of useful action and to come back to itself as to a pure creative energy? Many problems, which appear foreign to each other as long as we are bound by the letter of the terms in which these two sciences state them, are seen to be very near akin, and to be able to solve each other when we thus penetrate into their inner meaning. We little thought, at the beginning of our inquiry, that there could be any connection between the analytical study of memory and the question, which is debated between realists and idealists or between mechanists and dynamists, with regard to the existence or the essence of matter. Yet this connection is real, it is even intimate; and, if we take it into account, a cardinal metaphysical problem is carried into the open field of observation, where it may be solved progressively, instead of forever giving rise to fresh disputes of the schools within the closed lists of pure dialectic. The complexity of some parts of the present work is due to the inevitable dovetailing of problems which results from approaching philosophy in such a way. But through this complexity, which is due to the complexity of reality itself, we believe that the reader will find his way if he keeps a fast hold on the two principles which we have used as a clue throughout our own researches. The first is that in psychological analysis we must never forget the utilitarian character of our mental functions, which are essentially turned toward action. The second is that the habits formed in action find their way up to the sphere of speculation, where they create fictitious problems, and that metaphysics must begin by dispersing this artificial obscurity.

H. BERGSON

PARIS,
October 1910

Images and Bodies[5]

We will assume for the moment that we know nothing of theories of matter and theories of spirit, nothing of the discussions as to the reality or ideality of the external world. Here I am in the presence of images, in the vaguest sense of the word, images perceived when my senses are opened to them, unperceived when they are closed. All these images act and react upon one another in all their elementary parts according to constant laws which I call laws of nature, and, as a perfect knowledge of these laws would probably allow us to calculate and to foresee what will happen in each of these images, the future of the images must be contained in their present and will add to them nothing new.

Yet there is *one* of them which is distinct from all the others, in that I do not know it only from without by perceptions, but from within by affections: it is my body. I examine the conditions in which these affections are produced: I find that they always interpose themselves between the excitations that I receive from without and the movements which I am about to execute, as though they had some undefined influence on the final issue. I pass in review my different affections: it seems to me that each of them contains, after its kind, an invitation to act, with at the same time leave to wait and even to do nothing. I look closer: I find movements begun, but not executed, the indication of a more or less useful decision, but not that constraint which precludes choice. I call up, I compare my recollections: I remember that everywhere, in the organic world, I have thought I saw this same sensibility appear at the very moment when nature, having conferred upon the living being the power of mobility in space, gives warning to the species, by means of sensation, of the general dangers which threaten it, leaving to the individual the precautions necessary for escaping from them. Lastly, I interrogate my consciousness as to the part which it plays in affection: consciousness replies that it is present indeed, in the form of feeling or of sensation, at all the steps in which I believe that I take the initiative, and that it fades and disappears as soon as my activity, by becoming automatic, shows that consciousness is no longer needed. Therefore, either all these appearances are deceptive, or the act in which the affective state issues is not one of those which might be rigorously deduced from antecedent phenomena, as a movement from a movement; and, hence, it really adds something new to the universe and to its history. Let us hold to the appearances; I will formulate purely and simply what I feel and what I see: *All seems to take place as if, in this aggregate of images which I call the universe, nothing really new could happen except through the medium of certain particular images, the type of which is furnished me by my body.*

I pass now to the study, in bodies similar to my own, of the structure of that particular image which I call my body. I perceive afferent nerves which transmit a disturbance to the nerve centres; then efferent nerves which start from the centre, conduct the disturbance to the periphery, and set in motion parts of the body or the body as a whole. I question the physiologist and the psychologist as to the purpose of both kinds. They answer that, as the centrifugal movements of the nervous system can call forth a movement of the body or of parts of the body, so the centripetal movements, or at least some of them, give birth to the representation[6] of the external world. What are we to think of this?

The afferent nerves are images, the brain is an image, the disturbance travelling through the sensory nerves and propagated in the brain is an image too. If the image which I term cerebral disturbance really begot external images, it would contain them in one way or another, and the representation of the whole material universe would be implied in that of this molecular movement. Now to state this proposition is enough to show its absurdity. The brain is part of the material world; the material world is not part of the brain. Eliminate the image which bears the name material world, and you destroy at the same time the brain and the cerebral disturbance which are parts of it. Suppose, on the contrary, that these two images, the brain and the cerebral disturbance, vanish: *ex hypothesi* you efface only these, that is to say very little, an insignificant detail from an immense picture. The picture in its totality, that is to say the whole universe, remains. To make of the brain the condition on which the whole image depends is, in truth, a contradiction in terms, since the brain is by hypothesis a part of this image. Neither nerves nor nerve centres can, then, condition the image of the universe.

Let us consider this last point. Here are external images, then my body, and, lastly, the changes brought about by my body in the surrounding images. I see plainly how external images influence the image that I call my body: they transmit movement to it. And I also see how this body influences external images: it gives back movement to them. My body is, then, in the aggregate of the material world, an image which acts like other images, receiving and giving back movement, with, perhaps, this difference only, that my body appears to choose, within certain limits, the manner in which it shall restore what it receives. But how could my body in general, and my nervous system in particular, beget the whole or a part of my representation of the universe? You may say that my body is matter, or that it is an image: the word is of no importance. If it is matter, it is a part of the material world; and the material world, consequently, exists around it and without it. If it is an image, that image can give but what has been put into it, and since it is, by hypothesis, the image of my body only, it would be absurd to expect to get from it that of the whole universe. *My body, an object destined to move other objects, is, then, a centre of action; it cannot give birth to a representation.*

But if my body is an object capable of exercising a genuine and therefore a *new* action upon the surrounding objects, it must occupy a privileged position in regard to them. As a rule, any image influences other images in a manner which is determined, and even calculable, through what are called the laws of nature. As it has not to choose, so neither has it any need to explore the region round about it, nor to try its hand at several merely *eventual* actions. The *necessary* action will take place automatically, when its hour strikes. But I have supposed that the office of the image which I call my body was to exercise on other images a real influence, and, consequently, to decide which step to take among several which are all materially possible. And since these steps are probably suggested to it by the greater or lesser advantage which it can derive from the surrounding images, these images must display in some way, upon the aspect which they present to my body, the profit which my body can gain from them. In fact, I note that the size, shape, even the colour, of external objects is modified as my body approaches or recedes from them; that the strength of an odour, the intensity of a sound, increases or diminishes with distance; finally, that this very distance represents, above all, the measure in which surrounding bodies are insured, in some way, against the immediate action of my body. To the degree that my horizon widens, the images which surround me seem to be painted upon a more uniform background and become to me more indifferent. The more I narrow this horizon, the more the objects which it circumscribes space themselves out distinctly according to the greater or lesser ease with which my body can touch and move them. They send back, then, to my body, as would a mirror, its eventual influence; they take rank in an order corresponding to the growing or decreasing powers of my body. *The objects which surround my body reflect its possible action upon them*.

I will now, without touching the other images, modify slightly that image which I call my body. In this image I cut asunder, in thought, all the afferent nerves of the cerebro-spinal system. What will happen? A few cuts with the scalpel have severed a few bundles of fibres: the rest of the universe, and even the rest of my body, remain what they were before. The change effected is therefore insignificant. As a matter of fact, my perception has entirely vanished. Let us consider more closely what has just occurred. Here are the images which compose the universe in general, then those which are near to my body, and finally my body itself. In this last image the habitual office of the centripetal nerves is to transmit movements to the brain and to the cord; the centrifugal nerves send back this movement to the periphery. Sectioning of the centripetal nerves can, therefore, produce only one intelligible effect: that is, to interrupt the current which goes from the periphery to the periphery by way of the centre, and, consequently, to make it impossible for my body to extract, from among all the things which surround it, the quantity and quality of movement necessary in order to act upon them. Here is something which concerns action, and action alone. Yet it is my perception which has vanished. What does this mean, if not that my perception displays, in the midst of the image world, as would their outward reflection or shadow, the eventual or possible actions of my body? Now the system of images in which the scalpel has effected only an insignificant change is what is generally called the material world; and, on the other hand, that which has just vanished is 'my perception' of matter. Whence, provisionally, these two definitions: *I call* matter *the aggregate of images, and* perception of matter *these same images referred to the eventual action of one particular image, my body*.

Let us go more deeply into this reference. I consider my body, with its centripetal and centrifugal nerves, with its nerve centres. I know that external objects make in the afferent nerves a disturbance which passes onward to the centres, that the centres are the theatre of very varied molecular movements, and that these movements depend on the nature and position of the objects. Change the objects, or modify their relation to my body, and everything is changed in the interior movements of my perceptive centres. But everything is also changed in 'my perception.' My perception is, then, a function of these molecular movements; it depends upon them. But how does it depend upon them? It will perhaps be said that it translates them, and that, in the main, I represent to myself nothing but the molecular movements of cerebral substance. But how should this have any meaning, since the image of the nervous system and of its internal movements is only, by hypothesis, that of a certain material object, whereas I represent to myself the whole material universe? It is true that many philosophers attempt to evade the difficulty. They show us a brain, analogous in its essence to the rest of the material universe, an image, consequently, if the universe is an image. Then, since they want the internal movements of this brain to create or determine the representation of the whole material world – an image infinitely greater than that of the cerebral vibrations – they maintain that these molecular movements, and movement in general, are not images like others, but something which is either more or less than an image – in any case is of another nature than an image – and from which representation will issue as by a miracle. Thus matter is made into something radically different from representation, something of which, consequently, we have no image; over against it they place a consciousness empty of images, of which we are unable to form any idea; lastly, to fill consciousness, they invent an incomprehensible action of this formless matter upon this matterless thought. But the truth is that the movements of matter are very clear, regarded as images, and that there is no need to look in movement for anything more than what we see in it. The sole difficulty would consist in bringing forth from these very particular images the infinite variety of representations; but why seek to do so, since we all agree that the cerebral vibrations *are contained in* the material world, and that these images, consequently, are only a part of the representation? What then are these movements, and what part do these particular images play in the representation of the whole? The answer is obvious: they are, within my body, the movements intended to prepare, while beginning it, the reaction of my body to the action of external objects. Images themselves cannot create images; but they indicate at each moment, like a compass that is being moved about, the position of a certain given image, my body, in relation to the surrounding images. In the totality of representation they are very little; but they are of capital importance for that part of representation which I call my body, since they foreshadow at each successive moment its virtual acts. There is, then, only a difference of degree – there can be no difference in kind – between what is called the perceptive faculty of the brain and the reflex functions of the spinal cord. The cord transforms into movements the stimulation received; the brain prolongs them into reactions which are merely nascent; but, in the one case as in the other, the function of the nerve substance is to conduct, to coordinate, or to inhibit movements. How then does it come about that 'my perception of the universe' appears to depend upon the internal movements of the cerebral substance, to change when they vary, and to vanish when they cease?

The difficulty of this problem is mainly due to the fact that the grey matter and its modifications are regarded as things which are sufficient to themselves and might be isolated from the rest of the universe. Materialists and dualists are fundamentally agreed on this point. They consider certain molecular movements of the cerebral matter apart: then, some see in our conscious perception a phosphorescence which follows these movements and illuminates their track; for others, our perceptions succeed each other like an unwinding scroll in a consciousness which expresses continuously, in its own way, the molecular vibrations of the cortical substance: in the one case, as in the other, our perception is supposed to *translate* or to *picture* the states of our nervous system. But is it possible to conceive the nervous system as living apart from the organism which nourishes it, from the atmosphere in which the organism breathes, from the earth which that atmosphere envelopes, from the sun round which the earth revolves?

More generally, does not the fiction of an isolated material object imply a kind of absurdity, since this object borrows its physical properties from the relations which it maintains with all others, and owes each of its determinations, and, consequently, its very existence, to the place which it occupies in the universe as a whole? Let us no longer say, then, that our perceptions depend simply upon the molecular movements of the cerebral mass. We must say rather that they *vary with* them, but that these movements themselves remain inseparably bound up with the rest of the material world. The question, then, is not only how our perceptions are connected with the modifications of the grey matter. The problem widens, and can also be put in much clearer terms.

It might be stated as follows: Here is a system of images which I term my perception of the universe, and which may be entirely altered by a very slight change in a certain privileged image – *my body*. This image occupies the centre; by it all the others are conditioned; at each of its movements everything changes, as though by a turn of a kaleidoscope. Here, on the other hand, are the same images, but referred each one to itself, influencing each other no doubt, but in such a manner that the effect is always in proportion to the cause: this is what I term *the universe*. The question is: how can these two systems co-exist, and why are the same images relatively invariable in the universe and infinitely variable in perception? The problem at issue between realism and idealism, perhaps even between materialism and spiritualism, should be stated, then, it seems to us, in the following terms: *How is it that the same images can belong at the same time to two different systems*: *one in which each image varies for itself and in the well-defined measure that it is patient of the real action of surrounding images*; *and another in which all images change for a single image and in the varying measure that they reflect the eventual action of this privileged image?*

Every image is within certain images and without others; but of the aggregate of images we cannot say that it is within us or without us, since interiority and exteriority are only relations among images. To ask whether the universe exists only in our thought, or outside of our thought, is to put the problem in terms that are insoluble, even if we suppose them to be intelligible; it is to condemn ourselves to a barren discussion, in which the terms *thought*, *being*, *universe*, will always be taken on either hand in entirely different senses. To settle the matter, we must first find a common ground where combatants may meet; and since on both sides it is agreed that we can only grasp things in the form of images, we must state the problem in terms of images, and of images alone. Now no philosophical doctrine denies that the same images can enter at the same time into two distinct systems, one belonging to *science*, wherein each image, related only to itself, possesses an absolute value; and the other, the world of *consciousness*, wherein all the images depend on a central image, our body, the variations of which they follow. The question raised between realism and idealism then becomes quite clear: what are the relations which these two systems of images maintain with each other? And it is easy to see that subjective idealism consists in deriving the first system from the second, materialistic realism in deriving the second from the first.

The realist starts, in fact, from the universe, that is to say from an aggregate of images governed, as to their mutual relations, by fixed laws, in which effects are in strict proportion to their causes, and of which the character is an absence of centre, all the images unfolding on one and the same plane indefinitely prolonged. But he is at once bound to recognize that, besides this system, there are *perceptions*, that is to say, systems in which these same images seem to depend on a single one among them, around which they range themselves on different planes, so as to be wholly transformed by the slightest modification of this central image. Now this perception is just what the idealist starts from: in the system of images which he adopts there is a privileged image, his body, by which the other images are conditioned. But as soon as he attempts to connect the present with the past and to foretell the future, he is obliged to abandon this central position, to replace all the images on the same plane, to suppose that they no longer vary for him, but for themselves; and to treat them as though they made part of a system in which every change gives the exact measure of its cause. On this condition alone a science of the universe becomes possible; and, since this science exists, since it succeeds in foreseeing the future, its fundamental hypothesis cannot be arbitrary. The first system alone is *given* to present experience; but we *believe* in the second, if only because we affirm the continuity of the past, present and future. Thus in idealism, as in realism, we posit one of the two systems and seek to deduce the other from it.

But in this deduction neither realism nor idealism can succeed, because neither of the two systems of images is implied in the other, and each of them is sufficient to itself. If you posit the system of images which has no centre, and in which each element possesses its absolute dimensions and value, I see no reason why to this system should accrue a second, in which each image has an undetermined value, subject to all the vicissitudes of a central image. You must, then, to engender perception, conjure up some *deus ex machina*, such as the materialistic hypothesis of the epiphenomenal consciousness, whereby you choose, among all the images that vary absolutely and that you posited to begin with, the one which we term our brain – conferring on the internal states of this image the singular and inexplicable privilege of adding to itself a reproduction, this time relative and variable, of all the others. It is true that you afterwards pretend to attach no importance to this representation, to see in it a mere phosphorescence which the cerebral vibrations leave behind them: as if the cerebral matter and cerebral vibrations, set in the images which compose this representation, could be of another nature than they are! All realism is thus bound to make perception an accident, and, consequently, a mystery. But, inversely, if you posit a system of unstable images disposed about a privileged centre, and profoundly modified by trifling displacements of this centre, you begin by excluding the order of nature, that order which is indifferent to the point at which we take our stand and to the particular end from which we begin. You will have to bring back this order by conjuring up in your turn a *deus ex machina*; I mean that you will have to assume, by an arbitrary hypothesis, some sort of pre-established harmony between things and mind, or, at least (to use Kant's terms), between sense and understanding. It is science now that will become an accident, and its success a mystery. You cannot, then, deduce the first system of images from the second, nor the second from the first; and these two antagonistic doctrines, realism and idealism, as soon as they decide to enter the same lists, hurl themselves from opposite directions against the same obstacle.

If we now look closely at the two doctrines, we shall discover in them a common postulate, which we may formulate thus: *perception has a wholly speculative interest*; *it is pure knowledge*. The whole discussion turns upon the importance to be attributed to this knowledge as compared with *scientific* knowledge. The one doctrine starts from the order required by science, and sees in perception only a confused and provisional science. The other puts perception in the first place, erects it into an absolute, and then holds science to be a symbolic expression of the real. But, for both parties, to perceive means above all to know.

Now it is just this postulate that we dispute. Even the most superficial examination of the structure of the nervous system in the animal series gives it the lie. And it is not possible to accept it without profoundly obscuring the threefold problem of matter, consciousness and their relation.

For if we follow, step by step, the progress of external perception from the monera to the higher vertebrates, we find that living matter, even as a simple mass of protoplasm, is already irritable and contractile, that it is open to the influence of external stimulation, and answers to it by mechanical, physical and chemical reactions. As we rise in the organic series, we find a division of physiological labour. Nerve cells appear, are diversified, tend to group themselves into a system; at the same time, the animal reacts by more varied movements to external stimulation. But even when the stimulation received is not at once prolonged into movement, it appears merely to await its occasion; and the same impression, which makes the organism aware of changes in the environment, determines it or prepares it to adapt itself to them. No doubt there is in the higher vertebrates a radical distinction between pure automatism, of which the seat is mainly in the spinal cord, and voluntary activity, which requires the intervention of the brain. It might be imagined that the impression received, instead of expanding into more movements, spiritualises itself into consciousness. But as soon as we compare the structure of the spinal cord with that of the brain, we are bound to infer that there is merely a difference of complication, and not a difference in kind, between the functions of the brain and the reflex activity of the medullary system. For what takes place in reflex action? The centripetal movement communicated by the stimulus is reflected at once, by the intermediary of the nerve centres of the spinal cord, in a centrifugal movement determining a muscular contraction. In what, on the other hand, does the function of the cerebral system consist? The peripheral excitation, instead of proceeding directly to the motor cells of the spinal cord and impressing on the muscle a necessary contraction, mounts first to the brain, and then descends again to the very same motor cells of the spinal cord which intervened in the reflex action. Now what has it gained by this roundabout course, and what did it seek in the so-called sensory cells of the cerebral cortex? I do not understand, I shall never understand, that it draws thence a miraculous power of changing itself into a representation of things; and, moreover, I hold this hypothesis to be useless, as will shortly appear. But what I do see clearly is that the cells of the various regions of the cortex which are termed sensory – cells interposed between the terminal branches of the centripetal fibres and the motor cells of the Rolandic area – allow the stimulation received to reach *at will* this or that motor mechanism of the spinal cord, and so to *choose* its effect. The more these intercalated cells are multiplied and the more they project amoeboid prolongations which are probably capable of approaching each other in various ways, the more numerous and more varied will be the paths capable of opening to one and the same disturbance from the periphery, and, consequently, the more systems of movements will there be among which one and the same stimulation will allow of choice. In our opinion, then, the brain is no more than a kind of central telephonic exchange: its office is to allow communication or to delay it. It adds nothing to what it receives; but, as all the organs of perception send to it their ultimate prolongations, and, as all the motor mechanisms of the spinal cord and of the medulla oblongata have in it their accredited representatives, it really constitutes a centre, where the peripheral excitation gets into relation with this or that motor mechanism, chosen and no longer prescribed. Yet, as a great multitude of motor tracks can open simultaneously in this substance to one and the same excitation from the periphery, this disturbance may subdivide to any extent, and consequently dissipate itself in innumerable motor reactions which are merely nascent. Hence the office of the brain is sometimes to conduct the movement received to a *chosen* organ of reaction, and sometimes to open to this movement the *totality* of the motor tracts, so that it may manifest there all the potential reactions with which it is charged, and may divide and so disperse. In other words, the brain appears to us to be an instrument of analysis in regard to the movement received and an instrument of selection in regard to the movement executed. But, in the one case as in the other, its office is limited to the transmission and division of movement. And no more in the higher centres of the cortex than in the spinal cord do the nervous elements work with a view to knowledge: they do but indicate a number of possible actions at once, or organize one of them.

That is to say that the nervous system is in no sense an apparatus which may serve to fabricate, or even to prepare, representations. Its function is to receive stimulation, to provide motor apparatus, and to present the largest possible number of these apparatuses to a given stimulus. The more it develops, the more numerous and the more distant are the points of space which it brings into relation with ever more complex motor mechanisms. In this way the scope which it allows to our action enlarges: its growing perfection consists in nothing else. But, if the nervous system is thus constructed, from one end of the animal series to the other, in view of an action which is less and less necessary, must we not think that perception, of which the progress is regulated by that of the nervous system, is also entirely directed toward action, and not toward pure knowledge? And, if this be so, is not the growing richness of this perception likely to symbolize the wider range of indetermination left to the choice of the living being in its conduct with regard to things? Let us start, then, from this indetermination as from the true principle, and try whether we cannot deduce from it the possibility, and even the necessity, of conscious perception. In other words, let us posit that system of closely linked images which we call the material world, and imagine here and there, within the system, *centres of real action*, represented by living matter: what we mean to prove is that *there must* be, ranged round each one of these centres, images that are subordinated to its position and variable with it; that conscious perception is *bound* to occur, and that, moreover, it is possible to understand how it arises.

We note, in the first place, that a strict law connects the amount of conscious perception with the intensity of action at the disposal of the living being. If our hypothesis is well founded, this perception appears at the precise moment when a stimulation received by matter is not prolonged into a necessary action. In the case of a rudimentary organism, it is true that immediate contact with the object which interests it is necessary to produce the stimulation and that reaction can then hardly be delayed. Thus, in the lower organisms, touch is active and passive at one and the same time, enabling them to recognize their prey and seize it, to feel a danger and make the effort to avoid it. The various prolongations of the protozoa, the ambulacra of the echinodermata, are organs of movement as well as of tactile perception; the stinging apparatus of the coelenterata is an instrument of perception as well as a means of defence. In a word, the more immediate the reaction is compelled to be, the more must perception resemble a mere contact;

and the complete process of perception and of reaction can then hardly be distinguished from a mechanical impulsion followed by a necessary movement. But in the measure that the reaction becomes more uncertain, and allows more room for suspense, does the distance increase at which the animal is sensible of the action of that which interests it. By sight, by hearing, it enters into relation with an ever greater number of things, and is subject to more and more distant influences; and, whether these objects promise an advantage or threaten a danger, both promises and threats defer the date of their fulfilment. The degree of independence of which a living being is master, or, as we shall say, the zone of indetermination which surrounds its activity, allows, then, of an *a priori* estimate of the number and the distance of the things with which it is in relation. Whatever this relation may be, whatever be the inner nature of perception, we can affirm that its amplitude gives the exact measure of the indetermination of the act which is to follow. So that we can formulate this law: *perception is master of space in the exact measure in which action is master of time*.

But why does this relation of the organism to more or less distant objects take the particular form of conscious perception? We have examined what takes place in the organized body, we have seen movements transmitted or inhibited, metamorphosed into accomplished actions or broken up into nascent actions. These movements appear to us to concern action, and action alone; they remain absolutely foreign to the process of representation. We then considered action itself, and the indetermination which surrounds it and is implied in the structure of the nervous system – an indetermination to which this system seems to point much more than to representation. From this indetermination, accepted as a fact, we have been able to infer the necessity of a perception, that is to say, a *variable* relation between the living being and the more-or-less distant influence of the objects which interest it. How is it that this perception is consciousness, and why does everything happen *as if* this consciousness were born of the internal movements of the cerebral substance?

To answer this question, we will first simplify considerably the conditions under which conscious perception takes place. In fact, there is no perception which is not full of memories. With the immediate and present data of our senses, we mingle a thousand details out of our past experience. In most cases these memories supplant our actual perceptions, of which we then retain only a few hints, thus using them merely as 'signs' that recall to us former images. The convenience and the rapidity of perception are bought at this price; but hence also springs every kind of illusion. Let us, for the purposes of study, substitute for this perception, impregnated with our past, a perception that a consciousness would have if it were supposed to be ripe and full-grown, yet confined to the present and absorbed, to the exclusion of all else, in the task of moulding itself upon the external object. It may be urged that this is an arbitrary hypothesis, and that such an ideal perception, obtained by the elimination of individual accidents, has no correspondence with reality. But we hope to show that the individual accidents are merely grafted on to this impersonal perception, which is at the very root of our knowledge of things; and that just because philosophers have overlooked it, because they have not distinguished it from that which memory adds to or subtracts from it, they have taken perception as a whole for a kind of *interior* and *subjective* vision, which would then differ from memory only by its greater intensity. This will be our first hypothesis. But it leads naturally to another. However brief we suppose any perception to be, it always occupies a certain duration, and involves, consequently, an effort of memory which prolongs, one into another, a plurality of moments. As we shall endeavour to show, even the 'subjectivity' of sensible qualities consists above all else in a kind of contraction of the real, effected by our memory. In short, memory in these two forms, covering as it does with a cloak of recollections a core of immediate perception, and also contracting a number of external moments into a single internal moment, constitutes the principal share of individual consciousness in perception, the subjective side of the knowledge of things; and, since we must neglect this share in order to make our idea clearer, we shall go too far along the path we have chosen. But we shall only have to retrace our steps and to correct, especially by bringing memory back again, whatever may be excessive in our conclusions. What follows, therefore, must be regarded as only a schematic rendering, and we ask that perception should be provisionally understood to mean not my concrete and complex perception – that which is enlarged by memories and offers always a certain breadth of duration – but a *pure* perception. By this I mean a perception which exists in theory rather than in fact and would be possessed by a being placed where I am, living as I live, but absorbed in the present and capable, by giving up every form of memory, of obtaining a vision of matter both immediate and instantaneous. Adopting this hypothesis, let us consider how conscious perception may be explained.

To deduce consciousness would be, indeed, a bold undertaking; but it is really not necessary here, because by positing the material world we assume an aggregate of images, and, moreover, because it is impossible to assume anything else. No theory of matter escapes this necessity. Reduce matter to atoms in motion: these atoms, though denuded of physical qualities, are determined only in relation to an eventual vision and an eventual contact, the one without light and the other without materiality. Condense atoms into centres of force, dissolve them into vortices revolving in a continuous fluid: this fluid, these movements, these centres, can themselves be determined only in relation to an impotent touch, an ineffectual impulsion, a colourless light; they are still images. It is true that an image may *be* without *being perceived* – it may be present without being represented – and the distance between these two terms, presence and representation, seems just to measure the interval between matter itself and our conscious perception of matter. But let us examine the point more closely and see in what this difference consists. If there were *more* in the second term than in the first, if, in order to pass from presence to representation, it were necessary to add something, the barrier would indeed be insuperable, and the passage from matter to perception would remain wrapped in impenetrable mystery. It would not be the same if it were possible to pass from the first term to the second by way of diminution, and if the representation of an image were *less* than its presence; for it would then suffice that the images present should be compelled to abandon something of themselves in order that their mere presence should convert them into representations. Now, here is the image which I call a material object; I have the representation of it. How then does it not appear to be in itself that which it is for me? It is because, being bound up with all other images, it is continued in those which follow it, just as it prolonged those which preceded it. To transform its existence into representation, it would be enough to suppress what follows it, what precedes it, and also all that fills it, and to retain only its external crust, its superficial skin. That which distinguishes it as a *present* image, as an objective reality, from a *represented* image is the necessity which obliges it to act through every one of its points upon all the points of all other images, to transmit the whole of what it receives, to oppose to every action an equal and contrary reaction, to be, in short, merely a road by which pass, in every direction, the modifications propagated throughout the immensity of the universe. I should convert it into representation if I could isolate it, especially if I could isolate its shell. Representation is there, but always virtual – being neutralized, at the very moment when it might become actual, by the obligation to continue itself and to lose itself in something else. To obtain this conversion from the virtual to the actual, it would be necessary, not to throw more light on the object, but, on the contrary, to obscure some of its aspects, to diminish it by the greater part of itself, so that the remainder, instead of being encased in its surroundings as a *thing*, should detach itself from them as a *picture*. Now, if living beings are, within the universe, just 'centres of indetermination,' and if the degree of this indetermination is measured by the number and rank of their functions, we can conceive that their mere presence is equivalent to the suppression of all those parts of objects in which their functions find no interest. They allow to pass through them, so to speak, those external influences which are indifferent to them; the others isolated, become 'perceptions' by their very isolation. Everything thus happens for us as though we reflected back to surfaces the light which emanates from them, the light which, had it passed on unopposed, would never have been revealed. The images which surround us will appear to turn toward our body the side, emphasized by the light upon it, which interests our body. They will detach from themselves that which we have arrested on its way, that which we are capable of influencing. Indifferent to each other because of the radical mechanism which binds them together, they present each to the others all their sides at once: which means that they act and react mutually by all their elements, and that none of them perceives or is perceived consciously. Suppose, on the contrary, that they encounter somewhere a certain spontaneity of reaction: their action is so far diminished, and this diminution of their action is just the representation which we have of them. Our representation of things would thus arise from the fact that they are thrown back and reflected by our freedom.

When a ray of light passes from one medium into another, it usually traverses it with a change of direction. But the respective densities of the two media may be such that, for a given angle of incidence, refraction is no longer possible. Then we have total reflection. The luminous point gives rise to a *virtual* image which symbolizes, so to speak, the fact that the luminous rays cannot pursue their way. Perception is just a phenomenon of the same kind. That which is given is the totality of the images of the material world, with the totality of their internal elements. But, if we suppose centres of real, that is to say of spontaneous, activity, the rays which reach it, and which interest that activity, instead of passing through those centres, will appear to be reflected and thus to indicate the outlines of the object which emits them. There is nothing positive here, nothing added to the image, nothing new. The objects merely abandon something of their real action in order to manifest their virtual influence of the living being upon them. Perception therefore resembles those phenomena of reflexion which result from an impeded refraction; it is like an effect of mirage.

This is as much as to say that there is for images merely a difference of degree, and not of kind, between *being* and *being consciously perceived*. The reality of matter consists in the totality of its elements and of their actions of every kind. Our representation of matter is the measure of our possible action upon bodies: it results from the discarding of what has no interest for our needs, or more generally, for our functions. In one sense we might say that the perception of any unconscious material point whatever, in its instantaneousness, is infinitely greater and more complete than ours, since this point gathers and transmits the influences of all the points of the material universe, whereas our consciousness only attains to certain parts and to certain aspects of those parts. Consciousness – in regard to external perception – lies in just this choice. But there is, in this necessary poverty of our conscious perception, something that is positive, that foretells spirit: it is, in the etymological sense of the word, discernment.

The whole difficulty of the problem that occupies us comes from the fact that we imagine perception to be a kind of photographic view of things, taken from a fixed point by that special apparatus which is called an organ of perception – a photograph which would then be developed in the brain-matter by some unknown chemical and psychical process of elaboration. But is it not obvious that the photograph, if photograph there be, is already taken, already developed in the very heart of things and at all the points of space? No metaphysics, no physics even, can escape this conclusion. Build up the universe with atoms: each of them is subject to the action, variable in quantity and quality according to the distance, exerted on it by all material atoms. Bring in Faraday's centres of force: the lines of force emitted in every direction from every centre bring to bear upon each the influences of the whole material world. Call up the Leibnizian monads: each is the mirror of the universe. All philosophers, then, agree on this point. Only if, when we consider any other given place in the universe, we can regard the action of all matter as passing through it without resistance and without loss, and the photograph of the whole as translucent: here there is wanting behind the plate the black screen on which the image could be shown. Our 'zones of indetermination' play in some sort the part of the screen. They add nothing to what is there; they effect merely this: that the real action passes through, the virtual action remains.

This is no hypothesis. We content ourselves with formulating data with which no theory of perception can dispense. For no philosopher can begin the study of external perception without assuming the possibility at least of a material world, that is to say, in the main, the virtual perception of all things. From this merely possible material mass he will then isolate the particular object which I call my body, and, in this body, centres of perception: he will show me the disturbance coming from a certain point in space, propagating itself along the nerves, and reaching the centres. But here I am confronted by a transformation scene from fairyland. The material world, which surrounds the body; the body, which shelters the brain; the brain, in which we distinguish centres; he abruptly dismisses, and, as by a magician's wand, he conjures up, as a thing entirely new the representation of what he began by postulating. This representation he drives out of space, so that it may have nothing in common with the matter from which he started. As for matter itself, he would fain go without it, but cannot, because its phenomena present relatively to each other an order so strict and so indifferent as to the point of origin chosen, that this regularity and this indifference really constitute an independent existence. So he must resign himself to retaining at least the phantasm of matter. But then he manages to deprive it of all the qualities which give it life. In an amorphous space he carves out moving figures; or else (and it comes to nearly the same thing), he imagines relations of magnitude which adjust themselves one to another, mathematical functions which go on evolving and developing their own content: representation, laden with the spoils of matter, thenceforth displays itself freely in an unextended consciousness. But it is not enough to cut out, it is necessary to sew the pieces together. You must now explain how those qualities which you have detached from their material support can be joined to it again. Each attribute which you take away from matter widens the interval between representation and its object. If you make matter unextended, how will it acquire extension? If you reduce it to homogeneous movements, whence arises quality? Above all, how are we to imagine a relation between a thing and its image, between matter and thought, since each of these terms possesses, by definition, only that which is lacking to the other? Thus difficulties spring up beneath our feet; and every effort that you make to dispose of one of them does but resolve it into many more. What then do we ask of you? Merely to give up your magician's wand, and to continue along the path on which you first set out. You showed us external images reaching the organs of sense, modifying the nerves, propagating their influence in the brain. Well, follow the process to the end. The movement will pass through the cerebral substance (although not without having tarried there), and will then expand into voluntary action. There you have the whole mechanism of perception. As for perception itself, in so far as it is an image, you are not called upon to retrace its genesis, since you posited it to begin with, and since, moreover, no other course was open to you. In assuming the brain, in assuming the smallest portion of matter, did you not assume the totality of images? *What you have to explain, then, is not how perception arises, but how it is limited, since it should be the image of the whole, and is in fact reduced to the image of that which interests you.* But if it differs from the mere image, precisely in that its parts range themselves with reference to a variable centre, its limitation is easy to understand: unlimited *de jure*, it confines itself *de facto* to indicating the degree of indetermination allowed to the acts of the special image which you call your body. And, inversely, it follows that the indetermination of the movements of your body, such as it results from the structure of the grey matter of the brain, gives the exact measure of the extent of your perception. It is no wonder, then, that everything happens *as though* your perception were a result of the internal motions of the brain and issued in some sort from the cortical centres. It could not actually come from them, since the brain is an image like others, enveloped in the mass of other images, and it would be absurd that the container should issue from the content. But since the structure of the brain is like the detailed plan of the movements among which you have the choice, and since that part of the external images which appears to return upon itself in order to constitute perception includes precisely all the points of the universe which these movements could affect, conscious perception and cerebral movement are in strict correspondence. The reciprocal dependence of these two terms is therefore simply due to the fact that both are functions of a third, which is the indetermination of the will.

Take, for example, a luminous point P, of which the rays impinge on the different parts *a*, *b*, *c*, of the retina. At this point P, science localizes vibrations of a certain amplitude and duration. At the same point P, consciousness perceives light. We propose to show, in the course of this study, that both are right; and that there is no essential difference between the light and the movements, provided we restore to movement the unity, indivisibility, and qualitative heterogeneity denied to it by abstract mechanics; provided also that we see in sensible qualities *contractions* effected by our memory. Science and consciousness would then coincide in the instantaneous. For the moment all we need say, without examining too closely the meaning of the words, is that the point P sends to the retina vibrations of light. What happens then? If the visual image of the point P were not already given, we should indeed have to seek the manner in which it had been engendered, and should soon be confronted by an insoluble problem. But, whatever we do, we cannot avoid assuming it to begin with: the sole question is, then, to know how and why this image *is chosen* to form part of my perception, while an infinite number of other images remain excluded from it. Now I see that the vibrations transmitted from the point P to the various parts of the retina are conducted to the cortical optic centres, often to other centres as well, and that these centres sometimes transmit them to motor mechanisms, sometimes provisionally arrest them. The nervous elements concerned are, therefore, what give efficacy to the disturbance received; they symbolize the indetermination of the will; on their soundness this indetermination depends; consequently, any injury to these elements, by diminishing our possible action, diminishes perception in the same degree. In other words, if there exist in the material world places where the vibrations received are not mechanically transmitted, if there are, as we said, zones of indetermination, these zones must occur along the path of what is termed the sensori-motor process; and hence all must happen as though the rays P*a*, P*b*, P*c* were *perceived* along this path and afterwards *projected* into P. Further, while the indetermination is something which escapes experiment and calculation, this is not the case with the nervous elements by which the impression is received and transmitted. These elements are the special concern of the physiologist and the psychologist; on them all the details of external perception would seem to depend and by them they may be explained. So we may say, if we like, that the disturbance, after having travelled along these nervous elements, after having gained the centre, there changes into a conscious image which is subsequently exteriorised at the point P. But, when we so express ourselves, we merely bow to the exigencies of the scientific method; we in no way describe the real process. There is not, in fact, an unextended image which forms itself in consciousness and then projects itself into P. The truth is that the point P, the rays which it emits, the retina and the nervous elements affected, form a single whole; that the luminous point P is a part of this whole; and that it is really in P, and not elsewhere, that the image of P is formed and perceived.

When we represent things to ourselves in this manner, we do but return to the simple convictions of common sense. We all of us began by believing that we grasped the very object, that we perceived it in itself and not in us. When philosophers disdain an idea so simple and so close to reality, it is because the intracerebral process – that diminutive part of perception – appears to them the equivalent of the whole of perception. If we suppress the object perceived and keep the internal process, it seems to them that the image of the object remains. And their belief is easily explained: there are many conditions, such as hallucination and dreams, in which images arise that resemble external perception in all their details. Because as, in such cases, the object has disappeared while the brain persists, he holds that the cerebral phenomenon is sufficient for the production of the image. But it must not be forgotten that in all psychical states of this kind memory plays the chief part. We shall try to show later that, when perception, as we understand it, is once admitted, memory *must* arise, and that this memory has not, any more than perception itself, a cerebral state as its true and complete condition. But, without as yet entering upon the examination of these two points, we will content ourselves with a very simple observation which has indeed no novelty. In many people who are blind from birth, the visual centres are intact; yet they live and die without having formed a single visual image. Such an image, therefore, cannot appear unless the external object has, at least, once played its part: it must, once at any rate, have been part and parcel with representation. Now this is what we claim and for the moment all that we require, for we are dealing here with *pure* perception, and not with perception complicated by memory. Reject then the share of memory, consider perception in its unmixed state, and you will be forced to recognize that there is no image without an object. But, from the moment that you thus posit the intracerebral processes in addition to the external object which causes them, we can clearly see how the image of that object is given with it and in it: how the image should arise from the cerebral movement we shall never understand.

When a lesion of the nerves or of the centres interrupts the passage of the nerve vibration, perception is to that extent diminished. Need we be surprised? The office of the nervous system is to utilize that vibration, to convert it into practical deeds, really or virtually accomplished. If, for one reason or another, the disturbance cannot pass along, it would be strange if the corresponding perception still took place, since this perception would then connect our body with points of space which no longer directly invite it to make a choice. Sever the optic nerve of an animal: the vibrations issuing from the luminous point can no longer be transmitted to the brain and thence to the motor nerves; the thread, of which the optic nerve is a part and which binds the external object to the motor mechanisms of the animal, is broken: visual perception has therefore become impotent, and this very impotence is unconsciousness. That matter should be perceived without the help of a nervous system and without organs of sense, is not theoretically inconceivable; but it is practically impossible because such perception would be of no use. It would suit a phantom, not a living, and, therefore, acting, being. We are too much inclined to regard the living body as a world within a world, the nervous system as a separate being, of which the function is, first, to elaborate perceptions, and, then, to create movements. The truth is that my nervous system, interposed between the objects which affect my body and those which I can influence, is a mere conductor, transmitting, sending back or inhibiting movement. This conductor is composed of an enormous number of threads which stretch from the periphery to the centre, and from the centre to the periphery. As many threads as pass from the periphery to the centre, so many points of space are there able to make an appeal to my will and to put, so to speak, an elementary question to my motor activity. Every such question is what is termed a perception. Thus perception is diminished by one of its elements each time one of the threads termed sensory is cut, because some part of the external object then becomes unable to appeal to activity; and it is also diminished whenever a stable habit has been formed, because this time the ready-made response renders the question unnecessary. What disappears in either case is the apparent reflection of the stimulus upon itself, the return of the light on the image whence it comes; or rather that dissociation, that *discernment*, whereby the perception is disengaged from the image. We may therefore say that while the detail of perception is moulded exactly upon that of the nerves termed sensory, perception as a whole has its true and final explanation in the tendency of the body to movement.

The cause of the general illusion on this point lies in the apparent indifference of our movements to the stimulation which excites them. It seems that the movement of my body in order to reach and to modify an object is the same, whether I have been told of its existence by the ear or whether it has been revealed to me by sight or touch. My motor activity thus appears as a separate entity, a sort of reservoir whence movements issue at will, always the same for the same action, whatever the kind of image which has called it into being. But the truth is that the character of movements which are externally identical is internally different, according as they respond to a visual, an auditory or a tactile impression. Suppose I perceive a multitude of objects in space; each of them, inasmuch as it is a visual form, solicits my activity. Now I suddenly lose my sight. No doubt I still have at my disposal the same quantity and the same quality of movements in space; but these movements can no longer be coordinated to visual impressions; they must in future follow tactile impressions, for example, and a new arrangement will take place in the brain. The protoplasmic expansions of the motor nervous elements in the cortex will now be in relation with a much smaller number of the nervous elements termed sensory. My activity is then really diminished, in the sense that although I can produce the same movements, the occasion comes more rarely from the external objects. Consequently, the sudden interruption of optical continuity has brought with it, as its essential and profound effect, the suppression of a large part of the queries or demands addressed to my activity. Now such a query or demand is, as we have seen, a perception. Here we put our finger on the mistake of those who maintain that perception springs from what is properly called the sensory vibration, and not from a sort of question addressed to motor activity. They sever this motor activity from the perceptive process; and, as it appears to survive the loss of perception, they conclude that perception is localized in the nervous elements termed sensory. But the truth is that perception is no more in the sensory centres than in the motor centres; it measures the complexity of their relations, and is, in fact, where it appears to be.

Psychologists who have studied infancy are well aware that our representation is at first impersonal. Only little by little, and as a result of experience, does it adopt our body as a centre and become *our* representation. The mechanism of this process is, moreover, easy to understand. As my body moves in space, all the other images vary, while that image, my body, remains invariable. I must, therefore, make it a centre, to which I refer all the other images. My belief in an external world does not come, cannot come, from the fact that I project outside myself sensations that are unextended: how could these sensations ever acquire extension, and whence should I get the notion of exteriority? But, if we allow that, as experience testifies, the aggregate of images is given to begin with, I can see clearly how my body comes to occupy, within this aggregate, a privileged position. And I understand also whence arises the notion of interiority and exteriority, which is, to begin with, merely the distinction between my body and other bodies. For, if you start from my body, as is usually done, you will never make me understand how impressions received on the surface of my body, impressions which concern that body alone, are able to become for me independent objects and form an external world. But if, on the contrary, all images are posited at the outset, my body will necessarily end by standing out in the midst of them as a distinct thing, since they change unceasingly, and it does not vary. The distinction between the inside and the outside will then be only a distinction between the part and the whole. There is, first of all, the aggregate of images; and, then, in this aggregate, there are 'centres of action,' from which the interesting images appear to be reflected: thus perceptions are born and actions made ready. *My body* is that which stands out as the centre of these perceptions; my *personality* is the being to which these actions must be referred. The whole subject becomes clear if we travel thus from the periphery to the centre, as the child does, and as we ourselves are invited to do by immediate experience and by common sense. On the contrary everything becomes obscure, and problems are multiplied on all sides, if we attempt, with the theorists, to travel from the centre to the periphery. Whence arises, then, this idea of an external world constructed artificially, piece by piece, out of unextended sensations, though we can neither understand how they come to form an extended surface, nor how they are subsequently projected outside our body? Why insist, in spite of appearances, that I should go from my conscious self to my body, then from my body to other bodies, whereas in fact I place myself at once in the material world in general, and then gradually cut out within it the centre of action which I shall come to call my body and to distinguish from all others? There are so many illusions gathered round this belief in the originally unextended character of our external perception; there are, in the idea that we project outside ourselves states which are purely internal, so many misconceptions, so many lame answers to badly stated questions, that we cannot hope to throw light on the whole subject at once. We believe that light will increase, as we show more clearly, behind these illusions, the metaphysical error which confounds 'pure perception' with memory. But these illusions are, nevertheless, connected with real facts, which we may here indicate in order to correct their interpretation.

The first of these facts is that our senses require education. Neither sight nor touch is able at the outset to localize impressions. A series of comparisons and inductions is necessary, whereby we gradually coordinate one impression with another. Hence philosophers may jump to the belief that sensations are in their essence inextensive and that they constitute extensity by their juxtaposition. But is it not clear that, upon the hypothesis just advanced, our senses are equally in need of education – not, of course, in order to accommodate themselves to each other? Here, in the midst of all the images, there is a certain image which I term my body and of which the virtual action reveals itself by an apparent reflection of the surrounding images upon themselves. Suppose there are so many kinds of possible action for my body: there must be an equal number of systems of reflection for other bodies; each of these systems will be just what is perceived by one of my senses. My body, then, acts like an image which reflects others, and which, in so doing, analyses them along lines corresponding to the different actions which it can exercise upon them. And, consequently, each of the qualities perceived in the same object by my different senses symbolizes a particular direction of my activity, a particular need. Now, will all these perceptions of a body by my different senses give me, when united, the complete image of that body? Certainly not, because they have been gathered from a larger whole. To perceive all the influences from all the points of all bodies would be to descend to the condition of a material object. Conscious perception signifies choice, and consciousness mainly consists in this practical discernment. The diverse perceptions of the same object, given by my different senses, will not, then, when put together, reconstruct the *complete* image of the object; they will remain separated from each other by intervals which measure, so to speak, the gaps in my needs. It is to fill these intervals that an education of the senses is necessary. The aim of this education is to harmonize my senses with each other, to restore between their data a continuity which has been broken by the discontinuity of the needs of my body, in short, to reconstruct, as nearly as may be, the whole of the material object. This, on our hypothesis, explains the need for an education of the senses. Now let us compare it with the preceding explanation. In the first, unextended sensations of sight combine with unextended sensations of touch and of the other senses to give, by their synthesis, the idea of a material object. But, to begin with, it is not easy to see how these sensations can acquire extension, nor how, above all, when extension in general has been acquired, we can explain in particular the preference of a given one of these sensations for a given point of space. And then we may ask: by what happy agreement, in virtue of what pre-established harmony, do these sensations of different kinds coordinate themselves to form a stable object, henceforth solidified, common to my experience and to that of all men, subject, in its relation to other objects, to those inflexible rules which we call the laws of nature? In the second, 'the data of our different senses' are, on the contrary, the very qualities of things, perceived first in the things rather than in us: is it surprising that they come together, since abstraction alone has separated them? On the first hypothesis, the material object is nothing of all that we perceive: you put, on one side, the conscious principle with the sensible qualities and, on the other, a matter of which you can predicate nothing, which you define by negations because you have begun by despoiling it of all that reveals it to us. On the second hypothesis, an ever-deepening knowledge of matter becomes possible. Far from depriving matter of anything perceived, we must on the contrary, bring together all sensible qualities, restore their relationship, and re-establish among them the continuity broken by our needs. Our perception of matter is, then, no longer either relative or subjective, at least in principle, and apart, as we shall see presently, from affection and especially from memory; it is merely dissevered by the multiplicity of our needs. On the first hypothesis, spirit is as unknowable as matter, for (we) attribute to it the indefinable power of evoking sensations we know not whence, and of projecting them, we know not why, into a space where they will form bodies. On the second, the part played by consciousness is clearly defined: consciousness means virtual action, and the forms acquired by mind, those which hide the essence of spirit from us, should, with the help of this second principle, be removed as so many concealing veils. Thus, on our hypothesis, we begin to see the possibility of a clearer distinction between spirit and matter, and of a reconciliation between them. But we will leave this first point and come to the second.

The second fact brought forward consists of what was long termed the 'specific energy of the nerves.' We know that stimulation of the optic nerve by an external shock or by an electric current will produce a visual sensation and that this same electric current applied to the acoustic or to the glossopharyngeal nerve will cause a sound to be heard or a taste to be perceived. From these very particular facts have been deduced two very general laws: that different causes acting on the same nerve excite the same sensation and that the same cause, acting on different nerves, provokes different sensations. And from these laws it has been inferred that our sensations are merely signals and that the office of each sense is to translate into its own language homogeneous and mechanical movements occurring in space. Hence, as a conclusion, the idea of cutting our perception into two distinct parts, thenceforth incapable of uniting: on the one hand, homogeneous movements in space and, on the other hand, unextended sensations in consciousness. Now it is not our part to enter into an examination of the physiological problems raised by the interpretation of the two laws: in whatever way these laws are understood, whether the specific energy is attributed to the nerves or whether it is referred to the centres, insurmountable difficulties arise. But the very existence of the laws themselves appears more and more problematical. Lotze himself already suspected a fallacy in them. He awaited, before putting faith in them, 'sound waves which should give to the eye the sensation of light, or luminous vibrations which should give to the ear a sound.'[7] The truth is that all the facts alleged can be brought back to a single type: the one stimulus capable of producing different sensations, the multiple stimuli capable of inducing the same sensation, are either an electric current or a mechanical cause capable of determining in the organ a modification of electrical equilibrium. Now we may well ask whether the electrical stimulus does not include different *components*, answering objectively to sensations of different kinds, and whether the office of each sense is not merely to extract from the whole the component that concerns it. We should then have, indeed, the same stimuli giving the same sensations and different stimuli provoking different sensations. To speak more precisely, it is difficult to admit, for instance, that applying an electrical stimulus to the tongue would not occasion chemical changes, and these changes are what, in all cases, we term tastes. On the other hand, while the physicist has been able to identify light with an electromagnetic disturbance, we may say, inversely, that what he calls here an electromagnetic disturbance *is* light, so that it is really light that the optic nerve perceives objectively when subject to electrical stimulus. The doctrine of specific energy appears to be nowhere more firmly based than in the case of the ear: nowhere also has the real existence of the thing perceived become more probable. We will not insist on these facts, because they will be found stated and exhaustively discussed in a recent work.[8] We will only remark that the sensations here spoken of are not images perceived by us outside our body, but rather affections localized within the body. Now it results from the nature and use of our body, as we shall see, that each of its so-called sensory elements has its own *real* action, which must be of the same kind as its *virtual* action on the external objects which it usually perceives; and thus we can understand how it is that each of the sensory nerves appears to vibrate according to a fixed manner of sensation. But to elucidate this point we must consider the nature of affection. Thus we are led to the third and last argument which we have to examine.

This third argument is drawn from the fact that we pass by insensible degrees from the representative state, which occupies space, to the affective state which appears to be unextended.

Hence it is inferred that all sensation is naturally and necessarily unextended, so that extensity is superimposed upon sensation, and the process of perception consists in an exteriorisation of internal states. The psychologist starts, in fact, from his body, and, as the impressions received at the periphery of this body seem to him sufficient for the reconstitution of the entire material universe, to his body he at first reduces the universe. But this first position is not tenable; his body has not, and cannot have, any more or any less reality than all other bodies. So he must go farther, follow to the end the consequences of his principle, and, after having narrowed the universe to the surface of the living body, contract this body itself into a centre which he will end by supposing unextended. Then, from this centre will start unextended sensations, which will swell, so to speak, will grow into extensity, and will end by giving extension first to his body and afterwards to all other material objects. But this strange supposition would be impossible if there were not, in point of fact, between images and ideas – the former extended and the latter unextended – a series of intermediate states, more or less vaguely localized, which are the *affective* states. Our understanding, yielding to its customary illusion, poses the dilemma that a thing either is or is not extended, and as the affective state participates vaguely in extension, is in fact imperfectly localized, we conclude that this state is absolutely unextended. But then the successive degrees of extension, and extensity itself, will have to be explained by I know not what acquired property of unextended states; the history of perception will become that of internal unextended states which acquire extension and project themselves without. Shall we put the argument in another form? There is hardly any perception which may not, by the increase of the action of its object upon our body, become an affection, and, more particularly, pain. Thus we pass insensibly from the contact with a pin to its prick. Inversely the decreasing pain coincides with the lessening perception of its cause, and exteriorises itself, so to speak, into a representation. So it does seem, then, as if there were a difference of degree and not of nature between affection and perception. Now the first is intimately bound up with my personal existence: what, indeed, would be a pain detached from the subject that feels it? It seems, therefore, that it must be so with the second and that external perception is formed by projecting into space an affection which has become harmless. Realists and idealists are agreed in this method of reasoning. The latter see in the material universe nothing but a synthesis of subjective and unextended states; the former add that, behind this synthesis, there is an independent reality corresponding to it, but both conclude, from the gradual passage of affection to representation, that our representation of the material universe is relative and subjective and that it has, so to speak, emerged from us, rather than that we have emerged from it.

Before criticizing this questionable interpretation of an unquestionable fact, we may show that it does not succeed in explaining, or even in throwing light upon, the nature either of pain or of perception. That affective states, essentially bound up with my personality, and vanishing if I disappear, should acquire extensity by losing intensity, should adopt a definite position in space, and build up a firm, solid experience, always in accord with itself and with the experience of other men – is very difficult to realize. Whatever we do, we shall be forced to give back to sensations, in one form or another, first the extension and then the independence which we have tried to do without. But, what is more, affection, on this hypothesis, is hardly clearer than representation. For if it is not easy to see how affections, by diminishing in intensity, become representations, neither can we understand how the same phenomenon, which was given at first as perception, becomes affection by an increase of intensity. There is in pain something positive and active, which is ill explained by saying, as do some philosophers, that it consists in a *confused* representation. But still this is not the principal difficulty. That the gradual augmentation of the stimulus ends by transforming perception into pain, no one will deny; it is none the less true that this change arises at a definite moment: why at this moment rather than at another? And what special reason causes a phenomenon of which I was at first only an indifferent spectator to suddenly acquire for me a vital interest? Therefore, on this hypothesis I fail to see either why, at a given moment, a diminution of intensity in the phenomenon confers on it a right to extension and to an apparent independence, or why an increase of intensity should create, at one moment rather than at another, this new property, the source of positive action, which is called pain.

Let us return now to our hypothesis and show that affection *must*, at a given moment, arise out of the image. We shall thus understand how it is that we pass from a perception, which has extensity, to an affection which is believed to be unextended. But some preliminary remarks on the real significance of pain are indispensable.

When a foreign body touches one of the prolongations of the amoeba, that prolongation is retracted; every part of the protoplasmic mass is equally able to receive a stimulation and to react against it; perception and movement being here blended in a single property – contractility. But, as the organism grows more complex, there is a division of labour; functions become differentiated, and the anatomical elements thus determined forego their independence. In such an organism as our own, the nerve fibres termed sensory are exclusively empowered to transmit stimulation to a central region whence the vibration will be passed on to motor elements. It would seem then that they have abandoned individual action to take their share, as outposts, in the manoeuvres of the whole body. But nonetheless they remain exposed, singly, to the same causes of destruction which threaten the organism as a whole, and while this organism is able to move – and thereby to escape a danger or to repair a loss – the sensitive element retains the relative immobility to which the division of labour condemns it. Thence arises pain, which, in our view, is nothing but the effort of the damaged element to set things right – a kind of motor tendency in a sensory nerve. Every pain, then, must consist in an effort – an effort which is doomed to be unavailing. Every pain is a *local* effort, and in its very isolation lies the cause of its impotence, because the organism, by reason of the solidarity of its parts, is able to move only as a whole. It is also because the effort is local that pain is entirely disproportioned to the danger incurred by the living being. The danger may be mortal and the pain slight; the pain may be unbearable (as in a toothache) and the danger insignificant. There is then, there must be, a precise moment when pain intervenes: it is when the interested part of the organism, instead of accepting the stimulation, repels it. And it is not merely a difference of degree that separates perception from affection but a difference in kind.

Now we have considered the living body as a kind of centre whence is reflected on the surrounding objects the action which these objects exercise upon it: in that reflection external perception consists. But this centre is not a mathematical point; it is a body, exposed, like all natural bodies, to the action of external causes which threaten to disintegrate it. We have just seen that it resists the influence of these causes. It does not merely reflect action received from without; it struggles, and thus absorbs some part of this action. Here is the source of affection. We might therefore say, metaphorically, that while perception measures the reflecting power of the body, affection measures its power to absorb.

But this is only a metaphor. We must consider the matter more carefully in order to understand clearly that the necessity of affection follows from the very existence of perception. Perception, understood as we understand it, measures our possible action upon things, and thereby, inversely, the possible action of things upon us. The greater the body's power of action (symbolized by a higher degree of complexity in the nervous system), the wider is the field that perception embraces. The distance which separates our body from an object perceived really measures, therefore, the greater or less imminence of a danger, the nearer or more remote fulfilment of a promise. And, consequently, our perception of an object distinct from our body, separated from our body by an interval, never expresses anything but a *virtual* action. But the more distance decreases between this object and our body (the more, in other words, the danger becomes urgent or the promise immediate), the more does virtual action tend to pass into *real* action. Suppose the distance reduced to zero, that is to say that the object to be perceived coincides with our body, that is to say again, that our body is the object to be perceived. Then it is no longer virtual action, but real action, that this specialized perception will express, and this is exactly what affection is. Our sensations are, then, to our perceptions that which the real action of our body is to its possible, or virtual, action. Its virtual action concerns other objects and is manifested within those objects; its real action concerns itself, and is manifested within its own substance. Everything then will happen as if, by a true return of real and virtual actions to their points of application or of origin, the external images were reflected by our body into surrounding space and the real actions arrested by it within itself. And that is why its surface, the common limit of the external and the internal, is the only portion of space which is both perceived and felt.

That is to say once more, that my perception is outside my body and my affection within it. Just as external objects are perceived by me where they are, in themselves and not in me, so my affective states are experienced where they occur, that is, at a given point in my body. Consider the system of images which is called the material world. My body is one of them. Around this image is grouped the representation, i.e., its eventual influence on the others. Within it occurs affection, i.e., its actual effort upon itself. Such is indeed the fundamental difference which every one of us naturally makes between an image and a sensation. When we say that the image exists outside us, we signify by this that it is external to our body. When we speak of sensation as an internal state, we mean that it arises within our body. And this is why we affirm that the totality of perceived images subsists, even if our body disappears, whereas we know that we cannot annihilate our body without destroying our sensations.

Hence we begin to see that we must correct, at least in this particular, our theory of pure perception. We have argued as though our perception were a part of the images, detached, as such, from their entirety, as though, expressing the virtual action of the object upon our body, or of our body upon the object, perception merely isolated from the total object that aspect of it which interests us. But we have to take into account the fact that our body is not a mathematical point in space, that its virtual actions are complicated by, and impregnated with, real actions, or, in other words, that there is no perception without affection. Affection is, then, that part or aspect of the inside of our body which we mix with the image of external bodies; it is what we must first of all subtract from perception to get the image in its purity. But the psychologist who shuts his eyes to the difference of function and nature between perception and sensation – the latter involving a real action, and the former a merely possible action – can only find between them a difference of degree. Because sensation (on account of the *confused* effort which it involves) is only vaguely localized, he declares it unextended, and thence makes sensation in general the simple element from which we obtain by composition all external images. The truth is that affection is not the primary matter of which perception is made; it is rather the impurity with which perception is alloyed.

Here we grasp, at its origin, the error which leads the psychologist to consider sensation as unextended and perception as an aggregate of sensations. This error is reinforced, as we shall see, by illusions derived from a false conception of the role of space and of the nature of extensity. But it has also the support of misinterpreted facts, which we must now examine.

It appears, in the first place, as if the localization of an affective sensation in one part of the body were a matter of gradual training.

A certain time elapses before the child can touch with the finger the precise point where it has been pricked. The fact is indisputable, but all that can be concluded from it is that some tentative essays are required to coordinate the painful impressions on the skin, which has received the prick, with the impressions of the muscular sense, which guides the movement, of arm and hand. Our internal affections, like our external perceptions, are of different kinds. These kinds of affections, like those of perception, are discontinuous, separated by intervals which are filled up in the course of education. But it does not at all follow that there is not, for each affection, an immediate localization of a certain kind, a local colour which is proper to it. We may go further: if the affection has not this local colour at once, it will never have it. For all that education can do is to associate with the actual affective sensation the idea of a certain potential perception of sight and touch, so that a definite affection may evoke the image of a visual or tactile impression, equally definite. There must be, therefore, in this affection itself, something which distinguishes it from other affections of the same kind and permits of its reference to this or that potential datum of sight or touch rather than to any other. But is not this equivalent to saying that affection possesses, from the outset, a certain determination of extensity?

Again, it is alleged that there are erroneous localizations, for example, the illusion of those who have lost a limb (an illusion which requires, however, further examination). But what can we conclude from this beyond the fact that education, once acquired, persists and that such data of memory as are more useful in practical life supplant those of immediate consciousness? It is indispensable, in view of action, that we should translate our affective experience into eventual data of sight, touch and muscular sense. When this translation is made, the original pales, but it never could have been made if the original had not been there to begin with, and if sensation had not been, from the beginning, localized by its own power and in its own way.

But the psychologist has much difficulty in accepting this idea from common sense. Just as perception, in his view, could be in the things perceived only if they had perception, so a sensation cannot be in the nerve unless the nerve feels. Now it is evident that the nerve does not feel. So he takes sensation away from the point where common sense localizes it, carries it toward the brain, on which, more than on the nerve, it appears to depend, and logically should end by placing it *in* the brain. But it soon becomes clear that if it is not at the point where it appears to arise, neither can it be anywhere else: if it is not in the nerve, neither is it in the brain; for to explain its projection from the centre to the periphery a certain force is necessary, which must be attributed to a consciousness that is to some extent active. Therefore, he must go further, and, after having made sensations converge toward the cerebral centre, must push them out of the brain and thereby out of space. So he has to imagine, on the one hand, sensations that are absolutely unextended, and, on the other hand, an empty space indifferent to the sensations which are projected into it: henceforth he will exhaust himself in efforts of every kind to make us understand how unextended sensations acquire extensity and why they choose for their abode this or that point of space rather than any other. But this doctrine is not only incapable of showing us clearly how the unextended takes on extension; it renders affection, extension and representation equally inexplicable. It must assume affective states as so many absolutes, of which it is impossible to say why they appear in or disappear from consciousness at definite moments. The passage from affection to representation remains wrapped in an equally impenetrable mystery because, once again, you will never find in internal states, which are supposed to be simple and unextended, any reason why they should prefer this or that particular order in space. And, finally, representation itself must be posited as an absolute: we cannot guess either its origin or its goal.

Everything becomes clearer, on the other hand, if we start from representation itself, that is to say, from the totality of perceived images. My perception, in its pure state, isolated from memory, does not go on from my body to other bodies; it is, to begin with, in the aggregate of bodies, then gradually limits itself and adopts my body as a centre. And it is led to do so precisely by experience of the double faculty, which this body possesses, of performing actions and feeling affections; in a word, it is led to do so by experience of the sensori-motor power of a certain image, privileged among other images. For, on the one hand, this image always occupies the centre of representation, so that the other images range themselves round it in the very order in which they might be subject to its action; on the other hand, I know it from within, by sensations which I term affective, instead of knowing only, as in the case of the other images, its outer skin. There is, then, in the aggregate of images, a privileged image, perceived in its depths and no longer only on the surface – the seat of affection and, at the same time, the source of action: it is this particular image which I adopt as the centre of my universe and as the physical basis of my personality.

But before we go on to establish the precise relation between the personality and the images in which it dwells, let us briefly sum up, contrasting it with the analyses of current psychology, the theory of pure perception which we have just sketched out.

We will return, for the sake of simplicity, to the sense of sight, which we chose as our example. Psychology has accustomed us to assume the elementary sensations corresponding to the impressions received by the rods and cones of the retina. With these sensations it goes on to reconstitute visual perception. But, in the first place, there is not one retina, there are two; so that we have to explain how two sensations, held to be distinct, combine to form a single perception corresponding to what we call a point in space.

Suppose this problem is solved. The sensations in question are unextended; how will they acquire extension? Whether we see in extensity a framework ready to receive sensations, or an effect of the mere simultaneity of sensations coexisting in consciousness without coalescing, in either case something new is introduced with extensity, something unaccounted for: the process by which sensation arrives at extension, and the choice by each elementary sensation of a definite point in space, remain alike unexplained.

We will leave this difficulty, and suppose visual extension constituted. How does it in its turn reunite with tactile extension? All that my vision perceives in space is verified by my touch. Shall we say that objects are constituted by just the cooperation of sight and touch and that the agreement of the two senses in perception may be explained by the fact that the object perceived is their common product? But how could there be anything common, in the matter of quality, between an elementary visual sensation and a tactile sensation, since they belong to two different genera? The correspondence between visual and tactile extension can only be explained, therefore, by the parallelism of the *order* of the visual sensations with the order of the tactile sensations. So we are now obliged to suppose, over and above visual sensations, over and above tactile sensations, a certain order which is common to both and which, consequently, must be independent of either. We may go further: this order is independent of our individual perception, since it is the same for all men and constitutes a material world in which effects are linked with causes, in which phenomena obey laws. We are thus led at last to the hypothesis of an *objective* order, independent of ourselves, that is to say, of a material world distinct from sensation.

We have had, as we advanced, to multiply our irreducible data and to complicate more and more the simple hypothesis from which we started. But have we gained anything by it? Though the matter which we have been led to posit is indispensable in order to account for the marvellous accord of sensations among themselves, we still know nothing of it, since we must refuse to it all the qualities perceived, all the sensations of which it has only to explain the correspondence. It is not, then, it cannot be, anything of what we know, anything of what we imagine. It remains a mysterious entity.

But our own nature, the office and the function of our personality, remain enveloped in equal mystery. For these elementary unextended sensations which develop themselves in space, whence do they come, how are they born, what purpose do they serve? We must posit them as so many absolutes, of which we see neither the origin nor the end. And even supposing that we must distinguish, in each of us, between the spirit and the body, we can know nothing either of body or of spirit or of the relation between them.

Now in what does this hypothesis of ours consist, and at what precise point does it part company with the other? Instead of starting from *affection*, of which we can say nothing, since there is no reason why it should be what it is rather than anything else, we start from *action*, that is to say from our faculty of effecting changes in things, a faculty attested to by consciousness and toward which all the powers of the organized body are seen to converge. So we place ourselves at once in the midst of extended images, and in this material universe we perceive centres of indetermination, characteristic of life. In order that actions may radiate from these centres, the movements or influences of the other images must be, on the one hand, received and, on the other hand, utilized. Living matter, in its simplest form and in a homogeneous state, accomplishes this function simultaneously with those of nourishment and repair. The progress of such matter consists in sharing this double labour between two categories of organs, the purpose of the first, called organs of nutrition, being to maintain the second: the second, in their turn, are made for *action*; they have as their simple type a chain of nervous elements, connecting two extremities, of which the one receives external impressions and the other executes movements. Thus, to return to the example of visual perception, the office of the rods and cones is merely to receive excitations which will be subsequently elaborated into movements, either accomplished or nascent. No perception can result from this, and nowhere in the nervous system are there conscious centres, but perception arises from the same cause which has brought into being the chain of nervous elements, with the organs which sustain them and with life in general. It expresses and measures the power of action in the living being, the indetermination of the movement or of the action which will follow the receipt of the stimulus. This indetermination, as we have shown, will express itself in a reflection upon themselves or, better, in a division, of the images which surround our body, and, as the chain of nervous elements which receives, arrests and transmits movements is the seat of this indetermination and gives its measure, our perception will follow all the detail and will appear to express all the variations of the nervous elements themselves. Perception, in its pure state, is, then, in very truth, a part of things. And, as for affective sensation, it does not spring spontaneously from the depths of consciousness to extend itself, as it grows weaker, in space; it is one with the necessary modifications to which, in the midst of the surrounding images that influence it, the particular image that each one of us terms his body is subject.

Such is our simplified, schematic theory of external perception. It is the theory of *pure* perception. If we went no further, the part of consciousness in perception would thus be confined to threading on the continuous string of memory an uninterrupted series of instantaneous visions, which would be a part of things rather than of ourselves. That this *is* the chief office of consciousness in external perception is indeed what we may deduce *a priori* from the very definition of living bodies. For though the function of these bodies is to receive stimulations in order to elaborate them into unforeseen reactions, still the choice of the reaction cannot be the work of chance. This choice is likely to be inspired by past experience, and the reaction does not take place without an appeal to the memories which analogous situations may have left behind them. The indetermination of acts to be accomplished requires, then, if it is not to be confounded with pure caprice, the preservation of the images perceived. It may be said that we have no grasp of the future without an equal and corresponding outlook over the past, that the onrush of our activity makes a void behind it into which memories flow, and that memory is thus the reverberation, in the sphere of consciousness, of the indetermination of our will. But the action of memory goes further and deeper than this superficial glance would suggest. The moment has come to reinstate memory in perception, to correct in this way the element of exaggeration in our conclusions, and so to determine with more precision the point of contact between consciousness and things, between the body and the spirit.

We assert, at the outset, that if there be memory, that is, the survival of past images, these images must constantly mingle with our perception of the present and may even take its place. For if they have survived, it is with a view to utility; at every moment they complete our present experience, enriching it with experience already acquired, and, as the latter is ever increasing, it must end by covering up and submerging the former. It is indisputable that the basis of real, and so to speak instantaneous, intuition, on which our perception of the external world is developed, is a small matter compared with all that memory adds to it.[9] Just because the recollection of earlier analogous intuitions is more useful than the intuition itself, being bound up in memory with the whole series of subsequent events and capable thereby of throwing a better light on our decision, it supplants the real intuition of which the office is then merely – we shall prove it later – to call up the recollection, to give it a body, to render it active and thereby actual. We had every right, then, to say that the coincidence of perception with the object perceived exists in theory rather than in fact. We must take into account that perception ends by being merely an occasion for remembering, that we measure in practice the degree of reality by the degree of utility, and, finally, that it is our interest to regard as mere signs of the real those immediate intuitions which are, in fact, part and parcel of reality. But here we discover the mistake of those who say that to perceive is to project externally unextended sensations, which have been drawn from our own depths, and then to develop them in space. They have no difficulty in showing that our *complete* perception is filled with images which belong to us personally, with exteriorised (that is to say, recollected) images, but they forget that an impersonal basis remains in which perception coincides with the object perceived and which is, in fact, externality itself.

The capital error, the error which, passing over from psychology into metaphysic, shuts us out in the end from the knowledge both of body and spirit, is that which sees only a difference of intensity instead of a difference of nature, between pure perception and memory. Our perceptions are undoubtedly interlaced with memories, and, inversely, a memory, as we shall show later, only becomes actual by borrowing the body of some perception into which it slips. These two acts, perception and recollection, always interpenetrate each other, are always exchanging something of their substance as by a process of endosmosis. The proper office of psychologists would be to dissociate them, to give back to each its natural purity; in this way many difficulties raised by psychology, and perhaps also by metaphysics, might be lessened. But they will have it that these mixed states, compounded, in unequal proportions, of pure perception and pure memory, are simple. And so we are condemned to an ignorance both of pure memory and of pure perception; to knowing only a single kind of phenomenon which will be called now memory and now perception, according to the predominance in it of one or other of the two aspects; and, consequently, to finding between perception and memory only a difference in degree, and not in kind. The first effect of this error, as we shall see in detail, is to vitiate profoundly the theory of memory; for, if we make recollection merely a weakened perception, we misunderstand the essential difference between the past and the present, we abandon all hope of understanding the phenomena of recognition, and, more generally, the mechanism of the unconscious. But, inversely, if recollection is regarded as a weakened perception, perception must be regarded as a stronger recollection. We are driven to argue as though it was given to us after the manner of a memory, as an internal state, a mere modification of our personality; and our eyes are closed to the primordial and fundamental act of perception – the act, constituting pure perception, whereby we place ourselves in the very heart of things. And thus the same error, which manifests itself in psychology by a radical incapacity to explain the mechanism of memory, will in metaphysics profoundly influence the idealistic and realistic conceptions of matter.

For realism, in fact, the invariable order of the phenomena of nature lies in a cause distinct from our perceptions, whether this cause must remain unknowable, or whether we can reach it by an effort (always more or less arbitrary) of metaphysical construction. For the idealist, on the contrary, these perceptions are the whole of reality, and the invariable order of the phenomena of nature is but the symbol whereby we express, alongside of real perceptions, perceptions that are possible. But, for realism as for idealism, perceptions are 'veridical hallucinations,' states of the subject, projected outside himself, and the two doctrines differ merely in this: that, in the one, these states constitute reality; in the other, they are sent forth to unite with it.

But behind this illusion lurks yet another that extends to the theory of knowledge in general. We have said that the material world is made up of objects, or, if you prefer it, of images, of which all the parts act and react upon each other by movements. And that which constitutes our pure perception, is our dawning action, in so far as it is prefigured in those images. The *actuality* of our perception thus lies in its *activity*, in the movements which prolong it, and not in its greater intensity: the past is only idea, the present is ideo-motor. But this is what our opponents are determined not to see because they regard perception as a kind of contemplation, attribute to it always a purely speculative end, and maintain that it seeks some strange disinterested knowledge, as though, by isolating it from action, and thus severing its links with the real, they were not rendering it both inexplicable and useless. But thenceforward all difference between perception and recollection is abolished, since the past is essentially *that which acts no longer*, and since, by misunderstanding this characteristic of the past, they become incapable of making a real distinction between it and the present, i.e., *that which is acting*. No difference but that of mere degree will remain between perception and memory and neither in the one nor in the other will the subject be acknowledged to pass beyond himself. Restore, on the contrary, the true character of perception; recognize in pure perception a system of nascent acts which plunges roots deep into the real; and at once perception is seen to be radically distinct from recollection; the reality of things is no more constructed or reconstructed, but touched, penetrated, lived, and the problem at issue between realism and idealism, instead of giving rise to interminable metaphysical discussions, is solved, or rather, dissolved, by intuition.

In this way also we shall plainly see what position we ought to take up between idealism and realism, which are both condemned to see in a matter only a construction or a reconstruction executed by the mind. For if we follow to the end the principle according to which the subjectivity of our perception consists, above all, in the share taken by memory, we shall say that even the sensible qualities of matter would be known *in themselves*, from within and not from without, could we but disengage them from that particular rhythm of duration which characterizes our consciousness. Pure perception, in fact, however rapid we suppose it to be, occupies a certain depth of duration, so that our successive perceptions are never the real moments of things, as we have hitherto supposed, but are moments of our consciousness. Theoretically, we said, the part played by consciousness in external perception would be to join together, by the continuous thread of memory, instantaneous visions of the real. But, in fact, there is for us nothing that is instantaneous. In all that goes by that name there is already some work of our memory, and consequently, of our consciousness, which prolongs into each other, so as to grasp them in one relatively simple intuition, an endless number of moments of an endlessly divisible time. Now what is, in truth, the difference between matter as the strictest realism might conceive it and the perception which we have of it? Our perception presents us with a series of pictorial, but discontinuous, views of the universe; from our present perceptions we could not deduce subsequent perceptions because there is nothing in an aggregate of sensible qualities which foretells the new qualities into which they will change. On the contrary, matter, as realism usually posits it, evolves in such a manner that we can pass from one moment to the next by a mathematical deduction. It is true that, between this matter and this perception, scientific realism can find no point of contact because it develops matter into homogeneous changes in space, while it contracts perception into unextended sensations within consciousness. But, if our hypothesis is correct, we can easily see how perception and matter are distinguished and how they coincide. The qualitative heterogeneity of our successive perceptions of the universe results from the fact that each, in itself, extends over a certain depth of duration and that memory condenses in each an enormous multiplicity of vibrations which appear to us all at once, although they are successive. If we were only to divide, ideally, this undivided depth of time, to distinguish in it the necessary multiplicity of moments, in a word, to eliminate all memory, we should pass thereby from perception to matter, from the subject to the object. Then matter, becoming more and more homogeneous as our extended sensations spread themselves over a greater number of moments, would tend more and more toward that system of homogeneous vibrations of which realism tells us, although it would never coincide entirely with them. There would be no need to assume, on the one hand, space with unperceived movements, and, on the other, consciousness with unextended sensations. Subject and object would unite in an extended perception, the subjective side of perception being the contraction effected by memory, and the objective reality of matter fusing with the multitudinous and successive vibrations into which this perception can be internally broken up. Such at least is the conclusion which, we hope, will issue clearly from the last part of this essay. *Questions relating to subject and object, to their distinction and their union, should be put in terms of time rather than of space.*

But our distinction between 'pure perception' and 'pure memory' has yet another aim. Just as pure perception, by giving us hints as to the nature of matter, allows us to take an intermediate position between realism and idealism, so pure memory, on the other hand, by opening to us a view of what is called spirit should enable us to decide between those other two doctrines, materialism and spiritualism.[10] Indeed, it is this aspect of the subject which will first occupy our attention in the two following chapters because it is in this aspect that our hypothesis allows some degree of experimental verification.

For it is possible to sum up our conclusions as to pure perception by saying that *there is in matter something more than, but not something different from, that which is actually given.* Undoubtedly, conscious perception does not compass the whole of matter, since it consists, in as far as it is conscious, in the separation, or the 'discernment,' of that which, in matter, interests our various needs. But between this perception of matter and matter itself there is but a difference of degree and not of kind, pure perception standing toward matter in the relation of the part to the whole. This amounts to saying that matter cannot exercise powers of any kind other than those which we perceive. It has no mysterious virtue; it can conceal none. To take a definite example, one, moreover, which interests us most nearly, we may say that the nervous system, a material mass presenting certain qualities of colour, resistance, cohesion, etc., may well possess unperceived physical properties, but physical properties only. And hence it can have no other office than to receive, inhibit or transmit movement.

Now the essence of every form of materialism is to maintain the contrary, since it holds that consciousness, with all its functions, is born of the mere interplay of material elements. Hence it is led to consider even the perceived qualities of matter – sensible, and consequently felt, qualities – as so many phosphorescences which follow the track of the cerebral phenomena in the act of perception. Matter, thus supposed capable of creating elementary facts of consciousness, might therefore just as well engender intellectual facts of the highest order. It is, then, the essence of materialism to assert the perfect relativity of sensible qualities, and it is not without good reason that this thesis, which Democritus has formulated in precise terms, is as old as materialism.

But spiritualism has always followed materialism along this path. As if everything lost to matter *must* be gained by spirit, spiritualism has never hesitated to despoil matter of the qualities with which it is invested in our perception, and which, on this view, are subjective appearances. Matter has thus too often been reduced to a mysterious entity which, just because all we know of it is an empty show, might as well engender thought as well as any other phenomenon.

The truth is that there is one, and only one, method of refuting materialism: it is to show that matter is precisely that which it appears to be. Thereby we eliminate all virtuality, all hidden power, from matter and establish the phenomena of spirit as an independent reality. But to do this we must leave to matter those qualities which materialists and spiritualists alike strip from it: the latter that they may make of them representations of the spirit, the former that they may regard them only as the accidental garb of space.

This, indeed, is the attitude of common sense with regard to matter, and for this reason common sense believes in spirit. It seems to us that philosophy should here adopt the attitude of common sense, although correcting it in one respect. Memory, inseparable in practice from perception, imports the past into the present, contracts into a single intuition many moments of duration, and thus by a twofold operation compels us, *de facto*, to perceive matter in ourselves, whereas we, *de jure*, perceive matter within matter.

Hence the capital importance of the problem of memory. If it is memory above all that lends to perception its subjective character, the philosophy of matter must aim, in the first instance, we said, at eliminating the contributions of memory. We must now add that, as pure perception gives us the whole or at least the essential part of matter (since the rest comes from memory and is superadded to matter), it follows that memory must be, in principle, a power absolutely independent of matter. If, then, spirit is a reality, it is here, in the phenomenon of memory, that we may come into touch with it experimentally. And hence any attempt to derive pure memory from an operation of the brain should reveal on analysis a radical illusion.

Let us put the same statement in clearer language. We maintain that matter has no occult or unknowable power and that it coincides, in essentials, with pure perception. Therefore we conclude that the living body in general, and the nervous system in particular, are only channels for the transmission of movements, which, received in the form of stimulation, are transmitted in the form of action, reflex or voluntary. That is to say, it is vain to attribute to the cerebral substance the property of engendering representations. Now the phenomena of memory, in which we believe that we can grasp spirit in its most tangible form, are precisely those of which a superficial psychology is most ready to find the origin in cerebral activity alone; just because they are at the point of contact between consciousness and matter, and because even the adversaries of materialism have no objection to treating the brain as a storehouse of memories. But if it could be positively established that the cerebral process answers only to a very small part of memory, that it is rather the effect than the cause, that matter is here as elsewhere the vehicle of an *action* and not the substratum of a *knowledge*, then the thesis which we are maintaining would be demonstrated by the very example which is commonly supposed to be most unfavorable to it, and the necessity might arise of erecting spirit into an independent reality. In this way also, perhaps some light would be thrown on the nature of what is called spirit and on the possibility of the interaction of spirit and matter. For a demonstration of this kind could not be purely negative. Having shown what memory is not, we should have to try to discover what it is. Having attributed to the body the sole function of preparing actions, we are bound to enquire why memory appears to be one with this body, how bodily lesions influence it, and in what sense it may be said to mold itself upon the state of the brain matter. It is, moreover, impossible that this enquiry should fail to give us some information as to the psychological mechanism of memory and the various mental operations connected therewith. And, inversely, if the problems of pure psychology seem to acquire some light from our hypothesis, this hypothesis itself will thereby gain in certainty and weight.

But we must present this same idea in yet a third form, so as to make it quite clear why the problem of memory is in our eyes a privileged problem. From our analysis of pure perception issue two conclusions, which are in some sort divergent, one of them going beyond psychology in the direction of psycho-physiology and the other in that of metaphysics, but neither allowing of immediate verification. The first concerns the office of the brain in perception: we maintain that the brain is an instrument of action, and not of representation. We cannot demand from facts the direct confirmation of this thesis, because pure perception bears, by definition, upon *present* objects, acting on our organs and our nerve centres; and because everything always happens, in consequence, *as though* our perceptions emanated from our cerebral state and were subsequently projected upon an object which differs absolutely from them. In other words, with regard to external perception, the thesis which we dispute and that which we substitute for it lead to precisely the same consequence, so that it is possible to invoke in favour of either the one or the other its greater intelligibility, but not the authority of experience. On the contrary, the empirical study of memory may and must decide between them. For pure recollection is, by hypothesis, the representation of *an absent* object. If the necessary and sufficient cause of perception lies in a certain activity of the brain, this same cerebral activity, repeating itself more or less completely in the absence of the object, will suffice to reproduce perception: memory will be entirely explicable by the brain. But if we find that the cerebral mechanism does indeed in some sort condition memories, but is in no way sufficient to ensure their survival; if it concerns, in remembered perception, our action rather than our representation; we shall be able to infer that it plays an analogous part in perception itself and that its office is merely to ensure our effective action on the object present. Our first conclusion may thus find its verification. There would still remain this second conclusion, which is of a more metaphysical order – viz.: that in pure perception we are actually placed outside ourselves; we touch the reality of the object in an immediate intuition. Here also an experimental verification is impossible, since the practical results are absolutely the same whether the reality of the object is intuitively perceived or whether it is rationally constructed. But here again a study of memory may decide between the two hypotheses. For, in the second, there is only a difference of intensity, or more generally, of degree, between perception and recollection, since they are both self-sufficient phenomena of representation. But if, on the contrary, we find that the difference between perception and recollection is not merely in degree, but is a radical difference in kind, the presumption will be in favour of the hypothesis which finds in perception something which is entirely absent from memory, a reality intuitively grasped. Thus the problem of memory is in very truth a privileged problem, in that it must lead to the psychological verification of two theses which appear to be insusceptible to proof, and of which the second, being of a metaphysical order, appears to go far beyond the borders of psychology.

The road which we have to follow, then, lies clear before us. We shall first review evidence of various kinds borrowed from normal and from pathological psychology, by which philosophers might hold themselves justified in maintaining a physical explanation of memory. This examination must needs be minute or it would be useless. Keeping as close as possible to facts, we must seek to discover where, in the operations of memory, the office of the body begins and where it ends. And should we, in the course of this inquiry, find confirmation of our own hypothesis, we shall not hesitate to go further and, considering in itself the elementary work of the mind, complete the theory thereby sketched out, of the relation of spirit with matter.

The Persistence of the Past[11]

To sum up briefly the preceding chapters: we have distinguished three processes, pure memory, memory-image and perception, of which none of them, in fact, occurs apart from the others. Perception is never a mere contact of the mind with the object present; it is impregnated with memory-images which complete it as they interpret it. The memory-image, in its turn, partakes of the 'pure memory,' which it begins to materialize, and of the perception in which it tends to embody itself: regarded from the latter point of view, it might be defined as a nascent perception. Lastly, pure memory, though independent in theory, manifests itself as a rule only in the coloured and living image which reveals it. Symbolizing these three terms by the consecutive segments AB, BC, CD, of the same straight line AD, we may say that our thought describes this line in a single movement, which goes from A to D, and that it is impossible to say precisely where one of the terms ends and another begins.

In fact, this is just what consciousness bears witness to whenever, in order to analyse memory, it follows the movement of memory at work. Whenever we are trying to recover a recollection, to call up some period of our history, we become conscious of an act *sui generis* by which we detach ourselves from the present in order to replace ourselves, first, in the past in general, then, in a certain region of the past – a work of adjustment, something like the focusing of a camera. But our recollection still remains virtual; we simply prepare ourselves to receive it by adopting the appropriate attitude. Little by little it comes into view like a condensing cloud; from the virtual state it passes into the actual; and

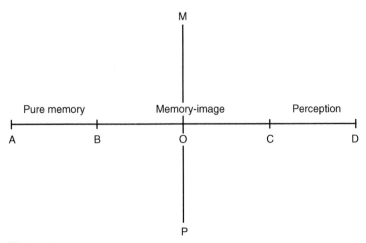

Figure 1

as its outlines become more distinct and its surface takes on colour, it tends to imitate perception. But it remains attached to the past by its deepest roots, and if, when once realized, it did not retain something of its original virtuality, if, being a present state, it were not also something which stands out distinct from the present, we should never know it for a memory.

The capital error of associationism is that it substitutes for this continuity of becoming, which is the living reality, a discontinuous multiplicity of elements, inert and juxtaposed. Just because each of the elements so constituted contains, by reason of its origin, something of what precedes and also of what follows, it must take to our eyes the form of a mixed and, so to speak, impure state. But the principle of associationism requires that each psychical state should be a kind of atom, a simple element. Hence the necessity for sacrificing, in each of the phases we have distinguished, the unstable to the stable, that is to say, the beginning to the end. If we are dealing with perception, we are asked to see in it nothing but the agglomerated sensations which colour it and to overlook the remembered images which form its dim nucleus. If it is the remembered image that we are considering, we are bidden to take it already made, realized in a weak perception, and to shut our eyes to the pure memory which this image has progressively developed. In the rivalry which associationism thus sets up between the stable and the unstable, perception is bound to expel the memory-image, and the memory-image to expel pure memory. And thus the pure memory disappears altogether. Associationism, cutting in two, by a line MO, the totality of the progress AD, sees, in the part OD, only the sensations which terminate it and which have been supposed to constitute the whole of perception; yet it also reduces the part AO to the realized image which pure memory attains to as it expands. Psychical life, then, is entirely summed up in these two elements, sensation and image. And as, on the one hand, this theory drowns in the image the pure memory, which makes the image into an original state, and, on the other hand, brings the image yet closer to perception by putting into perception, in advance, something of the image itself, it ends up by finding between these two states only a difference of degree, or of intensity. Hence the distinction between *strong states* and *weak states*, of which the first are supposed to be set up by us as perceptions of the present, and the second (why, no man knows) as representations of the past. But the truth is that we shall never reach the past unless we frankly place ourselves within it. Essentially virtual, it cannot be known as something past unless we follow and adopt the movement by which it expands into a present image, thus emerging from obscurity into the light of day. In vain do we seek its trace in anything actual and already realized: we might as well look for darkness beneath the light. This is, in fact, the error of associationism: placed in the actual, it exhausts itself in vain attempts to discover in a realized and present state the mark of its past origin, to distinguish memory from perception, and to erect into a difference in kind that which it condemned in advance to be but a difference of magnitude.

To *picture* is not to *remember*. No doubt a recollection, as it becomes actual, tends to live in an image; however, the converse is not true, and the image, pure and simple, will not be referred to the past unless, indeed, it was in the past that I sought it, thus following the continuous progress which brought it from darkness into light. This is what psychologists too often forget when they conclude, from the fact that a remembered sensation becomes more actual the more we dwell upon it, that the memory of the sensation is the sensation itself beginning to be. The fact which they allege is undoubtedly true: the more I strive to recall a past pain, the nearer I come to feeling it in reality. But this is easy to understand, since the progress of a memory precisely consists, as we have said, in its becoming materialized. The question is: was the memory of a pain, when it began, really pain? Because the hypnotized subject ends by feeling hot when he is repeatedly told that he is hot, it does not follow that the words of the suggestion were themselves hot. Neither must we conclude that, because the memory of a sensation prolongs itself into that very sensation, the memory was a nascent sensation: perhaps, indeed, this memory plays, with regard to the sensation which follows it, precisely the part of the hypnotiser who makes the suggestion. The argument we are criticizing, presented in this form, is then already of no value as proof; still, it is not yet a vicious argument, because it profits by the incontestable truth that memory passes into something else by becoming actual. The absurdity becomes patent when the argument is inverted (although this ought to be legitimate on the hypothesis adopted), that is to say, when the intensity of the sensation is decreased instead of the intensity of pure memory being increased. For then, if the two states differ merely in degree, there should be a given moment at which the sensation changed into a memory. If the memory of an acute pain, for instance, is but a slight pain, inversely, an intense pain which I feel, will end, as it grows less, by being an acute pain remembered. Now the moment will come, undoubtedly, when it is impossible for me to say whether what I feel is a slight sensation, which I experience, or a slight sensation, which I imagine (and this is natural, because the memory-image is already partly sensation), but never will this weak state appear to me to be the memory of a strong state. Memory, then, is something quite different.

But the illusion which consists in establishing only a difference of degree between memory and perception is more than a mere consequence of associationism, more than an accident in the history of philosophy. Its roots lie deep. It rests, in the last analysis, on a false idea of the nature and of the object of external perception. We are bent on regarding perception as only an instruction addressed to a pure spirit, as having a purely speculative interest. Then, as memory is itself essentially a knowledge of this kind, since its object is no longer present, we can only find between perception and memory a difference of degree – perceptions being then supposed to throw memories back into the past, and thus to reserve to themselves the present simply because right is might. But there is much more between past and present than a mere difference of degree. My present is that which interests me, which lives for me, and in a word, that which summons me to action;

in contrast, my past is essentially powerless. We must dwell further on this point. By contrasting it with present perception we shall better understand the nature of what we call 'pure memory.'

For we should endeavour in vain to characterize the memory of a past state unless we began by defining the concrete note, accepted by consciousness, of present reality. What is, for me, the present moment? The essence of time is that it goes by; time already gone by is the past, and we call the present the instant in which it goes by. But there can be no question here of a mathematical instant. No doubt there is an ideal present – a pure conception, the indivisible limit which separates past from future. But the real, concrete, live present – that of which I speak when I speak of my present perception – that present necessarily occupies a duration. Where then is this duration placed? Is it on the nearer or on the further side of the mathematical point which I determine ideally when I think of the present instant? Quite evidently, it is both on this side and on that, and what I call 'my present' has one foot in my past and another in my future. In my past, first, because 'the moment in which I am speaking is already far from me'; in my future, next, because this moment is impending over the future: it is to the future that I am tending, and could I fix this indivisible present, this infinitesimal element of the curve of time, it is the direction of the future that it would indicate. The psychical state, then, that I call 'my present,' must be both a perception of the immediate past and a determination of the immediate future. Now the immediate past, in so far as it is perceived, is, as we shall see, sensation, since every sensation translates a very long succession of elementary vibrations, and the immediate future, in so far as it is being determined, is action or movement. My present, then, is both sensation and movement; since my present forms an undivided whole, then the movement must be linked with the sensation, must prolong it in action. Whence I conclude that my present consists in a joint system of sensations and movements. My present is, in its essence, sensori-motor.

This is to say that my present consists in the consciousness I have of my body. Having extension in space, my body experiences sensations and at the same time executes movements. Sensations and movements being localized at determined points of this extended body, there can only be, at a given moment, a single system of movements and sensations. That is why my present appears to me to be a thing absolutely determined, and contrasting with my past. Situated between the matter which influences it and that on which it has influence, my body is a centre of action, the place where the impressions received choose intelligently the path they will follow to transform themselves into movements accomplished. Thus it, indeed, represents the actual state of my becoming, that part of my duration which is in process of growth. More generally, in that continuity of becoming which is reality itself, the present moment is constituted by the quasi-instantaneous section effected by our perception in the flowing mass, and this section is precisely that which we call the material world. Our body occupies its centre; it is, in this material world, that part of which we directly feel the flux; in its actual state the actuality of our present lies. If matter, so far as extended in space, is to be defined (as we believe it must) as a present which is always beginning again, inversely, our present is the very materiality of our existence, that is to say, a system of sensations and movements and nothing else. And this system is determined, unique for each moment of duration, just because sensations and movements occupy space, and because there cannot be in the same place several things at the same time. Why is it that it has been possible to misunderstand so simple, so evident a truth, one which is, moreover, the very idea of common sense?

The reason lies simply in the fact that philosophers insist on regarding the difference between actual sensations and pure memory as a mere difference in degree, and not in kind. In our view the difference is radical. My actual sensations occupy definite portions of the surface of my body; pure memory, on the other hand, interests no part of my body. No doubt, it will beget sensations as it materializes, but at that very moment it will cease to be a memory and pass into the state of a present thing, something actually lived. I shall then only restore to it its character of memory by carrying myself back to the process by which I called it up, as it was virtual, from the depths of my past. It is just because I made it active that it has become actual, that is to say, a sensation capable of provoking movements. But most psychologists see in pure memory only a weakened perception, an assembly of nascent sensations. Having thus effaced, to begin with, all difference in kind between sensation and memory, they are led by the logic of their hypothesis to materialize memory and to idealize sensation. They perceive memory only in the form of an image, that is to say, already embodied in nascent sensations. Having thus attributed to it that which is essential to sensation, and refusing to see in the ideality of memory something distinct, something contrasted with sensation itself, they are forced, when they come back to pure sensation, to leave to it that ideality with which they have thus implicidy endowed nascent sensations. For if the past, which by hypothesis is no longer active, can subsist in the form of a weak sensation, there must be sensations that are powerless. If pure memory, which by hypothesis interests no definite part of the body, is a nascent sensation, then sensation is not essentially localized in any point of the body. Hence the illusion that consists in regarding sensation as an ethereal and unextended state which acquires extension and consolidates in the body by mere accident: an illusion which vitiates profoundly, as we have seen, the theory of external perception and raises a great number of the questions at issue between the various metaphysics of matter. We must make up our minds to it: sensation is, in its essence, extended and localized; it is a source of movement. Pure memory, being inextensive and powerless, does not in any degree share the nature of sensation.

That which I call my present is my attitude with regard to the immediate future; it is my impending action. My present is, then, sensori-motor. Of my past, that alone becomes image and, consequently, sensation, at least nascent, which can collaborate in that action, insert itself in that attitude, in a word make itself useful; but, from the moment that it becomes image, the past leaves the state of pure memory and coincides with a certain part of my present. Memory actualised in an image differs, then, profoundly from pure memory. The image is a present state, and its sole share in the past is the memory from which it arose. Memory, on the contrary, powerless as long as it remains without utility, is pure from all admixture of sensation, is without attachment to the present, and is, consequently, unextended.

This radical powerlessness of pure memory is just what will enable us to understand how it is preserved in a latent state. Without as yet going to the heart of the matter, we will confine ourselves to the remark that our unwillingness to conceive *unconscious psychical states* is due, above all, to the fact that we hold consciousness to be the essential property of psychical states: so a psychical state cannot, it seems, cease to be conscious without ceasing to exist. But if consciousness is but the characteristic note of the *present*, that is to say, of the actually lived, in short, of the *active*, then that which does not act may cease to belong to consciousness without therefore ceasing to exist in some manner. In other words, in the psychological domain, consciousness may not be the synonym of existence, but only of real action or of immediate efficacy; limiting thus the meaning of the term, we shall have less difficulty in representing to ourselves a psychical state which is unconscious, that is to say, ineffective. Whatever idea we may frame of consciousness in itself, such as it would be if it could work untrammelled, we cannot deny that, in a being which has bodily functions, the chief office of consciousness is to preside over action and to enlighten choice. Therefore, it throws light on the immediate antecedents of the decision, and on those past recollections which can usefully combine with it; all else remains in shadow.

[. . .]

But we are so much accustomed to reverse, for the sake of action, the real order of things, we are so strongly obsessed by images drawn from space, that we cannot hinder ourselves from asking *where* memories are stored up. We understand that physico-chemical phenomena take place *in* the brain, that the brain is *in* the body, the body *in* the air which surrounds it, etc.; but the past, once achieved, if it is retained, where is it? To locate it in the cerebral substance, in the state of molecular modification, seems clear and simple enough because then we have a receptacle, actually given, which we have only to open in order to let the latent images flow into consciousness. But if the brain cannot serve such a purpose, in what warehouse shall we store the accumulated images? We forget that the relation of container to content borrows its apparent clearness and universality from the necessity laid upon us of always opening out space in front of us and of always closing duration behind us. Because it has been shown that one thing is within another, the phenomenon of its preservation is not thereby made any clearer. We may even go further: let us admit for a moment that the past survives in the form of a memory stored in the brain; it is then necessary that the brain, in order to preserve the memory, should preserve itself. But the brain, insofar as it is an image extended in space, never occupies more than the present moment: it constitutes, with all the rest of the material universe, an ever-renewed section of universal becoming. Either, then, you must suppose that this universe dies and is born again miraculously at each moment of duration, or you must attribute to it that continuity of existence which you deny to consciousness, and make of its past a reality which endures and is prolonged into its present. So that you have gained nothing by depositing the memories in matter, and you find yourself, on the contrary, compelled to extend to the totality of the states of the material world that complete and independent survival of the past which you have just refused to psychical states. This survival of the past *per se* forces itself upon philosophers, then, under one form or another; the difficulty that we have in conceiving it comes simply from the fact that we extend to the series of memories, in time, that obligation of *containing* and *being contained* which applies only to the collection of bodies instantaneously perceived in space. The fundamental illusion consists in transferring to duration itself, in its continuous flow, the form of the instantaneous sections which we make in it.

But how can the past, which, by hypothesis, has ceased to be, preserve itself? Have we not here a real contradiction? We reply that the question is just whether the past has ceased to exist or whether it has simply ceased to be useful. You define the present in an arbitrary manner as *that which is*, whereas the present is simply *what is being made*. Nothing *is* less than the present moment, if you understand by that the indivisible limit which divides the past from the future. When we think this present as going to be, it exists not yet, and when we think it as existing, it is already past. If, on the other hand, what you are considering is the concrete present such as it is actually lived by consciousness, we may say that this present consists, in large measure, in the immediate past. In the fraction of a second which covers the briefest possible perception of light, billions of vibrations have taken place, of which the first is separated from the last by an interval which is enormously divided. Your perception, however instantaneous, consists then in an incalculable multitude of remembered elements; in truth, every perception is already memory. *Practically, we perceive only the past*, the pure present being the invisible progress of the past gnawing into the future.

Consciousness, then, illumines, at each moment of time, that immediate part of the past which, impending over the future, seeks to realize and to associate with it. Solely preoccupied in thus determining an undetermined future, consciousness may shed a little of its light on those of our states, more remote in the past, which can be usefully combined with our present state, that is to say, with our immediate past: the rest remains in the dark. It is in this illuminated part of our history that we remain seated, in virtue of the fundamental law of life, which is a law of action: hence the difficulty we experience in conceiving memories which are preserved in the shadow. Our reluctance to admit the integral survival of the past has its origin, then, in the very bent of our psychical life – an unfolding of states wherein our interest prompts us to look at that which is unrolling, and not at that which is entirely unrolled.

So we return, after a long digression, to our point of departure. There are, we have said, two memories which are profoundly distinct: the one, fixed in the organism, is nothing else but the complete set of intelligently constructed mechanisms which ensure the appropriate reply to the various possible demands. This memory enables us to adapt ourselves to the present situation; through it the actions to which we are subject prolong themselves into reactions that are sometimes accomplished, sometimes merely nascent, but always more or less appropriate. Habit rather than memory, it acts our past experience but does not call up its image. The other is the true memory. Coextensive with consciousness, it retains and ranges alongside of each other all our states in the order in which they occur, leaving to each fact its place and, consequently, marking its date, truly moving in the past and not, like the first, in an ever renewed present. But, in marking the profound distinction between these two forms of memory, we have not shown their connecting link. Above the body, with its mechanisms which symbolize the accumulated effort of past actions, the memory which imagines and repeats has been left to hang, as it were, suspended in the void. Now, if it be true that we never perceive anything but our immediate past, if our consciousness of the present is already memory, the two terms which had been separated to begin with cohere closely together. Seen from this new point of view, indeed, our body is nothing but that part of our representation which is ever being born again, the part always present, or rather that which, at each moment, is just past. Itself an image, the body cannot store up images, since it forms a part of the images, and this is why it is a chimerical enterprise to seek to localize past or even present perceptions in the brain: they are not in it; it is the brain that is in them. But this special image which persists in the midst of the others, and which I call my body, constitutes at every moment, as we have said, a section of the universal becoming. It is then the *place of passage* of the movements received and thrown back, a hyphen, a connecting link

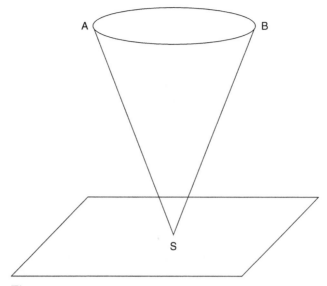

Figure 2

between the things which act upon me and the things upon which I act – the seat, in a word, of the sensori-motor phenomena. If I represent by a cone SAB, the totality of the recollections accumulated in my memory, the base AB, situated in the past, remains motionless, while the summit S, which indicates at all times my present, moves forward unceasingly, and unceasingly also touches the moving plane P of my actual representation of the universe. At S, the image of the body is concentrated, and, since it belongs to the plane P, this image does but receive and restore actions emanating from all the images of which the plane is composed.

The bodily memory, made up of the sum of the sensori-motor systems organized by habit, is then a quasi-instantaneous memory to which the true memory of the past serves as base. Since they are not two separate things, since the first is only, as we have said, the pointed end, ever moving, inserted by the second in the shifting plane of experience, it is natural that the two functions should lend each other a mutual support. So, on the one hand, the memory of the past offers to the sensori-motor mechanisms all the recollections capable of guiding them in their task and of giving to the motor reaction the direction suggested by the lessons of experience. It is in just this that the associations of contiguity and likeness consist. But, on the other hand, the sensori-motor apparatus furnish to ineffective, that is unconscious, memories, the means of taking on a body, of materializing themselves, in short of becoming present. For, that a recollection should reappear in consciousness, it is necessary that it should descend from the heights of pure memory down to the precise point where *action* is taking place. In other words, it is from the present that the appeal to which memory responds comes, and it is from the sensori-motor elements of present action that a memory borrows the warmth which gives it life.

Is it not by the constancy of this agreement, by the precision with which these two complementary memories insert themselves each into the other, that we recognize a 'well-balanced' mind, that is to say, in fact, a man nicely adapted to life? The characteristic of the man of action is the promptitude with which he summons to the help of a given situation all the memories which have reference to it; yet it is also the insurmountable barrier which encounters, when they present themselves on the threshold of his consciousness, memories that are useless or indifferent. To live only in the present, to respond to a stimulus by the immediate reaction which prolongs it, is the mark of the lower animals: the man who proceeds in this way is a man of *impulse*. But he who lives in the past for the mere pleasure of living there, and in whom recollections emerge into the light of consciousness without any advantage for the present situation, is hardly better fitted for action: here we have no man of impulse, but a *dreamer*. Between these two extremes lives the happy disposition of memory docile enough to follow with precision all the outlines of the present situation, but energetic enough to resist all other appeal. Good sense, or practical sense, is probably nothing but this.

The extraordinary development of spontaneous memory in most children is due to the fact that they have not yet persuaded their memory to remain bound up with their conduct. They usually follow the impression of the moment, and as with them action does not bow to the suggestions of memory, so neither are their recollections limited to the necessities of action. They seem to retain with greater facility only because they remember with less discernment. The apparent diminution of memory, as intellect develops, is then due to the growing organization of recollections with acts. Thus conscious memory loses in range what it gains in force of penetration: it had at first the facility of the memory of dreams, but then it was actually dreaming. Indeed we observe this same exaggeration of spontaneous memory in men whose intellectual development hardly goes beyond that of childhood. A missionary, after preaching a long sermon to some African savages, heard one of them repeat it textually, with the same gestures, from beginning to end.[12]

But, if almost the whole of our past is hidden from us because it is inhibited by the necessities of present action, it will find strength to cross the threshold of consciousness in all cases where we renounce the interests of effective action to replace ourselves, so to speak, in the life of dreams. Sleep, natural or artificial, brings about an indifference of just this kind. It has been recently suggested that in sleep there is an interruption of the contact between the nervous elements, motor and sensory.[13] Even if we do not accept this ingenious hypothesis, it is impossible not to see in sleep a relaxing, even if only functional, of the tension of the nervous system, ever ready, during waking hours, to prolong by an appropriate reaction the stimulation received. Now the exaltation of the memory in certain dreams and in certain somnambulistic states is well known. Memories, which we believed abolished, then reappear with striking completeness; we live over again, in all their detail, forgotten scenes of childhood; we speak languages which we no longer even remember to have learned. But there is nothing more instructive in this regard than what happens in cases of sudden suffocation, in men drowned or hanged. Such a man, when brought to life again, states that he saw, in a very short time, all the forgotten events of his life passing before him with great rapidity, with their smallest circumstances and in the very order in which they occurred.[14]

A human being who should *dream* his life instead of living it would no doubt thus keep before his eyes at each moment the infinite multitude of the details of his past history. And, conversely, the man who should repudiate this memory with all that it begets would be continually acting his life instead of truly representing it to himself: a conscious automaton, he would follow the lead of useful habits which prolong into an appropriate reaction the stimulation received. The first would never rise above the particular, or even above the individual; leaving to each image its date in time and its position in space, he would see wherein it *differs* from others and not how it resembles them. The other, always swayed by habit, would only distinguish in any situation that aspect in which it practically *resembles* former situations; incapable, doubtless, of *thinking* universals, since every general idea implies the representation, at least virtual, of a number of remembered images, he would, nevertheless, move in the universal, habit being to action what generality is to thought. But these two extreme states, the one of an entirely contemplative memory which apprehends only the singular in its *vision*, the other of a purely motor memory which stamps the note of generality on its *action*, are really separate and are fully visible only in exceptional cases. In normal life they are interpenetrating, so that each has to abandon some part of its original purity. The first reveals itself in the recollection of differences, the second in the perception of resemblances: at the meeting of the two currents appears the general idea.

[. . .]

The essence of the general idea, in fact, is to be unceasingly going backwards and forwards between the plane of action and that of pure memory. Let us refer once more to the diagram we traced above. At S is the present perception which I have of my body, that is to say, of a certain sensori-motor equilibrium. Over the surface of the base AB are spread, we may say, my recollections in their totality. Within the cone so determined, the general idea oscillates continually between the summit S and the base AB. In S, it would take the clearly defined form of a

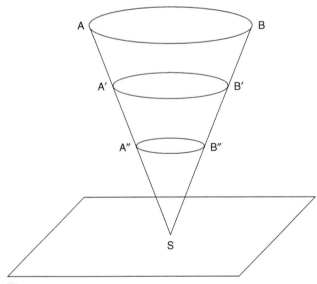

Figure 3

bodily attitude or of an uttered word; at AB, it would wear the aspect, no less defined, of the thousand individual images into which its fragile unity would break up. And that is why a psychology which abides by the *already done*, which considers only that which is made and ignores that which is in the making, will never perceive in this movement anything more than the two extremities between which it oscillates; it makes the general idea coincide sometimes with the action which manifests it or the word which expresses it and at other times with the multitudinous images, unlimited in number, which are its equivalent in memory. But the truth is that the general idea escapes us as soon as we try to fix it at either of the two extremities. It consists in the double current which goes from the one to the other – always ready either to crystallize into uttered words or to evaporate into memories.

This amounts to saying that between the sensori-motor mechanisms figured by the point S and the totality of the memories disposed in AB there is room, as we indicated in the preceding chapter, for a thousand repetitions of our psychical life, figured by as many sections A'B', A"B", etc., of the same cone. We tend to scatter ourselves over AB in the measure that we detach ourselves from our sensory and motor state to live in the life of dreams; we tend to concentrate ourselves in S in the measure that we attach ourselves more firmly to the present reality, responding by motor reactions to sensory stimulation. In point of fact, the normal self never stays in either of these extreme positions; it moves between them, adopts in turn the positions corresponding to the intermediate sections, or, in other words, gives to its representations just enough image and just enough idea for them to be able to lend useful aid to the present action.

Planes of Consciousness[15]

[. . .]

What is the cardinal error of associationism? It is to have set all recollections on the same plane, to have misunderstood the greater or lesser distance which separates them from the present bodily state, that is from action. Thus associationism is unable to explain either how the recollection clings to the perception which evokes it, or why association is effected by similarity or contiguity rather than in any other way, or, finally, by what caprice a particular recollection is chosen among the thousand others which similarity or contiguity might equally well attach to the present perception. This means that associationism has mixed and confounded all the different *planes of consciousness* and that it persists in regarding a less complete recollection as one that is less complex, whereas it is in reality a recollection less *dreamed*, more impersonal, nearer to action and, therefore, more capable of moulding itself – like a ready-made garment – upon the new character of the present situation. The opponents of associationism have, moreover, followed it onto this ground. They combat the theory because it explains the higher operations of the mind by association, but not because it misunderstands the true nature of association itself. Yet this is the original vice of associationism.

Between the plane of action – the plane in which our body has condensed its past into motor habits – and the plane of pure memory, where our mind retains in all its details the picture of our past life, we believe that we can discover thousands of different planes of consciousness, a thousand integral and yet diverse repetitions of the whole of the experience through which we have lived. To complete a recollection by more personal details does not at all consist in mechanically juxtaposing other recollections to this, but in transporting ourselves to a wider plane of consciousness, in going away from action in the direction of dream. Neither does the localizing of a recollection consist in inserting it mechanically among other memories, but in describing, by an increasing expansion of the memory as a whole, a circle large enough to include this detail from the past. These planes, moreover, are not given as ready-made things superposed the one on the other. Rather they exist virtually, with that existence which is proper to things of the spirit. The intellect, forever moving in the interval which separates them, unceasingly finds them again or creates them anew: the life of intellect consists in this very movement. Then we understand why the laws of association are similarity and contiguity rather than any other laws, and why memory chooses among recollections which are similar or contiguous certain images rather than other images, and, finally, how by the combined work of body and mind the earliest general ideas are formed. The interest of a living being lies in discovering in the present situation that which resembles a former situation, and then in placing alongside of that present situation what preceded and followed the previous one, in order to profit by past experience. Of all the associations which can be imagined, those of resemblance and contiguity are therefore at first the only associations that have a vital utility. But, in order to understand the mechanism of these associations and above all the apparently capricious selection which they make of memories, we must place ourselves alternately on the two extreme planes of consciousness which we have called the plane of action and the plane of dream. In the first are displayed only motor habits; these may be called associations which are acted or lived, rather than represented. Here resemblance and contiguity are fused together, for analogous external situations, as they recur, and have ended by connecting together certain bodily movements; thenceforth, the same automatic reaction, in which we unfold these contiguous movements, will also draw from the situation which occasions them its resemblance to former situations. But, as we pass from movements to images and from poorer to richer images, resemblance and contiguity part company: they end by contrasting sharply with each other on that other extreme plane where no action is any longer affixed to the images. The choice of one resemblance among many, of one contiguity among others, is, therefore, not made at random: it depends on the ever-varying degree of the *tension* of memory, which, according to its tendency to insert itself in the present act or to withdraw from it, transposes itself as a whole from one key into another. And this double movement of memory between its two extreme limits also sketches out, as we have shown, the first general ideas – motor habits ascending to seek similar images, in order to extract resemblances from them, and similar images coming down toward motor habits, to fuse themselves, for instance, in the automatic utterance of the word which makes them one. The nascent generality of the idea consists, then, in a certain activity of the mind, in a *movement* between action and representation. And this is why, as we have said, it will always be easy for a certain philosophy to localize the general idea at one of the two extremities, to make it crystallize into words or evaporate into memories, whereas it really consists in the transit of the mind as it passes from one term to the other.

Mind-Energy

Memory of the Present and False Recognition

An Article in the Revue Philosophique, *December 1908.*[1]

[. . .]

However, a remark must first be made concerning all psychical facts that are morbid or abnormal. Among them are some which evidently point to an impoverishment of the normal life. Such are the anaesthesias, the amnesias, the aphasias, the paralyses, all those states, in fact, which are characterized by the loss of particular sensations, particular memories, or particular movements. In order to define these states we simply have to indicate what has disappeared from consciousness. They consist in an absence. We all agree in seeing in them a psychic deficiency.

On the contrary, there are morbid or abnormal states which appear to add something to normal life and enrich it instead of impoverishing it. A delirium, a hallucination, an obsession, are positive facts. They consist in the presence, not in the absence, of something. They seem to introduce into the mind certain new ways of feeling and thinking. To define them, we have to consider what they are and what they bring, instead of what they are not and what they take away. If most of the symptoms of insanity belong to this second category, so also do a great many psychical anomalies and singularities. False recognition is one. As we shall see later, it presents an aspect *sui generis*, far different from that of true recognition.

However, the philosopher may very well question whether, in the mental domain, disorder and degeneration can really be capable of creating something, and whether the apparently positive characters which give the abnormal phenomenon an aspect of novelty are not, when we come to study their nature, reducible to an internal void, a shortcoming of normality. Disease, we generally say, is a diminution. True; but this is a vague way of expressing it, and we should indicate precisely, when no actual part of consciousness is missing, wherein the consciousness is diminished. I made an attempt of this kind in a former work to which I have already referred. I pointed out that, besides the diminution which affects the *number* of the states of consciousness, there is another which concerns their solidity or their *weight*. In the first case, the disorder simply and only eliminates some states without affecting others. In the second, no psychical state disappears but all are affected, all lose something of their ballast, that is to say, of their power of insertion and penetration into the reality. (See *Matter and Memory*, Chapter III.) It is the 'attention to life' which is diminished, and the new phenomena which are started are only the visible aspect, the outward appearance of this detachment.

I recognize, however, that even under this form the idea is still too general to be applied to the explanation of particular psychical facts. But it points the direction we must follow to find an explanation.

For, if we accept this principle, we shall not, in the case of a morbid or abnormal phenomenon presenting special characters, have to seek any active cause, because the phenomenon, despite appearances, has nothing positive and nothing new about it. It was already being manufactured while the conditions were normal; but it was prevented from emerging, when about to appear, by one of those continually active inhibitory mechanisms which secure *attention to life*. This means that normal psychical life, as I conceive it, is a system of functions, each with its own psychic organ. Were each of these organs to work by itself, there would result a host of useless or untoward effects, liable to disturb the functioning of the others and so upset that adjustable equilibrium by which our adaptation to the environment is continually maintained. But a work of elimination, of correction, of bringing back to the point, is constantly going on, and it is precisely this work which secures a healthy mind. Wherever this work is slackened, symptoms seem to be created, fresh and new, but in reality they were always there, or rather would have been there if nothing had interfered. I quite understand that the investigator should be struck with the *sui generis* character of the morbid facts. As they are complex and yet present a certain order in their complication, his first inclination is to relate them to an acting cause, capable of organizing the elements of them. But if, in the mental domain, disease is unable to create, it can only consist in the slackening or stopping of certain mechanisms which in the normal state prevent others from having their full effect. If this be so, then, in this case *the principal task of psychology is not to explain why certain phenomena are produced in disordered minds, but why they are not found in the normally healthy mind.*

Already I have applied that method to the study of dreams. We are too much inclined to look upon dreams as if they were phantoms superadded to the solid perceptions and conceptions of our waking life, will-o-the-wisps which hover above it. They are supposed to be facts of a special order, to which psychology ought simply to devote a special chapter and then be quit of them. And it is natural they should appear so, because the waking state is what matters to us, whilst the dreaming state is most foreign to action and most useless. From the practical point of view dream is merely an accessory, so from the theoretical point of view we come to regard it as an accident. But let us set aside this preconceived idea, and the dream-state will then be seen, on the contrary, to be the substratum of our normal state. The dream is not something fantastic hovering above and additional to the reality of being awake; on the contrary, that reality of the waking state is gained by limitation, by concentration and by tension of a diffuse psychical life, which is the dream-life. In a sense, the perception and memory we exercise in the dream-state are more natural than those in the waking state: there does consciousness disport itself, perceiving just to perceive, remembering just to remember, with no care for life, that is, for the action to be accomplished. But the waking state consists in eliminating, in choosing, in concentrating unceasingly the totality of the diffuse dream-life at the point where a practical problem is presented. To be awake means to will. Cease to will, detach yourself from life, disinterest yourself, and by that mere abstention you pass from the awake-self to the dream-self – less *tense* but more *extended*. The mechanism of the awake-state is, then, the more complex, more delicate and more *positive* of the two, and it is the awake-state, rather than the dream-state, which requires explanation.

Now, if dreams are in every respect an imitation or counterfeit of insanity, we may expect our remarks on dreams to apply as well to many forms of insanity. Of course, we must avoid approaching the study of mental diseases with anything like a stereotyped system. It is doubtful if all the phenomena of insanity are to be explained on one and the same principle. And for many of them, still undefined, it is hardly possible yet to attempt an explanation. As I said at first, I offer my view simply as a methodological indication, with no other object than that of pointing a direction for theoretical inquiry. There are, however, some pathological or abnormal facts to which I believe it is even now applicable. One of the chief of these is false recognition. For the mechanism of perception and the mechanism of memory seem to me such that false recognition would arise naturally from the joint play of the two faculties, were there not a special mechanism intervening at the same time in order to prevent it. The important thing to know, then, is not why it arises in certain persons at particular moments, but why it is not being produced at every moment in everybody.

How is a recollection formed? Let it first be clear, however, that the recollections of which I am going to speak are always psychical, although they may be more often unconscious than conscious or semi-conscious. Concerning recollections considered as traces left in the brain, I have given my view in *Matter and Memory*, the work to which I have had frequent occasion to refer. I have attempted there to prove that the various memories are indeed localized in the brain, in the meaning that the brain possesses for each category of memory-images a special contrivance whose purpose is to convert the pure memory into a nascent perception or image; but if we go further than this, and suppose every recollection to be localized in the matter of the brain, we are simply translating undoubted psychical facts into very questionable anatomical language, and we end in consequences which are contradicted by observation. Indeed, when we speak of our recollections, we think of something our consciousness possesses or can always recover by drawing in, so to say, the thread which holds it. The recollection, in fact, passes to and fro from consciousness to unconsciousness, and the transition from one to the other is so continuous, the limit between the two states so little marked, that we have no right to suppose a radical difference of nature between them. It is memory in this purely psychical meaning of which I am going to speak. On the other hand, let us agree to call 'perception' the consciousness of anything that is present, whether it be an internal or an external object. Both definitions being granted, I hold that *the formation of memory is never posterior to the formation of perception; it is contemporaneous with it*. Step by step, as perception is created, the memory of it is projected beside it, as the shadow falls beside the body. But, in the normal condition, there is no consciousness of it, just as we should be unconscious of our shadow were our eyes to throw light on it each time they turn in that direction.

For suppose memory is not created at the same moment as the perception: at what moment will it begin to exist? Does it wait till the perception is vanished that it may then arise? This is what we usually suppose, whether we think unconscious recollections are psychical states or cerebral modifications. In the one case we suppose a present psychical state, the perception, then, when that no longer exists, the remembrance of that absent perception. In the other case, we think that when certain cells come into play there is perception, and that the action of those cells has left traces so that, when the perception has vanished, there is memory. But, if things happen in this way, the course of our conscious existence must be composed of clear-cut states, each of which must begin objectively, and also objectively end. Now, is it not clear that dividing psychical life into states, as we divide a play into scenes, is relative to the varied and changing interpretations we give of our past and has nothing absolute about it? According to the point of view in which I am placed, or the centre of interest which I choose, I divide yesterday differently, discovering several very different series of situations or states in it. Though these divisions are not all equally artificial, not one existed in itself, because the unrolling of psychical life is continuous. The afternoon I happen to have spent in the country with friends has broken up into luncheon + walk + dinner, or into conversation + conversation + conversation, etc., and of none of these conversations, treading as it were on the heels of another, could it be said that it forms a distinct entity. Scores of systems of carving are possible; no system corresponds with joints of reality. What right have we, then, to suppose that memory chooses one particular system, or that it divides psychical life into definite periods and awaits the end of each period in order to rule up its accounts with perception?

Is it alleged that the perception of an external object begins when the object appears, and ends when it disappears, and that therefore we can, in this case at least, mark the precise moment when memory replaces perception? But this is to ignore the fact that the perception is ordinarily composed of successive parts, and that these parts have just as much individuality, or rather just as little, as the whole. Of each of them we can as well say that its object is disappearing all along: how, then, could the recollection arise only when everything is over? And how could memory know, at any particular moment of the operation, that everything was not over yet, that perception was still incomplete?

The more we reflect, the more impossible it is to imagine any way in which the recollection can arise if it is not created step by step with the perception itself. Either the present leaves no trace in memory, or it is twofold at every moment, its very up-rush being in two jets exactly symmetrical, one of which falls back towards the past whilst the other springs forward towards the future. But the forward-springing one, which we call perception, is that alone which interests us. We have no need of the memory of things whilst we hold the things themselves. Practical consciousness throwing this memory aside as useless, theoretical reflexion holds it to be non-existent. Thus the illusion arises that memory *succeeds* perception. But this illusion has another source deeper still.

The main cause is that the reanimated and conscious memory produces on us the effect of the perception itself, and appears to be the resurrection of the perception, feebler but not substantially different. Between the perception and the memory there seems to be a difference of intensity or degree, but not of nature. The perception being defined a strong state and the remembrance a weak state, the remembrance of a perception being necessarily then nothing else than that same perception weakened, it seems to us that memory, in order to register a perception in the unconscious, must wait until the whole of it goes to sleep. And so we suppose the remembrance of a perception cannot be created while the perception is being created nor be developed at the same time.

But the theory that present perception is a strong state, and revived recollection a feeble state, that perception passes into recollection by way of diminution, is contradicted by the most elementary observation of fact. Take an intense sensation and make it gradually decrease to zero. If there is only a difference of degree between the remembrance of the sensation and the sensation itself, the sensation will become memory before it disappears. Now, a moment may come when you are unable to say whether you are dealing with a weak sensation experienced or a weak sensation imagined, but the weak state never becomes the recollection, thrown back into the past, of the strong state. The recollection, then, is a totally different thing.

The recollection of a sensation is capable of *suggesting* the sensation, I mean of causing it to be born again, feeble at first, then stronger and stronger in proportion as the attention is more fixed upon it. But the recollection is distinct from the sensation it suggests; and it is precisely because we feel it behind the sensation it suggests, as the hypnotiser is behind the hallucination he provokes, that we localize its cause in the past. Sensation is essentially what is actual and now; but the recollection which suggests it from the depths of the unconscious, hardly emerging upwards, has that power *sui generis* of suggestion which belongs to things that are no more and would fain exist again. Hardly has the suggestion touched the imagination than the thing suggested is outlined in its nascent state, and this is why it is so difficult to distinguish between a weak sensation experienced and a weak sensation which we remember without dating it. But the suggestion is in no degree what it suggests. The pure recollection of a sensation or of a perception is not a degree of the sensation or the perception itself. To suppose it so would be like saying that the word of the hypnotiser, in order to suggest to the hypnotized patient that he has in his mouth sugar or salt, must already itself be a little sugared or salted.

If we try to discover the source and purpose of this illusion, we find that innate in our mind is the need to represent our whole inner life as modelled on that very small part of ourself which is inserted into the present reality, the part which perceives it and acts upon it. Our perceptions and our sensations are at once what is clearest in us and most important for us; they note at each moment the changing relation of our body to other bodies; they determine or direct our conduct. Thence our tendency to see in the other psychical facts nothing but perceptions or sensations obscured or diminished. Those, indeed, among us who resist this tendency, who believe thought to be something other than a play of images, yet have some trouble in persuading themselves that the remembrance of a perception is radically different from the perception itself. The remembrance must at any rate, it seems to them, be expressible in terms of perception. It must then be obtained by some operation effected on the image. What is the operation? Here a process of natural reasoning intervenes. We can say *a priori* that the operation must effect an alteration in the *quality* of the content of the image, or in its *quantity*, or in both at once. Now, it is certainly not in the quality, since memory must represent the past to us without altering it. It must be then in the quantity. But quantity, in its turn, may be extensive or intensive, for the image comprehends a definite number of parts and it presents a certain degree of force. Does, then, memory modify the extension of the image? Evidently not, for if it added anything to the past, it would be unfaithful to it, and if it subtracted something from the past, it would be incomplete. We conclude, then, that the modification bears on the intensity; and as it is evidently not an increase, it must be a diminution. Such is the instinctive, scarcely conscious dialectic by which we are led, from elimination to elimination, to see in the remembrance an enfeeblement of the image.

When once we have reached this conclusion, our whole psychology of memory is inspired by it; even our physiology feels the effect of it. In whatever way we then conceive the cerebral mechanism of perception, we see in recollection nothing but the same mechanism set going anew, an attenuated repetition of the same fact. Facts stand before us, however, and seem to point to the opposite direction. They evidence that a man can lose visual recollections without ceasing to see and auditory recollections without ceasing to hear, that psychic blindness and deafness do not necessarily imply loss of sight or of hearing: how would this be possible if perception and memory were concerned with the same centres, and put in play the same mechanisms? But we turn aside or pass on, rather than assent to a radical distinction between perception and memory.

In so far, then, as our reason reconstructs psychical life out of conscious states sharply delineated, and in so far as it judges that all those states are expressible in terms of images, it is following two paths which converge in making memory an enfeebled perception, something which follows the perception instead of being contemporaneous with it. Set aside this natural dialectic of the intellect, convenient though it be for expression in language, possibly indispensable in practice, but not suggested by inward observation, and observe what actually takes place. The memory will be seen to duplicate the perception at every moment, to arise with it, to be developed at the same time, and to survive it precisely because it is of a quite different nature.

What, then, is a memory? Every clear description of a psychical state is made up of images, and we are saying that the recollection of an image is not an image. The pure recollection, then, can only be described in a vague manner and in metaphoric terms. Let me repeat, then, an explanation I suggested in *Matter and Memory*. The memory seems to be to the perception what the image reflected in the mirror is to the object in front of it. The object can be touched as well as seen; acts on us as well as we on it; is pregnant with possible actions; it is *actual*. The image is *virtual*, and though it resembles the object, it is incapable of doing what the object does. Our actual existence then, whilst it is unrolled in time, duplicates itself all along with a virtual existence, a mirror-image. Every moment of our life presents two aspects, it is actual and virtual, perception on the one side and memory on the other. Each moment of life is split up as and when it is posited. Or rather, it consists in this very splitting, for the present moment, always going forward, fleeting limit between the immediate past which is now no more and the immediate future which is not yet, would be a mere abstraction were it not the moving mirror which continually reflects perception as a memory.

Let us imagine a mind to become conscious of this duplicating. Suppose the reflexion of our perception and of our action comes to consciousness not when the perception is complete and the action accomplished, but continuously and simultaneously, step by step, as we perceive and act. We must then see, at one and the same time, our real existence and its virtual image, the object on one side and its reflexion on the other. Moreover, the reflexion can not be confused with the object, for the object has all the characters of perception whilst the reflexion is already memory: were it not memory from the first, it never could become so. Later on, when performing its normal function, it will represent our past to us with the mark of the past; discerned at the very moment in which it is formed, it is already with the mark of the past, which is constitutive of its essence, that it appears to us. What past? A past that has no date and can have none; it is the past *in general*, it cannot be any past in particular. No doubt, if it were merely a past scene or a past emotion, we might be actually deceived and believe that we have already perceived the scene we are actually perceiving, that we have already experienced the motion we are experiencing. But it is far more than this. What is duplicating itself at each moment into perception and memory is the totality of what we are seeing, hearing and experiencing, all that we are with all that surrounds us. As we are becoming conscious of this duplication, it is the entirety of our present which must appear to us at once as perception and as memory. And yet we know full well that no life goes twice through the same moment of its history, that time does not remount its course. What is to be done? The case is most extraordinary and bewildering. It contradicts everything that we have been accustomed to. We feel that we are confronted with a recollection: a recollection it must be, for it bears the characteristic mark of states we usually call by this name and which only appear when their object has disappeared. And yet it does not present to us something which has been, but simply something which is; it advances *pari passu* with the perception which it reproduces. It is a recollection of the present moment in that actual moment itself. It is of the past in its form and of the present in its matter. It is *a memory of the present*.

Step by step, as the situation progresses, the memory which keeps pace with it gives to each of its stages the aspect of 'already seen,' the feeling of already known. But the situation, even before it has come to an end, seems to us something which must form a whole, being cut out of the continuity of our experience by the interest of the moment. Now, how could we have already lived a part of the situation if we had not lived the whole of it? Could we recognize what is being unrolled if we did not know what is still rolled up? Are we not able at each moment to anticipate at least the following moment? The instant which is about to come is already broken into by the instant which now is; the content of the one is inseparable from the content of the other: therefore, if the present instant belongs already to my past, must not the coming instant belong to it equally? If I recognize the present instant, am I not quite as surely going to recognize the coming one? So I am unceasingly, towards what is on the point of happening, in the attitude of a person who will recognize and who consequently knows. But this is only the *attitude* of knowledge, the form of it without the matter. As I cannot predict what is going to happen, I quite realize that I do not know it; but I foresee that I am going to have known it, in the sense that I shall recognize it when I shall perceive it; and this recognition to come, which I feel inevitable on account of the rush of my faculty of recognizing, exercises in advance a retroactive effect on my present, placing me in the strange position of a person who feels he knows what he knows he does not know.

Suppose we catch ourselves repeating mechanically something we once knew by heart but had long forgotten. As we recognize each word the moment we pronounce it, we have a feeling that we possess it before pronouncing it; and yet we only get it back while we pronounce it. Whoever becomes conscious of the continual duplicating of his present into perception and memory will be in the same state. If even slightly capable of self-analysis, he will compare himself to an actor playing his part automatically, listening to himself and beholding himself play. The more deeply he analyses his experience, the more he will split into two personages, one of which moves about on the stage while the other sits and looks. On the one hand, he knows that he continues to be what he was, a self who thinks and acts conformably to what the situation requires, a self inserted into real life and adapting itself to it by a free effort of will; this is what his perception of the present assures him. But the memory of this present, which is equally there, makes him believe that he is repeating what has been said already, seeing again what has been seen already, and so transforms him into an actor reciting his part. Thence two different selves, one of which, conscious of its liberty, erects itself into an independent spectator of a scene which the other seems to be playing in a mechanical way. But this duplication does not go through to the end. It is rather an oscillation between two standpoints from which one views oneself, a going and coming of the mind between perception which is only perception and perception duplicated with memory. The first implies the habitual feeling we have of our freedom and quite naturally inserts itself into the real world. The second makes us believe we are repeating a part we have learned, converts us into automata, transports us into a stage-world or a world of dream. Whoever has experienced during a few seconds a pressing danger, from which he has only been able to escape by a rapid series of actions imperatively called for and boldly executed, knows something of the kind. It is a duplication rather virtual than actual. We act and yet 'are acted.' We feel that we choose and will, but that we are choosing what is imposed on us and willing the inevitable. Thence a compenetration of states which melt into one another and even coincide in immediate consciousness, but which are none the less logically incompatible.

Because they are logically incompatible, reflective consciousness will represent them by a duplication of the self into two different personages, one of which appropriates freedom, the other necessity: the one, a free spectator, beholds the other automatically playing his part.

To sum up: I have imagined a mind, in its normal state, to become conscious of the duplication which is constantly but unconsciously going on, and I have described, in the last three pages, the three principal aspects under which that mind would appear to itself if it could thus witness the splitting of its present. Now, these are the very characteristics of false recognition. We find them the more accentuated the more definite the phenomenon is, the more complete it is, and the more profoundly analysed it is by the person who experiences it.

Several of those who have experienced it have spoken, to begin with, of a feeling of automatism, and of a state comparable to that of an actor playing a part. What is said and what is done, what the person himself says and does, appear 'inevitable.' He is looking on at his own movements, thoughts and actions.[2] Things happen *as though* his personality were duplicated, without, however, there being actual duplication. One of them writes: 'This feeling of duplication only exists in the sensation; the two persons are only one from the material standpoint.' He means probably that he experiences a feeling of duality, but accompanied with the consciousness that there is only one person.[3]

On the other hand, as I said at the beginning of this essay, the subject of this experience often finds himself in the singular state of mind of a person who believes he knows what is about to happen at the same time that he feels quite unable to predict it. 'It seems always to me,' says one, 'that I am foreseeing what is going to happen, yet I cannot actually announce it.' Another recalls what is going to happen 'as one recalls a name which is at the uttermost ends of memory.'[4] One of the earliest observations is that of one who believed he knew beforehand what the people around him would do.[5] We have in this a second characteristic of false recognition.

But the most general characteristic of all is the one to which I first called attention. The memory evoked is a loose memory, with no point of attachment in the past. It does not correspond with any former experience. The subject knows it, is convinced of it, and the conviction is not the effect of reasoning, it is immediate. It is a feeling that the recollection evoked must be simply a duplicate of the actual perception. Is it, then, a 'memory of the present'? If he does not use these words, it is probably because the expression would appear to him contradictory, because he only conceives memory as a repetition of the past, because it does not seem possible that a representation can bear the mark of the past independently of what it represents. In fact, he theorizes without knowing it, and holds all memory to have been formed after the perception which it reproduces. Yet he affirms something very like it when he speaks of a past which no interval separates from the present. 'I felt within me a kind of click which did away with all the past lying between that minute of long ago and the minute in which I then was.'[6] These words give expression to the most distinctive mark of the phenomenon. When we speak of it as 'false recognition,' we ought to add that it is a process which does not really counterfeit true recognition and which does not give the illusion of it. What, in fact, is normal recognition? It may be produced in two ways, either by a feeling of familiarity which accompanies the present perception, or by the evoking of a past perception which the present perception seems to repeat. Now false recognition is neither of these two operations. What characterizes the first kind of recognition is that it excludes any recall of a definite personal situation in which the recognized object had formerly been perceived. My desk, my table, my books form around me an atmosphere of familiarity only so long as they do not call up the recollection of any definite event of my history. If they evoke the exact recollection of an incident in which they have been mixed up, I recognize them as having been a part of that incident, but this recognition is superadded to the first and is fundamentally distinct from it, as distinct as the personal from the impersonal. Now false recognition is something quite different from this feeling of familiarity. It always bears on a personal situation, which we are convinced is the identical reproduction of another personal situation, just as precise and as definite. It would seem, then, that it must be recognition of the second kind, one which implies the recall of a former situation like the present one. But then it should be noticed that we have always to do in such cases with situations similar and not identical. Recognition of the second kind is brought about by the idea of what differentiates the two situations and not only of what is common to them. If I am at a play which I have seen before, I recognize one by one each of the words and each of the scenes; at last I recognize the whole piece and recall having seen it before; but I had then a different seat, and other neighbours, and was taken up with other preoccupations; in any case I could not have been then what I am today, since I have lived in the meanwhile. If, then, the two images are the same, they are not presented in the same frame, and the vague feeling of the difference of the frames surrounds, like a fringe, the consciousness I have of the identity of the images, and allows me at every moment to distinguish them. In false recognition, on the contrary, the frames are just as identical as the images themselves. I am present at the same play with the same sensations, the same preoccupations, I am at this very moment in the very same position, at the same date, at the same instant of my history where and when I then was. It is, then, hardly fit to speak here of illusion, since the illusory knowledge is the imitation of a real knowledge, and since the phenomenon with which we are dealing imitates no other phenomenon of our experience. And it is hardly fit to speak of false recognition, since there is no true recognition, of the one kind or of the other, of which it could be the exact counterfeit. We are in fact dealing with a phenomenon unique of its kind, the very phenomenon which the memory of the present would produce, were it to rise up instantaneously from the unconscious where it must lie. It would appear as memory, since memory bears a distinctive mark, different from that of perception; but it could not be carried back to any past experience, because each of us knows indeed that we do not live twice through one and the same moment of our history.

I turn now to the problem why this memory is ordinarily concealed, and how it is revealed in extraordinary cases. In a general way, or *by right*, the past only reappears to consciousness in the measure in which it can aid us to understand the present and to foresee the future. It is the forerunner of action. We go wrong when we study the functions of thought in their isolated state as if they were an end in themselves, and we pure minds occupied in contemplating ideas and images. The present perception would in that case attract to itself a resembling memory with no suspicion of utility, without purpose, for mere pleasure – the pleasure of introducing into the mental world a law of attraction analogous to that which governs the material world. Without questioning the 'law of similarity,' I may point out that any two ideas and any two images taken at random, however distant from one another we may suppose them to be, must have some relation of similarity since we can always find a common genus into which to make them enter: so that any perception would recall any recollection if there were nothing more, here, than a mechanical attraction of like for like. But the fact is that if a perception recalls a memory, it is in order that the circumstances which have preceded, accompanied and followed the past situation, should throw some light on the present situation and indicate the way out of it. Thousands and thousands of memories evoked by resemblance are possible, but the memory which tends to reappear is the one which resembles the perception by a particular side, that namely which may illumine and direct the action in preparation. Even this memory need not show itself; it is enough if, without showing itself, it recall the circumstances which have been given in contiguity with it, what has preceded and what has followed, what in short it is important to know in order to understand the present and anticipate the future. We may even suppose that the contiguous circumstances need not be manifested to consciousness, so long as the conclusion can appear, that is to say, the exact suggestion of a certain thing to do. It is in this mode, probably, that consciousness works in most animals. But the more the consciousness is developed, the more it illumines the work of the memory, and the more, too, it lets association by resemblance, which is the means, shine through association by contiguity, which is the end. When once the association has had official recognition in consciousness, it allows the introduction of a crowd of fancy memories, which resemble the present state but may be devoid of actual interest. In this way we may explain why we can dream as well as act; but it is the needs of action which determine the laws of recall; they alone hold the keys of consciousness, and fancy memories only slip in by taking advantage of what is lax and ill-defined in the relation of resemblance which legally entitles to a pass. In short, if the totality of our recollections be at every moment pushing upward from the depth of the unconscious, consciousness, attentive to life, only admits, legally, those which can offer their assistance to the present action, although, in fact, many others slip in because there must be a general rule, and because the rule, here, is that resemblance secures admittance.

But what can be more unavailing for our present action than memory of the present? Rather would any other kind of memory be entitled to lay a claim, for it at least brings with it some information, though it be of no actual interest. Alone, memory of the present has nothing to teach us, being only the double of perception. We have the real object, what are we to do with the virtual image of it? As well let go the substance for the shadow. This is why there is no memory from which our attention is more obstinately turned away.

By attention, of course, I do not mean here that individual attention which varies in its intensity, direction and duration according to personal temperament. I am alluding to what I should call racial attention, an attention naturally turned towards certain regions of psychical life, naturally turned away from others. Within each of these regions our individual attention may be directed, no doubt by its own caprice, but it then simply supervenes on that racial attention, as the choice that the individual eye makes of particular visual objects is superposed on the choice which the human eye has made once for all, of a certain definite region of the spectrum in which it sees light. Now, while a slight failure of individual attention is only absent-mindedness, – a normal thing – any failure of racial attention takes the form of a pathological or abnormal fact.

False recognition is such an anomaly. It indicates a temporary enfeebling of general attention to life: consciousness, no longer turning in its natural direction, allows itself to look at what it has no interest in perceiving. But what are we to understand here by 'attention to life'? What is the particular kind of inattention which ends in false recognition? Attention and inattention are vague terms. Can we define them more exactly in this particular case? Let me try to do so, without claiming, however, to attain in so obscure a subject complete clearness and definite precision.

We hardly notice the extent to which our present consists in an anticipation of our future. The vision reflective consciousness gives us of our inner life is that of one state succeeding another state, each commencing at one point, finishing at another, and provisionally self-sufficing. Consciousness, in this reflective vision, is preparing the way for language; it is distinguishing, separating and juxtaposing; it is only at its ease in the definite and the immobile; it stops at a static conception of reality. But immediate consciousness grasps quite another thing. Immanent in the inward life, it feels rather than sees it, but feels it as a movement, as a continual treading on a future which recoils without ceasing. Indeed, this feeling becomes very clear when it concerns a definite act we are called on to perform. The end of the action appears to us immediately; and, during the whole time that we are acting, we are conscious not so much of the successive states as of a decreasing distance between our actual position and the end towards which we are approaching. This end, moreover, is perceived only as a provisional end; we know there is something else behind; in the spring we take to leap the first obstacle we are already preparing to leap a second, until other leaps will take place and succeed one another indefinitely. Again, when we listen to a sentence, we need not pay attention to each word taken separately, it is the meaning of the whole which matters: from the very beginning we are reconstructing this meaning hypothetically; our mind darts forward in a certain general direction, only having to inflect it here and there according as the sentence, unrolling, pushes our attention towards one meaning or another. Here again the present is perceived in the future on which it treads, rather than apprehended in itself. This vital impulse gives to all the psychical states it causes us to pass or leap over, a particular aspect which is so constant and to which we are so accustomed that we only become aware of it when it is missing. Every one may have observed the strange character a familiar word sometimes takes when we fix our attention on it. The word appears new, and really is so, for till then our consciousness had not made it a stopping place; we had always passed it by to come to the end of a sentence. We cannot compress the impulse of our whole psychical life as completely as we compress that of our speech; but whenever the general impulse is enfeebled, the situation passed through must appear as strange as the sound of a word immobilized in the course of the movement of the sentence. It is no longer part and parcel of real life. Looking in our past experience for what resembles it most, we are likely to compare it with dream.

Now, it is remarkable that most of the recorded cases of false recognition just describe the experience as an impression of dream. Paul Bourget, for example, observes that the illusion is accompanied by 'a kind of unanalysable feeling that reality is a dream.'[7] And an English writer some years ago, describing his own experience, applied the epithet 'shadowy' to the whole phenomenon, adding that it appeared later, when it was recollected, as 'the half-forgotten relic of a dream.' Thus we have observers, unknown to one another, speaking different languages, expressing themselves in actually equivalent terms. The impression of dream, then, is almost general.

It is also remarkable that persons subject to false recognition are often liable to finding a familiar word strange. An inquiry instituted by G. Heymans has shown that these two dispositions are connected together. He adds very justly that current theories of the first phenomenon do not explain why it is associated with the second.

In these conditions, ought we not to look for the initial cause of false recognition in a momentary stop of the impulse of our consciousness, a stop which, no doubt, does not change anything in the materiality of our present, but detaches it from the future to which it cleaves and from the action which would be its normal conclusion, so giving it the aspect of a mere picture, of a play which is being presented to the player, of a reality transposed into dream? Let me now describe an impression derived from my own personal experience. I am not subject to false recognition, but I have tried very often, since I have studied it, to place myself in the state of mind described by observers and to induce experimentally the phenomenon in myself. I have never quite succeeded, but I have obtained on various occasions something approaching it, although very fugitive. The scene in which I find myself must be not only new to me, but in strong contrast with the course of my habitual life. It may be, for example, a scene when I am on a journey, but this journey must have been improvised, not premeditated. The first condition is, then, that I should experience a certain quite peculiar astonishment, which I will call *the astonishment at finding myself there*. On this astonishment there comes to be grafted a feeling rather different from it, but yet in relationship with it, the feeling that *the future is closed*, that the situation is detached from everything although I am attached to it. In the degree that these emotions interpenetrate, the reality loses its solidity and my perception of the present tends to duplicate itself with something which is behind it. Is this the *memory of the present* appearing through? I do not venture to say so; but it seems to me that I am then verily on the road to false recognition, and that a very little would bring me to it.

Now, why does *memory of the present* wait, before it can be revealed, for the *impulse of consciousness* to slacken or to stop? We know nothing of the mechanism by which an idea comes out of the unconscious or falls back into it. All we can do is to have recourse to a provisional scheme by which we can symbolize the operation. Let us come back to the one which we have already used. Let us imagine the totality of unconscious recollections pressing against consciousness, – consciousness laying down the general rule that only what can serve action is allowed to pass. The memory of the present is striving like the rest; moreover, it is nearer to us than any other memory. Hanging on to our perception of the present, it is always on the point of entering into it. Perception only escapes from it by a continual movement forward to keep itself in front. In other words, a memory can only be actualised by means of a perception: the memory of the present would therefore penetrate into consciousness, could it insinuate itself into the perception of the present. But this is always in advance of it: thanks to the impulse which animates it, perception is less in the present than in the future. Suppose now the impulse suddenly to stop: memory rejoins perception, the present is cognised and recognised at the same time.

False recognition seems then to be, upon the whole, the most harmless form of inattention to life. A constant lowering of tone of the fundamental attention is expressed outwardly by actual disorder or disease, more or less enduring, more or less severe. But it may happen that this attention is maintained ordinarily at its normal tone, and that its insufficiency is manifested in a quite different manner, namely by temporary arrests of functioning, generally very short, separated and far apart. As soon as the arrest occurs, false recognition overtakes consciousness, covers it for some instants and then falls back, like a wave.

Let me conclude with a final hypothesis, at which I hinted in the beginning of this essay. If inattention to life can take two forms unequally severe, should we not be right in supposing that the more benign form is nature's means of preserving the individual from the more severe form? In cases when fundamental attention is insufficient and when, therefore, there is a perpetual risk of passing completely from the state of waking to the state of dream, consciousness localizes the evil at a few points where attention stops for a short time and resigns entirely: attention is thus made able, all the rest of the time, to remain steadily fixed on reality. Certain distinct cases of false recognition appear to confirm this hypothesis. The patient begins by feeling himself detached from everything, as in a dream. He experiences false recognition immediately afterwards, as he begins to be self-possessed again.[8]

Such then seems to be the defect in will which occasions false recognition. Such, at least, seems to be its deep source and furthest origin. As for its actual cause and mechanism, it must be sought in the combined play of perception and memory. False recognition results from the natural functioning of these two faculties, each allowed its own way. It would take place at every moment if the will, unceasingly striving towards action, did not prevent the present turning back on itself by continually pressing it forward into the future. The darting forward of consciousness, which reveals the life-impetus, escapes analysis by its simplicity. We can however study, in the moments when it slackens, the conditions of mobile equilibrium which till then it had maintained, and so analyse a manifestation which foreshadows its essence.

Brain and Thought:
A Philosophical Illusion[9]

A paper read at the International Congress of Philosophy at Geneva in 1904, and published in the Revue de métaphysique et de morale *under the title 'Le Paralogisme psycho-physiologique.'*

The idea that there is an equivalence between a psychic state and its corresponding cerebral state is widely accepted in modern philosophy. Philosophers have discussed the causes and the significance of this equivalence rather than the equivalence itself. By some, it has been held that the cerebral state is reduplicated in certain cases by a psychical phosphorescence which illumines its outline. By others, it is supposed that the cerebral state and the psychic state form respectively two series of phenomena which correspond point to point, without it being necessary to attribute to the cerebral series the creation of the psychic. All, however, agree in admitting an equivalence or, as it is more usual to say, a *parallelism* of the two series. In order to express the idea, I will formulate it as a thesis: 'Given a cerebral state, there will ensue a definite psychic state.' Or it may be stated thus: 'A super-human intelligence, watching the dance of the atoms of which the human brain consists and possessing the psycho-physiological key, would be able to read, in the working of the brain, all that is occurring in the corresponding consciousness.' Or, finally, it may be put in this way: 'Consciousness tells no more than what is going on in the brain; it only tells it in a different language.'

There can be no doubt that the origin of this thesis is entirely metaphysical. It comes to us in a direct line from the Cartesian philosophy of the seventeenth century. Implicitly contained (with certain restrictions, it is true) in the philosophy of Descartes, accepted and pushed to extremes by his successors, it has passed from them, through the 'medical philosophers' of the eighteenth century, to the psycho-physiology of today.

It is easy to understand why the physiologists should have accepted it without demur. In the first place they had no choice, for the problem came to them from metaphysics, and the metaphysicians proposed no other solution. And, secondly, it was in the interest of physiology to rally to it, and to proceed *as if* it were some day to give us a complete translation of psychical activity into physiological language. Only on some such supposition could physiology advance, pushing ever farther its analysis of the cerebral conditions of thought. It was, and it still is, an excellent principle of research, signifying that we ought not to be too hasty in assigning limits to physiology, any more indeed than to any other scientific investigation. But the dogmatic affirmation of psycho-physiological parallelism is another matter altogether. It is no longer a scientific rule, but a metaphysical hypothesis. In so far as it is intelligible, it is the metaphysics of science as science was conceived in the time of Descartes, that is, in a purely mathematical framework. I believe that the facts, examined without prejudice and without the bias towards a mathematical mechanism, suggest a more subtle hypothesis concerning the correspondence between the psychic and the cerebral state. The latter only expresses the action which is pre-figured in the former; it marks out, so to say, the motor articulations of thought. Posit a psychical fact, and no doubt you therewith determine the concomitant cerebral state. But the converse is not true, for to the same cerebral state there may equally well correspond many different psychic facts. I have expounded this theory in *Matter and Memory*, and I will not repeat it here. The argument I propose to bring forward now is independent of it altogether. I am not going to substitute another hypothesis for that of psycho-physiological parallelism; what I want to show is that this hypothesis itself implies, in its usual form, a fundamental self-contradiction. It is, moreover, a self-contradiction full of instruction.

In the perception that there is a self-contradiction we are given the clue to the direction in which to seek the solution of the problem, at the same time that the mechanism of a most subtle metaphysical illusion is exposed. In pointing it out, we are not therefore engaged merely in critical and destructive work.

My contention is that the thesis rests on an ambiguity in the terms, that it cannot be stated in correct language without crumbling to pieces, that it implies a dialectical artifice, the surreptitious passing from one definite notation-system to an opposite notation-system without giving or taking notice of the substitution. Need I add that the fallacy is in one respect voluntary? It is suggested by the very terms in which the question is put; and it comes so naturally to our mind that we have no way of avoiding it except by forcing ourselves to formulate the thesis, *by turns*, in each of the two notation-systems of which philosophy makes use.

When we speak of external objects, we have to choose, in fact, between two notation-systems. We can treat external objects, and the changes they exhibit, as a system of *things* or as a system of *ideas*. And either of these two systems will work provided we keep strictly to the one we have chosen.

Let us, first of all, try to distinguish the two systems with precision. When realism speaks of things and idealism of ideas, it is not merely a dispute about words; realism and idealism are two different notation-systems, that is to say, two different ways of setting about the analysis of reality. For the idealist, there is nothing in reality over and above what appears to his consciousness or to consciousness in general. It would be absurd to speak of a property of matter which could not be represented in idea. There is no virtuality, or, at least, nothing definitely virtual; whatever exists is actual or could become so. Idealism is, then, a notation-system which implies that everything essential in matter is displayed or displayable in the idea which we have of it, and that the real world is articulated in the very same way as it is presented in idea. The hypothesis of realism is the exact reverse. When realism affirms that matter exists independently of the idea, the meaning is that beneath our idea of matter there is an inaccessible cause of that idea, that behind perception, which is actual, there are hidden powers and virtualities; in short, realism assumes that the divisions and articulations visible in our perception are purely relative to our manner of perceiving.

I am not questioning that profounder definitions could be given of the two tendencies, realist and idealist, such as they are to be found throughout the history of philosophy. I have myself indeed used the words 'realism' and 'idealism' in a somewhat different meaning. This is as much as to say that I have no particular liking for the definitions I have just given. They may characterize an idealism like that of Berkeley and the realism opposed to it. They may also fairly well represent our ordinary notion of the two tendencies – the tendency of idealism to include the whole reality in what can be presented to our mind, the tendency of realism to claim to pass beyond what is presented to our mind. But the argument I am about to put forward is independent of any historical conception of realism and idealism. If any one is inclined to dispute the generality of my two definitions, I simply ask him to accept the words *realism* and *idealism* as conventional terms by which I intend to indicate, in the course of this study, two notations of reality, one of which implies the possibility, the other the impossibility, of identifying things with their ideas, that is with the presentations, spread out and articulated in space, which they offer to a human consciousness. That these two postulates are mutually exclusive, that consequently it is illegitimate to apply the two notation-systems at the same time to the same object, everyone will agree. Now, I require nothing more for my present purpose.

I propose to establish the three following points: (1) If we choose the idealist notation, the affirmation of parallelism (in the meaning of equivalence) between the psychic state and the cerebral state is a self-contradiction. (2) If, on the other hand, we choose the realist notation, there is the same contradiction, but transposed. (3) The thesis of parallelism appears consistent only when we employ at the same time, in the same proposition, both notation-systems together. That is to say, the thesis is intelligible only because, by an unconscious trick of intellectual conjuring, we pass instantly from realism to idealism and from idealism to realism, showing ourselves in the one at the very moment when we are going to be caught in the act of self-contradiction in the other. The trick, moreover, is quite natural; we are, in this case, born conjurors, because the problem we are concerned with, the psycho-physiological problem of the relation of brain and thought, itself suggests by its very terms the two points of view of realism and idealism – the term 'brain' making us think of a *thing*, the term 'thought' of an *idea*. By the very wording of the question is prepared the double meaning which vitiates the answer.

First of all, then, we will place ourselves at the idealist standpoint, and consider, as an example, the perception of the objects which at any given moment occupy the visual field. These objects act on the visual centres in the brain through the retina and the optic nerve. There they bring about a modification of atomic and molecular dispositions. What is the relation of this cerebral modification to the external objects?

The thesis of parallelism is that the cerebral state caused by the objects, and not the objects themselves, determines conscious perception, and therefore, so long as the cerebral state exists, all the objects perceived might, by a touch as it were of a magic wand, cease to exist, it would in no way alter what is going on in consciousness. But it is obvious that on the idealist hypothesis such a proposition is absurd. External objects are for the idealist images, and the brain is one of them. There is nothing in things themselves over and above what is displayed or displayable in the images. There is nothing, then, in the dancing about of cerebral atoms over and above a dance of atoms. Since this is all we have supposed to be in the brain, it is all that will be found there or that can be got out of it. To say that an image of the surrounding world issues from this image of a dance of atoms, or that the image of the one expresses the image of the other, or that given the one the other is also given, is self-contradictory, since these two images – the external world and the intra-cerebral movement – have been assumed to be of like nature, and since the latter image is, by the very hypothesis, a tiny part of the field of images presented, while the external world is that field in its entirety. To say that the cerebral movements contain virtually the image presentation which is the external world may indeed seem intelligible if we hold the doctrine that movement is something *underlying* the idea of it, a mysterious power whose effect upon us is alone perceived. But this is evidently self-contradictory if we hold the doctrine that movement is itself idea, for it amounts to saying that a small patch of the field of presentation is the whole of presentation.

I can understand, assuming the idealist hypothesis, that cerebral modifications may be an *effect* of the action of external objects; they may be movements received by the organism which lead it to prepare the appropriate reactions. The nerve-centres, – images in the midst of images, moving pictures like all the other pictures, – contain movable parts which take in certain movements from outside and turn them into internal movements of reaction, either carried out or simply started. But, then, the work of the brain – a picture – is limited to receiving the influence of the other pictures and to marking out, as I said, their motor articulations. In this, and in this alone, is the brain indispensable to the remainder of our world presentation, and that is why it cannot be injured without there resulting a partial or total destruction of that presentation. But it does not provide or exhibit the presentation, because, itself idea, it could not present the whole of the presentation unless it ceased to be a part of the presentation and became the whole. Formulated in strictly idealist language, the thesis of parallelism would therefore have to be summed up in the self-contradictory proposition: *the part is the whole*.

But the truth is that *the philosopher unconsciously passes from the idealist to a pseudo-realist point of view*. He began by viewing the brain as an idea or picture exactly like all other ideas or pictures, encased in the other pictures and inseparable from them: the internal motion of the brain, being then a picture in the midst of pictures, was not required to provide the other pictures, since these were given with it and around it. But insensibly he comes to changing the brain and the intra-cerebral motion into *things*, that is to say, into *causes* hidden behind a particular picture and whose power extends far beyond what is presented. Whence this sliding from idealism to realism? It is favoured by many subtle fallacies; yet it would not be so smooth and easy were there not facts that seem to point in the same direction.

For, besides perception, there is memory. When I remember objects once perceived, the objects may be gone. One only has remained, my body; and yet the other objects may become visible again in the form of memory-images. Surely, then, it seems, my body, or some part of my body, has the power of evoking these images. Let us assume it does not create them; at least it is able to arouse them. How could it do this, were it not that to definite cerebral states correspond definite memory-images, and were there not, in this precise meaning, a parallelism between cerebral work and thought?

The reply is obvious: in the idealist hypothesis it is impossible for an object to be presented as an idea in the complete absence of the object itself. If there be nothing in the object over and above what is ideally present, if the presence of the object coincide with the idea we have of it, any part of the idea of the object must be in some sort a part of its presence. The recollection is no longer the object itself, I grant. Many things are wanted before it can be that. In the first place, it is fragmentary, for usually the recollection retains only some elements of the primitive perception. Again, it exists only for the person who evokes it, whereas the object forms part of a common experience. Lastly, when the memory-image arises, the accompanying modifications of the brain-image are no longer, as in perception, movements strong enough to excite the organism-image to react immediately. The body no longer feels uplifted by the perceived object, and since it is in the *suggestion of activity* that the *feeling of actuality* consists, the object presented no longer appears actual: this is what we express by saying that it is no longer present. The fact is that, in the idealist hypothesis, the memory-image can only be a pellicle detached from the primitive presentation or, what amounts to the same thing, from the object. It is always present, but consciousness turns its attention away from it so long as there is no reason for consciousness to consider it. Consciousness has an interest in perceiving it only when it feels itself capable of making use of it, that is to say, when the present cerebral state already outlines some of the nascent motor reactions which the real object (that is, the complete idea) would have determined: this beginning of bodily activity confers on the idea a beginning of actuality. But, then, there is no such thing as 'parallelism' or 'equivalence' between the memory-image and the cerebral state. For the nascent motor reactions portray some of the possible effects of the idea which is about to reappear, but they do not portray the idea; and as the same motor reaction may follow many very different recollections, it is not a definite recollection which is evoked by a definite bodily state; on the contrary, many different recollections are equally possible, and among them consciousness exercises a choice. They are subject to only one common condition – that of entering the same motor frame: in this lies their 'resemblance,' a term which is vague in current association theories, but which acquires a precise meaning when we define it by the identity of motor articulations. However, I shall not press this. I am content to say that in the idealist hypothesis the perceived objects are coincident with the complete and completely acting presentation, the remembered objects with the same, but incomplete and incompletely acting, presentation, and that neither in the case of perception nor in the case of memory is the cerebral state equivalent to the presentation, for the simple reason that it is part of it.

Let us turn, then, to realism and see whether it will make the thesis of psycho-physiological parallelism clearer.

Again, objects fill my visual field; my brain is in the midst of them; in my sensory nerve-centres are displacements of molecules and atoms occasioned by the action of external objects. From the idealist standpoint, I had no right to attribute to these internal movements a mysterious power of duplicating themselves with the idea of external things, for they were supposed to be in reality what they are in idea, and since, by the hypothesis, they present themselves as movements of certain atoms of the brain, they are movements of atoms of the brain and nothing else. But it is the essence of realism to suppose that behind ideas is a cause which is not idea. There seems no reason, then, why realism should not hold that the idea of external objects is implied in the cerebral modifications. According to some theories, the cerebral states are actually the creators of the ideas, which are then only their 'epiphenomenon.' According to other theories it is supposed, following the Cartesian distinction, that the cerebral movements are the occasion, not the cause, of the apparition of conscious perceptions, or even that the perceptions and the movements are only two aspects of a reality which is neither movement nor perception. All, however, believe that to a definite cerebral state there corresponds a definite conscious state, and that the internal movements of the cerebral substance, considered by themselves, would reveal to one who should possess the cipher the complete detail of whatever might be going on in the corresponding consciousness.

But is it not at once clear that to consider the brain separately, and separately also the movement of its atoms, involves now an actual self-contradiction? An idealist has the right to declare any object isolable which gives him an isolated idea, because for him the object is not distinct from the idea. But realism consists precisely in the rejection of this view; it holds that the lines of separation which we draw in the field of presentation are artificial or relative; it supposes that beneath presentations there is a system of reciprocal actions and entangled potentialities; in short, it defines the object not by its entry into our presentation, but by its solidarity with the whole of a reality supposed to be unknowable. The more science investigates the nature of the body in the direction of its 'reality,' the more it sees each property of the body, consequently its very existence, melt into the relations in which it stands with the matter outside it capable of influencing it. Indeed, the terms which reciprocally influence one another (whatever the names we give them: atoms, material points, centres of force, etc.) are only, for science, provisional terms; it is the reciprocal influence, or *interaction*, which is for it the final reality.

Now, – should I say to the realist, – you began by giving yourself a brain, and saying that objects external to it modify it in such a way as to raise up ideas of themselves. Then you did away with these objects external to the brain, and ascribed to the cerebral modification the power of providing by its own resources the idea of the objects. But, in withdrawing the objects which encase it, you are withdrawing also, whether you will or no, the cerebral state, for it owes to them all its properties and its reality. You *only preserve this cerebral state because you pass surreptitiously to the idealist notation-system, where you can posit as isolable by right what is isolated in idea*.

Keep to your hypothesis. External objects and the brain being compresent, the idea is produced. You ought to say that this idea is a function not of the cerebral state alone, but of cerebral state *and* the objects determining it, cerebral state and external objects now forming together one indivisible block. Here again, then, the thesis of parallelism that the cerebral states, detached from the external objects, are themselves alone able to create, occasion or at least express the ideas of the objects, cannot be stated without falling to pieces. In strictly realist language it would be formulated thus: *A part, which owes all that it is to the remainder of the whole, can be conceived as subsisting when the remainder of the whole has vanished. Or, still more simply: A relation between two terms is the equivalent of one of them*.

Either the movements of atoms going on in the brain are just what they purport to be in our idea of them, or they are different. In the first hypothesis, they are perceived as they are, and whatever else we perceive is then another thing: between the cerebral movements and the rest of what we perceive there is, consequently, the relation of contained to container. This is the idealist standpoint. In the second hypothesis, the fundamental reality of the cerebral movements consists in their solidarity with all that is behind the totality of our other perceptions, and by the very fact of considering this fundamental reality we consider the whole of the reality with which the cerebral movements form an undivided system: which amounts to saying that the intra-cerebral movement, envisaged as an isolated phenomenon, has vanished, and that there can be no longer any pretence of making into the substratum of presentation, as a whole, a phenomenon which is only a part, and a part artificially carved out of the middle of it.

But the fact is that realism never does maintain itself in a pure unalloyed state. We can posit the existence of the real in general behind the ideas; but as soon as we begin to speak of particular reals, we must, whether we will or no, assume that things more or less coincide with the ideas we have of them. In front of the hidden background which he assumes to be reality itself, and where everything must be implied in everything, since it is behind space, the realist sets side by side, just as the idealist does, the distinct and explicit ideas or pictures which make up the whole of presentation. Realist when he posits the real, he becomes idealist directly he affirms anything concerning it, because realist-notation, when applied to explanations of detail, can hardly consist in anything else but inscribing, beneath each term of idealist notation, a *mark* which indicates its provisional character. Be it so: but then, what we have just said of idealism now applies to realism which has taken up idealism on its own account. And therefore, by whatever name we denote the system, to say that cerebral states are the equivalent of perceptions and memories comes always to affirming that the part is the whole.

Comparing the two systems, we see that it is essential to idealism to stop at what is displayed and spread out in space and at spatial divisions, whilst realism regards the display as superficial and the divisions as artificial: realism assumes behind the juxtaposed ideas a system of reciprocal actions, consequently a mutual *implication* of the pictures or ideas. Now, as our knowledge of matter can never get clean away from space, and as the reciprocal implication with which realism deals, however deep it be, can never become extraneous to space without becoming extraneous to science, realism in its explanations can never get beyond idealism. We are always more or less in idealism (in the sense defined) when we have to do with knowledge or science: were we not, we should not even think of taking isolated parts of reality and relating them to each other, – which is the very essence of science. The hypothesis of the realist is therefore here only an ideal, whose purpose is to remind him that he has never gone deep enough down in his explanation of reality, and that he must discover more and more fundamental relations between the parts of the real which to our eyes are juxtaposed in space. But the realist cannot help hypostatising this ideal. He hypostatises it in the ideas or pictures, set side by side, which for the idealist are reality itself. These ideas become therefore for the realist so many *things* – that is to say, reservoirs of hidden potentialities – and he can now think of the intra-cerebral movement (no longer simple ideas, but things) as enclosing potentially the whole complete world as idea. In this consists his affirmation of psycho-physiological parallelism. He forgets that he had placed his reservoir outside the world of idea and not within it, out of space and not within it, and that in any case his original hypothesis consisted in supposing reality either undivided or articulated in itself otherwise than it is in idea. In making a particular part of the world as reality correspond to each part of the world as idea, he articulates the real as he articulates the idea, he displays reality in space, and abandons his realism in order to enter into idealism, in which the relation of the brain as idea to the rest of the world as idea is clearly that of the part to the whole.

You began by speaking – should I say again to the philosopher – of the brain such as we see it, such as it stands out in the midst of the presentation: so you assumed it to be a part of presentation, an idea, and you were in idealism. There, I repeat, the relation of the brain to the rest of presentation can only be the relation of part to whole. Thence, all of a sudden, you have fled to a reality supposed to *lie beneath* the presentation. Very good: but such reality is subspatial, which amounts to saying that the brain is no more an independent entity. What you have to do with now is the totality of the real, in itself unknowable, over which is spread the totality of the presentation. You are now, indeed, in realism; and no more in this realism than in the idealism of a moment ago are the cerebral states the equivalent of the whole of presentation: it is – I must repeat it – the whole world of things which is again implied (but, this time, concealed and unknowable) in the whole of perception. But lo! taking the brain apart and dealing with things separately, you are actually continuing to decompose and recompose reality along the same lines and according to the same laws as presentation, which means that you no longer distinguish the one from the other. Back you are, then, in idealism; there you ought to remain. But not at all! You do indeed preserve the brain as it is given in presentation, therefore as an idea, but you forget that if the real is thus spread out in the presentation, if it is *extension* and not *tension*, it can no longer compress within itself the powers and virtualities postulated by realism; unheedingly you erect the cerebral movements into the equivalent of the whole of presentation. You are therefore oscillating from idealism to realism and from realism to idealism, but so quickly that you do not perceive the see-saw motion and you think yourself all the time astride the two systems joined into one. This apparent reconciliation of two irreconcilable affirmations is the very essence of the thesis of parallelism.

I have tried to dissipate the illusion. It is not likely that I have entirely succeeded, because so many sympathetic ideas are grouped around the thesis of parallelism and protect it. Some of these ideas were born of the thesis itself; others, on the contrary, preceded it and were the instigators of the illegitimate union which gave it birth; others again, with no blood relationship, have modelled themselves on it by constantly living beside it. All form round it today an imposing line of defence, which, when broken through on one point, calls up renewed resistance on another. I may specify some of these in particular.

1. There is the implicit (I might even say the unconscious) hypothesis of a *cerebral soul*, I mean the hypothesis that the world as idea is concentrated in the cortical substance. As our presentation-world seems to accompany us when our body moves, we reason that there must be, inside that body, the equivalent of the world-presentation. The cerebral movements are thought to be this equivalent. Consciousness, then, can perceive the whole of the universe without putting itself out of the way; it has only to range within the limited space of the cerebral cortex, – a *camera obscura* where a miniature reproduction is to be found of the whole world.

2. There is the idea that all causality is mechanical and that there is nothing in the universe which is not mathematically calculable. Then, as our actions result from our ideas (past as well as present), we must, under pain of admitting a breach in mechanical causality, suppose that the brain, from which the action is started, contains the equivalent of perception, memory and even thought itself. But the idea that the whole world, including the living beings in it, can be treated as the subject of pure mathematics, is an *a priori* view of mind which goes back to the Cartesians. We may express it in modern terms, we may translate it into the language of present science, we may call in support of it an ever-increasing number of actual observations (the idea itself has prompted

us to make them) and so attribute to it an experimental origin, the effectively measurable part of reality remains limited none the less, and the law, regarded as absolute, retains the character of a metaphysical hypothesis, which it already had in the time of Descartes.

3. There is the idea that all that is required, in order to pass from the idealist standpoint of *image-presentation* to the realist standpoint of *thing in itself*, is to substitute for the pictorial presented image that same image reduced to a colourless design and to the mathematical relations of its parts to one another. Hypnotized, so to speak, by the void which our mental power of abstraction is creating, we accept the suggestion that some, I know not what, marvellous significance is inherent in the mere motion of material points in space, that is to say, in an impoverished perception. We endow this blank abstraction with a virtue we should never have thought of bestowing on the concrete image, far richer, given in our immediate perception. But the truth is that we have to choose between the conception of reality which represents it spread out in space and consequently in idea, thus considering it as altogether actual or ready to become so, and the conception of reality which represents it as a reservoir of potentialities shrunk into itself, so to say, and outside space. No work of abstracting, of eliminating, – in short, of impoverishing, – performed on the first conception brings us any nearer to the second. Whatever you say concerning the relation of the brain to the idea from the standpoint of a pictorial idealism, which takes immediate presentations as they are, coloured and living, applies *a fortiori* to an abstruse idealism which reduces them to their mathematical skeleton, and which, by emphasizing the spatial character and reciprocal externality of the ideas, only shows more clearly how impossible it is for one of them to include all the others. Because, by rubbing extensive presentations against one another, you have blotted out the qualities which differentiated them in perception, you have not thereby advanced one step towards a reality which you assumed to be tension, not extension, and consequently so much the more real as it is more inextensive. As well might we imagine that a worn-out coin, by losing the precise mark which denotes its value, had gained an unlimited purchasing power.

4. Lastly, there is the idea that if two wholes are solidary, each part of the one is solidary with a definite part of the other. And so, as there is no state of consciousness without its cerebral accompaniment, as a

variation of this cerebral state does not take place without bringing on a variation of the conscious state (although the converse is not necessarily true in all cases), as an injury which interferes with cerebral activity may entail an injury to conscious activity, we conclude that to any fraction whatsoever of the state of consciousness there corresponds a definite part of the cerebral state, and then that one of the two terms can be substituted for the other. As though we had the right to extend to the detail of the parts, thus supposing them to be related each to each, what has only been observed or inferred of the two wholes, and so convert a relation of solidarity into a relation of equivalent to equivalent! The presence or absence of a screw may decide whether or not a machine will work: does it follow that each part of the screw corresponds to a particular part of the machine, and that the equivalent of the machine is the screw? The relation of the cerebral state to the idea or presentation may very well be that of the screw to the machine, that is, of the part to the whole.

These four ideas themselves imply a great number of others, which it would be interesting to analyse in their turn, because they would be found to be, in a kind of way, so many harmonics the fundamental tone of which is the thesis of parallelism. In this study I have only tried to bring to light the contradiction inherent in the thesis itself. Just because the consequences to which it leads, and the postulates which it contains, cover, so to say, the whole domain of philosophy, it has seemed to me that this critical examination is incumbent on, and may serve as the starting-point of, a theory of the mind considered in its relation to the determinism of nature.

Creative Evolution

The Endurance of Life[1]

The existence of which we are most assured and which we know best is unquestionably our own, for of every other object we have notions which may be considered external and superficial, whereas, of ourselves, our perception is internal and profound. What, then, do we find? In this privileged case, what is the precise meaning of the word 'exist'? Let us recall here briefly the conclusions of an earlier work.

I find, first of all, that I pass from state to state. I am warm or cold, I am merry or sad, I work or I do nothing, I look at what is around me or I think of something else. Sensations, feelings, volitions, ideas – such are the changes into which my existence is divided and which colour it in turns. I change, then, without ceasing. But this is not saying enough. Change is far more radical than we are at first inclined to suppose.

For I speak of each of my states as if it formed a block and were a separate whole. I say indeed that I change, but the change seems to me to reside in the passage from one state to the next: of each state, taken separately, I am apt to think that it remains the same during all the time that it prevails. Nevertheless, a slight effort of attention would reveal to me that there is no feeling, no idea, no volition which is not undergoing change every moment: if a mental state ceased to vary, its duration would cease to flow. Let us take the most stable of internal states, the visual perception of a motionless external object. The object may remain the same, I may look at it from the same side, at the same angle, in the same light; nevertheless the vision I now have of it differs from that which I have just had, even if only because the one is an instant older than the other. My memory is there, which conveys something of the past into the present. My mental state, as it advances on the road of time, is continually swelling with the duration which it accumulates: it goes on increasing – rolling upon itself, as a snowball on the snow. Still more is this the case with states more deeply internal, such as sensations, feelings, desires, etc., which do not correspond, like a simple visual perception, to an unvarying external object. But it is expedient to disregard this uninterrupted change, and to notice it only when it becomes sufficient to impress a new attitude on the body, a new direction on the attention. Then, and then only, we find that our state has changed. The truth is that we change without ceasing, and that the state itself is nothing but change.

This amounts to saying that there is no essential difference between passing from one state to another and persisting in the same state. If the state which 'remains the same' is more varied than we think, on the other hand the passing from one state to another resembles, more than we imagine, a single state being prolonged; the transition is continuous. But, just because we close our eyes to the unceasing variation of every psychical state, we are obliged, when the change has become so considerable as to force itself on our attention, to speak as if a new state were placed alongside the previous one. Of this new state we assume that it remains unvarying in its turn, and so on endlessly. The apparent discontinuity of the psychical life is then due to our attention being fixed on it by a series of separate acts: actually there is only a gentle slope; but in following the broken line of our acts of attention, we think we perceive separate steps. True, our psychic life is full of the unforeseen. A thousand incidents arise, which seem to be cut off from those which precede them, and to be disconnected from those which follow. Discontinuous though they appear, however, in point of fact they stand out against the continuity of a background on which they are designed, and to which indeed they owe the intervals that separate them; they are the beats of the drum which break forth here and there in the symphony. Our attention fixes on them because they interest it more, but each of them is borne by the fluid mass of our whole psychical existence. Each is only the best illuminated point of a moving zone which comprises all that we feel or think or will – all, in short, that we are at any given moment. It is this entire zone which in reality makes up our state. Now, states thus defined cannot be regarded as distinct elements. They continue each other in an endless flow.

But, as our attention has distinguished and separated them artificially, it is obliged next to reunite them by an artificial bond. It imagines, therefore, a formless *ego*, indifferent and unchangeable, on which it threads the psychic states which it has set up as independent entities. Instead of a flux of fleeting shades merging into each other, it perceives distinct and, so to speak, *solid* colours, set side by side like the beads of a necklace; it must perforce then suppose a thread, also itself solid, to hold the beads together. But if this colourless substratum is perpetually coloured by that which covers it, it is for us, in its indeterminateness, as if it did not exist, since we only perceive what is coloured, or, in other words, psychic states. As a matter of fact, this substratum has no reality; it is merely a symbol intended to recall unceasingly to our consciousness the artificial character of the process by which the attention places clean-cut states side by side, where actually there is a continuity which unfolds. If our existence were composed of separate states with an impassive ego to unite them, for us there would be no duration. For an ego which does not change does not *endure*, and a psychic state which remains the same so long as it is not replaced by the following state does not *endure* either. Vain, therefore, is the attempt to range such states beside each other on the ego supposed to sustain them: never can these solids strung upon a solid make up that duration which flows. What we actually obtain in this way is an artificial imitation of the internal life, a static equivalent which will lend itself better to the requirements of logic and language, just because we have eliminated from it the element of real time. But, as regards the psychical life unfolding beneath the symbols which conceal it, we readily perceive that time is just the stuff it is made of.

There is, moreover, no stuff more resistant nor more substantial. For our duration is not merely one instant replacing another; if it were, there would never be anything but the present – no prolonging of the past into the actual, no evolution, no concrete duration. Duration is the continuous progress of the past which gnaws into the future and which swells as it advances. And as the past grows without ceasing, so also there is no limit to its preservation. Memory, as we have tried to prove,[2] is not a faculty of putting away recollections in a drawer, or of inscribing them in a register. There is no register, no drawer; there is not even, properly speaking, a faculty, for a faculty works intermittently, when it will or when it can, whilst the piling up of the past upon the past goes on without relaxation. In reality, the past is preserved by itself, automatically. In its entirety, probably, it follows us at every instant; all that we have felt, thought and willed from our earliest infancy is there, leaning over the present which is about to join it, pressing against the portals of consciousness that would fain leave it outside. The cerebral mechanism is arranged just so as to drive back into the unconscious almost the whole of this past, and to admit beyond the threshold only that which can cast light on the present situation or further the action now being prepared – in short, only that which can give *useful* work. At the most, a few superfluous recollections may succeed in smuggling themselves through the half-open door. These memories, messengers from the unconscious, remind us of what we are dragging behind us unawares. But, even though we may have no distinct idea of it, we feel vaguely that our past remains present to us. What are we, in fact, what is our *character*, if not the condensation of the history that we have lived from our birth – nay, even before our birth, since we bring with us prenatal dispositions? Doubtless we think with only a small part of our past, but it is with our entire past, including the original bent of our soul, that we desire, will and act. Our past, then, as a whole, is made manifest to us in its impulse; it is felt in the form of tendency, although a small part of it only is known in the form of idea.

From this survival of the past it follows that consciousness cannot go through the same state twice. The circumstances may still be the same, but they will act no longer on the same person, since they find him at a new moment of his history. Our personality, which is being built up each instant with its accumulated experience, changes without ceasing. By changing, it prevents any state, although superficially identical with another, from ever repeating it in its very depth. That is why our duration is irreversible. We could not live over again a single moment, for we should have to begin by effacing the memory of all that had followed. Even could we erase this memory from our intellect, we could not from our will.

Thus our personality shoots, grows and ripens without ceasing. Each of its moments is something new added to what was before. We may go further: it is not only something new, but something unforeseeable. Doubtless, my present state is explained by what was in me and by what was acting on me a moment ago. In analysing it I should find no other elements. But even a superhuman intelligence would not have been able to foresee the simple indivisible form which gives to these purely abstract elements their concrete organization. For to foresee consists of projecting into the future what has been perceived in the past, or of imagining for a later time a new grouping, in a new order, of elements already perceived. But that which has never been perceived, and which is at the same time simple, is necessarily unforeseeable. Now such is the case with each of our states, regarded as a moment in a history that is gradually unfolding: it is simple, and it cannot have been already perceived, since it concentrates in its indivisibility all that has been perceived and what the present is adding to it besides. It is an original moment of a no less original history.

The finished portrait is explained by the features of the model, by the nature of the artist, by the colours spread out on the palette; but, even with the knowledge of what explains it, no one, not even the artist, could have foreseen exactly what the portrait would be, for to predict it would have been to produce it before it was produced – an absurd hypothesis which is its own refutation. Even so with regard to the moments of our life, of which we are the artisans. Each of them is a kind of creation. And just as the talent of the painter is formed or deformed – in any case, is modified – under the very influence of the works he produces, so each of our states, at the moment of its issue, modifies our personality, being indeed the new form that we are just assuming. It is then right to say that what we do depends on what we are; but it is necessary to add also that we are, to a certain extent, what we do, and that we are creating ourselves continually. This creation of self by self is the more complete, the more one reasons on what one does. For reason does not proceed in such matters as in geometry, where impersonal premises are given once for all, and an impersonal conclusion must perforce be drawn. Here, on the contrary, the same reasons may dictate to different persons, or to the same person at different moments, acts profoundly different, although equally reasonable. The truth is that they are not quite the same reasons, since they are not those of the same person, nor of the same moment. That is why we cannot deal with them in the abstract, from outside, as in geometry, nor solve for another the problems by which he is faced in life. Each must solve them from within, on his own account. But we need not go more deeply into this. We are seeking only the precise meaning that our consciousness gives to this word 'exist,' and we find that, for a conscious being, to exist is to change, to change is to mature, to mature is to go on creating oneself endlessly. Should the same be said of existence in general?

A material object, of whatever kind, presents opposite characters to those which we have just been describing. Either it remains as it is, or else, if it changes under the influence of an external force, our idea of this change is that of a displacement of parts which themselves do not change. If these parts took to changing, we should split them up in their turn. We should thus descend to the molecules of which the fragments are made, to the atoms that make up the molecules, to the corpuscles that generate the atoms, to the 'imponderable' within which the corpuscle is perhaps a mere vortex. In short, we should push the division or analysis as far as necessary. But we should stop only before the unchangeable.

Now, we say that a composite object changes by the displacement of its parts. But when a part has left its position, there is nothing to prevent its return to it. A group of elements which has gone through a state can therefore always find its way back to that state, if not by itself, at least by means of an external cause able to restore everything to its place. This amounts to saying that any state of the group may be repeated as often as desired, and consequently that the group does not grow old. It has no history.

Thus nothing is created therein, neither form nor matter. What the group will be is already present in what it is, provided 'what it is' includes all the points of the universe with which it is related. A superhuman intellect could calculate, for any moment of time, the position of any point of the system in space. And as there is nothing more in the form of the whole than the arrangement of its parts, the future forms of the system are theoretically visible in its present configuration.

All our belief in objects, all our operations on the systems that science isolates, rest in fact on the idea that time does not bite into them. We have touched on this question in an earlier work, and shall return to it in the course of the present study. For the moment, we will confine ourselves to pointing out that the abstract time t attributed by science to a material object or to an isolated system consists only in a certain number of simultaneities or more generally of correspondences, and that this number remains the same, whatever be the nature of the intervals between the correspondences. With these intervals we are never concerned when dealing with inert matter; or, if they are considered, it is in order to count therein fresh correspondences, between which again we shall not care what happens. Common sense, which is occupied with detached objects, and also science, which considers isolated systems, are concerned only with the ends of the intervals and not with the intervals themselves. Therefore the flow of time might assume an infinite rapidity, the entire past, present, and future of material objects or of isolated systems might be spread out all at once in space, without there being anything to change either in the formulae of the scientist or even in the language of common sense. The number t would always stand for the same thing; it would still count the same number of correspondences between the states of the objects or systems and the points of the line, ready drawn, which would be then the 'course of time.'

Yet succession is an undeniable fact, even in the material world. Though our reasoning on isolated systems may imply that their history, past, present, and future, might be instantaneously unfurled like a fan, this history, in point of fact, unfolds itself gradually, as if it occupied a duration like our own. If I want to mix a glass of sugar and water, I must, willy nilly, wait until the sugar melts. This little fact is big with meaning. For here the time I have to wait is not that mathematical time which would apply equally well to the entire history of the material world, even if that history were spread out instantaneously in space. It coincides with my impatience, that is to say, with a certain portion of my own duration, which I cannot protract or contract as I like. It is no longer something *thought*, it is something *lived*. It is no longer a relation, it is an absolute. What else can this mean than that the glass of water, the sugar, and the process of the sugar's melting in the water are abstractions, and that the Whole within which they have been cut out by my senses and understanding progresses, it may be, in the manner of a consciousness?

Certainly, the operation by which science isolates and closes a system is not altogether artificial. If it had no objective foundation, we could not explain why it is clearly indicated in some cases and impossible in others. We shall see that matter has a tendency to constitute *isolable* systems, that can be treated geometrically. In fact, we shall define matter by just this tendency. But it is only a tendency. Matter does not go to the end, and the isolation is never complete. If science does go to the end and isolate completely, it is for convenience of study; it is understood that the so-called isolated system remains subject to certain external influences. Science merely leaves these alone, either because it finds them slight enough to be negligible, or because it intends to take them into account later on. It is none the less true that these influences are so many threads which bind up the system to another more extensive, and to this a third which includes both, and so on to the system most objectively isolated and most independent of all, the solar system complete. But, even here, the isolation is not absolute. Our sun radiates heat and light beyond the farthest planet. And, on the other hand, it moves in a certain fixed direction, drawing with it the planets and their satellites. The thread attaching it to the rest of the universe is doubtless very tenuous. Nevertheless it is along this thread that is transmitted down to the smallest particle of the world in which we live the duration immanent to the whole of the universe.

The universe *endures*. The more we study the nature of time, the more we shall comprehend that duration means invention, the creation of forms, the continual elaboration of the absolutely new. The systems marked off by science *endure* only because they are bound up inseparably with the rest of the universe. It is true that in the universe itself two opposite movements are to be distinguished, as we shall see later on, 'descent' and 'ascent.' The first only unwinds a roll ready prepared. In principle, it might be accomplished almost instantaneously, like releasing a spring. But the ascending movement, which corresponds to an inner work of ripening or creating, *endures* essentially, and imposes its rhythm on the first, which is inseparable from it.

There is no reason, therefore, why a duration, and so a form of existence like our own, should not be attributed to the systems that science isolates, provided such systems are reintegrated into the Whole. But they must be so reintegrated. The same is even more obviously true of the objects cut out by our perception. The distinct outlines which we see in an object, and which give it its individuality, are only the design of a certain kind of *influence* that we might exert on a certain point of space: it is the plan of our eventual actions that is sent back to our eyes, as though by a mirror, when we see the surfaces and edges of things. Suppress this action, and with it consequently those main directions which by perception are traced out for it in the entanglement of the real, and the individuality of the body is re-absorbed in the universal interaction which, without doubt, is reality itself.

Now, we have considered material objects generally. Are there not some objects privileged? The bodies we perceive are, so to speak, cut out of the stuff of nature by our *perception*, and the scissors follow, in some way, the marking of lines along which *action* might be taken. But the body which is to perform this action, the body which marks out upon matter the design of its eventual actions even before they are actual, the body that has only to point its sensory organs on the flow of the real in order to make that flow crystallize into definite forms and thus to create all the other bodies – in short, the *living* body – is this a body as others are?

Doubtless it, also, consists in a portion of extension bound up with the rest of extension, an intimate part of the Whole, subject to the same physical and chemical laws that govern any and every portion of matter. But, while the subdivision of matter into separate bodies is relative to our perception, while the building up of closed-off systems of material points is relative to our science, the living body has been separated and closed off by nature herself. It is composed of unlike parts that complete each other. It performs diverse functions that involve each other. It is an *individual*, and of no other object, not even of the crystal, can this be said, for a crystal has neither difference of parts nor diversity of functions. No doubt, it is hard to decide, even in the organized world, what is individual and what is not. The difficulty is great, even in the animal kingdom; with plants it is almost insurmountable. This difficulty is, moreover, due to profound causes, on which we shall dwell later. We shall see that individuality admits of any number of degrees, and that it is not fully realized anywhere, even in man. But that is no reason for thinking it is not a characteristic property of life. The biologist who proceeds as a geometrician is too ready to take advantage here of our inability to give a precise and general definition of individuality. A perfect definition applies only to a completed reality; now, vital properties are never entirely realized, though always on the way to become so; they are not so much *states* as *tendencies*. And a tendency achieves all that it aims at only if it is not thwarted by another tendency. How, then, could this occur in the domain of life, where, as we shall show, the interaction of antagonistic tendencies is always implied? In particular, it may be said of individuality that, while the tendency to individuate is everywhere present in the organized world, it is everywhere opposed by the tendency towards reproduction. For the individuality to be perfect, it would be necessary that no detached part of the organism could live separately. But then reproduction would be impossible. For what is reproduction, but the building up of a new organism with a detached fragment of the old? Individuality therefore harbours its enemy at home. Its very need of perpetuating itself in time condemns it never to be complete in space. The biologist must take due account of both tendencies in every instance, and it is therefore useless to ask him for a definition of individuality that shall fit all cases and work automatically.

But too often one reasons about the things of life in the same way as about the conditions of crude matter. Nowhere is the confusion so evident as in discussions about individuality. We are shown the stumps of a Lumbriculus, each regenerating its head and living thenceforward as an independent individual; a hydra whose pieces become so many fresh hydras; a sea-urchin's egg whose fragments develop complete embryos: where then, we are asked, was the individuality of the egg, the hydra, the worm? – But, because there are several individuals now, it does not follow that there was not a single individual just before. No doubt, when I have seen several drawers fall from a chest, I have no longer the right to say that the article was all of one piece. But the fact is that there can be nothing more in the present of the chest of drawers than there was in its past, and if it is made up of several different pieces now, it was so from the date of its manufacture. Generally speaking, unorganised bodies, which are what we have need of in order that we may act, and on which we have modelled our fashion of thinking, are regulated by this simple law: *the present contains nothing more than the past, and what is found in the effect was already in the cause.* But suppose that the distinctive feature of the organized body is that it grows and changes without ceasing, as indeed the most superficial observation testifies, there would be nothing astonishing in the fact that it was *one* in the first instance, and afterwards *many*. The reproduction of unicellular organisms consists in just this – the living being divides into two halves, of which each is a complete individual. True, in the more complex animals, nature localizes in the almost independent sexual cells the power of producing the whole anew. But something of this power may remain diffused in the rest of the organism, as the facts of regeneration prove, and it is conceivable that in certain privileged cases the faculty may persist integrally in a latent condition and manifest itself on the first opportunity. In truth, that I may have the right to speak of individuality, it is not necessary that the organism should be without the power to divide into fragments that are able to live. It is sufficient that it should have presented a certain systematisation of parts before the division, and that the same systematisation tend to be reproduced in each separate portion afterwards. Now, that is precisely what we observe in the organic world. We may conclude, then, that individuality is never perfect, and that it is often difficult, sometimes impossible, to tell what is an individual, and what is not, but that life nevertheless manifests a search for individuality, as if it strove to constitute systems naturally isolated, naturally closed.

By this is a living being distinguished from all that our perception or our science isolates or closes artificially. It would therefore be wrong to compare it to an *object*. Should we wish to find a term of comparison in the inorganic world, it is not to a determinate material object, but much rather to the totality of the material universe that we ought to compare the living organism. It is true that the comparison would not be worth much, for a living being is observable, whilst the whole of the universe is constructed or reconstructed by thought. But at least our attention would thus have been called to the essential character of organization. Like the universe as a whole, like each conscious being taken separately, the organism which lives is a thing that *endures*. Its past, in its entirety, is prolonged into its present, and abides there, actual and acting. How otherwise could we understand that it passes through distinct and well-marked phases, that it changes its age – in short, that it has a history? If I consider my body in particular, I find that, like my consciousness, it matures little by little from infancy to old age; like myself, it grows old. Indeed, maturity and old age are, properly speaking, attributes only of my body; it is only metaphorically that I apply the same names to the corresponding changes of my conscious self. Now, if I pass from the top to the bottom of the scale of living beings, from one of the most to one of the least differentiated, from the multicellular organism of man to the unicellular organism of the Infusorian, I find, even in this simple cell, the same process of growing old. The Infusorian is exhausted at the end of a certain number of divisions, and though it may be possible, by modifying the environment, to put off the moment when a rejuvenation by conjugation becomes necessary, this cannot be indefinitely postponed.[3] It is true that between these two extreme cases, in which the organism is completely individualized, there might be found a multitude of others in which the individuality is less well marked, and in which, although there is doubtless an ageing somewhere, one cannot say exactly what it is that grows old. Once more, there is no universal biological law which applies precisely and automatically to every living thing. There are only *directions* in which life throws out species in general. Each particular species, in the very act by which it is constituted, affirms its independence, follows its caprice, deviates more or less from the straight line, sometimes even remounts the slope and seems to turn its back on its original direction. It is easy enough to argue that a tree never grows old, since the tips of its branches are always equally young, always equally capable of engendering new trees by budding. But in such an organism – which is, after all, a society rather than an individual – *something* ages, if only the leaves and the interior of the trunk. And each cell, considered separately, evolves in a specific way. *Wherever anything lives, there is, open somewhere, a register in which time is being inscribed.*

This, it will be said, is only a metaphor. – It is of the very essence of mechanism, in fact, to consider as metaphorical every expression which attributes to time an effective action and a reality of its own. In vain does immediate experience show us that the very basis of our conscious existence is memory, that is to say, the prolongation of the past into the present, or, in a word, *duration*, acting and irreversible. In vain does reason prove to us that the more we get away from the objects cut out and the systems isolated by common sense and by science and the deeper we dig beneath them, the more we have to do with a reality which changes as a whole in its inmost states, as if an accumulative memory of the past made it impossible to go back again. The mechanistic instinct of the mind is stronger than reason, stronger than immediate experience. The metaphysician that we each carry unconsciously within us, and the presence of which is explained, as we shall see later on, by the very place that man occupies amongst the living beings, has its fixed requirements, its ready-made explanations, its irreducible propositions: all unite in denying concrete duration. Change *must* be reducible to an arrangement or rearrangement of parts; the irreversibility of time *must* be an appearance relative to our ignorance; the impossibility of turning back *must* be only the inability of man to put things in place again. So growing old can be nothing more than the gradual gain or loss of certain substances, perhaps both together. Time is assumed to have just as much reality for a living being as for an hour-glass, in which the top part empties while the lower fills, and all goes where it was before when you turn the glass upside down.

True, biologists are not agreed on what is gained and what is lost between the day of birth and the day of death. There are those who hold to the continual growth in the volume of protoplasm from the birth of the cell right to its death.[4] More probable and more profound is the theory according to which the diminution bears on the quantity of nutritive substance contained in that 'inner environment' in which the organism is being renewed, and the increase on the quantity of unexcreted residual substances which, accumulating in the body, finally 'crust it over.'[5] Must we however – with an eminent bacteriologist – declare any explanation of growing old insufficient that does not take account of phagocytosis?[6] We do not feel qualified to settle the question. But the fact that the two theories agree in affirming the constant accumulation or loss of a certain kind of matter, even though they have little in common as to what is gained and lost, shows pretty well that the frame of the explanation has been furnished *a priori*. We shall see this more and more as we proceed with our study: it is not easy, in thinking of time, to escape the image of the hour-glass.

The cause of growing old must lie deeper. We hold that there is unbroken continuity between the evolution of the embryo and that of the complete organism. The impetus which causes a living being to grow larger, to develop and to age, is the same that has caused it to pass through the phases of the embryonic life. The development of the embryo is a perpetual change of form. Anyone who attempts to note all its successive aspects becomes lost in an infinity, as is inevitable in dealing with a continuum. Life does but prolong this prenatal evolution. The proof of this is that it is often impossible for us to say whether we are dealing with an organism growing old or with an embryo continuing to evolve; such is the case, for example, with the larvae of insects and crustacea. On the other hand, in an organism such as our own, crises like puberty or the menopause, in which the individual is completely transformed, are quite comparable to changes in the course of larval or embryonic life – yet they are part and parcel of the process of our aging. Although they occur at a definite age and within a time that may be quite short, no one would maintain that they appear then *ex abrupto*, from without, simply because a certain age is reached, just as a legal right is granted to us on our twenty-first birthday. It is evident that a change like that of puberty is in course of preparation at every instant from birth, and even before birth, and that the aging up to that crisis consists, in part at least, of this gradual preparation. In short, what is properly vital in growing old is the insensible, infinitely graduated, continuance of the change of form. Now, this change is undoubtedly accompanied by phenomena of organic destruction: to these, and to these alone, will a mechanistic explanation of aging be confined. It will note the facts of sclerosis, the gradual accumulation of residual substances, the growing hypertrophy of the protoplasm of the cell. But under these visible effects an inner cause lies hidden. The evolution of the living being, like that of the embryo, implies a continual recording of duration, a persistence of the past in the present, and so an appearance, at least, of organic memory.

The present state of an unorganised body depends exclusively on what happened at the previous instant; and likewise the position of the material points of a system defined and isolated by science is determined by the position of these same points at the moment immediately before. In other words, the laws that govern unorganised matter are expressible, in principle, by differential equations in which time (in the sense in which the mathematician takes this word) would play the role of independent variable. Is it so with the laws of life? Does the state of a living body find its complete explanation in the state immediately before? Yes, if it is agreed *a priori* to liken the living body to other bodies, and to identify it, for the sake of the argument, with the artificial systems on which the chemist, physicist, and astronomer operate. But in astronomy, physics, and chemistry the proposition has a perfectly definite meaning: it signifies that certain aspects of the present, important for science, are calculable as functions of the immediate past. Nothing of the sort in the domain of life. Here calculation touches, at most, certain phenomena of organic *destruction*. Organic *creation*, on the contrary, the evolutionary phenomena which properly constitute life, we cannot in any way subject to a mathematical treatment. It will be said that this impotence is due only to our ignorance. But it may equally well express the fact that the present moment of a living body does not find its explanation in the moment immediately before, that *all* the past of the organism must be added to that moment, its heredity – in fact, the whole of a very long history. In the second of these two hypotheses, not in the first, is really expressed the present state of the biological sciences, as well as their direction. As for the idea that the living body might be treated by some superhuman calculator in the same mathematical way as our solar system, this has gradually arisen from a metaphysic which has taken a more precise form since the physical discoveries of Galileo, but which, as we shall show, was always the natural metaphysic of the human mind. Its apparent clearness, our impatient desire to find it true, the enthusiasm with which so many excellent minds accept it without proof – all the seductions, in short, that it exercises on our thought, should put us on our guard against it. The attraction it has for us proves well enough that it gives satisfaction to an innate inclination. But, as will be seen further on, the intellectual tendencies innate today, which life must have created in the course of its evolution, are not at all meant to supply us with an explanation of life: they have something else to do.

Any attempt to distinguish between an artificial and a natural system, between the dead and the living, runs counter to this tendency at once. Thus it happens that we find it equally difficult to imagine that the organized has duration and that the unorganised has not. When we say that the state of an artificial system depends exclusively on its state at the moment before, does it not seem as if we were bringing time in, as if the system had something to do with real duration? And, on the other hand, though the whole of the past goes into the making of the living being's present moment, does not organic memory press it into the moment immediately before the present, so that the moment immediately before becomes the sole cause of the present one? – To speak thus is to ignore the cardinal difference between *concrete* time, along which a real system develops, and that *abstract* time which enters into our speculations on artificial systems. What does it mean, to say that the state of an artificial system depends on what it was at the moment immediately before? There is no instant immediately before another instant; there could not be, any more than there could be one mathematical point touching another. The instant 'immediately before' is, in reality, that which is connected with the present instant by the interval dt. All that you mean to say, therefore, is that the present state of the system is defined by equations into which differential coefficients enter, such as ds/dt, dv/dt, that is to say, at bottom, present velocities and *present* accelerations. You are therefore really speaking only of the present – a present, it is true, considered along with its *tendency*. The systems science works with are, in fact, in an instantaneous present that is always being renewed; such systems are never in that real, concrete duration in which the past remains bound up with the present. When the mathematician calculates the future state of a system at the end of a time t, there is nothing to prevent him from supposing that the universe vanishes from this moment till that, and suddenly reappears. It is the *t*-th moment only that counts – and that will be a mere instant. What will flow on in the interval – that is to say, real time – does not count, and cannot enter into the calculation. If the mathematician says that he puts himself inside this interval, he means that he is placing himself at a certain point, at a particular moment, therefore at the extremity again of a certain time *t'*; with the interval up to *T'* he is not concerned. If he divides the interval into infinitely small parts by considering the differential *dt*, he thereby expresses merely the fact that he will consider accelerations and velocities – that is to say, numbers which denote tendencies and enable him to calculate the state of the system at a given moment. But he is always speaking of a given moment – a static moment, that is – and not of flowing time. In short, *the world the mathematician deals with is a world that dies and is reborn at every instant – the world which Descartes was thinking of when he spoke of continued creation*. But, in time thus conceived, how could evolution, which is the very essence of life, ever take place? Evolution implies a real persistence of the past in the present, a duration which is, as it were, a hyphen, a connecting link. In other words, to know a living being or *natural system* is to get at the very interval of duration, while the knowledge of an *artificial* or *mathematical system* applies only to the extremity.

Continuity of change, preservation of the past in the present, real duration – the living being seems, then, to share these attributes with consciousness. Can we go further and say that life, like conscious activity, is invention, is unceasing creation?

[. . .]

[W]e think the language of transformism forces itself now upon all philosophy, as the dogmatic affirmation of transformism forces itself upon science.

But then, we must no longer speak of *life in general* as an abstraction, or as a mere heading under which all living beings are inscribed. At a certain moment, in certain points of space, a visible current has taken rise; this current of life, traversing the bodies it has organized one after another, passing from generation to generation, has become divided amongst species and distributed amongst individuals without losing anything of its force, rather intensifying in proportion to its advance. It is well known that, on the theory of the 'continuity of the germ-plasm,' maintained by Weismann,[7] the sexual elements of the generating organism pass on their properties directly to the sexual elements of the organism engendered. In this extreme form, the theory has seemed debatable, for it is only in exceptional cases that there are any signs of sexual glands at the time of segmentation of the fertilized egg. But, though the cells that engender the sexual elements do not generally appear at the beginning of the embryonic life, it is none the less true that they are always formed out of those tissues of the embryo which have not undergone any particular functional differentiation, and whose cells are made of unmodified protoplasm.[8] In other words, the genetic power of the fertilized ovum weakens, the more it is spread over the growing mass of the tissues of the embryo; but, while it is being thus diluted, it is concentrating anew something of itself on a certain special point, to wit, the cells, from which the ova or spermatozoa will develop. It might therefore be said that, though the germ-plasm is not continuous, there is at least continuity of genetic energy, this energy being expended only at certain instants, for just enough time to give the requisite impulsion to the embryonic life, and being recouped as soon as possible in new sexual elements, in which, again, it bides its time. Regarded from this point of view, *life is like a current passing from germ to germ through the medium of a developed organism*. It is as if the organism itself were only an excrescence, a bud caused to sprout by the former germ endeavouring to continue itself in a new germ. The essential thing is the *continuous progress* indefinitely pursued, an invisible progress, on which each visible organism rides during the short interval of time given it to live.

Now, the more we fix our attention on this continuity of life, the more we see that organic evolution resembles the evolution of a consciousness, in which the past presses against the present and causes the upspringing of a new form of consciousness, incommensurable with its antecedents. That the appearance of a vegetable or animal species is due to specific causes, nobody will gainsay. But this can only mean that if, after the fact, we could know these causes in detail, we could explain by them the form that has been produced; foreseeing the form is out of the question.[9] It may perhaps be said that the form could be foreseen if we could know, in all their details, the conditions under which it will be produced. But these conditions are built up into it and are part and parcel of its being; they are peculiar to that phase of its history in which life finds itself at the moment of producing the form: how could we know beforehand a situation that is unique of its kind, that has never yet occurred and will never occur again? Of the future, only that is foreseen which is like the past or can be made up again with elements like those of the past. Such is the case with astronomical, physical and chemical facts, with all facts which form part of a system in which elements supposed to be unchanging are merely put together, in which the only changes are changes of position, in which there is no theoretical absurdity in imagining that things are restored to their place; in which, consequently, the same total phenomenon, or at least the same elementary phenomena, can be repeated. But an original situation, which imparts something of its own originality to its elements, that is to say, to the partial views that are taken of it, how can such a situation be pictured as given before it is actually produced?[10] All that can be said is that, once produced, it will be explained by the elements that analysis will then carve out of it. Now, what is true of the production of a new species is also true of the production of a new individual, and, more generally, of any moment of any living form. For, though the variation must reach a certain importance and a certain generality in order to give rise to a new species, it is being produced every moment, continuously and insensibly, in every living being. And it is evident that even the sudden 'mutations' which we now hear of are possible only if a process of incubation, or rather of maturing, is going on throughout a series of generations that do not seem to change. In this sense it might be said of life, as of consciousness, that at every moment it is creating something.[11]

But against this idea of the absolute originality and unforeseeability of forms our whole intellect rises in revolt. The essential function of our intellect, as the evolution of life has fashioned it, is to be a light for our conduct, to make ready for our action on things, to foresee, for a given situation, the events, favourable or unfavourable, which may follow thereupon. Intellect therefore instinctively selects in a given situation whatever is like something already known; it seeks this out, in order that it may apply its principle that 'like produces like.' In just this does the prevision of the future by common sense consist. Science carries this faculty to the highest possible degree of exactitude and precision, but does not alter its essential character. Like ordinary knowledge, in dealing with things science is concerned only with the aspect of *repetition*. Though the whole be original, science will always manage to analyse it into elements or aspects which are approximately a reproduction of the past. Science can work only on what is supposed to repeat itself – that is to say, on what is withdrawn, by hypothesis, from the action of real time. Anything that is irreducible and irreversible in the successive moments of a history eludes science. To get a notion of this irreducibility and irreversibility, we must break with scientific habits which are adapted to the fundamental requirements of thought, we must do violence to the mind, go counter to the natural bent of the intellect. But that is just the function of philosophy.

In vain, therefore, does life evolve before our eyes as a continuous creation of unforeseeable form: the idea always persists that form, unforeseeability and continuity are mere appearance – the outward reflection of our own ignorance. What is presented to the senses as a continuous history would break up, we are told, into a series of successive states. 'What gives you the impression of an original state resolves, upon analysis, into elementary facts, each of which is the repetition of a fact already known. What you call an unforeseeable form is only a new arrangement of old elements. The elementary causes, which in their totality have determined this arrangement, are themselves old causes repeated in a new order. Knowledge of the elements and of the elementary causes would have made it possible to foretell the living form which is their sum and their resultant. When we have resolved the biological aspect of phenomena into physico-chemical factors, we will leap, if necessary, over physics and chemistry themselves; we will go from masses to molecules, from molecules to atoms, from atoms to corpuscles: we must indeed at last come to something that can be treated as a kind of solar system, astronomically. If you deny it, you oppose the very principle of scientific mechanism, and you arbitrarily affirm that living matter is not made of the same elements as other matter.' – We reply that we do not question the fundamental identity of inert matter and organized matter. The only question is whether the natural systems which we call living beings must be assimilated to the artificial systems that science cuts out within inert matter, or whether they must not rather be compared to that natural system which is the whole of the universe. That life is a kind of mechanism I cordially agree. But is it the mechanism of parts artificially isolated within the whole of the universe, or is it the mechanism of the real whole? The real whole might well be, we conceive, an indivisible continuity. The systems we cut out within it would, properly speaking, not then be *parts* at all; they would be *partial views* of the whole. And, with these partial views put end to end, you will not make even a beginning of the reconstruction of the whole, any more than, by multiplying photographs of an object in a thousand different aspects, you will reproduce the object itself. So of life and of the physico-chemical phenomena to which you endeavour to reduce it. Analysis will undoubtedly resolve the process of organic creation into an ever-growing number of physico-chemical phenomena, and chemists and physicists will have to do, of course, with nothing but these. But it does not follow that chemistry and physics will ever give us the key to life.

Mechanism and Finalism[12]

The more duration marks the living being with its imprint, the more obviously the organism differs from a mere mechanism, over which duration glides without penetrating. And the demonstration has most force when it applies to the evolution of life as a whole, from its humblest origins to its highest forms, inasmuch as this evolution constitutes, through the unity and continuity of the animated matter which supports it, a single indivisible history. Thus viewed, the evolutionist hypothesis does not seem so closely akin to the mechanistic conception of life as it is generally supposed to be. Of this mechanistic conception we do not claim, of course, to furnish a mathematical and final refutation. But the refutation which we draw from the consideration of real time, and which is, in our opinion, the only refutation possible, becomes the more rigorous and cogent the more frankly the evolutionist hypothesis is assumed. We must dwell a good deal more on this point. But let us first show more clearly the notion of life to which we are leading up.

The mechanistic explanations, we said, hold good for the systems that our thought artificially detaches from the whole. But of the whole itself and of the systems which, within this whole, seem to take after it, we cannot admit *a priori* that they are mechanically explicable, for then time would be useless, and even unreal. The essence of mechanical explanation, in fact, is to regard the future and the past as calculable functions of the present, and thus to claim that *all is given*. On this hypothesis, past, present and future would be open at a glance to a superhuman intellect capable of making the calculation. Indeed, the scientists who have believed in the universality and perfect objectivity of mechanical explanations have, consciously or unconsciously, acted on a hypothesis of this kind. Laplace formulated it with the greatest precision: 'An intellect which at a given instant knew all the forces with which nature is animated, and the respective situations of the beings that compose nature – supposing the said intellect were vast enough to subject these data to analysis – would embrace in the same formula the motions of the greatest bodies in the universe and those of the slightest atom: nothing would be uncertain for it, and the future, like the past, would be present to its eyes.'[13] And Du Bois-Reymond: 'We can imagine the knowledge of nature arrived at a point where the universal process of the world might be represented by a single mathematical formula, by one immense system of simultaneous differential equations, from which could be deduced, for each moment, the position, direction, and velocity of every atom of the world.'[14] Huxley has expressed the same idea in a more concrete form:[15] 'If the fundamental proposition of evolution is true, that the entire world, living and not living, is the result of the mutual interaction, according to definite laws, of the forces possessed by the molecules of which the primitive nebulosity of the universe was composed, it is no less certain that the existing world lay, potentially, in the cosmic vapour, and that a sufficient intellect could, from a knowledge of the properties of the molecules of that vapour, have predicted, say the state of the Fauna of Great Britain in 1869, with as much certainty as one can say what will happen to the vapour of the breath in a cold winter's day.' In such a doctrine, time is still spoken of: one pronounces the word, but one does not think of the thing. For time is here deprived of efficacy, and if it *does* nothing, it *is* nothing. Radical mechanism implies a metaphysic in which the totality of the real is postulated complete in eternity, and in which the apparent duration of things expresses merely the infirmity of a mind that cannot know everything at once. But duration is something very different from this for our consciousness, that is to say, for that which is most indisputable in our experience. We perceive duration as a stream against which we cannot go. It is the foundation of our being, and, as we feel, the very substance of the world in which we live. It is of no use to hold up before our eyes the dazzling prospect of a universal mathematic; we cannot sacrifice experience to the requirements of a system. That is why we reject radical mechanism.

But radical finalism is quite as unacceptable, and for the same reason. The doctrine of teleology, in its extreme form, as we find it in Leibniz for example, implies that things and beings merely realize a programme previously arranged. But if there is nothing unforeseen, no invention or creation in the universe, time is useless again. As in the mechanistic hypothesis, here again it is supposed that *all is given*. Finalism thus understood is only inverted mechanism. It springs from the same postulate, with this sole difference, that in the movement of our finite intellects along successive things, whose successiveness is reduced to a mere appearance, it holds in front of us the light with which it claims to guide us, instead of putting it behind. It substitutes the attraction of the future for the impulsion of the past. But succession remains none the less a mere appearance, as indeed does movement itself. In the doctrine of Leibniz, time is reduced to a confused perception, relative to the human standpoint, a perception which would vanish, like a rising mist, for a mind seated at the centre of things.

Yet finalism is not, like mechanism, a doctrine with fixed rigid outlines. It admits of as many inflections as we like. The mechanistic philosophy is to be taken or left: it must be left if the least grain of dust, by straying from the path foreseen by mechanics, should show the slightest trace of spontaneity. The doctrine of final causes, on the contrary, will never be definitively refuted. If one form of it be put aside, it will take another. Its principle, which is essentially psychological, is very flexible. It is so extensible, and thereby so comprehensive, that one accepts something of it as soon as one rejects pure mechanism. The theory we shall put forward in this book will therefore necessarily partake of finalism to a certain extent. For that reason it is important to intimate exactly what we are going to take of it, and what we mean to leave.

Let us say at once that to thin out the Leibnizian finalism by breaking it into an infinite number of pieces seems to us a step in the wrong direction. This is, however, the tendency of the doctrine of finality. It fully realizes that if the universe as a whole is the carrying out of a plan, this cannot be demonstrated empirically, and that even of the organized world alone it is hardly easier to prove all harmonious: facts would equally well testify to the contrary. Nature sets living beings at discord with one another. She everywhere presents disorder alongside of order, retrogression alongside of progress. But, though finality cannot be affirmed either of the whole of matter or of the whole of life, might it not yet be true, says the finalist, of each organism taken separately? Is there not a wonderful division of labour, a marvellous solidarity among the parts of an organism, perfect order in infinite complexity? Does not each living being thus realize a plan immanent in its substance? – This theory consists, at bottom, in breaking up the original notion of finality into bits. It does not accept, indeed it ridicules, the idea of an *external* finality, according to which living beings are ordered with regard to each other: to suppose the grass made for the cow, the lamb for the wolf – that is all acknowledged to be absurd. But there is, we are told, an *internal* finality: each being is made for itself, all its parts conspire for the greatest good of the whole and are intelligently organized in view of that end. Such is the notion of finality which has long been classic. Finalism has shrunk to the point of never embracing more than one living being at a time. By making itself smaller, it probably thought it would offer less surface for blows.

The truth is, it lay open to them a great deal more. Radical as our own theory may appear, finality is external or it is nothing at all.

Consider the most complex and the most harmonious organism. All the elements, we are told, conspire for the greatest good of the whole. Very well, but let us not forget that each of these elements may itself be an organism in certain cases, and that in subordinating the existence of this small organism to the life of the great one we accept the principle of an *external* finality. The idea of a finality that is *always* internal is therefore a self-destructive notion. An organism is composed of tissues, each of which lives for itself. The cells of which the tissues are made have also a certain independence. Strictly speaking, if the subordination of all the elements of the individual to the individual itself were complete, we might contend that they are not organisms, reserve the name organism for the individual, and recognize only internal finality. But everyone knows that these elements may possess a true autonomy. To say nothing of phagocytes, which push independence to the point of attacking the organism that nourishes them, or of germinal cells, which have their own life alongside the somatic cells – the facts of regeneration are enough: here an element or a group of elements suddenly reveals that, however limited its normal space and function, it can transcend them occasionally; it may even, in certain cases, be regarded as the equivalent of the whole.

There lies the stumbling-block of the vitalistic theories. We shall not reproach them, as is ordinarily done, with replying to the question by the question itself: the 'vital principle' may indeed not explain much, but it is at least a sort of label affixed to our ignorance, so as to remind us of this occasionally,[16] while mechanism invites us to ignore that ignorance. But the position of vitalism is rendered very difficult by the fact that, in nature, there is neither purely internal finality nor absolutely distinct individuality. The organized elements composing the individual have themselves a certain individuality, and each will claim its vital principle if the individual pretends to have its own. But, on the other hand, the individual itself is not sufficiently independent, not sufficiently cut off from other things, for us to allow it a 'vital principle' of its own. An organism such as a higher vertebrate is the most individuated of all organisms; yet, if we take into account that it is only the development of an ovum forming part of the body of its mother and of a spermatozoon belonging to the body of its father, that the egg (i.e. the ovum fertilized) is a connecting link between the two progenitors since it is common to their two substances, we shall realize that every individual organism, even that of a man, is merely a bud that has sprouted on the combined body of both its parents. Where, then, does the vital principle of the individual begin or end? Gradually we shall be carried further and further back, up to the individual's remotest ancestors: we shall find him solidary with each of them, solidary with that little mass of protoplasmic jelly which is probably at the root of the genealogical tree of life. Being, to a certain extent, one with this primitive ancestor, he is also solidary with all that descends from the ancestor in divergent directions. In this sense each individual may be said to remain united with the totality of living beings by invisible bonds. So it is of no use to try to restrict finality to the individuality of the living being. If there is finality in the world of life, it includes the whole of life in a single indivisible embrace. This life common to all the living undoubtedly presents many gaps and incoherences, and again it is not so mathematically *one* that it cannot allow each being to become individualized to a certain degree. But it forms a single whole, none the less; and we have to choose between the out-and-out negation of finality and the hypothesis which co-ordinates not only the parts of an organism with the organism itself, but also each living being with the collective whole of all others.

Life as *Creative* Change[17]

Such is the philosophy of life to which we are leading up. It claims to transcend both mechanism and finalism; but, as we announced at the beginning, it is nearer the second doctrine than the first. It will not be amiss to dwell on this point, and show more precisely how far this philosophy of life resembles finalism and wherein it is different.

Like radical finalism, although in a vaguer form, our philosophy represents the organized world as a harmonious whole. But this harmony is far from being as perfect as it has been claimed to be. It admits of much discord, because each species, each individual even, retains only a certain impetus from the universal vital impulsion and tends to use this energy in its own interest. In this consists *adaptation*. The species and the individual thus think only of themselves – whence arises a possible conflict with other forms of life. Harmony, therefore, does not exist in fact; it exists rather in principle; I mean that the original impetus is a *common* impetus, and the higher we ascend the stream of life the more do diverse tendencies appear complementary to each other. Thus the wind at a street-corner divides into diverging currents which are all one and the same gust. Harmony, or rather 'complementarity,' is revealed only in the mass, in tendencies rather than in states. Especially (and this is the point on which finalism has been most seriously mistaken) harmony is rather behind us than before. It is due to an identity of impulsion and not to a common aspiration. It would be futile to try to assign to life an end, in the human sense of the word. To speak of an end is to think of a pre-existing model which has only to be realized. It is to suppose, therefore, that all is given, and that the future can be read in the present. It is to believe that life, in its movement and in its entirety, goes to work like our intellect, which is only a motionless and fragmentary view of life, and which naturally takes its stand outside of time. Life, on the contrary, progresses and *endures* in time. Of course, when once the road has been travelled, we can glance over it, mark its direction, note this in psychological terms and speak as if there had been pursuit of an end. Thus shall we speak ourselves. But, of the road which was going to be travelled, the human mind could have nothing to say, for the road has been created *pari passu* with the act of travelling over it, being nothing but the direction of this act itself. At every instant, then, evolution must admit of a psychological interpretation which is, from our point of view, the best interpretation; but this explanation has neither value nor even significance except retrospectively. Never could the finalistic interpretation, such as we shall propose it, be taken for an anticipation of the future. It is a particular mode of viewing the past in the light of the present. In short, the classic conception of finality postulates at once too much and too little: it is both too wide and too narrow. In explaining life by intellect, it limits too much the meaning of life: intellect, such at least as we find it in ourselves, has been fashioned by evolution during the course of progress; it is cut out of something larger, or, rather, it is only the projection, necessarily on a plane, of a reality that possesses both relief and depth. It is this more comprehensive reality that true finalism ought to reconstruct, or, rather, if possible, embrace in one view. But, on the other hand, just because it goes beyond intellect – the faculty of connecting the same with the same, of perceiving and also of producing repetitions – this reality is undoubtedly creative, i.e., productive of effects in which it expands and transcends its own being. These effects were therefore not given in it in advance, and so it could not take them for ends, although, when once produced, they admit of a rational interpretation, like that of the manufactured article that has reproduced a model. In short, the theory of final causes does not go far enough when it confines itself to ascribing some intelligence to nature, and it goes too far when it supposes a pre-existence of the future in the present in the form of idea. And the second theory, which sins by excess, is the outcome of the first, which sins by defect. In place of intellect proper must be substituted the more comprehensive reality of which intellect is only the contraction. The future then appears as expanding the present: it was not, therefore, contained in the present in the form of a represented end. And yet, once realized, it will explain the present as much as the present explains it, and even more; it must be viewed as an end as much as, and more than, a result. Our intellect has a right to consider the future abstractly from its habitual point of view, being itself an abstract view of the cause of its own being.

It is true that the cause may then seem beyond our grasp. Already the finalist theory of life eludes all precise verification. What if we go beyond it in one of its directions? Here, in fact, after a necessary digression, we are back at the question which we regard as essential: can the insufficiency of mechanism be proved by facts? We said that if this demonstration is possible, it is on condition of frankly accepting the evolutionist hypothesis. We must now show that if mechanism is insufficient to account for evolution, the way of proving this insufficiency is not to stop at the classic conception of finality, still less to contract or attenuate it, but, on the contrary, to go further.

Let us indicate at once the principle of our demonstration. We said of life that, from its origin, it is the continuation of one and the same impetus, divided into divergent lines of evolution. Something has grown, something has developed by a series of additions which have been so many creations. This very development has brought about a dissociation of tendencies which were unable to grow beyond a certain point without becoming mutually incompatible. Strictly speaking, there is nothing to prevent our imagining that the evolution of life might have taken place in one single individual by means of a series of transformations spread over thousands of ages. Or, instead of a single individual, any number might be supposed, succeeding each other in a unilinear series. In both cases evolution would have had, so to speak, one dimension only. But evolution has actually taken place through millions of individuals, on divergent lines, each ending at a crossing from which new paths radiate, and so on indefinitely. If our hypothesis is justified, if the essential causes working along these diverse roads are of psychological nature, they must keep something in common in spite of the divergence of their effects, as school-fellows long separated keep the same memories of boyhood. Roads may fork or by-ways be opened along which dissociated elements may evolve in an independent manner, but nevertheless it is in virtue of the primitive impetus of the whole that the movement of the parts continues. Something of the whole, therefore, must abide in the parts; and this common element will be evident to us in some way, perhaps by the presence of identical organs in very different organisms. Suppose, for an instant, that the mechanistic explanation is the true one: evolution must then have occurred through a series of accidents added to one another, each new accident being preserved by selection if it is advantageous to that sum of former advantageous accidents which the present form of the living being represents. What likelihood is there that, by two entirely different series of accidents being added together, two entirely different evolutions will arrive at similar results? The more two lines of evolution diverge, the less probability is there that accidental outer influences or accidental inner variations bring about the construction of the same apparatus upon them, especially if there was no trace of this apparatus at the moment of divergence. But such similarity of the two products would be natural, on the contrary, on a hypothesis like ours: even in the latest channel there would be something of the impulsion received at the source. *Pure mechanism, then, would be refutable, and finality, in the special sense in which we understand it, would be demonstrable in a certain aspect, if it could be proved that life may manufacture the like apparatus, by unlike means, on divergent lines of evolution; and the strength of the proof would be proportional both to the divergency between the lines of evolution thus chosen and to the complexity of the similar structures found in them.*

It will be said that resemblance of structure is due to sameness of the general conditions in which life has evolved, and that these permanent outer conditions may have imposed the same direction on the forces constructing this or that apparatus, in spite of the diversity of transient outer influences and accidental inner changes. We are not, of course, blind to the role which the concept of *adaptation* plays in the science of today. Biologists certainly do not all make the same use of it. Some think the outer conditions capable of causing change in organisms in a *direct* manner, in a definite direction, through physico-chemical alterations induced by them in the living substance; such is the hypothesis of Eimer, for example.[18] Others, more faithful to the spirit of Darwinism, believe the influence of conditions works *indirectly* only, through favoring, in the struggle for life, those representatives of a species which the chance of birth has best adapted to the environment. In other words, some attribute a *positive* influence to outer conditions, and say that they actually *give rise to* variations, while the others say these conditions have only a *negative* influence and merely *eliminate* variations. But, in both cases, the outer conditions are supposed to bring about a precise adjustment of the organism to its circumstances. Both parties, then, will attempt to explain mechanically, by adaptation to similar conditions, the similarities of structure which we think are the strongest argument against mechanism. So we must at once indicate in a general way, before passing to the detail, why explanations from 'adaptation' seem to us insufficient.

Let us first remark that, of the two hypotheses just described, the latter is the only one which is not equivocal. The Darwinian idea of adaptation by automatic elimination of the unadapted is a simple and clear idea. But, just because it attributes to the outer cause which controls evolution a merely negative influence, it has great difficulty in accounting for the progressive and, so to say, rectilinear development of complex apparatus such as we are about to examine. How much greater will this difficulty be in the case of the similar structure of two extremely complex organs on two entirely different lines of evolution! An accidental variation, however minute, implies the working of a great number of small physical and chemical causes. An accumulation of accidental variations, such as would be necessary to produce a complex structure, requires therefore the concurrence of an almost infinite number of infinitesimal causes. Why should these causes, entirely accidental, recur the same, and in the same order, at different points of space and time? No one will hold that this is the case, and the Darwinian himself will probably merely maintain that identical effects may arise from different causes, that more than one road leads to the same spot. But let us not be fooled by a metaphor. The place reached does not give the form of the road that leads there; while an organic structure is just the accumulation of those small differences which evolution has had to go through in order to achieve it. The struggle for life and natural selection can be of no use to us in solving this part of the problem, for we are not concerned here with what has perished, we have to do only with what has survived. Now, we see that identical structures have been formed on independent lines of evolution by a gradual accumulation of effects. How can accidental causes, occurring in an accidental order, be supposed to have repeatedly come to the same result, the causes being infinitely numerous and the effect infinitely complicated?

The principle of mechanism is that 'the same causes produce the same effects.' This principle, of course, does not always imply that the same effects must have the same causes; but it does involve this consequence in the particular case in which the causes remain visible in the effect that they produce and are indeed its constitutive elements. That two walkers starting from different points and wandering at random should finally meet, is no great wonder. But that, throughout their walk, they should describe two identical curves exactly superposable on each other, is altogether unlikely. The improbability will be the greater, the more complicated the routes; and it will become impossibility, if the zigzags are infinitely complicated. Now, what is this complexity of zigzags as compared with that of an organ in which thousands of different cells, each being itself a kind of organism, are arranged in a definite order?

Let us turn, then, to the other hypothesis, and see how it would solve the problem. Adaptation, it says, is not merely elimination of the unadapted; it is due to the positive influence of outer conditions that have moulded the organism on their own form. This time, similarity of effects will be explained by similarity of cause. We shall remain, apparently, in pure mechanism. But if we look closely, we shall see that the explanation is merely verbal, that we are again the dupes of words, and that the trick of the solution consists in taking the term 'adaptation' in two entirely different senses at the same time.

If I pour into the same glass, by turns, water and wine, the two liquids will take the same form, and the sameness in form will be due to the sameness in adaptation of content to container. Adaptation, here, really means mechanical adjustment. The reason is that the form to which the matter has adapted itself was there, ready-made, and has forced its own shape on the matter. But, in the adaptation of an organism to the circumstances it has to live in, where is the pre-existing form awaiting its matter? The circumstances are not a mould into which life is inserted and whose form life adopts: this is indeed to be fooled by a metaphor. There is no form yet, and the life must create a form for itself, suited to the circumstances which are made for it. It will have to make the best of these circumstances, neutralize their inconveniences and utilize their advantages – in short, respond to outer actions by building up a machine which has no resemblance to them. Such adapting is not *repeating*, but *replying*, – an entirely different thing. If there is still adaptation, it will be in the sense in which one may say of the solution of a problem of geometry, for example, that it is adapted to the conditions. I grant indeed that adaptation so understood explains why different evolutionary processes result in similar forms: the same problem, of course, calls for the same solution. But it is necessary then to introduce, as for the solution of a problem of geometry, an intelligent activity, or at least a cause which behaves in the same way. This is to bring in finality again, and a finality this time more than ever charged with anthropomorphic elements. In a word, if the adaptation is passive, if it is mere repetition in the relief of what the conditions give in the mould, it will build up nothing that one tries to make it build; and if it is active, capable of responding by a calculated solution to the problem which is set out in the conditions, that is going further than we do – too far, indeed, in our opinion – in the direction we indicated in the beginning. But the truth is that there is a surreptitious passing from one of these two meanings to the other, a flight for refuge to the first whenever one is about to be caught *in flagrante delicto* of finalism by employing the second. It is really the second which serves the usual practice of science, but it is the first that generally provides its philosophy. In any *particular* case one talks as if the process of adaptation were an effort of the organism to build up a machine capable of turning external circumstances to the best possible account: then one speaks of adaptation *in general* as if it were the very impress of circumstances, passively received by an indifferent matter. [. . .]

So we come back, by a somewhat roundabout way, to the idea we started from, that of an *original impetus* of life, passing from one generation of germs to the following generation of germs through the developed organisms which bridge the interval between the generations. This impetus, sustained right along the lines of evolution among which it gets divided, is the fundamental cause of variations, at least of those that are regularly passed on, that accumulate and create new species. In general, when species have begun to diverge from a common stock, they accentuate their divergence as they progress in their evolution. Yet, in certain definite points, they may evolve identically; in fact, they must do so if the hypothesis of a common impetus be accepted. This is just what we shall have to show now in a more precise way, by the same example we have chosen, the formation of the eye in molluscs and vertebrates. The idea of an 'original impetus,' moreover, will thus be made clearer.

Two points are equally striking in an organ like the eye: the complexity of its structure and the simplicity of its function. The eye is composed of distinct parts, such as the sclerotic, the cornea, the retina, the crystalline lens, etc. In each of these parts the detail is infinite. The retina alone comprises three layers of nervous elements – multipolar cells, bipolar cells, visual cells – each of which has its individuality and is undoubtedly a very complicated organism: so complicated, indeed, is the retinal membrane in its intimate structure, that no simple description can give an adequate idea of it. The mechanism of the eye is, in short, composed of an infinity of mechanisms, all of extreme complexity. Yet vision is one simple fact. As soon as the eye opens, the visual act is effected. Just because the act is simple, the slightest negligence on the part of nature in the building of the infinitely complex machine would have made vision impossible. This contrast between the complexity of the organ and the unity of the function is what gives us pause.

A mechanistic theory is one which means to show us the gradual building-up of the machine under the influence of external circumstances intervening either directly by action on the tissues or indirectly by the selection of better-adapted ones. But, whatever form this theory may take, supposing it avails at all to explain the detail of the parts, it throws no light on their correlation.

Then comes the doctrine of finality, which says that the parts have been brought together on a preconceived plan with a view to a certain end. In this it likens the labour of nature to that of the workman, who also proceeds by the assemblage of parts with a view to the realization of an idea or the imitation of a model. Mechanism, here, reproaches finalism with its anthropomorphic character, and rightly. But it fails to see that itself [*sic*] proceeds according to this method – somewhat mutilated! True, it has got rid of the end pursued or the ideal model. But it also holds that nature has worked like a human being by bringing parts together, while a mere glance at the development of an embryo shows that life goes to work in a very different way. *Life does not proceed by the association and addition of elements, but by dissociation and division*.

We must get beyond both points of view, both mechanism and finalism being, at bottom, only standpoints to which the human mind has been led by considering the work of man. But in what direction can we go beyond them? We have said that in analysing the structure of an organ, we can go on decomposing for ever, although the function of the whole is a simple thing. This contrast between the infinite complexity of the organ and the extreme simplicity of the function is what should open our eyes.

In general, when the same object appears in one aspect as simple and in another as infinitely complex, the two aspects have by no means the same importance, or rather the same degree of reality. In such cases, the simplicity belongs to the object itself, and the infinite complexity to the views we take in turning around it, to the symbols by which our senses or intellect represent it to us, or, more generally, to elements *of a different order*, with which we try to imitate it artificially, but with which it remains incommensurable, being of a different nature. An artist of genius has painted a figure on his canvas. We can imitate his picture with many-coloured squares of mosaic. And we shall reproduce the curves and shades of the model so much the better as our squares are smaller, more numerous and more varied in tone. But an infinity of elements infinitely small, presenting an infinity of shades, would be necessary to obtain the exact equivalent of the figure that the artist has conceived as a simple thing, which he has wished to transport as a whole to the canvas, and which is the more complete the more it strikes us as the projection of an indivisible intuition. Now, suppose our eyes so made that they cannot help seeing in the work of the master a mosaic effect. Or suppose our intellect so made that it cannot explain the appearance of the figure on the canvas except as a work of mosaic. We should then be able to speak simply of a collection of little squares, and we should be under the mechanistic hypothesis. We might add that, beside the materiality of the collection, there must be a plan on which the artist worked; and then we should be expressing ourselves as finalists. But in neither case should we have got at the real process, for there are no squares brought together. It is the picture, *i.e.* the simple act, projected on the canvas, which, by the mere fact of entering into our perception, is *de*composed before our eyes into thousands and thousands of little squares which present, as *re*composed, a wonderful arrangement. So the eye, with its marvellous complexity of structure, may be only the simple act of vision, divided *for us* into a mosaic of cells, whose order seems marvellous to us because we have conceived the whole as an assemblage.

If I raise my hand from A to B, this movement appears to me under two aspects at once. Felt from within, it is a simple, indivisible act. Perceived from without, it is the course of a certain curve, AB. In this curve I can distinguish as many positions as I please, and the line itself might be defined as a certain mutual coordination of these positions. But the positions, infinite in number, and the order in which they are connected, have sprung automatically from the indivisible act by which my hand has gone from A to B. Mechanism, here, would consist in seeing only the positions. Finalism would take their order into account. But both mechanism and finalism would leave on one side the movement, which is reality itself. In one sense, the movement is *more* than the positions and than their order; for it is sufficient to make it in its indivisible simplicity to secure that the infinity of the successive positions as also their order be given at once – with something else which is neither order nor position but which is essential, the mobility. But, in another sense, the movement is *less* than the series of positions and their connecting order; for, to arrange points in a certain order, it is necessary first to conceive the order and then to realize it with points, there must be the work of assemblage and there must be intelligence, whereas the simple movement of the hand contains nothing of either. It is not intelligent, in the human sense of the word, and it is not an assemblage, for it is not made up of elements. Just so with the relation of the eye to vision. There is in vision *more* than the component cells of the eye and their mutual coordination: in this sense, neither mechanism nor finalism go far enough. But, in another sense, mechanism and finalism both go too far, for they attribute to Nature the most formidable of the labours of Hercules in holding that she has exalted to the simple act of vision an infinity of infinitely complex elements, whereas Nature has had no more trouble in making an eye than I have in lifting my hand. Nature's simple act has divided itself automatically into an infinity of elements which are then found to be coordinated to one idea, just as the movement of my hand has dropped an infinity of points which are then found to satisfy one equation.

We find it very hard to see things in that light, because we cannot help conceiving organization as manufacturing. But it is one thing to manufacture, and quite another to organize. Manufacturing is peculiar to man. It consists in assembling parts of matter which we have cut out in such manner that we can fit them together and obtain from them a common action. The parts are arranged, so to speak, around the action as an ideal centre. To manufacture, therefore, is to work from the periphery to the centre, or, as the philosophers say, from the many to the one. Organization, on the contrary, works from the centre to the periphery. It begins in a point that is almost a mathematical point, and spreads around this point by concentric waves which go on enlarging. The work of manufacturing is the more effective, the greater the quantity of matter dealt with. It proceeds by concentration and compression. The organizing act, on the contrary, has something explosive about it: it needs at the beginning the smallest possible place, a minimum of matter, as if the organizing forces only entered space reluctantly. The spermatozoon, which sets in motion the evolutionary process of the embryonic life, is one of the smallest cells of the organism; and it is only a small part of the spermatozoon which really takes part in the operation.

But these are only superficial differences. Digging beneath them, we think, a deeper difference would be found.

A manufactured thing delineates exactly the form of the work of manufacturing it. I mean that the manufacturer finds in his product exactly what he has put into it. If he is going to make a machine, he cuts out its pieces one by one and then puts them together: the machine, when made, will show both the pieces and their assemblage. The whole of the result represents the whole of the work; and to each part of the work corresponds a part of the result.

Now I recognize that positive science can and should proceed as if organization was like making a machine. Only so will it have any hold on organized bodies. For its object is not to show us the essence of things, but to furnish us with the best means of acting on them. Physics and chemistry are well advanced sciences, and living matter lends itself to our action only so far as we can treat it by the processes of our physics and chemistry. Organization can therefore only be studied scientifically if the organized body has first been likened to a machine. The cells will be the pieces of the machine, the organism their assemblage, and the elementary labours which have organized the parts will be regarded as the real elements of the labour which has organized the whole. This is the standpoint of science. Quite different, in our opinion, is that of philosophy.

For us, the whole of an organized machine may, strictly speaking, represent the whole of the organizing work (this is, however, only approximately true), yet the parts of the machine do not correspond to parts of the work, because *the materiality of this machine does not represent a sum of means employed, but a sum of obstacles avoided*: it is a negation rather than a positive reality. So, as we have shown in a former study, vision is a power which should attain *by right* an infinity of things inaccessible to our eyes. But such a vision would not be continued into action; it might suit a phantom, but not a living being. The vision of a living being is an *effective* vision, limited to objects on which the being can act: it is a vision that is *canalised*, and the visual apparatus simply symbolizes the work of canalising. Therefore the creation of the visual apparatus is no more explained by the assembling of its anatomic elements than the digging of a canal could be explained by the heaping-up of the earth which might have formed its banks. A mechanistic theory would maintain that the earth had been brought cart-load by cart-load; finalism would add that it had not been dumped down at random, that the carters had followed a plan. But both theories would be mistaken, for the canal has been made in another way.

With greater precision, we may compare the process by which nature constructs an eye to the simple act by which we raise the hand. But we supposed at first that the hand met with no resistance. Let us now imagine that, instead of moving in air, the hand has to pass through iron filings which are compressed and offer resistance to it in proportion as it goes forward. At a certain moment the hand will have exhausted its effort, and, at this very moment, the filings will be massed and coordinated in a certain definite form, to wit, that of the hand that is stopped and of a part of the arm. Now, suppose that the hand and arm are invisible. Lookers-on will seek the reason of the arrangement in the filings themselves and in forces within the mass. Some will account for the position of each filing by the action exerted upon it by the neighbouring filings: these are the mechanists. Others will prefer to think that a plan of the whole has presided over the detail of these elementary actions: they are the finalists. But the truth is that there has been merely one indivisible act, that of the hand passing through the filings: the inexhaustible detail of the movement of the grains, as well as the order of their final arrangement, expresses negatively, in a way, this undivided movement, being the unitary form of a resistance, and not a synthesis of positive elementary actions. For this reason, if the arrangement of the grains is termed an 'effect' and the movement of the hand a 'cause,' it may indeed be said that the whole of the effect is explained by the whole of the cause, but to parts of the cause parts of the effect will in no wise correspond. In other words, neither mechanism nor finalism will here be in place, and we must resort to an explanation of a different kind. Now, in the hypothesis we propose, the relation of vision to the visual apparatus would be very nearly that of the hand to the iron filings that follow, canalise and limit its motion.

The greater the effort of the hand, the farther it will go into the filings. But at whatever point it stops, instantaneously and automatically the filings coordinate and find their equilibrium. So with vision and its organ. According as the undivided act constituting vision advances more or less, the materiality of the organ is made of a more or less considerable number of mutually coordinated elements, but the order is necessarily complete and perfect. It could not be partial, because, once again, the real process which gives rise to it has no parts. That is what neither mechanism nor finalism takes into account, and it is what we also fail to consider when we wonder at the marvellous structure of an instrument such as the eye. At the bottom of our wondering is always this idea, that it would have been possible for a part only of this coordination to have been realized, that the complete realization is a kind of special favour. This favour the finalists consider as dispensed to them all at once, by the final cause; the mechanists claim to obtain it little by little, by the effect of natural selection; but both see something positive in this coordination, and consequently something fractionable in its cause, – something which admits of every possible degree of achievement. In reality, the cause, though more or less intense, cannot produce its effect except in one piece, and completely finished. According as it goes further and further in the direction of vision, it gives the simple pigmentary masses of a lower organism, or the rudimentary eye of a Serpula, or the slightly differentiated eye of the Alciope, or the marvellously perfected eye of the bird; but all these organs, unequal as is their complexity, necessarily present an equal coordination. For this reason, no matter how distant two animal species may be from each other, if the progress toward vision has gone equally far in both, there is the same visual organ in each case, for the form of the organ only expresses the degree in which the exercise of the function has been obtained.

But, in speaking of a progress toward vision, are we not coming back to the old notion of finality? It would be so, undoubtedly, if this progress required the conscious or unconscious idea of an end to be attained.

But it is really effected in virtue of the original impetus of life; it is implied in this movement itself, and that is just why it is found in independent lines of evolution. If now we are asked why and how it is implied therein, we reply that life is, more than anything else, a tendency to act on inert matter. The direction of this action is not predetermined; hence the unforeseeable variety of forms which life, in evolving, sows along its path. But this action always presents, to some extent, the character of contingency; it implies at least a rudiment of choice. Now a choice involves the anticipatory idea of several possible actions. Possibilities of action must therefore be marked out for the living being before the action itself. Visual perception is nothing else:[19] the visible outlines of bodies are the design of our eventual action on them. Vision will be found, therefore, in different degrees in the most diverse animals, and it will appear in the same complexity of structure wherever it has reached the same degree of intensity.

Duration and Simultaneity[1]

Concerning the Nature of Time

There is no doubt but that for us time is at first identical with the continuity of our inner life. What is this continuity? That of a flow or passage, but a self-sufficient flow or passage, the flow not implying a thing that flows, and the passing not presupposing states through which we pass; the *thing* and the *state* are only artificially taken snapshots of the transition; and this transition, all that is naturally experienced, is duration itself. It is memory, but not personal memory, external to what it retains, distinct from a past whose preservation it assures; it is a memory within change itself, a memory that prolongs the before into the after, keeping them from being mere snapshots and appearing and disappearing in a present ceaselessly reborn. A melody to which we listen with our eyes closed, heeding it alone, comes close to coinciding with this time which is the very fluidity of our inner life; but it still has too many qualities, too much definition, and we must first efface the difference among the sounds, then do away with the distinctive features of sound itself, retaining of it only the continuation of what precedes into what follows and the uninterrupted transition, multiplicity without divisibility and succession without separation, in order finally to rediscover basic time. Such is immediately perceived duration, without which we would have no idea of time.

How do we pass this inner time to the time of things? We perceive the physical world and this perception appears, rightly or wrongly, to be inside and outside us at one and the same time; in one way, it is a state of consciousness; in another, a surface film of matter in which perceiver and perceived coincide. To each moment of our inner life there thus corresponds a moment of our body and of all environing matter that is 'simultaneous' with it; this matter then seems to participate in our conscious duration.[2] Gradually, we extend this duration to the whole physical world, because we see no reason to limit it to the immediate vicinity of our body. The universe seems to us to form a single whole; and, if the part that is around us endures in our manner, the same must hold, we think, for that part by which it, in turn, is surrounded, and so on indefinitely. Thus is born the idea of a duration of the universe, that is to say, of an impersonal consciousness that is the link among all individual consciousnesses, as between these consciousnesses and the rest of nature.[3] Such a consciousness would grasp, in a single, instantaneous perception, multiple events lying at different points in space; simultaneity would be precisely the possibility of two or more events entering within a single, instantaneous perception. What is true and what illusory, in this way of seeing things? What matters at the moment is not allotting it shares of truth or error but seeing clearly where experience ends and theory begins. There is no doubt that our consciousness feels itself enduring, that our perception plays a part in our consciousness, and that something of our body and environing matter enters into our perception.[4] Thus, our duration and a certain felt, lived participation of our physical surroundings in this inner duration are facts of experience. But, in the first place, the nature of this participation is unknown, as we once demonstrated; it may relate to a property that things outside us have, without themselves enduring, of manifesting themselves in our duration in so far as they act upon us, and of thus scanning or staking out the course of our conscious life.[5] Next, in assuming that this environment 'endures', there is no strict proof that we may find the same duration again when we change our surroundings; different durations, differently rhythmed, might co-exist. We once advanced a theory of that kind with regard to living species. We distinguished durations of higher and lower tension, characteristic of different levels of consciousness, ranging over the animal kingdom. Still, we did not perceive then, nor do we see even today, any reason for extending this theory of a multiplicity of durations to the physical universe. We had left open the question of whether or not the universe was divisible into independent worlds; we were sufficiently occupied with our own world and the particular impetus that life manifests there. But if we had to decide the question, we would, in our present state of knowledge, favour the hypothesis of a physical time that is one and universal.[6] This is only a hypothesis, but it is based upon an argument by analogy that we must regard as conclusive as long as we are offered nothing more satisfactory. We believe this scarcely conscious argument reduces to the following: All human consciousnesses are of like nature, perceive in the same way, keep in step, as it were, and live the same duration. But, nothing prevents us from imagining as many human consciousnesses as we please, widely scattered through the whole universe, but brought close enough to one another for any two consecutive ones, taken at random, to overlap the fringes of their fields of outer experience. Each of these two outer experiences participates in the duration of each of the two consciousnesses. And, since the two consciousnesses have the same rhythm of duration, so must the two experiences. But the two experiences have a part in common. Through this connecting link, then, they are reunited in a single experience, unfolding in a single duration which will be, at will, that of either of the two consciousnesses. Since the same argument can be repeated step by step, a single duration will gather up the events of the whole physical world along its way; and we shall then be able to eliminate the human consciousness that we had at first laid out at wide intervals like so many relays for the motion of our thought; there will be nothing more than an impersonal time in which all things will pass. In thus formulating mankind's belief, we are perhaps putting more precision into it than is proper. Each of us is generally content with indefinitely enlarging, by a vague effort of imagination, his immediate physical environment, which, being perceived by him, participates in the duration of his consciousness. But as soon as this effort is precisely stated, as soon as we seek to justify it, we catch ourselves doubling and multiplying our consciousness, transporting it to the limits of our outer experience, then, to the edge of the new field of experience that it has thus disclosed, and so on indefinitely – they are really multiple consciousnesses sprung from ours, similar to ours, which we entrust with forging a chain across the immensity of the universe and with attesting, through the identity of their inner durations and the contiguity of their outer experiences, the singleness of an impersonal time. Such is the hypothesis of common sense. We maintain that it could as readily be considered Einstein's and that the theory of relativity was, if anything, meant to bear out the idea of a time common to all things. This idea, hypothetical in any case, even appears to us to take on special rigor and consistency in the theory of relativity, correctly understood. Such is the conclusion that will emerge from our work of analysis. But that is not the important point at the moment. Let us put aside the question of a single time. What we wish to establish is that we cannot speak of a reality that endures without inserting consciousness into it. The metaphysician will have a universal consciousness intervene directly. Common sense will vaguely ponder it. The mathematician, it is true, will not have to occupy himself with it, since he is concerned with the measurement of things, not their nature. But if he were to wonder what he was measuring, if he were to fix his attention upon time itself, he would necessarily picture succession, and therefore a before and after, and consequently a bridge between the two (otherwise, there would be only one of the two, a mere snapshot); but, once again, it is impossible to imagine or conceive a connecting link between the before and after without an element of memory and, consequently, of consciousness.

We may perhaps feel averse to the use of the word 'consciousness' if an anthropomorphic sense is attached to it. But to imagine a thing that endures, there is no need to take one's own memory and transport it, even attenuated, into the interior of the thing. However much we may reduce the intensity of our memory, we risk leaving in it some degree of the variety and richness of our inner life; we are then preserving the personal, at all events, human character of memory. It is the opposite course we must follow. We shall have to consider a moment in the unfolding of the universe, that is, a snapshot that exists independently of any consciousness, then we shall try conjointly to summon another moment brought as close as possible to the first, and thus have a minimum of time enter into the world without allowing the faintest glimmer of memory to go with it. We shall see that this is impossible. Without an elementary memory that connects the two moments, there will be only one or the other, consequently a single instance, no before or after, no succession, no time. We can bestow upon this memory just what is needed to make the connection; it will be, if we like, this very connection, a mere continuing of the before into the immediate after with a perpetually renewed forgetfulness of what is not the immediately prior moment. We shall nonetheless have introduced memory. To tell the truth, it is impossible to distinguish between the duration, however short it may be, that separates two instants and a memory that connects them, because duration is essentially a continuation of what no longer exists into what does exist. This is real time, perceived and lived. This is also any conceived time, because we cannot conceive a time without imagining it as perceived and lived. Duration therefore implies consciousness; and we place consciousness at the heart of things for the very reason that we credit them with a time that endures.

However, the time that endures is not measurable, whether we think of it as within us or imagine it outside of us. Measurement that is not merely conventional implies, in effect, division and superimposition. But we cannot superimpose successive durations to test whether they are equal or unequal; by hypothesis, the one no longer exists when the other appears; the idea of verifiable equality loses all meaning here. Moreover if real duration becomes divisible, as we shall see, by means of the community that is established between it and the line symbolizing it, it consists in itself of an indivisible and total progress. Listen to a melody with your eyes closed, thinking of it alone, no longer juxtaposing on paper or an imaginary keyboard notes which you thus preserved one for the other, which then agreed to become simultaneous and renounced their fluid continuity in time to congeal in space; you will rediscover, undivided and indivisible, the melody or portion of the melody that you will have replaced within pure duration. Now, our inner duration, considered from the first to the last moment of our conscious life, is something like this melody. Our attention may turn away from it and, consequently, from its indivisibility; but when we try to cut it, it is as if we suddenly passed a blade through a flame – divide only the space it occupied. When we witness a very rapid motion, like that of a shooting star, we quite clearly distinguish its fiery line divisible at will, from the indivisible mobility that it subtends; it is this mobility that is pure duration. Impersonal and universal time, if it exists, is in vain endlessly prolonged from past to future; it is all of a piece; the parts we single out in it are merely those of a space that delineates its track and becomes its equivalent in our eyes; we are dividing the unfolded, not the unfolding. How do we first pass from the unfolding to the unfolded, from pure duration to measurable time? It is easy to reconstruct the mechanism of this operation.

If I draw my finger across a sheet of paper without looking at it, the motion I perform is, perceived from within, a continuity of consciousness, something of my own flow, in a word, duration. If I now open my eyes, I see that my finger is tracing on the sheet of paper a line that is preserved, where all is juxtaposition and no longer succession; this is the unfolded, which is the record of the result of motion, and which will be its symbol as well.

Now, this line is divisible, measurable. In dividing and measuring it, I can then say, if it suits me, that I am dividing and measuring the duration of the motion that is tracing it out. It is therefore quite true that time is measured through the intermediary of motion. But it is necessary to add that, if this measurement of time by motion is possible, it is, above all, because we are capable of performing motions ourselves and because these motions then have a dual aspect. As muscular sensation, they are a part of the stream of our conscious life, they endure; as visual perception, they describe a trajectory, they claim a space. I say 'above all' because we could, at a pinch, conceive of a conscious creature reduced to visual perception who would yet succeed in framing the idea of measurable time. Its life would then have to be spent in the contemplation of an outside motion continuing without end. It would also have to be able to extract from the motion perceived in space and sharing the divisibility of its trajectory, the 'pure mobility,' the uninterrupted solidarity of the before and after that is given in consciousness as an indivisible fact. We drew this distinction just before when we were speaking of the fiery path traced out by the shooting star. Such a consciousness would have a continuity of life constituted by the uninterrupted sensation of an external, endlessly unfolding mobility. And the uninterruption of unfolding would still remain distinct from the divisible track left in space, which is still of the unfolded. The latter is divisible and measurable because it is space. The other is duration. Without the continual unfolding, there would be only space, and a space that, no longer subtending a duration, would no longer represent time.

Now, nothing prevents us from assuming that each of us is tracing an uninterrupted motion in space from the beginning to the end of his conscious life. We could be walking day and night. We would thus complete a journey coextensive with our conscious life. Our entire history would then unfold in a measurable time.

Are we thinking of such a journey when we speak of an impersonal time? Not entirely, for we live a social and even cosmic life. Quite naturally we substitute any other person's journey for the one we would make, then any uninterrupted motion that would be contemporaneous with it. I call two flows 'contemporaneous' when they are equally *one* or *two* for my consciousness, the latter perceiving them together as a single flowing if it sees fit to engage in an undivided act of attention, and, on the other hand, separating them throughout if it prefers to divide its attention between them, even doing both at one and the same time if it decides to divide its attention and yet not cut it in two. I call two instantaneous perceptions 'simultaneous' that are apprehended in one and the same mental act, the attention here again being able to make one or two out of them at will. This granted, it is easy to see that it is entirely in our interest to take for the 'unfolding of time' a motion independent of that of our own body. In truth, we find it already taken. Society has adopted it for us. It is the earth's rotational motion. But if we accept it, if we understand it as time and not just space, it is because a journey of our own body is always virtual in it, and *could have been* for us the unfolding of time.

It matters little, moreover, what moving body we adopt as our recorder of time. Once we have exteriorised our own duration as motion in space, the rest follows. Thenceforth, time will seem to us like the unwinding of a thread, that is, like the journey of the mobile entrusted with computing it. We shall say that we have measured the time of this unwinding and, consequently, that of the universal unwinding as well.

But all things would not seem to us to be unwinding along with the thread, each actual moment of the universe would not be for us the tip of the thread, if we did not have the concept of simultaneity at our disposal. We shall soon see the role of this concept in Einstein's theory. For the time being, we would like to make clear its psychological origin, about which we have already said something. The theoreticians of relativity never mention any simultaneity but that of two instants. Anterior to that one, however, is another, the idea of which is more natural: the simultaneity of two flows. We stated that it is of the very essence of our attention to be able to be divided without being split up. When we are seated on the bank of a river, the flowing of the water, the gliding of a boat or the flight of a bird, the ceaseless murmur in our life's deeps are for us three separate things or only one, as we choose. We can interiorise the whole, dealing with a single perception that carries along the three flows, mingled, in its course; or we can leave the first two outside and then divide our attention between the inner and the outer; or, better yet, we can do both at one and the same time, our attention uniting and yet differentiating the three flows, thanks to its singular privilege of being one and several. Such is our primary idea of simultaneity. We therefore call two external flows that occupy the same duration 'simultaneous' because they both depend upon the duration of a like third, our own; this duration is ours only when our consciousness is concerned with us alone, but it becomes equally theirs when our attention embraces the three flows in a single indivisible act.

Now from the simultaneity of two flows, we would never pass to that of two instants, if we remained within pure duration, for every duration is thick; real time has no instants. But we naturally form the idea of instant, as well as of simultaneous instants, as soon as we acquire the habit of converting time into space. For, if a duration has no instants, a line terminates in points.[7] And, as soon as we make a line correspond to a duration, to portions of this line there must correspond 'portions of duration' and to an extremity of the line, an 'extremity of duration'; such is the instant – something that does not exist actually, but virtually. The instant is what would terminate duration if the latter came to a halt. But it does not halt. Real time cannot therefore supply the instant; the latter is born of the mathematical point, that is to say, of space. And yet, without real time, the point would be only a point, not an instant. Instantaneity thus involves two things, a continuity of real time, that is, duration, and a Spatialised time, that is, a line which, described by a motion, has thereby become symbolic of time. This spatialised time, which admits of points, ricochets onto real time and there gives rise to the instant. This would not be possible without the tendency – fertile in illusions – which leads us to apply the motion *against* the distance travelled, to make the trajectory coincide with the journey, and then to decompose the motion over the line as we decompose the line itself; if it has suited us to single out points on the line, these points will then become 'positions' of the moving body (as if the latter, moving, could ever *coincide* with something at rest, as if it would not thus stop moving at once!). Then, having dotted the path of motion with positions, that is, with the extremities of the subdivisions of the line, we have them correspond to 'instants' of the continuity of the motion – mere virtual stops, purely mental views. We once described the mechanism of this process; we have also shown how the difficulties raised by philosophers over the question of motion vanish as soon as we perceive the relation of the instant to spatialised time, and that of spatialised time to pure duration. Let us confine ourselves here to remarking that no matter how much this operation appears learned, it is native to the human mind; we practice it instinctively. Its recipe is deposited in the language.

Simultaneity of the instant and simultaneity of flow are therefore distinct but complementary things. Without simultaneity of flow, we would not consider these three terms interchangeable; continuity of our inner life, continuity of a voluntary motion which our mind indefinitely prolongs, and continuity of any motion through space. Real duration and spatialised time would not then be equivalent, and consequently time in general would no longer exist for us; there would be only each one's duration. But, on the other hand, this time can be computed thanks only to the simultaneity of the instant. We need this simultaneity of the instant in order (1) to note the simultaneity of a phenomenon with a clock moment, (2) to point off, all along our own duration, the simultaneities of these moments with moments of our duration which are created in the very act of pointing. Of these two acts, the first is the essential one in the measurement of time. But without the second, we would have no particular measurement, we would end up with a figure *t* representing anything at all, we would not be thinking of time. It is therefore the simultaneity between two instants of two motions outside of us that enables us to measure time; but it is the simultaneity of these moments with moments pricked by them along our inner duration that makes this measurement one of time.

We shall have to dwell upon these two points. But let us first open a parenthesis. We have just distinguished between two 'simultaneities of the instant'; neither of the two is the simultaneity most in question in the theory of relativity, namely, the simultaneity between readings given by two separated clocks. Of that we have spoken in our first chapter; we shall soon be especially occupied with it. But it is clear that the theory of relativity itself cannot help acknowledging the two simultaneities that we have just described; it confines itself to adding a third, one that depends upon a synchronizing of clocks. Now we shall no doubt show how the readings of two separated clocks *C* and *C'*, synchronized and showing the same time, are or are not simultaneous according to one's point of view. The theory of relativity is correct in so stating; we shall see upon what condition. But it thereby recognizes that an event *E* occurring beside clock *C* is given in simultaneity with a reading on clock *C* in a quite different sense – in the psychologist's sense of the word simultaneity. And likewise for the simultaneity of event *E'* with the reading on its 'neighbouring' clock *C'*. For if we did not begin by admitting a simultaneity of this kind, one which is absolute and has nothing to do with the synchronizing of clocks, the clocks would serve no purpose. They would be bits of machinery with which we would amuse ourselves by comparing them with one another; they would not be employed in classifying events; in short, they would exist for their own sake and not to serve us. They would lose their *raison d'être* for the theoretician of relativity as for everyone else, for he too calls them in only to designate the time of an event. Now, it is very true that simultaneity thus understood is easily established between moments in two flows only if the flows pass by 'at the same place.' It is also very true that common sense and science itself until now have, *a priori*, extended this conception of simultaneity to events separated by any distance. They no doubt imagined, as we said further back, a consciousness coextensive with the universe, capable of embracing the two events in a unique and instantaneous perception. But, more than anything else, they applied a principle inherent in every mathematical representation of things and asserting itself in the theory of relativity as well. We find in it the idea that the distinction between 'small' and 'large,' 'not far apart' and 'very far apart,' has no scientific validity and that if we can speak of simultaneity outside of any synchronizing of clocks, independently of any point of view, when dealing with an event and a clock not much distant from one another, we have this same right when the distance is great between the clock and the event or between the two clocks. No physics, no astronomy, no science is possible if we deny the scientist the right to represent the whole universe schematically on a piece of paper. We therefore implicitly grant the possibility of reducing without distorting. We believe that size is not an absolute, that there are only relations among sizes, and that everything would turn out the same in a universe made smaller at will, if the relations among parts were preserved. But in that case how can we prevent our imagination, and even our understanding, from treating the simultaneity of the readings of two very widely separated clocks like the simultaneity of two clocks slightly separated, that is, situated 'at the same place'? A thinking microbe would find an enormous interval between two 'neighbouring' clocks. And it would not concede the existence of an absolute, intuitively perceived simultaneity between their readings. More Einsteinian than Einstein, it would see simultaneity here only if it had been able to note identical readings on two microbial clocks, synchronized by optical signals, which it had substituted for our two 'neighbouring' clocks. Our absolute simultaneity would be its relative simultaneity because it would refer our absolute simultaneity to the readings on its two microbial clocks which it would, in its turn, perceive (which it would, moreover, be equally wrong to perceive) 'at the same place.' But this is of small concern at the moment; we are not criticizing Einstein's conception; we merely wish to show to what we owe the natural extension that has always been made of the idea of simultaneity, after having actually derived it from the ascertainment of two 'neighbouring' events. This analysis, which has until now hardly been attempted, reveals a fact that the theory of relativity could make use of. We see that if our understanding passes here so easily from a short to a long distance, from simultaneity between neighbouring events to simultaneity between widely separated events, if it extends to the second case the absolute character of the first, it is because it is accustomed to believing that we can arbitrarily modify the dimensions of all things on condition of retaining their relations. But it is time to close the parenthesis. Let us return to the intuitively perceived simultaneity which we first mentioned and the two propositions we had set forth: (1) it is the simultaneity between two instants of two motions outside us that allows us to measure an interval of time; (2) it is the simultaneity of these moments with moments dotted by them along our inner duration that makes this measurement one of time.

The first point is obvious. We saw above how inner duration exteriorises itself as spatialised time and how the latter, space rather than time, is measurable. It is henceforth through the intermediary of space that we shall measure every interval of time. As we shall have divided it into parts corresponding to equal spaces, equal by definition, we shall have at each division point an extremity of the interval, an instant, and we shall regard the interval itself as the unit of time. We shall then be able to consider any motion, any change, occurring beside this model motion; we shall point off the whole length of its unfolding with 'simultaneities of the instant.' As many simultaneities as we shall have established, so many units of time shall we record for the duration of the phenomenon. Measuring time consists therefore in counting simultaneities. All other measuring implies the possibility of directly or indirectly laying the unit of measurement over the object measured. All other measuring therefore bears upon the interval between the extremities even though we are, in fact, confined to counting these extremities. But in dealing with time, we can only count extremities; we merely *agree* to say that we have measured the interval in this way. If we now observe that science works exclusively with measurements, we become aware that, with respect to time, science counts instants, takes note of simultaneities, but remains without a grip on what happens in the intervals. It may indefinitely increase the number of extremities, indefinitely narrow the intervals; but always the interval escapes it, shows it only its extremities. If every motion in the universe was to accelerate in proportion, including the one that serves as the measure of time, something would change for a consciousness not bound up with intracerebral molecular motions; it would not receive the same enrichment between sunup and sundown; it would therefore detect a change; in fact, the hypothesis of a simultaneous acceleration of every motion in the universe makes sense only if we imagine a spectator-consciousness whose completely qualitative duration admits of a more or a less without being thereby accessible to measurement.[8] But the change would exist only for that consciousness able to compare the flow of things with that of the inner life. In the view of science nothing would have changed. Let us go further. The speed of unfolding of this external, mathematical time might become infinite; all the past, present, and future states of the universe might be found experienced at a stroke; in place of the unfolding there might be only the unfolded. The motion representative of time would then have become a line; to each of the divisions of this line there would correspond the same portion of the unfolded universe that corresponded to it before in the unfolding universe; nothing would have changed in the eyes of science. Its formulae and calculations would remain what they were.

It is true that exactly at the moment of our passing from the unfolding to the unfolded, it would have been necessary to endow space with an extra dimension. More than thirty years ago,[9] we pointed out that spatialised time is really a fourth dimension of space. Only this fourth dimension allows us to juxtapose what is given as succession: without it, we would have no room. Whether a universe has three, two, or a single dimension, or even none at all and reduces to a point, we can always convert the indefinite succession of all its events into instantaneous or eternal juxtaposition by the sole act of granting it an additional dimension.

If it has none, reducing to a point that changes quality indefinitely, we can imagine the rapidity of succession of the qualities becoming infinite and these *points of quality* being given all at once, provided we bring to this world without dimension a line upon which the points are juxtaposed. If it already had one dimension, if it were linear, two dimensions would be needed to juxtapose the *lines of quality* – each one indefinite – which were the successive moments of its history. The same observation again if it had two dimensions, if it were a surface universe, an indefinite canvas upon which flat images would indefinitely be drawn, each one covering it completely; the rapidity of succession of these images will again be able to become infinite, and we shall again go over from a universe that unfolds to an unfolded universe, provided that we have been accorded an extra dimension. We shall then have all the endless, piled-up canvases giving us all the successive images that make up the entire history of the universe; we shall possess them all together; but we shall have had to pass from a flat to a volumed universe. It is easy to understand, therefore, why the sole act of attributing an infinite speed to time, of substituting the unfolded for the unfolding, would require us to endow our solid universe with a fourth dimension. Now, for the very reason that science cannot specify the 'speed of unfolding' of time, that it counts simultaneities but necessarily neglects intervals, it deals with a time whose speed of unfolding we may as well assume to be infinite, thereby virtually conferring an additional dimension upon space.

Immanent in our measurement of time, therefore, is the tendency to empty its content into a space of four dimensions in which past, present, and future are juxtaposed or superimposed for all eternity. This tendency simply expresses our inability mathematically to translate time itself, our need to replace it, in order to measure it, by simultaneities which we count. These simultaneities are instantaneities; they do not partake of the nature of real time; they do not endure. They are purely mental views that stake out conscious duration and real motion with virtual stops, using for this purpose the mathematical point that has been carried over from space to time.

But if our science thus attains only to space, it is easy to see why the dimension of space that has come to replace time is still called time. It is because our consciousness is there. It infuses living duration into a time dried up as space. Our mind, interpreting mathematical time, retraces the path it has travelled in obtaining it. From inner duration it had passed to a certain undivided motion which was still closely bound up with it and which had become the model motion, the generator or computer of time; from what there is of pure mobility in this motion, that mobility which is the link between motion and duration, it passed to the trajectory of the motion, which is pure space; dividing the trajectory into equal parts, it passed from the points of division of this trajectory to the corresponding or 'simultaneous' points of division of the trajectory of any other motion. The duration of this last motion was thus measured; we have a definite number of simultaneities; this will be the measure of time; it will henceforth be time itself. But this is time only because we can look back at what we have done. From the simultaneities staking out the continuity of motions, we are always prepared to reascend the motions themselves and, through them, the inner duration that is contemporaneous with them, thus replacing a series of simultaneities of the instant, which we count but which are no longer time, by the simultaneity of flows that leads us back to inner, real duration.

Some will wonder whether it is useful to return to it, and whether science has not, as a matter of fact, corrected a mental imperfection, brushed aside a limitation of our nature, by spreading out 'pure duration' in space. These will say: 'Time, which is pure duration, is always in the course of flowing; we apprehend only its past and its present, which is already past; the future appears closed to our knowledge, precisely because we believe it open to our action – it is the promise or anticipation of unforeseeable novelty. But the operation by which we convert time into space for the purpose of measuring it informs us implicitly of its content. The measurement of a thing is sometimes the revealer of its nature, and precisely at this point mathematical expression turns out to have a magical property: created by us or risen at our bidding, it does more than we asked of it; for we cannot convert into space the time already elapsed without treating all of time the same way. The act by which we usher the past and present into space spreads out the future there without consulting us. To be sure, this future remains concealed from us by a screen; but now we have it there, all complete, given along with the rest. Indeed, what we called the passing of time was only the steady sliding of the screen and the gradually obtained vision of what lay waiting, globally, in eternity. Let us then take this duration for what it is, for a negation, a barrier to seeing all, steadily pushed back; our acts themselves will no longer seem like a contribution of unforeseeable novelty. They will be part of the universal weave of things, given at one stroke. We do not introduce them into the world; it is the world that introduces them ready-made into us, into our consciousness, as we reach them. Yes, it is we who are passing when we say time passes; it is the motion before our eyes which, moment by moment, actualises a complete history given virtually.' Such is the metaphysic immanent in the spatial representation of time. It is inevitable. Clear or confused, it was always the natural metaphysic of the mind speculating upon becoming. We need not discuss it here, still less replace it by another. We have explained elsewhere why we see in duration the very stuff of our existence and of all things, and why, in our eyes, the universe is a continuity of creation. We thus kept as close as possible to the immediate; we asserted nothing that science could not accept and use; only recently, in an admirable book, a philosopher-mathematician affirmed the need to admit of an 'advance of Nature' and linked this conception with ours.[10] For the present, we are confining ourselves to drawing a demarcation line between what is theory, metaphysical construction, and what is purely and simply given in experience; for we wish to keep to experience. Real duration is *experienced*; we *learn* that time unfolds and, moreover, we are unable to measure it without converting it into space and without assuming all we know of it to be unfolded. But, it is impossible mentally to spatialize only a part; the act, once begun, by which we unfold the past and thus abolish real succession involves us in a total unfolding of time; inevitably we are then led to blame human imperfection for our ignorance of a future that is present and to consider duration a pure negation, a 'deprivation of eternity.' Inevitably we come back to the Platonic theory. But since this conception *must* arise because we have no way of limiting our spatial representation of elapsed time to the past, it is *possible* that the conception is erroneous, and in any case *certain* that it is purely a mental construction. Let us therefore keep to experience.

If time has a positive reality, if the delay of duration at instantaneity represents a certain hesitation or indetermination inherent in a certain part of things which holds all the rest suspended within it; in short, if there is a creative evolution, I can very well understand how the portion of time already unfolded may appear as juxtaposition in space and no longer as pure succession; I can also conceive how every part of the universe which is mathematically linked to the present and past – that is, the future unfolding of the inorganic world – may be representable in the same schema (we once demonstrated that in astronomical and physical matters *prevision* is really a *vision*). We believe that a philosophy in which duration is considered real and even active can quite readily admit Minkowski's and Einstein's space-time (in which, it must be added, the fourth dimension called time is no longer, as in our examples above, a dimension completely similar to the others). On the other hand, you will never derive the idea of a temporal flow from Minkowski's schema. Is it not better, in that case, to confine ourselves, until further notice, to that one of the two points of view which sacrifices nothing of experience, and therefore – not to prejudge the question – nothing of appearances? Besides, how can a physicist wholly reject inner experience if he operates with perceptions and, therefore, with the data of consciousness? It is true that a certain doctrine accepts the testimony of the senses, that is, of consciousness, in order to obtain terms among which to establish relations, then retains only the relations and regards the terms as nonexistent. But this is a metaphysic grafted upon science, it is not science. And, to tell the truth, it is by abstraction that we distinguish both terms and relations: a continual flow from which we simultaneously derive both terms and relations and which is, over and above all that, fluidity; this is the only immediate datum of experience.

But we must close this overly long parenthesis. We believe we have achieved our purpose, which was to describe the salient features of a time in which there really is succession. Abolish these features and there is no longer succession, but juxtaposition. You can say that you are still dealing with time – we are free to give words any meaning we like, as long as we begin by defining that meaning – but we shall know that we are no longer dealing with an experienced time; we shall be before a symbolic and conventional time, an auxiliary magnitude introduced with a view to calculating real magnitudes. It is perhaps for not having first analysed our mental view of the time that flows, our feeling of real duration, that there has been so much trouble in determining the philosophical meaning of Einstein's theories, that is, their relation to reality. Those whom the paradoxical appearance of the theories inconvenienced have declared Einstein's multiple times to be purely mathematical entities. But those who would like to dissolve things into relations, who regard every reality, even ours, as a confusedly perceived mathematics, are apt to declare that Minkowski's and Einstein's space-time is reality itself, that all of Einstein's times ate equally real, as much and perhaps more so than the time that flows along with us. We are too hasty in both instances. We have just stated, and we shall soon demonstrate in greater detail, why the theory of relativity cannot express all of reality. But it is impossible for it not to express some. For the time that intervenes in the Michelson-Morley experiment is a real time – real again is the time to which we return with the application of the Lorentz formulae. If we leave real time to end with real time, we have perhaps made use of mathematical artifices in between, but these must have some connection with things. It is therefore a question of allotting shares to the real and to the conventional. Our analyses were simply intended to pave the way for this task.

But we have just uttered the word 'reality'; and in what follows, we shall constantly be speaking of what is real and not real. What shall we mean by that? If it were necessary to define reality in general, to say by what sign we recognize it, we could not do so without classifying ourselves within a school; philosophers are not in agreement, and the problem has received as many solutions as there are shades of realism and idealism. We would, besides, have to distinguish between the standpoints of philosophy and science; the former rather regards the concrete, all charged with quality, as the real; the latter extracts or abstracts a certain aspect of things and retains only size or relation among sizes. Very happily, we have only to be occupied, in all that follows, with a single reality, time. This being so, it will be easy for us to follow the rule we have imposed upon ourselves in the present essay, that of advancing nothing that cannot be accepted by any philosopher or scientist – even nothing that is not implied in all philosophy and science.

Everyone will surely agree that time is not conceived without a *before* and an *after* – time is succession. Now we have just shown that where there is not some memory, some consciousness, real or virtual, established or imagined, actually present or ideally introduced, there cannot be a before *and* an after; there is one *or* the other, not both; and both are needed to constitute time. Hence, in what follows, whenever we shall wish to know whether we are dealing with a real or an imaginary time, we shall merely have to ask ourselves whether the object before us can or cannot be perceived, whether we can or cannot become conscious of it. The case is privileged; it is even unique. If it is a question of colour, for example, consciousness undoubtedly intervenes at the beginning of the study in order to give the physicist the perception of the thing; but the physicist has the right and the duty to substitute for the datum of consciousness something measurable and numerable with which he will henceforward work while granting it the name of the original perception merely for greater convenience. He can do so because, with this original perception eliminated, something remains, or at the very least, is deemed to remain. But what will be left of time if you take succession out of it? And what is left of succession if you remove even the possibility of perceiving a before and an after? I grant you the right to substitute, say, a line for time, since to measure it is quite in order. But a line can be called time only when the juxtaposition it affords is convertible into succession; otherwise you are arbitrarily and conventionally giving that line the name of time. We must be forewarned of this so as not to lay ourselves open to a serious error. What will happen if you introduce into your reasoning and figuring the hypothesis that the thing you called 'time' *cannot*, on pain of contradiction, be perceived by a consciousness, either real or imaginary? Will you not then be working, by definition, with an imaginary, unreal time? Now such is the case with the times with which we shall often be dealing in the theory of relativity. We shall meet with perceived or perceptible ones – those will be considered real. But there are others that the theory prohibits, as it were, from being perceived or becoming perceptible: if they became so, they would change in scale, so that measurement, correct if it bears upon what we do not perceive, would be false as soon as we do perceive. Why not declare these latter unreal, at least as far as their being 'temporal' goes? I admit that the physicist still finds it convenient to call them time; we shall soon see why. But if we liken these times to the other, we fall into paradoxes that have certainly hurt the theory of relativity, even if they have helped popularise it. It will therefore be no surprise if, in the present study, we require the property of being perceived or perceptible for everything held up as real. We shall not be deciding the question of whether all reality possesses this salient feature. We are only dealing here with the reality of time.

The Creative Mind[1]

itself in its accomplishment realizes something willed and consequently foreseen, it has none the less its own particular form in all its originality. – Granted, someone will say; there is perhaps something original and unique in a state of soul; but matter is repetition; the external world yields to mathematical laws; a superhuman intelligence which would know the position, the direction, and the speed of all the atoms and electrons of the material universe at a given moment could calculate any future state of this universe as we do, in the case of an eclipse of the sun or the moon. – I admit all this for the sake of argument, if it concerns only the inert world and at least with regard to elementary phenomena, although this is beginning to be a much debated question. But this 'inert' world is only an abstraction. Concrete reality comprises those living, conscious beings enframed in inorganic matter. I say living and conscious, for I believe that the living is conscious by right; it becomes unconscious in fact where consciousness falls asleep, but even in the regions where consciousness is in a state of somnolence, in the vegetable kingdom for example, there is regulated evolution, definite progress, aging; in fact, all the external signs of the duration which characterizes consciousness. And why must we speak of an inert matter into which life and consciousness would be inserted as in a frame? By what right do we put the inert first? The ancients had imagined a World Soul supposed to assure the continuity of existence of the material universe. Stripping this conception of its mythical element, I should say that the inorganic world is a series of infinitely rapid repetitions or quasi-repetitions which, when totalled, constitute visible and previsible changes. I should compare them to the swinging of the pendulum of a clock: the swingings of the pendulum are coupled to the continuous unwinding of a spring linking them together and whose unwinding they mark; the repetitions of the inorganic world constitute rhythm in the life of conscious beings and measure their duration. Thus the living being essentially has duration; it has duration precisely because it is continuously elaborating what is new and because there is no elaboration without searching, no searching without groping. Time is this very hesitation, or it is nothing. Suppress the conscious and the living (and you can do this only through an artificial effort of abstraction, for the material world once again implies perhaps the necessary presence of consciousness and of life), you obtain in fact a universe whose successive states are in theory calculable in advance, like the images placed side by side along the cinematographic film, prior to its unrolling. Why, then, the unrolling? Why does reality unfurl? Why is it not spread out? What good is time? (I refer to real, concrete time, and not to that abstract time which is only a fourth dimension of space.)[3] This, in days gone by, was the starting-point of my reflections. Some fifty years ago I was very much attached to the philosophy of Spencer. I perceived one fine day that, in it, time served no purpose, did nothing. Nevertheless, I said to myself, time is something. Therefore it acts. What can it be doing? Plain common sense answered: time is what hinders everything from being given at once. It retards, or rather it is retardation. It must, therefore, be elaboration. Would it not then be a vehicle of creation and of choice? Would not the existence of time prove that there is indetermination in things? Would not time be that indetermination itself?

If such is not the opinion of most philosophers, it is because human intelligence is made precisely to take things by the other end. I say intelligence, I do not say thought, I do not say mind. Alongside of intelligence there is in effect the immediate perception by each of us of his own activity and of the conditions in which it is exercised. Call it what you will; it is the feeling we have of being creators of our intentions, of our decisions, of our acts, and by that, of our habits, our characters, ourselves. Artisans of our life, even artists when we so desire, we work continually, with the material furnished us by the past and present, by heredity and opportunity, to mould a figure unique, new, original, as unforeseeable, as the form given by the sculptor to the clay. Of this work and what there is unique about it we are warned, no doubt, even while it is being done, but the essential thing is that we do it. It is up to us to go deeply into it; it is not even necessary that we be fully conscious of it, any more than the artist needs to analyse his creative ability; he leaves that to the philosopher to worry about, being content, himself, simply to create. On the other hand, the sculptor must be familiar with the technique of his art and know everything that can be learned about it: this technique deals especially with what his work has in common with other works; it is governed by the demands of the material upon which he operates and which is imposed upon him as upon all artists; it concerns in art what is repetition or fabrication, and has nothing to do with creation itself. On it is concentrated the attention of the artist, what I should call his intellectuality. In the same way, in the creation of our character we know very little about our creative ability: in order to learn about it we should have to turn back upon ourselves, to philosophise, and to climb back up the slope of nature; for nature desired action, it hardly thought about speculation. The moment it is no longer simply a question of feeling an impulse within oneself and of being assured that one can act, but of turning thought upon itself in order that it may seize this ability and catch this impulse, the difficulty becomes great, as if the whole normal direction of consciousness had to be reversed. On the contrary we have a supreme interest in familiarizing ourselves with the technique of our action, that is to say in extracting from the conditions in which it is exercised, all that can furnish us with recipes and general rules upon which to base our conduct. There will be novelty in our acts thanks only to the repetition we have found in things. Our normal faculty of knowing is then essentially a power of extracting what stability and regularity there is in the flow of reality. Is it a question of perceiving? Perception seizes upon the infinitely repeated shocks which are light or heat, for example, and contracts them into relatively invariable sensations: trillions of external vibrations are what the vision of a colour condenses in our eyes in the fraction of a second. Is it a question of conceiving? To form a general idea is to abstract from varied and changing things a common aspect which does not change or at least offers an invariable hold to our action. The invariability of our attitude, the identity of our eventual or virtual reaction to the multiplicity and variability of the objects represented is what first marks and delineates the generality of the idea. Finally, is it a question of understanding? It is simply finding connections, establishing stable relations between transitory facts, evolving laws; an operation which is much more perfect as the relation becomes more definite and the law more mathematical. All these functions are constitutives of the intellect. And the intellect is in the line of truth so long as it attaches itself, in its penchant for regularity and stability, to what is stable and regular in the real, that is to say to materiality. In so doing it touches one of the sides of the absolute, as our consciousness touches another when it grasps within us a perpetual efflorescence of novelty or when, broadening out, it comes into sympathy with that effort of nature which is constantly renewing. Error begins when the intellect claims to think one of the aspects as it thought the other, directing its powers on something for which it was not intended.

I believe that the great metaphysical problems are in general badly stated, that they frequently resolve themselves of their own accord when correctly stated, or else are problems formulated in terms of illusion which disappear as soon as the terms of the formula are more closely examined. They arise in fact from our habit of transposing into fabrication what is creation. Reality is global and undivided growth, progressive invention, duration: it resembles a gradually expanding rubber balloon assuming at each moment unexpected forms. But our intelligence imagines its origin and evolution as an arrangement and rearrangement of parts which supposedly merely shift from one place to another; in theory therefore, it should be able to foresee any one state of the whole: by positing a definite number of stable elements one has, predetermined, all their possible combinations. That is not all. Reality, as immediately perceived, is fullness constantly swelling out, to which emptiness is unknown. It has extension just as it has duration; but this concrete extent is not the infinite and infinitely divisible space the intellect takes as a place in which to build. Concrete space has been extracted from things. They are not in it; it is space which is in them. Only, as soon as our thought reasons about reality, it makes space a receptacle. As it has the habit of assembling parts in a relative vacuum, it imagines that reality fills up some absolute kind of vacuum. Now, if the failure to recognize radical novelty is the original cause of those badly stated metaphysical questions, the habit of proceeding from emptiness to fullness is the source of problems which are non-existent. Moreover, it is easy to see that the second mistake is already implied in the first. But I should like first of all to define it more precisely.

I say that there are pseudo-problems, and that they are the agonizing problems of metaphysics. I reduce them to two. One gave rise to theories of being, the other to theories of knowledge. The first false problem consists in asking oneself why there is being, why something or someone exists. The nature of what is is of little importance; say that it is matter, or mind, or both, or that matter and mind are not self-sufficient and manifest a transcendent Cause: in any case, when existences and causes are brought into consideration and the causes of these causes, one feels as if pressed into a race – if one calls a halt, it is to avoid dizziness. But just the same one sees, or thinks one sees, that the difficulty still exists, that the problem is still there and will never be solved. It will never, in fact, be solved, but it should never have been raised. It arises only if one posits a nothingness which supposedly precedes being. One says: 'There could be nothing,' and then is astonished that there should be something – or someone. But analyse that sentence: 'There could be nothing.' You will see you are dealing with words, not at all with ideas, and that 'nothing' here has no meaning. 'Nothing' is a term in ordinary language which can only have meaning in the sphere, proper to man, of action and fabrication. 'Nothing' designates the absence of what we are seeking, we desire, expect. Let us suppose that absolute emptiness was known to our experience: it would be limited, have contours, and would therefore be something. But in reality there is no vacuum. We perceive and can conceive only occupied space. One thing disappears only because another replaces it. Suppression thus means substitution. We say 'suppression,' however, when we envisage, in the case of substitution, only one of its two halves, or rather the one of its two sides which interests us; in this way we indicate a desire to turn our attention to the object which is gone, and away from the one replacing it.

We say then that there is nothing more, meaning by that, that what exists does not interest us, that we are interested in what is no longer there or in what might have been there. The idea of absence, or of nothingness, or of nothing, is therefore inseparably bound to that of suppression, real or eventual, and the idea of suppression is itself only an aspect of the idea of substitution. Those are the ways of thinking we use in practical life; it is particularly essential to our industry that our thought should be able to lag behind reality and remain attached, when need be, to what was or to what might be, instead of being absorbed by what is. But when we go from the domain of fabrication to that of creation, when we ask ourselves why there is being, why something or someone, why the world or God, exists and why not nothingness, when, in short, we set ourselves the most agonizing of metaphysical problems, we virtually accept an absurdity; for if all suppression is a substitution, if the idea of a suppression is only the truncated idea of a substitution, then to speak of a suppression of everything is to posit a substitution which would not be one, that is, to be self-contradictory. Either the idea of a suppression of everything has just about as much existence as that of a round square – the existence of a sound, *flatus vocis* – or else, if it does represent something, it translates a movement of the intellect from one object to another, preferring the one it has just left to the object it finds before it, and designates by 'absence of the first' the presence of the second. We have posited the whole, then made each of its parts disappear one by one, without consenting to see what replaced it; it is therefore the totality of presences, simply arranged in a new order, that one has in mind in attempting to total up the absences. In other words, this so-called representation of absolute emptiness is, in reality, that of universal fullness in a mind which leaps indefinitely from part to part, with the fixed resolution never to consider anything but the emptiness of its dissatisfaction instead of the fullness of things. All of which amounts to saying that the idea of Nothing, when it is not that of a simple word, implies as much matter as the idea of All, with, in addition, an operation of thought.

I should say as much of the idea of disorder. Why is the universe well-ordered? How is rule imposed upon what is without rule, and form upon matter? How is it that our thought recognizes itself in things? This problem, which among the moderns has become the problem of knowledge after having been, among the ancients, the problem of being, was born of an illusion of the same order. It disappears if one considers that the idea of disorder has a definite meaning in the domain of human industry or, as we say, of fabrication, but not in that of creation. Disorder is simply the order we are not looking for. You cannot suppress one order even by thought, without causing another to spring up. If there is not finality or will, it is because there is mechanism; if the mechanism gives way, so much the gain for will, caprice, finality. But when you expect one of these two orders and you find the other, you say there is disorder, formulating what is in terms of what might or should be, and objectifying your regret. All disorder thus includes two things: outside us, one order; within us, the representation of a different order which alone interests us. Suppression therefore again signifies substitution. And the idea of a suppression of all order, that is to say, the idea of an absolute disorder, then contains a veritable contradiction, because it consists in leaving only a single aspect to the operation which, by hypothesis, embraced two. Either the idea of an absolute disorder represents no more than a combination of sounds, *flatus vocis*, or else, if it corresponds to something, it translates a movement of the mind which leaps from mechanism to finality, from finality to mechanism, and which, in order to mark the spot where it is, prefers each time to indicate the point where it is not. Therefore, in wishing to suppress order, you find yourself with two or more 'orders.' This is tantamount to saying that the conception of an order which is superadded to an 'absence of order' implies an absurdity, and that the problem disappears.

The two illusions I have just mentioned are in reality only one. They consist in believing that there is *less* in the idea of the empty than in the idea of the full, *less* in the concept of disorder than in that of order. In reality, there is more intellectual content in the ideas of disorder and nothingness when they represent something than in those of order and existence, because they imply several orders, several existences and, in addition, a play of wit which unconsciously juggles with them.

Very well then, I find the same illusion in the case in point. Underlying the doctrines which disregard the radical novelty of each moment of evolution there are many misunderstandings, many errors. But there is especially the idea that the possible is *less* than the real, and that, for this reason, the possibility of things precedes their existence. They would thus be capable of representation beforehand; they could be thought of before being realized.

But it is the reverse that is true. If we leave aside the closed systems, subjected to purely mathematical laws, isolable because duration does not act upon them, if we consider the totality of concrete reality or simply the world of life, and still more that of consciousness, we find there is more and not less in the possibility of each of the successive states than in their reality. For the possible is only the real with the addition of an act of mind which throws its image back into the past, once it has been enacted. But that is what our intellectual habits prevent us from seeing.

During the great war certain newspapers and periodicals sometimes turned aside from the terrible worries of the day to think of what would happen later once peace was restored. They were particularly preoccupied with the future of literature. Someone came one day to ask me my ideas on the subject. A little embarrassed, I declared I had none. 'Do you not at least perceive,' I was asked, 'certain possible directions? Let us grant that one cannot foresee things in detail; you as a philosopher have at least an idea of the whole. How do you conceive, for example, the great dramatic work of tomorrow?' I shall always remember my interlocutor's surprise when I answered, 'If I knew what was to be the great dramatic work of the future, I should be writing it.' I saw distinctly that he conceived the future work as being already stored up in some cupboard reserved for possibles; because of my long-standing relations with philosophy, I should have been able to obtain from it the key to the storehouse. 'But,' I said, 'the work of which you speak is not yet possible.' – 'But it must be, since it is to take place.' – 'No, it is not. I grant you, at most, that it *will have been possible*.' 'What do you mean by that?' – 'It's quite simple. Let a man of talent or genius come forth, let him create a work: it will then be real, and by that very fact it becomes retrospectively or retroactively possible. It would not be possible, it would not have been so, if this man had not come upon the scene. That is why I tell you that it will have been possible today, but that it is not yet so.' 'You're nor serious! You are surely not going to maintain that the future has an effect upon the present, that the present brings something into the past, that action works back over the course of time and imprints its mark afterwards?' – 'That depends. That one can put reality into the past and thus work backwards in time is something I have never claimed. But that one can put the possible there, or rather that the possible may put itself there at any moment, is not to be doubted. As reality is created as something unforeseeable and new, its image is reflected behind it into the indefinite past; thus it finds that it has from all time been possible, but it is at this precise moment that it begins to have been always possible, and that is why I said that its possibility, which does not precede its reality, will have preceded it once the reality has appeared. The possible is therefore the mirage of the present in the past; and as we know the future will finally constitute a present and the mirage effect is continually being produced, we are convinced that the image of tomorrow is already contained in our actual present, which will be the past of tomorrow, although we did not manage to grasp it. That is precisely the illusion. It is as though one were to fancy, in seeing his reflection in the mirror in front of him, that he could have touched it had he stayed behind it. Thus in judging that the possible does not presuppose the real, one admits that the realization adds something to the simple possibility: the possible would have been there from all time, a phantom awaiting its hour; it would therefore have become reality by the addition of something, by some transfusion of blood or life. One does not see that the contrary is the case, that the possible implies the corresponding reality with, moreover, something added, since the possible is the combined effect of reality once it has appeared and of a condition which throws it back in time. The idea immanent in most philosophies and natural to the human mind, of possibles which would be realized by an acquisition of existence, is therefore pure illusion. One might as well claim that the man in flesh and blood comes from the materialization of his image seen in the mirror, because in that real man is everything found in this virtual image with, in addition, the solidity which makes it possible to touch it. But the truth is that more is needed here to obtain the virtual than is necessary for the real, more for the image of the man than for the man himself, for the image of the man will not be portrayed if the man is not first produced, and in addition one has to have the mirror.'

That is what my interlocutor was forgetting as he questioned me on the theatre of tomorrow. Perhaps too he was unconsciously playing on the meaning of the word 'possible.' *Hamlet* was doubtless possible before being realized, if that means that there was no insurmountable obstacle to its realization. In the particular sense one calls possible what is not impossible; and it stands to reason that this non-impossibility of a thing is the condition of its realization. But the possible thus understood is in no degree virtual, something ideally pre-existent. If you close the gate you know no one will cross the road; it does not follow that you can predict who will cross when you open it. Nevertheless, from the quite negative sense of the term 'impossible' you pass surreptitiously, unconsciously to the positive sense. Possibility signified 'absence of hindrance' a few minutes ago: now you make of it a 'pre-existence under the form of an idea,' which is quite another thing. In the first meaning of the word it was a truism to say that the possibility of a thing precedes its reality: by that you meant simply that obstacles, having been surmounted, were surmountable.[4] But in the second meaning it is an absurdity, for it is clear that a mind in which the *Hamlet* of Shakespeare had taken shape in the form of the possible would by that fact have created its reality: it would thus have been, by definition, Shakespeare himself. In vain do you imagine at first that this mind could have appeared before Shakespeare; it is because you are not thinking then of all the details in the play. As you complete them the predecessor of Shakespeare finds himself thinking all that Shakespeare will think, feeling all he will feel, knowing all he will know, perceiving therefore all he will perceive, and consequently occupying the same point in space and time, having the same body and the same soul: it is Shakespeare himself.

But I am putting too much stress on what is self-evident. We are forced to these considerations in discussing a work of art. I believe in the end we shall consider it evident that the artist in executing his work is creating the possible as well as the real. Whence comes it then that one might hesitate to say the same thing for nature? Is not the world a work of art incomparably richer than that of the greatest artist? And is there not as much absurdity, if not more, in supposing, in the work of nature, that the future is outlined in advance, that possibility existed before reality? Once more let me say I am perfectly willing to admit that the future states of a closed system of material points are calculable and hence visible in its present state. But, and I repeat, this system is extracted, or abstracted, from a whole which, in addition to inert and unorganised matter, comprises organization. Take the concrete and complete world, with the life and consciousness it encloses; consider nature in its entirety, nature the generator of new species as novel and original in form as the design of any artist: in these species concentrate upon individuals, plants or animals, each of which has its own character – I was going to say its personality (for one blade of grass does not resemble another blade of grass any more than a Raphael resembles a Rembrandt); lift your attention above and beyond individual man to societies which disclose actions and situations comparable to those of any drama: how can one still speak of possibles which would precede their own realization? How can we fail to see that if the event can always be explained afterwards by an arbitrary choice of antecedent events, a completely different event could have been equally well explained in the same circumstances by another choice of antecedents – nay, by the same antecedents otherwise cut out, otherwise distributed, otherwise perceived – in short, by our retrospective attention? Backwards over the course of time a constant remodelling of the past by the present, of the cause by the effect, is being carried out.

We do not see it, always for the same reason, always a prey to the same illusion, always because we treat as the more what is the less, as the less what is the more. If we put the possible back into its proper place, evolution becomes something quite different from the realization of a program: the gates of the future open wide; freedom is offered an unlimited field. The fault of those doctrines – rare indeed in the history of philosophy – which have succeeded in leaving room for indetermination and freedom in the world, is to have failed to see what their affirmation implied. When they spoke of indetermination, of freedom, they meant by indetermination a competition between possibles, by freedom a choice between possibles – as if possibility was not created by freedom itself! As if any other hypothesis, by affirming an ideal pre-existence of the possible to the real, did not reduce the new to a mere rearrangement of former elements! As if it were not thus to be led sooner or later to regard that rearrangement as calculable and foreseeable! By accepting the premise of the contrary theory one was letting the enemy in. We must resign ourselves to the inevitable: it is the real which makes itself possible, and not the possible which becomes real.

But the truth is that philosophy has never frankly admitted this continuous creation of unforeseeable novelty. The ancients already revolted against it because, Platonists to a greater or less degree, they imagined that Being was given once and for all, complete and perfect, in the immutable system of Ideas: the world which unfolds before our eyes could therefore add nothing to it; it was, on the contrary, only diminution or degradation; its successive states measured as it were the increasing or decreasing distance between what is, a shadow projected in time, and what ought to be, Idea set in eternity; they would outline the variations of a deficiency, the changing form of a void. It was Time which, according to them, spoiled everything. The moderns, it is true, take a quite different point of view. They no longer treat Time as an intruder, a disturber of eternity; but they would very much like to reduce it to a simple appearance. The temporal is, then, only the confused form of the rational. What we perceive as being a succession of states is conceived by our intellect, once the fog has settled, as a system of relations. The real becomes once more the eternal, with this single difference, that it is the eternity of the Laws in which the phenomena are resolved instead of being the eternity of the Ideas which serve them as models. But in each case, we are dealing with theories. Let us stick to the facts. Time is immediately given. That is sufficient for us, and until its inexistence or perversity is proved to us we shall merely register that there is effectively a flow of unforeseeable novelty.

Philosophy stands to gain in finding some absolute in the moving world of phenomena. But we shall gain also in our feeling of greater joy and strength. Greater joy because the reality invented before our eyes will give each one of us, unceasingly, certain of the satisfactions which art at rare intervals procures for the privileged; it will reveal to us, beyond the fixity and monotony which our senses, hypnotized by our constant needs, at first perceived in it, ever-recurring novelty, the moving originality of things. But above all we shall have greater strength, for we shall feel we are participating, creators of ourselves, in the great work of creation which is the origin of all things and which goes on before our eyes. By getting hold of itself, our faculty for acting will become intensified. Humbled heretofore in an attitude of obedience, slaves of certain vaguely-felt natural necessities, we shall once more stand erect, masters associated with a greater Master. To such a conclusion will our study bring us. In this speculation on the relation between the possible and the real, let us guard against seeing a simple game. It can be a preparation for the art of living.

Philosophical Intuition

Lecture given at the Philosophical Congress in Bologna, April 10th, 1911

I should like to submit to you some reflections on the philosophical mind. It seems to me – and more than one report presented at this Congress bears witness to the fact – that metaphysics at present is tending to become more simplified, to draw closer to life. I think this tendency is a correct one, and that it is along this line we should work. But in so doing we shall be doing nothing revolutionary; we shall merely be giving the most appropriate form to what is the foundation of all philosophy – I mean of any philosophy which is fully conscious of its function and destination. For the complication of the letter must not allow the simplicity of the spirit to be lost to view. If we confine ourselves entirely to doctrines already formulated, to the synthesis in which they then appear to embrace the conclusions of earlier philosophies and all the forms of acquired knowledge, we run the risk of underestimating the essentially spontaneous aspect of philosophical thought.

There is a remark that those of us who teach the history of philosophy might make, those who frequently have occasion to come back to the study of the same doctrines and to go ever more deeply into them. A philosophical system seems at first to appear as a complete edifice, expertly designed, where arrangements have been made for the commodious lodging of all problems. In contemplating it in that form we experience an aesthetic joy intensified by a professional satisfaction. Not only, in fact, do we find here order in complexity (an order to which we sometimes like to add our little word as we describe it) but we also have the satisfaction of telling ourselves that we know from whence come the materials and how the building is done. In the problems the philosopher has stated we recognize the questions that were being discussed around him. In the solutions he gives to them we think we recognize, arranged or disarranged, but only slightly modified, the elements of previous or contemporary philosophies. Such a view must have been given to him by this one, another has been suggested by someone else. With what we read, heard and learned we could doubtless reproduce most of what he did. We therefore set to work, we go back to the sources, we weigh the influences, we extract the similitudes, and in the end we distinctly see in the doctrine what we were looking for: a more or less original synthesis of the ideas among which the philosopher lived.

But if we go on constantly renewing contact with the philosopher's thought, we can, by a gradual impregnation, be brought to an entirely different view. I do not say that the work of comparison undertaken at the outset was time lost: without this preliminary effort to recompose a philosophy out of what is other than itself, and to link it up to the conditions which surrounded it, we should perhaps never succeed in grasping what it actually is; for the human mind is so constructed that it cannot begin to understand the new until it has done everything in its power to relate it to the old. But, as we seek to penetrate more fully the philosopher's thought instead of circling around its exterior, his doctrine is transformed for us. In the first place its complication diminishes. Then the various parts fit into one another. Finally the whole is brought together into a single point, which we feel could be ever more closely approached even though there is no hope of reaching it completely.

In this point is something simple, infinitely simple, so extraordinarily simple that the philosopher has never succeeded in saying it. And that is why he went on talking all his life. He could not formulate what he had in mind without feeling himself obliged to correct his formula, then to correct his correction: thus, from theory to theory, correcting when he thought he was completing, what he has accomplished, by a complication which provoked more complication, by developments heaped upon developments, has been to convey with an increasing approximation the simplicity of his original intuition. All the complexity of his doctrine, which would go on *ad infinitum*, is therefore only the incommensurability between his simple intuition and the means at his disposal for expressing it.

What is this intuition? If the philosopher has not been able to give the formula for it, we certainly are not able to do so. But what we shall manage to recapture and to hold is a certain intermediary image between the simplicity of the concrete intuition and the complexity of the abstractions which translate it, a receding and vanishing image, which haunts, unperceived perhaps, the mind of the philosopher, which follows him like his shadow through the ins and outs of his thought and which, if it is not the intuition itself, approaches it much more closely than the conceptual expression, of necessity symbolical, to which the intuition must have recourse in order to furnish 'explanation.' Let us look closely at this shadow: by doing so we shall divine the attitude of the body which projects it. And if we try to imitate this attitude, or better still to assume it ourselves, we shall see as far as it is possible what the philosopher saw.

What first of all characterizes this image is the power of *negation* it possesses. You recall how the demon of Socrates proceeded: it checked the philosopher's will at a given moment and prevented him from acting rather than prescribing what he should do. It seems to me that intuition often behaves in speculative matters like the demon of Socrates in practical life; it is at least in this form that it begins, in this form also that it continues to give the most clear-cut manifestations: it forbids. Faced with currently accepted ideas, theses which seemed evident, affirmations which had up to that time passed as scientific, it whispers into the philosopher's ear the word: *Impossible!* Impossible, even though the facts and the reasons appeared to invite you to think it possible and real and certain. Impossible, because a certain experience, confused perhaps but decisive, speaks to you through my voice, because it is incompatible with the facts cited and the reasons given, and because hence these facts must have been badly observed, these reasonings false. What a strange force this intuitive power of negation is! How is it that the historians of philosophy have not been more greatly struck by it? Is it not obvious that the first step the philosopher takes, when his thought is still faltering and there is nothing definite in his doctrine, is to reject certain things definitively? Later he will be able to make changes in what he affirms; he will vary only slightly what he denies. And if he varies in his affirmations, it will still be in virtue of the power of negation immanent in intuition or in its image. He will have allowed himself lazily to deduce consequences according to the rules of a rectilinear logic; and then suddenly, in the face of his own affirmation he has the same feeling of impossibility that he had in the first place in considering the affirmations of others. Having in fact left the curve of his thought, to follow straight along a tangent, he has become exterior to himself. He returns to himself when he gets back to intuition. Of these departures toward an affirmation and these returns to the primary intuition are constituted the zigzaggings of a doctrine which 'develops,' that is to say which loses itself, finds itself again, and endlessly corrects itself.

Let us get rid of this complication and get back to the simple intuition, or at least to the image which translates it: in so doing we see the doctrine freed of those conditions of time and place upon which it seemed to depend. Doubtless the problems which the philosopher worked upon were the problems which presented themselves in his day; the science he used or criticized was the science of his time; in the theories he expounds one might even find, by looking for them, the ideas of his contemporaries and his predecessors. How could it be otherwise? In order to have the new understood, it must be expressed in terms of the old; and the problems already stated, the solutions provided, the philosophy and science of the times in which he lived, all these have been for each great thinker the material he was obliged to use to give a concrete form to his thought. Not to mention that it has been traditional, from ancient times, to present all philosophy as a complete system, which includes everything one knows. But it would be a strange mistake to take for a constitutive element of doctrine what was only the means of expressing it. Such is the first error to which we are exposed, as I was just saying, when we undertake the study of a system. So many partial resemblances strike us, so many parallels seem to be indicated, so many pressing appeals to our ingenuity and erudition are sent out from all directions, that we are tempted to recompose the philosopher's thought with fragments of ideas gathered here and there, praising him afterwards, of course, for having been able – as we have just shown ourselves to be – to execute a pretty piece of mosaic. But the illusion does not last long, for we soon perceive that in the very places where the philosopher seems to be repeating things already said, he is thinking them in his own way. We then abandon the idea of recomposing; but in so doing we tumble more often than not into another illusion, less serious perhaps but more tenacious than the first. We are inclined to imagine the doctrine – even though it be that of a master – as growing out of earlier philosophies and representing 'a moment of an evolution.' This time, to be sure, we are not completely wrong, for a philosophy resembles an organism rather than an assemblage, and it is still better to speak of evolution in this case than of composition. But this new comparison, in addition to the fact that it attributes more continuity to the history of thought than is really in it, has the disadvantage of keeping our attention fixed upon the external complication of the system and upon what its superficial form allows us to foresee, instead of inviting us to put our finger on the novelty and simplicity of the inner content. A philosopher worthy of the name has never said more than a single thing: and even then it is something he has tried to say, rather than actually said. And he has said only one thing because he has seen only one point: and at that it was not so much a vision as a contact: this contact has furnished an impulse, this impulse a movement, and if this movement, which is as it were a kind of swirling of dust taking a particular form, becomes visible to our eyes only through what it has collected along its way, it is no less true that other bits of dust might as well have been raised and that it would still have been the same whirlwind. Thus a thought which brings something new into the world is of course obliged to manifest itself through the ready-made ideas it comes across and draws into its movement; it seems thus, as it were, relative to the epoch in which the philosopher lived; but that is frequently merely an appearance. The philosopher might have come several centuries earlier; he would have had to deal with another philosophy and another science; he would have given himself other problems; he would have expressed himself by other formulas; not one chapter perhaps of the books he wrote would have been what it is; and nevertheless he would have said the same thing.

Let me take an example. I have appealed to your professional memories: with your permission I am going to recall some of my own. As professor in the Collège de France I devote one of my courses each year to the history of philosophy. In that way I have been able, during several consecutive years, to practice at length upon Berkeley and Spinoza the experiment I have just described. I shall not discuss Spinoza; he would take us too far afield. Nevertheless I know of nothing more instructive than the contrast between the form and the matter of a book like the *Ethics*: on the one hand those tremendous things called Substance, Attribute and Mode, and the formidable array of theorems with the close network of definitions, corollaries and scholia, and that complication of machinery, that power to crush which causes the beginner, in the presence of the *Ethics*, to be struck with admiration and terror as though he were before a battleship of the Dreadnought class; on the other hand, something subtle, very light and almost airy, which flees at one's approach, but which one cannot look at, even from afar, without becoming incapable of attaching oneself to any part whatever of the remainder, even to what is considered essential, even to the distinction between Substance and Attribute, even to the duality of Thought and Extension. What we have behind the heavy mass of concepts of Cartesian and Aristotelian parentage, is that intuition which was Spinoza's, an intuition which no formula, no matter how simple, can be simple enough to express. Let us say, to be content with an approximation, that it is the feeling of a coincidence between the act by which our mind knows truth perfectly, and the operation by which God engenders it; the idea that the 'conversion' of the Alexandrians, when it becomes complete, is indistinguishable from their 'procession,' that when man, sprung from divinity, succeeds in returning to it, he perceives that what he had at first taken to be two opposed movements of coming and going are in fact a single movement – moral experience in this case undertaking to resolve a logical contradiction and to fuse, by an abrupt suppression of Time, the movement of coming with that of going. The closer we get to this original intuition the better we understand that if Spinoza had lived before Descartes he would doubtless have written something other than what he wrote, but that given Spinoza living and writing, we were certain to have Spinozism in any case.

I come to Berkeley, and since it is he whom I take as an example you will not think it amiss that I analyse him in detail: brevity here could only be at the expense of a strict examination of the subject. A mere glance over the work of Berkeley is enough to see that, as if of itself, it resolves into four fundamental theses. The first, which defines a certain idealism and to which is linked up the new theory of vision (although the philosopher had judged it wise to present the latter as independent), the first, I say, would be formulated thus: 'Matter is a cluster of ideas.' The second consists in the claim that abstract and general ideas are merely words: that is nominalism. The third thesis affirms the reality of minds and characterizes them by the will: let us say that it is spiritualism and voluntarism. The last, which we might call theism, posits the existence of God, basing itself principally on the consideration of matter. Now, nothing would be easier than to find these four theses, formulated in practically the same terms, among the contemporaries or predecessors of Berkeley. The fourth is found among the theologians. The third was in Duns Scotus; Descartes said somewhat the same thing. The second fed the controversies of the Middle Ages before becoming an integral part of the philosophy of Hobbes. As to the first, it greatly resembles the 'occasionalism' of Malebranche, the idea and even the formula of which we should already discover in certain texts of Descartes; nor, for that matter had Descartes been the first to point out that dreams have every appearance of reality and that there is nothing in any of our perceptions taken separately which guarantees us the existence of a thing outside us. Thus, with the philosophers of already distant times or even, if we do not care to go back too far, with Descartes and Hobbes to whom Locke might be added, we shall have the elements necessary for the external reconstitution of Berkeley's philosophy: we shall at most leave him his theory of vision, which would then constitute his own individual work and whose originality, reflected through the rest, would give to the doctrine as a whole its original aspect. Let us then take these slices of ancient and modern philosophy, put them in the same bowl, add by way of vinegar and oil a certain aggressive impatience with regard to mathematical dogmatism and the desire, natural in a philosopher bishop, to reconcile reason with faith, mix well and turn it over and over conscientiously, and sprinkle over the whole, like so many savoury herbs, a certain number of aphorisms culled from among the Neo-Platonists: we shall have – if I may be pardoned the expression – a salad which, at a distance, will have certain resemblance to what Berkeley accomplished.

Well, anyone who went about it in this way would be incapable of penetrating Berkeley's thought. I am not speaking of the difficulties and impossibilities which he would come up against in explaining the details: a strange sort of 'nominalism' that was, which ended by raising a number of general ideas to the dignity of eternal essences, immanent in the divine Intelligence! a strange negation of the reality of bodies that which is expressed by a positive theory of the nature of matter, a fertile theory, as far removed as possible from the sterile idealism which tries to assimilate perception to dreaming! What I mean to say is that it is impossible for us to examine Berkeley's philosophy carefully without seeing the four theses we have discovered in it first approach, then penetrate one another, in such a way that each of them seems to become pregnant with the other three, to take on breadth and depth, and become radically distinguished from the earlier or contemporary theories with which one could superficially identify it. Perhaps this second point of view from which the doctrine appears as an organism and not as a mere assemblage, is still not the definitive point of view. It is at least closer to the truth. I cannot go into all the details; but nevertheless I must indicate for at least one or two of the four theses, how any of the others could be extracted from them.

Let us take idealism. It does not consist merely in saying that bodies are ideas. What good would that do? We should indeed be obliged to continue to affirm everything about these ideas that experience has led us to affirm about bodies, and we should simply have substituted one word for another; for Berkeley surely does not think that matter will cease to exist when he has stopped living. What Berkeley's idealism signifies is that matter is coextensive with our representation of it; that it has no interior, no underneath; that it hides nothing, contains nothing; that it possesses neither power nor virtuality of any kind; that it is spread out as mere surface and that it is no more than what it presents to us at any given moment. The word 'idea' ordinarily indicates an existence of this kind, I mean to say a completely realized existence, whose being is indistinguishable from its seeming, while the word 'thing' makes us think of a reality which would be at the same time a reservoir of possibilities; that is why Berkeley prefers to call bodies ideas rather than things. But if we look upon his 'idealism' in that light, we see that it coincides with his 'nominalism'; for the more clearly this second thesis takes shape in the philosopher's mind, the more evidently it is restricted to the negation of general abstract ideas – *abstracted*, that is, *extracted* from matter: it is clear in fact that one cannot extract something from what contains nothing, nor consequently make a perception yield something other than the perception itself. Colour being but colour, resistance being only resistance, you will never find anything in common between resistance and colour, you will never discover in visual data any element shared by the data of touch. If you claim to abstract from the data of either something which will be common to all, you will perceive in examining that something that you are dealing with a word: therein lies the nominalism of Berkeley; but there also, at the same time, is the 'new theory of vision.' If an extension which would be at once visual and tactile is only a word, it is all the more so with an extension which would involve all the senses at once: there again is nominalism, but there too is the refutation of the Cartesian theory of matter. Let us not even talk any more about extension; let us simply note that in view of the structure of language the two expressions 'I have this perception' and 'this perception exists' are synonymous, but that the second, introducing the same word 'existence' into the description of totally different perceptions, invites us to believe that they have something in common between them and to imagine that their diversity conceals a fundamental unity, the unity of a 'substance' which is, in reality, only the word *existence* hypostasised: there you have the whole idealism of Berkeley; and this idealism, as I was saying, is identical with his nominalism. – Let us go on now, with your permission, to the theory of God and the theory of minds. If a body is made of 'ideas' or, in other words, if it is entirely passive and determinate, having neither power nor virtuality, it cannot act on other bodies; and consequently the movements of bodies must be the effect of an active power, which has produced these bodies themselves and which, because of the order which the universe reveals, can only be an intelligent cause. If we are mistaken when under the name of general ideas we set up as realities the names that we have given to groups of objects or perceptions more or less artificially constituted by us on the plane of matter, such is not the case when we think we discover, behind this plane, the divine intentions: the general idea which exists only on the surface and which links body to body is no doubt only a word, but the general idea which exists in depth, relating bodies to God or rather descending from God to bodies, is a reality; and thus the nominalism of Berkeley quite naturally calls for this development of the doctrine as found in the *Siris*, and which has wrongly been considered a Neo-Platonic fantasy; in other words, the idealism of Berkeley is only one aspect of the theory which places God behind all the manifestations of matter. Finally, if God imprints in each one of us perceptions, or as Berkeley says, 'ideas,' the being which gathers up these perceptions, or rather which goes to meet them, is quite the reverse of an idea: it is a will, though one which is constantly limited by divine will. The meeting-place of these two wills is precisely what we call matter. If the *percipi* is pure passivity the *percipere* is pure activity. Human mind, matter, divine mind therefore become terms which we can express only in terms of one another. And the spiritualism of Berkeley is itself found to be only an aspect of any one of the other three theses.

Thus the various parts of the system interpenetrate, as in a living being. But, as I was saying at the beginning, the spectacle of this reciprocal penetration doubtless gives us a more precise idea of the body of the doctrine; it still does not enable us to reach the soul.

We shall get closer to it, if we can reach the mediating *image* referred to above – an image which is almost matter in that it still allows itself to be seen, and almost mind in that it no longer allows itself to be touched – a phantom which haunts us while we turn about the doctrine and to which we must go in order to obtain the decisive signal, the indication of the attitude to take and of the point from which to look. Did the mediating image which takes shape in the mind of the interpreter, as he progresses in his study of the work, exist originally in the same form in the master's thought? If it was not that particular one, it was another, which could belong to a different order of perceptions and have no material resemblance whatsoever to it, but which nevertheless would equal it in value as two translations of the same work in different languages equal one another. Perhaps these two images, perhaps even other images, still equivalent, were present all at once, following the philosopher step by step in procession through the evolutions of his thought. Or perhaps he did not perceive any one of them clearly, being content only at rare intervals to make contact directly with that still more subtle thing, intuition itself; but then we are indeed forced, as interpreters, to re-establish the intermediary image, unless we are prepared to speak of the 'original intuition' as a vague thought and of the 'spirit of the doctrine' as an abstraction, whereas this spirit is as concrete and this intuition as precise as anything in the system.

In Berkeley's case, I think I see two different images and the one which strikes me most is not the one whose complete indication we find in Berkeley himself. It seems to me that Berkeley perceives matter as *a thin transparent film* situated between man and God. It remains transparent as long as the philosophers leave it alone, and in that case God reveals Himself through it. But let the metaphysicians meddle with it, or even common sense in so far as it deals in metaphysics: immediately the film becomes dull, thick and opaque, and forms a screen because such words as Substance, Force, abstract Extension, etc. slip behind it, settle there like a layer of dust, and hinder us from seeing God through the transparency. The image is scarcely indicated by Berkeley himself though he has said in so many words 'that we first raise a dust and then complain we cannot see.' But there is another comparison, often evoked by the philosopher, which is only the auditory transposition of the visual image I have just described: according to this, matter is a language which God speaks to us. That being so, the metaphysics of matter thickening each one of the syllables, marking it off, setting it up as an independent entity, turns our attention away from the meaning to the sound and hinders us from following the divine word. But, whether we attach ourselves to the one or to the other, in either case we are dealing with a simple image that we must keep in view, because if it is not the intuition generating the doctrine, it is immediately derived from it, and approximates it more than any of the theses taken individually, more even than the combination of all of them.

Is it possible for us to recapture this intuition itself? We have just two means of expression, concept and image. It is in concepts that the system develops; it is into an image that it contracts when it is driven back to the intuition from which it comes: so that, if one wishes to go beyond the image by rising above it, one necessarily falls back on concepts, and on concepts more vague, even more general than those from which one started in search of the image and the intuition. Reduced to this form, bottled as it were the moment it comes from the spring, the original intuition will then become superlatively insipid and uninteresting: it will be banal in the extreme. If we were to say for example that Berkeley considers the human soul as partially united with God and partially independent, that it is conscious of itself at every moment as of an imperfect activity which would join a higher activity if there were not, interposed between the two, something which is absolutely passive, we should be expressing all of the original intuition of Berkeley that can be directly translated into concepts, and still we should have something so abstract as to be almost empty. Let us stick to these formulas since we cannot find better ones, but let us try to put a little life into them. Let us take all that the philosopher has written, let us bring back these scattered ideas to the image from which they had descended; and let us raise them, enclosed now in the image, up to the abstract formula enlarged by its absorption of the image and ideas, let us now attach ourselves to this formula and watch it, simple as it is, grow simpler still, all the more simple for our having pushed into it a greater number of things; finally let us rise with it, go up to the point where everything that was given extended in the doctrine contracts in tension: we shall picture to ourselves this time how from this centre of force, which is moreover inaccessible, there springs the impulse which gives the impetus, that is to say the intuition itself. It is from this that the four theses of Berkeley came, because this movement met on its way the ideas and problems the contemporaries of Berkeley were raising. In other times Berkeley would doubtless have formulated other theses; but, the movement being the same, these theses would have been situated in the same way with regard to one another; they would have had the same relationship to one another, like new words of a new sentence through which runs the thread of an old meaning: and it would have been the same philosophy.

The relation of a philosophy to earlier and contemporary philosophies is not, then, what a certain conception of the history of systems would lead us to assume. The philosopher does not take pre-existing ideas in order to recast them into a superior synthesis or combine them with a new idea. One might as well believe that in order to speak we go hunting for words that we string together afterwards by means of a thought. The truth is that above the word and above the sentence there is something much more simple than a sentence or even a word: the meaning, which is less a thing thought than a movement of thought, less a movement than a direction. And just as the impulsion given to the embryonic life determines the division of an original cell into cells which in turn divide until the complete organism is formed, so the characteristic movement of each act of thought leads this thought, by an increasing sub-division of itself, to spread out more and more over the successive planes of the mind until it reaches that of speech. Once there it expresses itself by means of a sentence, that is, by a group of pre-existing elements; but it can almost arbitrarily choose the first elements of the group provided that the others are complementary to them; the same thought is translated just as well into diverse sentences composed of entirely different words, provided these words have the same connection between them. Such is the process of speech. And such also is the operation by which a philosophy is constituted. The philosopher does not start with pre-existing ideas; at most one can say that he arrives at them. And when he gets there the idea thus caught up into the movement of his mind, being animated with a new life like the word which receives its meaning from the sentence, is no longer what it was outside the vortex.

One would find the same kind of relationship between a philosophical system and the whole body of scientific knowledge of the epoch in which the philosopher lived. There is a certain conception of philosophy which requires that all the effort of the philosopher should be to embrace in one large synthesis the results of the particular sciences. Indeed, the philosopher, for a long time, was he who possessed universal knowledge; and today even, when the multiplicity of particular sciences, the diversity and complexity of methods, the enormous mass of facts collected make the accumulation of all human knowledge in a single mind impossible, the philosopher remains the man of universal knowledge, in this sense, that if he can no longer know everything, there is nothing that he should not have put himself in a position to learn. But does it necessarily follow, that his task is to take possession of existing science to bring it to increasing degrees of generality, and to proceed, from condensation to condensation, to what has been called the unification of knowledge? May I be pardoned if I consider it strange that this conception of philosophy is proposed to us in the name of science, out of respect for science: I know of no conception more offensive to science or more injurious to the scientist. Here, if you like, is a man who, over a long period of time, has followed a certain scientific method and laboriously gained his results, who says to us: 'Experience, with the help of reasoning, leads to this point; scientific knowledge begins here, it ends there; such are my conclusions'; and the philosopher would have the right to answer: 'Very well, leave it to me, and I'll show you what I can do with it! The knowledge you bring me unfinished, I shall complete. What you put before me in bits I shall put together. With the same materials, since it is understood that I shall keep to the facts which you have observed, with the same kind of work, since I must restrict myself as you did to induction and deduction, I shall do more and better than you have done.' Truly a very strange pretension! How could the profession of philosopher confer upon him who exercises it the power of advancing farther than science in the same direction as science? That certain scientists are more inclined than others to forge ahead and to generalize their results, more inclined also to turn back and to criticize their methods, that in this particular meaning of the word they should be dubbed philosophers, moreover that each science can and should have its own philosophy thus understood, I am the first to admit. But that particular philosophy is still science, and he who practices it is still a scientist. It is no longer a question, as it was a moment ago, of setting up philosophy as a synthesis of the positive sciences and of claiming, in virtue of the philosopher's mind alone, to raise oneself above science in the generalization of the same facts.

Such a conception of the role of the philosopher would be unfair to science. But how much more unfair to philosophy! Is it not evident that if the scientist stops at a certain point along the road of generalization and synthesis it is because beyond that point objective experience and sure reasoning do not permit us to advance? And hence in claiming to go further in the same direction, should we not be placing ourselves systematically in the arbitrary or at least the hypothetical? To make of philosophy an ensemble of generalities which goes beyond scientific generalization, is to insist that the philosopher be content with the plausible and that probability be sufficient for him. I am perfectly well aware that for most of those who follow our discussions from a distance, our domain is in fact that of the simple possible, at most that of the probable; they would be very much inclined to say that philosophy begins where certitude leaves off. But who among us would like philosophy to be in such a situation? Doubtless everything is not equally verified or verifiable in what a philosophy brings us, and it is the essence of the philosophical method to demand that at many moments, on many points, the mind should take risks. But the philosopher runs these risks only because he has insured himself and because there are things of which he feels himself unshakeably certain. He will make us certain in our turn to the extent that he is able to communicate to us the intuition from whence he draws his strength.

The truth is that philosophy is not a synthesis of particular sciences, and that if it often places itself on the terrain of science, if it sometimes embraces in a simpler vision the objects of science, it is not by intensifying science, it is not by carrying the results of science to a higher degree of generality. There would not be place for two ways of knowing, philosophy and science, if experience did not present itself to us under two different aspects; on the one hand in the form of facts side by side with other facts, which repeat themselves more or less, which can to a certain extent be measured, and which in fact open out in the direction of distinct multiplicity and spatiality; on the other hand in the form of a reciprocal penetration which is pure duration, refractory to law and measurement. In both cases, experience signifies consciousness; but in the first case, consciousness unfolds outward and externalises itself in relation to itself in the exact measure to which it perceives things as external to one another; in the second, it turns back within itself, it takes possession of itself and develops in depth. In thus probing its own depth does it penetrate more deeply into the interior of matter, of life, or reality in general? One could dispute this if consciousness had been superadded to matter as an accident; but I believe I have shown that such a hypothesis, according to the way in which it is generally taken, is absurd or false, self-contradictory or contradicted by the facts. One might still dispute it, if human consciousness, although related to a higher and vaster consciousness, had been put aside, as if man had to stand in a corner of nature like a child being punished. But no! the matter and life which fill the world are equally within us; the forces which work in all things we feel within ourselves; whatever may be the inner essence of what is and what is done, we are of that essence. Let us then go down into our own inner selves: the deeper the point we touch, the stronger will be the thrust which sends us back to the surface. Philosophical intuition is this contact, philosophy is this impetus. Brought back to the surface by an impulsion from the depth, we shall regain contact with science as our thought opens out and disperses. Philosophy then must be able to model itself upon science, and an idea of so-called intuitive origin which could not manage, by dividing itself and subdividing its divisions, to cover the facts observed outwardly and the laws by which science joins them to each other, which would not be capable even of correcting certain generalizations and of rectifying certain observations, would be pure fantasy; it would have nothing in common with intuition. But on the other hand the idea which succeeds in fitting perfectly this dispersion of itself upon the facts and laws, was not obtained by a unification of external experience; for the philosopher did not arrive at unity, he started from it. I am speaking, naturally, of a unity which is at once restricted and relative, like the unity which marks off a living being from the rest of the universe. The process by which philosophy seems to assimilate the results of positive science, like the operation in the course of which a philosophy appears to re-assemble in itself the fragments of earlier philosophies, is not a synthesis but an analysis.

Science is the auxiliary of action. And action aims at a result. The scientific intelligence asks itself therefore what will have to be done in order that a certain desired result be attained, or more generally, what conditions should obtain in order that a certain phenomenon take place. It goes from an arrangement of things to a rearrangement, from a simultaneity to a simultaneity. Of necessity it neglects what happens in the interval; or if it does concern itself with it, it is in order to consider other arrangements in it, still more simultaneities. With methods meant to seize the ready-made, it cannot in general enter into what is being done, it cannot follow the moving reality, adopt the becoming which is the life of things. This last task belongs to philosophy. While the scientist, obliged to take immobile views of movement and to gather repetitions along a path where nothing is repeated, intent also on dividing reality conveniently on successive planes where it is deployed in order to submit it to the action of man, is obliged to use craft with nature, to adopt toward it the wary attitude of an adversary, the philosopher treats nature as a comrade. The rule of science is the one posited by Bacon: obey in order to command. The philosopher neither obeys nor commands; he seeks to be at one with nature. From this point of view, moreover, the essence of philosophy is the spirit of simplicity. Whether we contemplate the philosophical spirit in itself or in its works, whether we compare philosophy to science or one philosophy with other philosophies, we always find that any complication is superficial, that the construction is a mere accessory, synthesis a semblance: the act of philosophising is a simple one.

The more we become imbued with this truth, the more we shall be inclined to take philosophy out of the school and bring it into closer contact with life. No doubt the attitude of common-sense, as it results from the structure of the senses, of intelligence and of language, is nearer to the attitude of science than to that of philosophy. By that I do not mean only that the general categories of our thought are the very categories of science, that the highways traced by our senses across the continuity of the real are those along which science will travel, that perception is a science in the process of being born, science an adult perception, and that ordinary knowledge and scientific knowledge, both destined to prepare our action upon things, are necessarily two visions of a kind, although of unequal precision and range; what I wish particularly to say, is that ordinary knowledge is forced, like scientific knowledge and for the same reasons, to take things in a time broken up into an infinity of particles, pulverized so to speak, where an instant which does not endure follows another equally without duration. Movement is for it a series of positions, change a series of qualities, and becoming, generally, a series of states. It starts from immobility (as though immobility could be anything but an appearance, comparable to the special effect that one moving body produces upon another when both move at the same rate in the same direction), and by an ingenious arrangement of immobilities it recomposes an imitation of movement which it substitutes for movement itself: an operation which is convenient from a practical standpoint but is theoretically absurd, pregnant with all the contradictions, all the pseudo-problems that Metaphysics and Criticism find before them.

But precisely because it is right there that common sense turns its back upon philosophy, all we shall have to do is to have it make a *volte-face* on that point in order to head it again in the direction of philosophical thought. Intuition doubtless admits of many degrees of intensity, and philosophy many degrees of depth; but the mind once brought back to real duration will already be alive with intuitive life and its knowledge of things will already be philosophy. Instead of a discontinuity of moments replacing one another in an infinitely divided time, it will perceive the continuous fluidity of real time which flows along, indivisible. Instead of surface states covering successively some neutral stuff and maintaining with it a mysterious relationship of phenomenon to substance, it will seize upon one identical change which keeps ever lengthening as in a melody where everything is becoming but where the becoming, being itself substantial, has no need of support. No more inert states, no more dead things; nothing but the mobility of which the stability of life is made. A vision of this kind, where reality appears as continuous and indivisible, is on the road which leads to philosophical intuition.

For, in order to reach intuition it is not necessary to transport ourselves outside the domain of the senses and of consciousness. Kant's error was to believe that it was. After having proved by decisive arguments that no dialectical effort will ever introduce us into the beyond and that an effective metaphysics would necessarily be an intuitive metaphysics, he added that we lack this intuition and that this metaphysics is impossible.

It would in fact be so if there were no other time or change than those which Kant perceived and which, moreover, we too must reckon with; for our usual perception cannot get out of time nor grasp anything else than change. But the time in which we are naturally placed, the change we habitually have before us, are a time and change that our senses and our consciousness have reduced to dust in order to facilitate our action upon things. Undo what they have done, bring our perception back to its origins, and we shall have a new kind of knowledge without having been obliged to have recourse to new faculties.

If this knowledge is generalized, speculation will not be the only thing to profit by it. Everyday life can be nourished and illuminated by it. For the world into which our senses and consciousness habitually introduce us is no more than the shadow of itself: and it is as cold as death. Everything in it is arranged for our maximum convenience, but in it, everything is in a present which seems constantly to be starting afresh; and we ourselves, fashioned artificially in the image of a no less artificial universe, see ourselves in the instantaneous, speak of the past as of something done away with, and see in memory a fact strange or in any case foreign to us, an aid given to mind by matter. Let us on the contrary grasp ourselves afresh as we are, in a present which is thick, and furthermore, elastic, which we can stretch indefinitely backward by pushing the screen which masks us from ourselves farther and farther away; let us grasp afresh the external world as it really is, not superficially, in the present, but in depth, with the immediate past crowding upon it and imprinting upon it its impetus; let us in a word become accustomed to see all things *sub specie durationis*: immediately in our galvanized perception what is taut becomes relaxed, what is dormant awakens, what is dead comes to life again. Satisfactions which art will never give save to those favoured by nature and fortune, and only then upon rare occasions, philosophy thus understood will offer to all of us, at all times, by breathing life once again into the phantoms which surround us and by revivifying us. In so doing philosophy will become complementary to science in practice as well as in speculation. With its applications which aim only at the convenience of existence, science gives us the promise of well-being, or at most, of pleasure. But philosophy could already give us joy.

The Perception of Change

First lecture

My first words are words of thanks to the University of Oxford for the great honour she has done me in inviting me to address her. I have always thought of Oxford as one of the few sanctuaries where, reverently maintained, passed on by each generation to the next, the warmth and radiance of ancient thought are preserved. But I also know that this attachment to antiquity does not prevent your University from being very modern and very much alive. More especially in what concerns philosophy, am I struck to see with what profundity and what originality the ancient philosophers are studied here (did not one of your most eminent masters only recently touch up the interpretation of the Platonic theory of Ideas on its essential points?); and I am also struck, on the other hand, by the fact that Oxford is in the vanguard of the philosophical movement with the two extreme conceptions of the nature of truth: integral rationalism and pragmatism. This alliance of past and present is fruitful in all fields, nowhere more so than in philosophy. To be sure, we have something new to do, and perhaps the moment has come to be fully alive to it; but the fact that it is new does not mean that it must be revolutionary. Let us rather study the ancients, become imbued with their spirit and try to do, as far as possible, what they themselves would be doing were they living among us. Endowed with our knowledge (I do not refer so much to our mathematics and physics, which would perhaps not radically alter their way of thinking, but especially our biology and psychology), they would arrive at very different results from those they obtained. That is what particularly strikes me in the problem I have undertaken to deal with here, that of change.

I chose it, because I consider it fundamental, and because I believe that if one were convinced of the reality of change and if one made an effort to grasp it, everything would become simplified, philosophical difficulties, considered insurmountable, would fall away. Not only would philosophy gain by it, but our everyday life – I mean the impression things make upon us and the reaction of our intelligence, our sensibility and our will upon things – would perhaps be transformed and, as it were, transfigured. The point is that usually we look at change but we do not see it. We speak of change, but we do not think about it. We say that change exists, that everything changes, that change is the very law of things: yes, we say it and we repeat it; but those are only words, and we reason and philosophise as though change did not exist. In order to think change and see it, there is a whole veil of prejudices to brush aside, some of them artificial, created by philosophical speculation, the others natural to common sense. I believe we shall end by coming to an agreement about them, and shall thus form a philosophy in which everyone will collaborate, upon which everyone will be able to agree. That is why I should like to fix two or three points upon which it seems to me agreement has already been reached; it will gradually be extended to the rest of them. The first lecture therefore will deal less with change itself than with the general characteristics of a philosophy attached to the intuition of change.

Here, first of all, is a point upon which everyone will agree. If the senses and consciousness had an unlimited scope, if in the double direction of matter and mind the faculty of perceiving was indefinite, one would not need to conceive any more than to reason. Conceiving is a make-shift when perception is not granted us, and reasoning is done in order to fill up the gaps of perception or to extend its scope. I do not deny the utility of abstract and general ideas – any more than I question the value of bank-notes. But just as the note is only a promise of gold, so a conception has value only through the eventual perceptions it represents. It is not, of course, merely a question of the perception of a thing, or a quality, or a state. One can conceive an order, a harmony, and more generally a *truth*, which then becomes a *reality*. I say that we agree on this point. Everyone could see for himself, in fact, that the most ingeniously assembled conceptions and the most learnedly constructed reasonings collapse like a house of cards the moment the fact – a single fact really seen – collides with these conceptions and these reasonings. There is not a single metaphysician, moreover, not one theologian, who is not ready to affirm that a perfect being is one who knows all things intuitively without having to go through reasoning, abstraction and generalization. There is no difficulty therefore about the first point.

And there will not be any more about the second, which we come to now. The insufficiency of our faculties of perception – an insufficiency verified by our faculties of conception and reasoning – is what has given birth to philosophy. The history of doctrines attests it. The conceptions of the earliest Greek thinkers were certainly very close to perception, since it was by the transformations of a sensible element like water, air or fire, that they completed the immediate sensation. But from the time the philosophers of the school of Elea, criticizing the idea of transformation, had shown or thought they had shown the impossibility of keeping so close to the sense-data, philosophy started off along the road it has since travelled, the road leading to a 'supra-sensible' world: one was to explain things henceforth with pure 'ideas.' It is true that for the ancient philosophers the intelligible world was situated outside and above the one our senses and consciousness perceive: our faculties of perception showed us only shadows projected in time and space by immutable and eternal Ideas. For the moderns, on the contrary, these essences are constitutive of sensible things themselves; they are veritable substances, of which phenomena are only the surface covering. But all of them, ancient and modern, are agreed in seeing in philosophy a substitution of the concept for the percept. They all appeal from the insufficiency of our senses and consciousness to the faculties of the mind no longer perceptive, I mean to the functions of abstraction, generalization and reasoning.

On the second point we can therefore be agreed. I come then to the third, which, I imagine, will not occasion any discussion either.

If such is really the philosophical method, there is not, there cannot be a philosophy as there is a science; on the contrary there will always be as many different philosophies as there are original thinkers. How could it be otherwise? No matter how abstract a conception may be it always has its starting point in a perception. The intellect combines and separates; it arranges, disarranges and co-ordinates; it does not create.

It must have a matter, and this matter can only reach it through the senses or consciousness. A philosophy which constructs or completes reality with pure ideas will therefore only be substituting for or adding to our concrete perceptions as a whole, some particular one of them it has elaborated, thinned down, refined and thereby converted into an abstract and general idea. But there will always be something arbitrary in its choice of that privileged perception, for positive science has taken for itself all that is incontestably common to different things; or in other words *quantity*, and all that remains for philosophy therefore is the domain of *quality*, where everything is heterogeneous to everything else, and where a part will never represent the whole except in virtue of a contestable if not arbitrary decree. One can always oppose other decrees to this one. And many different philosophies will spring up, armed with different concepts. They will struggle indefinitely with one another.

Here, then, is the question which arises, and which I consider essential. Since any attempt at purely conceptual philosophy calls forth antagonistic efforts, and since, in the field of pure dialectics there is no system to which one cannot oppose another, should we remain in that field or (without, of course, ceasing to exercise our faculties of conception and reasoning), ought we not rather return to perception, getting it to expand and extend? I was saying that it is the insufficiency of natural perception which has driven philosophers to complete perception by conception – the latter having as its function to fill in the spaces between the data of the senses or of consciousness and in that way to unify and systematize our knowledge of things. But the examination of doctrines shows us that the faculty of conceiving, as it advances in this work of integration, is forced to eliminate from the real a great number of qualitative differences, to extinguish in part our perceptions, and to weaken our concrete vision of the universe. For the very reason that each philosophy is led, willy-nilly, to proceed in this way, it gives rise to opposing philosophies, each of which picks up something of what the other has dropped. The method, therefore, goes contrary to the purpose: it should in theory extend and complete perception; it is obliged in fact to require that many perceptions stand aside so that some one of them may become representative of the others. – But suppose that instead of trying to rise above our perception of things we were to plunge into it for the purpose of deepening and widening it. Suppose that we were to insert our will into it, and that this will, expanding, were to expand our vision of things. We should obtain this time a philosophy where nothing in the data of the senses or consciousness would be sacrificed: no quality, no aspect of the real would be substituted for the rest ostensibly to explain it. But above all we should have a philosophy to which one could not oppose others, for it would have left nothing outside of itself that other doctrines could pick up; it would have taken everything. It would have taken everything that is given, and even more, for the senses and consciousness, urged on by this philosophy to an exceptional effort, would have given it more than they furnish naturally. To the multiplicity of systems contending with one another, armed with different concepts, would succeed the unity of a doctrine capable of reconciling all thinkers in the same perception – a perception which moreover would grow ever larger, thanks to the combined effort of philosophers in a common direction.

It will be said that this enlarging is impossible. How can one ask the eyes of the body, or those of the mind, to see more than they see? Our attention can increase precision, clarify and intensify; it cannot bring forth in the field of perception what was not there in the first place. That's the objection. – It is refuted in my opinion by experience. For hundreds of years, in fact, there have been men whose function has been precisely to see and to make us see what we do not naturally perceive. They are the artists.

What is the aim of art if not to show us, in nature and in the mind, outside of us and within us, things which did not explicitly strike our senses and our consciousness? The poet and the novelist who express a mood certainly do not create it out of nothing; they would not be understood by us if we did not observe within ourselves, up to a certain point, what they say about others. As they speak, shades of emotion and thought appear to us which might long since have been brought out in us but which remained invisible; just like the photographic image which has not yet been plunged into the bath where it will be revealed. The poet is this revealing agent. But nowhere is the function of the artist shown as clearly as in that art which gives the most important place to imitation, I mean painting. The great painters are men who possess a certain vision of things which has or will become the vision of all men. A Corot, a Turner – not to mention others – have seen in nature many an aspect that we did not notice. Shall it be said that they have not seen but created, that they have given us products of their imagination, that we adopt their inventions because we like them and that we get pleasure from looking at nature through the image the great painters have traced for us? It is true to a certain extent; but, if it were only that, why should we say of certain works – those of the masters – that they are true? Where would the difference be between great art and pure fancy? If we reflect deeply upon what we feel as we look at a Turner or a Corot, we shall find that, if we accept them and admire them, it is because we had already perceived something of what they show us. But we had perceived without seeing. It was, for us, a brilliant and vanishing vision, lost in the crowd of those visions, equally brilliant and equally vanishing, which become overcast in our ordinary experience like 'dissolving views' and which constitute, by their reciprocal interference, the pale and colourless vision of things that is habitually ours. The painter has isolated it; he has fixed it so well on the canvas that henceforth we shall not be able to help seeing in reality what he himself saw.

Art would suffice then to show us that an extension of the faculties of perceiving is possible. But how does this extension work? – Let us notice that the artist has always been considered an 'idealist.' We mean by that that he is less preoccupied than ourselves with the positive and material side of life. He is, in the real sense of the word, 'absent-minded.' Why then, being detached from reality to a greater degree, does he manage to see in it more things? We should not understand why if the vision we ordinarily have of external objects and of ourselves were not a vision which we had been obliged to narrow and drain by our attachment to reality, our need for living and acting. As a matter of fact, it would be easy to show that the more we are preoccupied with living, the less we are inclined to contemplate, and that the necessities of action tend to limit the field of vision. I cannot go into a demonstration of this point; I am of the opinion that an entirely new light would illuminate many psychological and psycho-physiological questions if we recognized that distinct perception is merely cut, for the purposes of practical existence, out of a wider canvas. In psychology and elsewhere, we like to go from the part to the whole, and our customary system of explanation consists in reconstructing ideally our mental life with simple elements, then in supposing that the combination of these elements has really produced our mental life. If things happened this way, our perception would as a matter of fact be inextensible; it would consist of the assembling of certain specific materials, in a given quantity, and we should never find anything more in it than what had been put there in the first place.

But the facts, taken as they are, without any mental reservation about providing a mechanical explanation of the mind, suggest an entirely different interpretation. They show us, in normal psychological life, a constant effort of the mind to limit its horizon, to turn away from what it has a material interest in not seeing. Before philosophising one must live; and life demands that we put on blinders, that we look neither to the right, nor to the left nor behind us, but straight ahead in the direction we have to go. Our knowledge, far from being made up of a gradual association of simple elements, is the effect of a sudden dissociation: from the immensely vast field of our virtual knowledge, we have selected, in order to make it into actual knowledge, everything which concerns our action upon things; we have neglected the rest. The brain seems to have been constructed with a view to this work of selection. That could easily be shown by the way in which the memory works. Our past, as we shall see in our next lecture, is necessarily automatically preserved. It survives complete. But our practical interest is to thrust it aside, or at least to accept of it only what can more or less usefully illuminate and complete the situation in the present. The brain serves to bring about this choice: it actualises the useful memories, it keeps in the lower strata of the consciousness those which are of no use. One could say as much for perception. The auxiliary of action, it isolates that part of reality as a whole that interests us; it shows us less the things themselves than the use we can make of them. It classifies, it labels them beforehand; we scarcely look at the object, it is enough for us to know to which category it belongs. But now and then, by a lucky accident, men arise whose senses or whose consciousness are less adherent to life. Nature has forgotten to attach their faculty of perceiving to their faculty of acting. When they look at a thing, they see it for itself, and not for themselves. They do not perceive simply with a view to action; they perceive in order to perceive – for nothing, for the pleasure of doing so. In regard to a certain aspect of their nature, whether it be their consciousness or one of their senses, they are born *detached*; and according to whether this detachment is that of a certain particular sense, or of consciousness, they are painters or sculptors, musicians or poets. It is therefore a much more direct vision of reality that we find in the different arts; and it is because the artist is less intent on utilizing his perception that he perceives a greater number of things.

Well, what nature does from time to time, by distraction, for certain privileged individuals, could not philosophy on such a matter attempt, in another sense and another way, for everyone? Would not the role of philosophy under such circumstances be to lead us to a completer [*sic*] perception of reality by means of a certain displacement of our attention? It would be a question of *turning* this attention *aside* from the part of the universe which interests us from a practical viewpoint and *turning it back* toward what serves no practical purpose. This conversion of the attention would be philosophy itself.

At first glance it would seem that this has long since been done. More than one philosopher has in fact said that in order to philosophise he had to be detached, and that speculation was the reverse of action. We were speaking a few moments ago of the Greek philosophers: not one of them expressed the idea more forcefully than Plotinus. 'All action,' he said (and he even added 'all fabrication') 'weakens contemplation.'

And, faithful to the spirit of Plato, he thought that the discovery of truth demanded a conversion of the mind, which breaks away from the appearances here below and attaches itself to the realities above: 'Let us flee to our beloved homeland!' – But as you see, it was a question of 'fleeing.' More precisely, for Plato and for all those who understand metaphysics in that way, breaking away from life and converting one's attention consisted in transporting oneself immediately into a world different from the one we inhabit, in developing other faculties of perception than the senses and consciousness. They did not believe that this education of the attention might most frequently consist in removing its blinders, in freeing it from the contraction that it is accustomed to by the demands of life. They were not of the opinion that the metaphysician, for at least half of his speculations, should continue to look at what everyone looks at: no, he had always to turn toward something else. That is why they invariably call upon faculties of vision other than those we constantly exercise in the knowledge of the external world and of ourselves.

And precisely because he disputed the existence of these transcendent faculties, Kant believed metaphysics to be impossible. One of the most profound and important ideas in the *Critique of Pure Reason* is this: if metaphysics is possible, it is through a vision and not through a dialectic. Dialectics leads to contrary philosophies; it demonstrates the thesis as well as the antithesis of antinomies. Only a superior intuition (which Kant calls an 'intellectual' intuition), that is, a *perception* of metaphysical reality, would enable metaphysics to be constituted. The most obvious result of the Kantian *Critique* is thus to show that one could only penetrate into the beyond by a vision, and that a doctrine has value in this domain only to the extent that it contains perception: take this perception, analyse it, recompose it, turn it round and round in all directions, cause it to undergo the most subtle operations of the highest intellectual chemistry, you will never get from your crucible anything more than you have put into it; as much vision as you have put into it, just so much will you find; and reasoning will not have made you go one step *beyond* what you had perceived in the first place. That is what Kant brought out so clearly and that, it seems to me, is the greatest service he rendered to speculative philosophy. He definitively established that, if metaphysics is possible, it can be so only through an effort of intuition. – Only, having proved that intuition alone would be capable of giving us a metaphysics, he added: this intuition is impossible.

Why did he consider it impossible? Precisely because he pictured a vision of the kind – I mean a vision of reality 'in itself' – that Plotinus had imagined, as those who have appealed to metaphysical intuition have imagined it. By that they all understood a faculty of knowing which would differ radically from consciousness as well as from the senses, which would even be orientated in the opposite direction. They have all believed that to break away from practical life was to turn one's back upon it.

Why did they believe that? Why did Kant, their adversary, share their mistake? How is it they one and all had this conception even if they drew opposite conclusions from it – they constructing a metaphysics, and he declaring metaphysics impossible?

They believed it because they imagined that our senses and consciousness, as they function in everyday life, make us grasp movement directly. They believed that by our senses and consciousness, working as they usually work, we actually perceive the change which takes place in things and in ourselves. Then, as it is incontestable that in following the usual data of our senses and consciousness we arrive in the speculative order at insoluble contradictions, they concluded that contradiction was inherent in change itself and that in order to avoid this contradiction one had to get out of the sphere of change and lift oneself above Time. Such is the position taken by the metaphysician as well as by those who, along with Kant, deny the possibility of metaphysics.

Metaphysics, as a matter of fact, was born of the arguments of Zeno of Elea on the subject of change and movement. It was Zeno who, by drawing attention to the absurdity of what he called movement and change, led the philosophers – Plato first and foremost – to seek the true and coherent reality in what does not change. And it is because Kant believed that our senses and consciousness are in fact exerted in a real Time, that is, in a Time which changes continuously, in a duration which endures; it is because, on the other hand, he took into account the relativity of the usual data of our senses and consciousness (a relativity which he laid down, furthermore, long before the transcendent conclusion of his endeavour that he considered metaphysics impossible without an entirely different kind of vision from that of the senses and consciousness – a vision, moreover, no trace of which he found in man).

But if we could prove that what was considered as movement and change by Zeno first, and then by metaphysicians in general, is neither change nor movement, that of change they retained what does not change, and of movement what does not move, that they took for an immediate and complete perception of movement and change a crystallization of this perception, a solidification with an eye to practice – and if we could show on the other hand, that what Kant took for time itself was a time which neither flows nor changes nor endures – then, in order to avoid such contradictions as those which Zeno pointed out and to separate our everyday knowledge from the relativity to which Kant considered it condemned, we should not have to get outside of time (we are already outside of it!), we should not have to free ourselves of change (we are already only too free of it!); on the contrary, what we should have to do is to grasp change and duration in their original mobility. Then we should not only see many difficulties drop away one by one, and more than one problem disappear; but through the extension and revivification of our faculty of perceiving, perhaps also (though for the moment it is not a question of rising to such heights) through a prolongation which privileged souls will give to intuition, we should re-establish continuity in our knowledge as a whole – a continuity which

The Possible and the Real[2]

[handwritten annotations: "Add to open-ended unfinalized, (ADD UNPREDICTABLE)" with circled "177" and arrow pointing to title]

I should like to come back to a subject on which I have already spoken, the continuous creation of unforeseeable novelty which seems to be going on in the universe. As far as I am concerned, I feel I am experiencing it constantly. No matter how I try to imagine in detail what is going to happen to me, still how inadequate, how abstract and stilted is the thing I have imagined in comparison to what actually happens! The realization brings along with it an unforeseeable nothing which changes everything. For example, I am to be present at a gathering; I know what people I shall find there, around what table, in what order, to discuss what problem. But let them come, be seated and chat as I expected, let them say what I was sure they would say: the whole gives me an impression at once novel and unique, as if it were but now designed at one original stroke by the hand of an artist. Gone is the image I had conceived of it, a mere prearrangeable juxtaposition of things already known! I agree that the picture has not the artistic value of a Rembrandt or a Velasquez: yet it is just as unexpected and, in this sense, quite as original. It will be alleged that I did not know the circumstances in detail, that I could not control the persons in question, their gestures, their attitudes, and that if the thing as a whole provided me with something new it was because they produced additional factors. But I have the same impression of novelty before the unrolling of my inner life. I feel it more vividly than ever, before the action I willed and of which I was sole master. If I deliberate before acting, the moments of deliberation present themselves to my consciousness like the successive sketches a painter makes of his picture, each one unique of its kind; and no matter whether the act would no longer be hypothetical and constructed, but experienced and lived. Is a work of this kind possible? That is what we shall seek to determine, at least as far as the knowledge of our surroundings is concerned, in our second lecture.

Second lecture

You gave me such sustained attention yesterday that you must not be surprised if I am tempted to take advantage of it today. I am going to ask you to make a strenuous effort to put aside some of the artificial schema we interpose unknowingly between reality and us. What is required is that we should break with certain habits of thinking and perceiving that have become natural to us. We must return to the direct perception of change and mobility. Here is an immediate result of this effort. *We shall think of all change, all movement, as being absolutely indivisible.*

Let us begin with movement. I have my hand at point *A*. I move it over to point *B*, traversing the interval *AB*. I say that this movement from *A* to *B* is by nature simple.

But of this each one of us has the immediate sensation. No doubt while we are moving our hand from *A* to *B* we say to ourselves that we could stop it at an intermediary point, but in that case we should not have to do with the same movement. There would no longer be a single movement from *A* to *B*; there would be, by hypothesis, two movements, with an interval. Neither from within, through the muscular sense, nor from without through sight, should we still have the same perception. If I leave my movement from *A* to *B* as it is, I feel it undivided and must declare it to be indivisible.

It is true that, when I watch my hand going from *A* to *B* and describing the interval *AB*, I say: 'The interval *AB* can be divided into as many parts as I wish, therefore the movement from A to B can be divided into as many parts as I like, since this movement is applied exactly upon this interval.' Or again: 'At each instant of its trajection, the mobile passes through a certain point, therefore one can distinguish in the movement as many stages as one likes, therefore the movement is infinitely divisible.' But let us reflect for a moment. How could the movement *be applied upon* the space it traverses? How can something moving coincide with something immobile? How could the moving object *be* in a point of its trajectory passage? *It passes through*, or in other terms, it *could be there*. It would be there if it stopped; but if it should stop there, it would no longer be the same movement we were dealing with. It is always by a single bound that a passing is completed, when there is no break in the passage. The bound may last a few seconds, or days, months, years: it matters little. The moment it is one single bound, it is indecomposable. Only, once the passage is effected, as the trajectory is space and space is indefinitely divisible, we imagine that movement itself is indefinitely divisible. We like to imagine it because, in a movement, it is not the change of position which interests us, it is the positions themselves, the one the movement has left, the one it will take, the one it would take if it stopped on the way. We need immobility, and the more we succeed in imagining movement as coinciding with the immobilities of the points of space through which it passes, the better we think we understand it. To tell the truth, there never is real immobility, if we understand by that an absence of movement. Movement is reality itself, and what we call immobility is a certain state of things analogous to that produced when two trains move at the same speed, in the same direction, on parallel tracks: each of the two trains is then immovable to the travellers seated in the other. But a situation of this kind which, after all, is exceptional, seems to us to be the regular and normal situation, because it is what permits us to act upon things and also permits things to act upon us: the travellers in the two trains can hold out their hands to one another through the door and talk to one another only if they are 'immobile,' that is to say, if they are going in the same direction at the same speed. 'Immobility' being the prerequisite for our action, we set it up as a reality, we make of it an absolute, and we see in movement something which is superimposed. Nothing is more legitimate in practice. But when we transport this habit of mind into the domain of speculation, we fail to recognize the true reality, we deliberately create insoluble problems, we close our eyes to what is most living in the real.

I need not recall the arguments of Zeno of Elea. They all involve the confusion of movement with the space covered, or at least the conviction that one can treat movement as one treats space, divide it without taking account of its articulations. Achilles, they say, will never overtake the tortoise he is pursuing, for when he arrives at the point where the tortoise was the latter will have had time to go further, and so on indefinitely. Philosophers have refuted this argument in numerous ways, and ways so difficult that each of these refutations deprives the others of the right to be considered definitive. There would have been, nevertheless, a very simple means of making short work of the difficulty: that would have been to question Achilles. For since Achilles finally catches up to the tortoise and even passes it, he must know better than anyone else how he goes about it. The ancient philosopher who demonstrated the possibility of movement by walking was right: his only mistake was to make the gesture without adding a commentary. Suppose then we ask Achilles to comment on his race: here, doubtless, is what he will answer: 'Zeno insists that I go from the point where I am to the point the tortoise has left, from that point to the next point it has left, etc., etc.; that is his procedure for making me run. But I go about it otherwise. I take a first step, then a second, and so on: finally, after a certain number of steps, I take a last one by which I skip ahead of the tortoise. I thus accomplish a series of indivisible acts. My course is the series of these acts. You can distinguish its parts by the number of steps it involves. But you have not the right to disarticulate it according to another law, or to suppose it articulated in another way. To proceed as Zeno does is to admit that the race can be arbitrarily broken up like the space which has been covered; it is to believe that the passage is in reality applied to the trajectory; it is making movement and immobility coincide and consequently confusing one with the other.'

But that is precisely what our usual method consists in. We argue about movement as though it were made of immobilities and, when we look at it, it is with immobilities that we reconstitute it. Movement for us is a position, then another position, and so on indefinitely. We say, it is true, that there must be something else, and that from one position to another there is the *passage* by which the interval is cleared. But as soon as we fix our attention on this passage, we immediately make of it a series of positions, even though we still admit that between two successive positions one must indeed assume a passage. We put this passage off indefinitely the moment we have to consider it. We admit that it exists, we give it a name; that is enough for us: once that point has been satisfactorily settled we turn to the positions preferring to deal with them alone. We have an instinctive fear of those difficulties which the vision of movement as movement would arouse in our thought; and quite rightly, once we have loaded movement down with immobilities. If movement is not everything, it is nothing; and if to begin with we have supposed that immobility can be a reality, movement will slip through our fingers when we think we have it.

I have spoken of movement; but I could say the same for any change whatever. All real change is an indivisible change. We like to treat it as a series of distinct states which form, as it were, a line in time. That is perfectly natural. If change is continuous in us and also in things, on the other hand, in order that the uninterrupted change which each of us calls 'me' may act upon the uninterrupted change that we call a 'thing,' these two changes must find themselves, with regard to one another, in a situation like that of the two trains referred to above. We say, for example, that an object changes colour, and that change here consists in a series of shades which would be the constitutive elements of change and which, themselves, would not change. But in the first place, if each shade has any objective existence at all, it is an infinitely rapid oscillation, it is change. And in the second place, the perception we have of it, to the extent that it is subjective, is only an isolated, abstract aspect of the general state of our person, and this state as a whole is constantly changing and causing this so-called invariable perception to participate in its change; in fact, there is no perception which is not constantly being modified. So that colour, outside of us, is mobility itself, and our own person is also mobility. But the whole mechanism of our perception of things, like the mechanism of our action upon things, has been regulated in such a way as to bring about, between the external and the internal mobility, a situation comparable to that of our two trains – more complicated, perhaps, but of the same kind: when the two changes, that of the object and that of the subject, take place under particular conditions, they produce the particular appearance that we call a 'state.' And once in possession of 'states,' our mind recomposes change with them. I repeat, there is nothing more natural: the breaking up of change into states enables us to act upon things, and it is useful in a practical sense to be interested in the states rather than in the change itself. But what is favourable to action in this case would be fatal to speculation. If you imagine a change as being really composed of states, you at once cause insoluble metaphysical problems to arise. They deal only with appearances. You have closed your eyes to true reality.

I shall not press the point. Let each of us undertake the experiment, let him give himself the direct vision of a change, of a movement: he will have a feeling of absolute indivisibility. I come then to the second point, closely allied to the first. *There are changes, but there are underneath the change no things which change: change has no need of a support. There are movements, but there is no inert or invariable object which moves: movement does not imply a mobile.*[5]

It is difficult to picture things in this way, because the sense 'par excellence' is the sense of sight, and because the eye has developed the habit of separating, in the visual field, the relatively invariable figures which are then supposed to change place without changing form, movement is taken as super-added to the mobile as an accident. It is, in fact, useful to have to deal in daily life with objects which are stable and, as it were, responsible, to which one can address oneself as to persons. The sense of sight contrives to take things in this way: as an advance-guard for the sense of touch, it prepares our action upon the external world. But we already have less difficulty in perceiving movement and change as independent realities if we appeal to the sense of hearing. Let us listen to a melody, allowing ourselves to be lulled by it: do we not have the clear perception of a movement which is not attached to a mobile, of a change without anything changing? This change is enough, it is the thing itself. And even if it takes time, it is still indivisible; if the melody stopped sooner it would no longer be the same sonorous whole, it would be another, equally indivisible. We have, no doubt, a tendency to divide it and to picture, instead of the uninterrupted continuity of melody, a juxtaposition of distinct notes. But why? Because we are thinking of the discontinuous series of efforts we should be making to recompose approximately the sound heard if we were doing the singing, and also because our auditory perception has acquired the habit of absorbing visual images. We therefore listen to the melody through the vision which an orchestra-leader would have of it as he watched its score. We picture notes placed next to one another upon an imaginary piece of paper. We think of a keyboard upon which someone is playing, of the bow going up and down, of the musicians, each one playing his part along with the others. If we do not dwell on these spatial images, pure change remains, sufficient unto itself, in no way divided, in no way attached to a 'thing' which changes.

Let us come back, then, to the sense of sight. In further concentrating our attention upon it we perceive that even here movement does not demand a vehicle nor change a substance in the ordinary meaning of the word. A suggestion of this vision of material things already comes to us from physical science. The more it progresses the more it resolves matter into actions moving through space, into movements dashing back and forth in a constant vibration so that mobility becomes reality itself. No doubt science begins by assigning a support to this mobility. But as it advances, the support recedes; masses are pulverized into molecules, molecules into atoms, atoms into electrons or corpuscles: finally, the support assigned to movement appears merely as a convenient schema – a simple concession on the part of the scholar to the habits of our visual imagination. But there is no need to go so far. What is the 'mobile' to which our eye attaches movement as to a vehicle? Simply a coloured spot which we know perfectly well amounts, in itself, to a series of extremely rapid vibrations. This alleged movement of a thing is in reality only a movement of movements.

But nowhere is the *substantiality* of change so visible, so palpable as in the domain of the inner life. Difficulties and contradictions of every kind to which the theories of personality have led come from our having imagined, on the one hand, a series of distinct psychological states, each one invariable, which would produce the variations of the ego by their very succession, and on the other hand an ego, no less invariable, which would serve as support for them. How could this unity and this multiplicity meet? How, without either of them having duration – the first because change is something superadded, the second because it is made up of elements which do not change – how could they constitute an ego which endures? But the truth is that there is neither a rigid, immovable substratum nor distinct states passing over it like actors on a stage. There is simply the continuous melody of our inner life – a melody which is going on and will go on, indivisible, from the beginning to the end of our conscious existence. Our personality is precisely that.

This indivisible continuity of change is precisely what constitutes true duration. I cannot here enter into the detailed examination of a question I have dealt with elsewhere. I shall confine myself therefore to saying, in reply to those for whom this 'real duration' is something inexpressible and mysterious, that it is the clearest thing in the world: *real duration* is what we have always called time, but time perceived as indivisible. That *time* implies succession I do not deny. But that succession is first presented to our consciousness, like the distinction of a 'before' and 'after' set side by side, is what I cannot admit. When we listen to a melody we have the purest impression of succession we could possibly have – an impression as far removed as possible from that of simultaneity – and yet it is the very continuity of the melody and the impossibility of breaking it up which make that impression upon us. If we cut it up into distinct notes, into so many 'befores' and 'afters,' we are bringing spatial images into it and impregnating the succession with simultaneity: in space, and only in space, is there a clear-cut distinction of parts external to one another. I recognize moreover that it is in spatialised time that we ordinarily place ourselves. We have no interest in listening to the uninterrupted humming of life's depths. And yet, that is where real duration is. Thanks to it, the more or less lengthy changes we witness within us and in the external world, take place in a single identical time.

Thus, whether it is a question of the internal or the external, of ourselves or of things, reality is mobility itself. That is what I was expressing when I said that there is change, but that there are not things which change.

Before the spectacle of this universal mobility there may be some who will be seized with dizziness. They are accustomed to terra firma; they cannot get used to the rolling and pitching. They must have 'fixed' points to which they can attach thought and existence. They think that if everything passes, nothing exists; and that if reality is mobility, it has already ceased to exist at the moment one thinks it – it eludes thought. The material world, they say, is going to disintegrate, and the mind will drown in the torrent-like flow of things. – Let them be reassured! Change, if they consent to look directly at it without an interposed veil, will very quickly appear to them to be the most substantial and durable thing possible. Its solidity is infinitely superior to that of a fixity which is only an ephemeral arrangement between mobilities. I have come, in fact, to the third point to which I should like to draw your attention.

It is this: if change is real and even constitutive of reality, we must envisage the past quite differently from what we have been accustomed to doing through philosophy and language. We are inclined to think of our past as inexistent, and philosophers encourage this natural tendency in us. For them and for us the present alone exists by itself: if something of the past does survive it can only be because of help given it by the present, because of some act of charity on the part of the present, in short – to get away from metaphor – by the intervention of a certain particular function called memory, whose role is presumed to be to preserve certain parts of the past, for which exception is made, by storing them away in a kind of box. – This is a profound mistake! A useful one, I admit, perhaps necessary to action, but fatal to speculation. One could find in it, 'in a nutshell' as you say, most of the illusions capable of vitiating philosophical thought.

Let us reflect for a moment on this 'present' which alone is considered to have existence. What precisely is the present? If it is a question of the present – I mean, of a mathematical instant which would be to time what the mathematical point is to the line – it is clear that such an instant is a pure abstraction, an aspect of the mind; it cannot have real existence. You could never create time out of such instants any more than you could make a line out of mathematical points. Even if it does exist, how could there be an instant anterior to it? The two instants could not be separated by an interval of time since, by hypothesis, you reduce time to a juxtaposition of instants. Therefore they would not be separated by anything, and consequently they would be only one: two mathematical points which touch are identical. But let us put such subtleties aside. Our consciousness tells us that when we speak of our present we are thinking of a certain interval of duration. What duration? It is impossible to fix it exactly, as it is something rather elusive. My present, at this moment, is the sentence I am pronouncing. But it is so because I want to limit the field of my attention to my sentence. This attention is something that can be made longer or shorter, like the interval between the two points of a compass. For the moment, the points are just far enough apart to reach from the beginning to the end of my sentence; but if the fancy took me to spread them further my present would embrace, in addition to my last sentence, the one that preceded it: all I should have had to do is to adopt another punctuation. Let us go further: an attention which could be extended indefinitely would embrace, along with the preceding sentence, all the anterior phrases of the lecture and the events which preceded the lecture, and as large a portion of what we call our past as desired. The distinction we make between our present and past is therefore, if not arbitrary, at least relative to the extent of the field which our attention to life can embrace. The 'present' occupies exactly as much space as this effort. As soon as this particular attention drops any part of what it held beneath its gaze, immediately that portion of the present thus dropped becomes *ipso facto* a part of the past. In a word, our present falls back into the past when we cease to attribute to it an immediate interest. What holds good for the present of individuals holds also for the present of nations: an event belongs to the past, and enters into history, when it is no longer of any direct interest to the politics of the day and can be neglected without the affairs of the country being affected by it. As long as its action makes itself felt, it adheres to the life of a nation and remains present to it.

Consequently nothing prevents us from carrying back as far as possible the line of separation between our present and our past. An attention to life, sufficiently powerful and sufficiently separated from all practical interest, would thus include in an undivided present the entire past history of the conscious person – not as instantaneity, not like a cluster of simultaneous parts, but as something continually present which would also be something continually moving: such, I repeat, is the melody which one perceives as indivisible, and which constitutes, from one end to the other – if we wish to extend the meaning of the word – a perpetual present, although this perpetuity has nothing in common with immutability, or this indivisibility with instantaneity. What we have is a present which endures.

That is not a hypothesis. It happens in exceptional cases that the attention suddenly loses the interest it had in life: immediately, as though by magic, the past once more becomes present. In people who see the threat of sudden death unexpectedly before them, in the mountain climber falling down a precipice, in drowning men, in men being hanged, it seems that a sharp conversion of the attention can take place – something like a change of orientation of the consciousness which, up until then turned toward the future and absorbed by the necessities of action, suddenly loses all interest in them. That is enough to call to mind a thousand different 'forgotten' details and to unroll the whole history of the person before him in a moving panorama.

Memory therefore has no need of explanation. Or rather, there is no special faculty whose role is to retain quantities of the past in order to pour it into the present. The past preserves itself automatically. Of course, if we shut our eyes to the indivisibility of change, to the fact that our most distant past adheres to our present and constitutes with it a single and identical uninterrupted change, it seems that the past is normally what is abolished and that there is something extraordinary about the preservation of the past: we think ourselves obliged to conjure up an apparatus whose function would be to record the parts of the past capable of reappearing in our consciousness.

But if we take into consideration the continuity of the inner life and consequently of its indivisibility, we no longer have to explain the preservation of the past, but rather its apparent abolition. We shall no longer have to account for remembering, but for forgetting. The explanation moreover will be found in the structure of the brain. Nature has invented a mechanism for canalising our attention in the direction of the future, in order to turn it away from the past – I mean of that part of our history which does not concern our present actions – in order to bring to it at most, in the form of 'memories,' one simplification or another of anterior experience, destined to complete the experience of the moment; it is in this that the function of the brain consists. We cannot here undertake the discussion of that theory which claims that the brain is useful for the preservation of the past, that it stores up memories like so many photographic plates from which we afterward develop proofs, or like so many phonograms destined to become sounds again. We have examined this thesis elsewhere. This doctrine was largely inspired by a certain metaphysics with which contemporary psychology and psycho-physiology are imbued, and which one accepts naturally: this accounts for its apparent clarity. But as we consider it more closely, we see what difficulties and impossibilities accumulate in it. Let us take the case most favourable to the thesis, that of a material object making an impression on the eye and leaving a visual memory in the mind. What can this memory possibly be, if it is really the result of the fixation in the brain of the impression received by the eye? The slightest movement on the part of the object or the eye and there would be not one image but ten, a hundred, a thousand images, as many and more than on a cinematographic film. Were the object merely considered for a certain time, or seen at various moments, the different images of that object could be counted by millions. And we have taken the simplest example! Let us suppose all those images are stored up; what good will they serve? which one shall we use? Let us grant that we have our reasons for choosing one of them, why, and how, shall we throw it back into the past when we perceive it? But to pass over these difficulties, how shall we explain the diseases of the memory? In those diseases which correspond to local lesions of the brain, that is in the various forms of aphasia, the psychological lesion consists less in an abolition of the memories than in an ability to recall them. An effort, an emotion, can bring suddenly to consciousness words believed definitely lost. These facts, with many others, unite to prove that in such cases the brain's function is to choose from the past, to diminish it, to simplify it, to utilize it, but not to preserve it. We should have no trouble in looking upon things from this angle if we had not acquired the habit of believing that the past is abolished. Then its partial reappearance creates the effect of an extraordinary event which demands an explanation. And that is why we imagine here and there in the brain, memory 'pigeon-holes' for preserving fragments of the past – the brain, moreover, being self-preserving. As though that were not postponing the difficulty and simply putting off the problem! As though, by positing that cerebral matter is preserved through time, or more generally that all matter endures, one did not attribute to it precisely the memory one claimed to explain by it! Whatever we do, even if we imagine that the brain stores up memories, we do not escape the conclusion that the past can preserve itself automatically.

This holds not only for our own past, but also for the past of any change whatsoever, always providing that it is a question of a single and therefore indivisible change: the preservation of the past in the present is nothing else than the indivisibility of change. It is true that, with regard to the changes which take place outside of us we almost never know whether we are dealing with a single change or one composed of several movements interspersed with stops (the stop never being anything but relative). We would have to be inside beings and things as we are inside ourselves before we could express our opinion on this point. But that is not where the importance lies. It is enough to be convinced once and for all that reality is change, that change is indivisible, and that in an indivisible change the past is one with the present.

Let us imbibe this truth and we shall see a good many philosophical enigmas melt away and evaporate. Certain great problems such as that of substance, of change, and of their relation to one another, will no longer arise. All the difficulties raised around these points – difficulties which caused substance to recede little by little to the regions of the unknowable – came from the fact that we shut our eyes to the indivisibility of change. If change, which is evidently constitutive of all our experience, is the fleeting thing most philosophers have spoken of, if we see in it only a multiplicity of states replacing other states, we are obliged to re-establish the continuity between these states by an artificial bond; but this immobile substratum of immobility, being incapable of possessing any of the attributes we know – since all are changes – recedes as we try to approach it: it is as elusive as the phantom of change it was called upon to fix. Let us, on the contrary, endeavour to perceive change as it is in its natural indivisibility: we see that it is the very substance of things, and neither does movement appear to us any longer under the vanishing form which rendered it elusive to thought, nor substance with the immutability which made it inaccessible to our experience. Radical instability and absolute immutability are therefore mere abstract views taken from outside of the continuity of real change, abstractions which the mind then hypostatises into multiple *states* on the one hand, into *thing* or substance on the other. The difficulties raised by the ancients around the question of movement and by the moderns around the question of substance disappear, the former because movement and change are substantial, the latter because substance is movement and change.

At the same time that theoretical obscurities disappear we get a glimpse of the possible solution of more than one reputedly unsolvable problem. The discussions on the subject of free will would come to an end if we saw ourselves where we are really, in a concrete duration where the idea of necessary determination loses all significance, since in it the past becomes identical with the present and continuously creates with it – if only by the fact of being added to it – something absolutely new. And we could gradually acquire a deeper appreciation of the relation of man to the universe if we took into account the true nature of *states*, of *qualities*, in fact of everything which presents itself to us with the appearance of stability. In such a case the object and the subject should be, with regard to one another, in a situation analogous to that of the two trains we spoke of at the beginning: it is a certain regulating of mobility on mobility which produces the effect of immobility. Let us then become imbued with this idea, let us never lose sight of the particular relation of the object to the subject translated by a static vision of things: everything that experience teaches us of the one will increase the knowledge we had of the other, and the light the latter receives will in turn be able, by reflection, to illuminate the former.

But as I said in the beginning, pure speculation will not be the only thing to benefit by this vision of universal becoming. We shall be able to make it penetrate into our everyday life, and through it, obtain from philosophy satisfactions similar to those we receive from art, but more frequent, more continual and more accessible to the majority of men. Art enables us, no doubt, to discover in things more qualities and more shades than we naturally perceive. It dilates our perception, but on the surface rather than in depth. It enriches our present, but it scarcely enables us to go beyond it. Through philosophy we can accustom ourselves never to isolate the present from the past which it pulls along with it. Thanks to philosophy, all things acquire depth – more than depth, something like a fourth dimension which permits anterior perceptions to remain bound up with present perceptions, and the immediate future itself to become partly outlined in the present. Reality no longer appears then in the static state, in its manner of being; it affirms itself dynamically, in the continuity and variability of its tendency. What was immobile and frozen in our perception is warmed and set in motion. Everything comes to life around us, everything is revivified in us. A great impulse carries beings and things along. We feel ourselves uplifted, carried away, borne along by it. We are more fully alive and this increase of life brings with it the conviction that grave philosophical enigmas can be resolved or even perhaps that they need not be raised, since they arise from a frozen vision of the real and are only the translation, in terms of thought, of a certain artificial weakening of our vitality. In fact, the more we accustom ourselves to think and to perceive all things *sub specie durationis*, the more we plunge into real duration. And the more we immerse ourselves in it, the more we set ourselves back in the direction of the principle, though it be transcendent, in which we participate and whose eternity is not to be an eternity of immutability, but an eternity of life: how, otherwise, could we live and move in it? *In ea vivimus et movemur et sumus*.

On the Pragmatism of William James: Truth and Reality[6]

To talk about pragmatism after William James might well seem superfluous. And indeed what is there for me to say about it that has not already been said, and much better, in the fascinating and delightful book for which we now have an excellent translation? I should in fact refrain from saying anything were it not that James's thought is frequently impoverished and falsified by the way in which it is interpreted. There are many ideas in circulation which threaten to come between the reader and the book and to cast an artificial obscurity over a work which is clarity itself.

One would have a mistaken idea of James's pragmatism if one did not begin by modifying the idea usually held of reality in general. We speak of the 'world' or the 'cosmos'; and these words, according to their origin, designate something simple or at least well composed. We say 'universe' and the word makes us think of a possible unification of things. One can be a spiritualist, a materialist, a pantheist, just as one can be indifferent to philosophy and satisfied with common sense: the fact remains that one always conceives of one or several simple principles by which the whole of material and moral things might be explained.

This is because our intelligence loves simplicity. It seeks to reduce effort, and insists that nature was arranged in such a way as to demand of us, in order to be thought, the least possible labour. It therefore provides itself with the exact minimum of elements and principles with which to recompose the indefinite series of objects and events.

But if instead of reconstructing things ideally for the greater satisfaction of our reason we confine ourselves purely and simply to what is given us by experience, we should think and express ourselves in quite another way. While our intelligence with its habits of economy imagines effects as strictly proportioned to their causes, nature, in its extravagance, puts into the cause much more than is required to produce the effect. While our motto is *Exactly what is necessary*, nature's motto is *More than is necessary* – too much of this, too much of that, too much of everything. Reality, as James sees it, is redundant and superabundant. Between this reality and the one constructed by the philosophers, I believe he would have established the same relation as between the life we live every day and the life which actors portray in the evening on the stage. On the stage, each actor says and does only what has to be said and done; the scenes are clear-cut; the play has a beginning, a middle and an end; and everything is worked out as economically as possible with a view to an ending which will be happy or tragic. But in life, a multitude of useless things are said, many superfluous gestures made, there are no sharply-drawn situations; nothing happens as simply or as completely or as nicely as we should like; the scenes overlap; things neither begin nor end; there is no perfectly satisfying ending, nor absolutely decisive gesture, none of those telling words which give us pause: all the effects are spoiled. Such is human life. And such, no doubt, in James's eyes, is reality in general.

To be sure, our experience is not incoherent. At the same time as it presents us with things and facts it shows us relationships between the things and connections between the facts: these relations are as real, as directly observable, according to William James, as the things and facts themselves. But the relations are fluctuating and the things fluid. This is vastly different from that dry universe constructed by the philosophers with elements that are clear-cut and well-arranged, where each part is not only linked to another part, as experience shows us, but also, as our reason would have it, is coordinated to the whole.

The 'Pluralism' of William James means little else than this. Antiquity had imagined a world shut off, arrested, finite: it is a hypothesis which answers certain demands of our reason. The moderns think rather of an infinite: it is another hypothesis which satisfies other needs of our reason. From the point of view taken by James, which is that of pure experience or of 'radical empiricism,' reality no longer appears as finite or as infinite, but simply as indefinite. It flows without our being able to say whether it is in a single direction, or even whether it is always and throughout the same river flowing.

Our reason is less satisfied. It feels less at ease in a world where it no longer finds, as in a mirror, its own image. And certainly the importance of human reason is diminished. But the importance of man himself – the whole of man, will and sensibility quite as much as intelligence – will thereby be immeasurably enhanced!

The universe our reason conceives is, in fact, a universe which extends infinitely beyond human experience, the characteristic of reason being to prolong the data of experience, to extend them by way of generalization, in order to make us conceive many more things than we shall ever perceive. In such a universe man is expected to do very little and to occupy very little space: what he gives to his intelligence he takes away from his will. Above all, having attributed to his thought the power of embracing everything, he is obliged to imagine all things in terms of thought; of his aspirations, his desires, his enthusiasms he cannot ask enlightenment in a world in which everything accessible to him has been first considered by him as translatable into pure ideas. His sensibility cannot enlighten his intelligence, for it is with his intelligence that he has made what light there is.

Most philosophies, therefore, restrict our experience on the side of feeling and will, as at the same time they indefinitely prolong it on the side of thought. What James asks of us is not to add too much to experience through hypothetical considerations, and also not to mutilate it in its solid elements. We are absolutely sure only of what experience gives us; but we should accept experience wholly, and our feelings are a part of it by the same right as our perceptions, consequently, by the same right as 'things.' In the eyes of William James, the whole man counts.

In fact, he counts for a great deal in a world which no longer overwhelms him with its immensity. Considerable surprise has been expressed at the importance James attributes, in one of his books,[7] to the curious theory of Fechner which makes of the Earth an independent being, endowed with a divine soul. He did so because he saw in it a convenient means of symbolizing – perhaps even of expressing – his own thought. The things and facts which make up our experience constitute for us a *human* world,[8] no doubt connected with others, but so far removed from them and so close to us that we must consider it, in practice, as sufficient for man and sufficient unto itself. We are an integral part of these things and these events – we, that is to say, all that we are conscious of being, all that we experience. The powerful feelings which stir the soul at certain special moments are forces as real as those that interest the physicist; man does not create them any more than he creates heat or light. According to James, we bathe in an atmosphere traversed by great spiritual currents. If many of us resist, others allow themselves to be carried along. And there are certain souls which open wide to the beneficent breeze. Those are the mystical souls. We know with what sympathy James studied them. When his book *Religious Experience* appeared, many saw in it only a series of very vivid descriptions and very penetrating analyses – a psychology, they said, of religious feeling. This was a complete misinterpretation of the author's thought. The truth is that James leaned out upon the mystic soul as, on a spring day, we lean out to feel the caress of the breeze on our cheek, or as, at the sea-side, we watch the coming and going of sail-boats to know how the wind blows. Souls filled with religious enthusiasm are truly uplifted and carried away: why could they not enable us to experience directly, as in a scientific experiment, this uplifting and exalting force? That is undoubtedly the origin, the inspiring idea of the 'pragmatism' of William James. For him those truths it is most important for us to know, are truths which have been felt and experienced before being thought.[9]

It has at all times been said that there are truths which have to do with feeling as much as with reason; and that along with those truths we find already made there are also others we assist in the making, which depend in part on our will. But it must be said that in James this idea takes on a new strength and significance. Thanks to his particular conception of reality it blossoms into a general theory of truth.

What constitutes a true judgment? If an affirmation agrees with reality we say that it is true. But in what does this agreement consist? Our inclination is to see in it something like the resemblance of a portrait to the model: the true affirmation would be the one which would *copy* reality. Upon reflection, however, we shall see that it is only in rare and exceptional cases that this definition of the true finds its application. What is real is any determined fact taking place at any point in space and time, it is singular – it is changing. On the contrary, most of our affirmations are general and imply a certain stability on the part of their object. Let us take a truth as close to experience as possible, for instance: 'heat expands bodies.' Of what model is this truth a copy? It is possible, in a certain sense, to copy the expansion of a specific body at particular moments, by photographing it in its various stages. Even by metaphor I can still say that the affirmation, 'that iron bar is expanding,' is the copy of what happens when I watch the expansion of the iron bar. But a truth which is applied to all bodies without concerning any one in particular that I have seen, copies nothing, reproduces nothing. We insist however that it copy something and as far back as one can go philosophy has always sought to give us satisfaction on this point. For the ancient philosophers there was, above time and space, a world in which were located from all eternity all possible truths: the truth of human affirmations was measured by the degree of faithfulness with which they copied these eternal truths. Modern philosophers have brought truth from heaven down to earth; but they still see in it something which is pre-existent to our affirmations. According to them, truth is lodged in things and facts: our science seeks it in them, draws it from its hiding-place and exposes it to the light of day. An affirmation, such as 'heat expands bodies,' would then be a law governing facts, which is enthroned if not above them, at least in their midst, a law veritably contained in our experience; all we should have to do would be to extract it therefrom. Even a philosophy like that of Kant, which insists that all scientific truth is relative to the human mind, considers true affirmations as given in advance in human experience: once that experience is organized by human thought in general, all the work of science consists, so to speak, in piercing the resisting envelope of the facts inside which the truth is lodged, like a nut in its shell.

This conception of truth is natural to our mind and natural also to philosophy, because it is natural to picture reality as a perfectly coherent and systematized whole sustained by a logical armature. This armature would be truth itself; all that our science does is to rediscover it. But experience pure and simple tells us nothing of the kind, and James confines himself to experience. Experience presents us a flow of phenomena: if a certain affirmation relating to one of them enables us to master those which follow or even simply to foresee them, we say of this affirmation that it is true. A proposition such as 'heat expands bodies,' a proposition suggested by seeing a certain body expand, means that we foresee how other bodies will act when exposed to heat; it helps us to proceed from a past experience to new experiences; it is a clue conducting to what will happen, nothing more. Reality flows; we flow with it; and we call true any affirmation which, in guiding us through moving reality, gives us a grip upon it and places us under more favourable conditions for acting.

The difference between this conception of the truth and the traditional one is plain to see. We ordinarily define the true by its conformity to what already exists; James defines it by its relation to what does not yet exist. The true, according to William James, does not copy something which has been or which is: it announces what will be, or rather it prepares our action upon what is going to be. Philosophy has a natural tendency to have truth look backward: for James, it looks ahead.

More precisely, other doctrines make of truth something anterior to the clearly-determined act of the man who formulates it for the first time. He was the first to see it, we say, but it was waiting for him, just as America was waiting for Christopher Columbus. Something hid it from view and, so to speak, covered it up: he uncovered it. – Quite different is William James's conception. He does not deny that reality is independent, at least to a great extent, of what we say or think of it; but the truth, which can be attached only to what we affirm about reality, is, for him, created by our affirmation. We invent the truth to utilize reality, as we create mechanical devices to utilize the forces of nature. It seems to me one could sum up all that is essential in the pragmatic conception of truth in a formula such as this: *while for other doctrines a new truth is a discovery, for pragmatism it is an invention.*[10]

It does not follow, of course, that the truth is arbitrary. The value of a mechanical invention lies solely in its practical usefulness. In the same way an affirmation, because it is true, should increase our mastery over things. It is no less the creation of a certain individual mind, and it was no more pre-existent to the effort of that mind than the phonograph, for example, existed before Edison. No doubt the inventor of the phonograph had to study the properties of sound, which is a reality. But his invention was superadded to that reality as a thing absolutely new, which might never have been produced had he not existed. Thus a truth, if it is to endure, should have its roots in realities; but these realities are only the ground in which that truth grows, and other flowers could just as well have grown there if the wind had brought other seeds.

Truth, according to pragmatism, has come little by little into being, thanks to the individual contributions of a great number of inventors. If these inventors had not existed, if there had been others in their place, we should have had an entirely different body of truths. Reality would evidently have remained what it is, or approximately the same; but quite different would have been the paths we should have traced in reality, for our convenience in finding our way about it. And this has to do not only with scientific truths. We cannot construct a sentence, we cannot even today pronounce a word, without accepting certain hypotheses which were created by our ancestors and which might have been very different from what they are. When I say: 'My pencil has just fallen under the table,' I am certainly not enunciating a fact of experience, for what sight and touch show me is simply that my hand opened and let fall what it held: the baby tied in his high-chair, who sees his plaything fall, probably does not imagine that this object continues to exist; or rather he has not the clear idea of an 'object,' that is to say, of something which subsists, invariable and independent, through the diversity and mobility of the appearances which pass before him. The first to venture to believe in this invariability and independence made a hypothesis: it is that hypothesis which we currently adopt every time we use a substantive, every time we speak. Our grammar would have been different, the articulations of our thought would have been other than what they are, had humanity in the course of its evolution preferred to adopt hypotheses of another kind.

The structure of our mind is therefore to a great extent our work, or at least the work of some of us. That, it seems to me, is the most important thesis of pragmatism, even though it has not been explicitly stated. It is in this way that pragmatism continues Kantianism. Kant had said that truth depends upon the general structure of the human mind. Pragmatism adds, or at least implies, that the structure of the human mind is the effect of the free initiative of a certain number of individual minds.

That, again, does not mean that truth depends upon each one of us: we might as well believe that each of us could invent the phonograph. But it does mean that of the various kinds of truth, the one which most nearly coincides with its object is not scientific truth, nor is it the truth of common sense, nor more generally truth of an intellectual order. Every truth is a path traced through reality: but among these paths there are some to which we could have given an entirely different turn if our attention had been orientated in a different direction or if we had aimed at another kind of utility; there are some, on the contrary, whose direction is marked out by reality itself: there are some, one might say, which correspond to currents of reality. Doubtless these also depend upon us to a certain extent, for we are free to go against the current or to follow it, and even if we follow it, we can variously divert it, being at the same time associated with and submitted to the force manifest within it. Nevertheless these currents are not created by us; they are part and parcel of reality. Pragmatism thus results in a reversal of the order in which we are accustomed to place the various kinds of truth. Apart from the truths which translate mere sensations, it is, according to pragmatism, the truths of feeling which would push their roots deepest into reality. If we agree to say that all truth is an invention, I believe we must, if we wish to remain faithful to the thought of William James, establish between the truths of feeling and the scientific truths the same kind of difference as there is, for example, between the sail-boat and the steamer: both are human inventions; but the first makes only slight use of artificial means – it takes the direction of the wind and makes the natural force it utilizes perceptible to the eye; on the contrary, in the second the artificial mechanism holds the most important place; it covers the force it puts into play and assigns to it a direction which we ourselves have chosen.

The definition that James gives to truth, therefore, is an integral part of his conception of reality. If reality is not that economic and systematic universe our logic likes to imagine, if it is not sustained by a framework of intellectuality, intellectual truth is a human invention whose effect is to utilize reality rather than to enable us to penetrate it. And if reality does not form a single whole, if it is multiple and mobile, made up of cross-currents, truth which arises from contact with one of these currents – truth felt before being conceived – is more capable of seizing and storing up reality than truth merely thought.

Therefore it is, in fact, with this theory of reality that a critique of pragmatism should first grapple. One may raise objections to it – and I myself should make certain reservations concerning it: but no one will challenge its depth and originality. Neither will anyone, after having closely examined the conception of truth allied with it, fail to recognize its high moral value. People have said that the pragmatism of James was only a form of scepticism, that it lowered truth, that it subordinated truth to material utility, that it advised against and discouraged disinterested scientific research. Such an interpretation will never enter the heads of those who read his work attentively. And it will greatly astonish those who have had the pleasure of knowing the man. No one loved truth with a more ardent love. No one sought it with greater passion. He was stirred by an immense unrest, and went from science to science, from anatomy and physiology to psychology, from psychology to philosophy, tense over great problems, heedless of anything else, forgetful of himself. All his life he observed, experimented, meditated. And as if he had not done enough, he still dreamed, as he fell into his last slumber, of extraordinary experiments and superhuman efforts by which he could continue even beyond death to work with us for the greater good of science, and the greater glory of truth.

Introduction to Metaphysics[11]

[. . .]

Of the propositions I am about to set forth, most have received in the present work a beginning of proof. I hope to demonstrate them more completely when we attack other problems.

I. *There is an external reality which is given immediately to our mind.* Common sense is right on this point against the idealism and realism of the philosophers.

II. This reality is mobility.[12] There do not exist things made, but only *things* in the making, not states that remain fixed, but only *states* in process of change. Rest is never anything but apparent, or rather, relative. The consciousness we have of our own person in its continual flowing, introduces us to the interior of a reality on whose model we must imagine the others. *All reality is, therefore, tendency, if we agree to call tendency a nascent change of direction.*

III. Our mind, which seeks solid bases of operation, [*points d'appui solides*] has as its principal function, in the ordinary course of life, to imagine *states* and *things*. Now and then it takes quasi-instantaneous views of the undivided mobility of the real. It thus obtains *sensations* and *ideas*. By that means it substitutes for the continuous the discontinuous, for mobility stability, for the tendency in process of change it substitutes fixed points which mark a direction of change and tendency. This substitution is necessary to common sense, to language, to practical life, and even, to a certain extent which we shall try to determine, to positive science. *Our intelligence, when it follows its natural inclination, proceeds by solid perceptions on the one hand, and by stable conceptions on the other*. It starts from the immobile and conceives and expresses movement only in terms of immobility. It places itself in ready-made concepts and tries to catch in them, as in a net, something of the passing reality. It does not do so in order to obtain an internal and metaphysical knowledge of the real. It is simply to make use of them, each concept (like each sensation) being a *practical question* which our activity asks of reality and to which reality will answer, as is proper in things, by a yes or a no. But in so doing it allows what is the very essence of the real to escape.

IV. The difficulties inherent in metaphysics, the antinomies it raises, the contradictions into which it falls, the division into opposing schools and the irreducible oppositions between systems, are due in large part to the fact that we apply to the disinterested knowledge of the real the procedures we use currently with practical utility as the aim. They are due principally to the fact that we place ourselves in the immobile to watch for the moving reality as it passes instead of putting ourselves back into the moving reality to traverse with it the immobile positions. They come from the fact that we claim to reconstitute reality, which is tendency and consequently mobility, with the percepts and concepts which have as their function to immobilize it. One will never create mobility with halts, however numerous: if one begins with mobility, one can draw from it through thought as many halts as one wishes. In other words, *it is understood that fixed concepts can be extracted by our thought from the mobile reality; but there is no means whatever of reconstituting with the fixity of concepts the mobility of the real*. Dogmatism, as the constructor of systems, has nevertheless always attempted this reconstitution.

V. It was bound to fail. This is the impotence, and this alone, pointed out by the sceptical, idealistic and critical doctrines, all those doctrines, in fact, which question our mind's ability to attain the absolute. But it does not follow from the fact that we fail to reconstitute living reality with concepts that are rigid and ready-made, that we could not grasp it in any other manner. *The demonstrations which have been given of the relativity of our knowledge are therefore tainted with an original vice: they assume, like the dogmatism they attack, that all knowledge must necessarily start from rigidly defined concepts in order to grasp by their means the flowing reality.*

VI. But the truth is that our mind is able to follow the reverse procedure. It can be installed in the mobile reality, adopt its ceaselessly changing direction, in short, grasp it intuitively. But to do that, it must do itself violence, reverse the direction of the operation by which it ordinarily thinks, continually upsetting its categories, or rather, recasting them. In so doing it will arrive at fluid concepts, capable of following reality in all its windings and of adopting the very movement of the inner life of things. Only in that way will a progressive philosophy be constituted, freed from the disputes which arise between the schools, capable of resolving problems naturally because it will be rid of the artificial terms chosen in stating them. *To philosophise means to reverse the normal direction of the workings of thought.*

VII. This reversal has never been practiced in a methodical manner; but a careful study of the history of human thought would show that to it we owe the greatest accomplishments in the sciences, as well as whatever living quality there is in metaphysics. The most powerful method of investigation known to the mind, infinitesimal calculus, was born of that very reversal.[13] Modern mathematics is precisely an effort to substitute for the *ready-made* what is in process of *becoming*, to follow the growth of magnitudes, to seize movement no longer from outside and in its manifest result, but from within and in its tendency towards change, in short, to adopt the mobile continuity of the pattern of things. It is true that it contents itself with the pattern, being but the science of magnitudes. It is also true that it has been able to realize these marvellous applications only through the invention of certain symbols, and that, if the intuition we have just mentioned is at the origin of the invention, it is the symbol alone which intervenes in the application. But metaphysics, which does not aim at any application, can and for the most part ought to abstain from converting intuition into symbol. Exempt from the obligation of arriving at results useful from a practical standpoint, it will indefinitely enlarge the domain of its investigations. What it will have lost with regard to science, in utility and occurrence, it will regain in scope and range. If mathematics is only the science of magnitudes, if mathematical procedures only apply to quantities, it must not be forgotten that quantity is always nascent quality: it is, one might say, its limiting case. It is therefore natural that metaphysics should adopt the generative idea of our mathematics in order to extend it to all qualities, that is, to reality in general. In so doing, it will in no way proceed to universal mathematics, that chimera of modern philosophy. Quite the contrary, as it makes more headway, it will meet with objects less and less translatable into symbols. But it will at least have begun by making contact with the continuity and mobility of the real exactly where this contact happens to be the most utilizable. It will have looked at itself in a mirror which sends back an image of itself no doubt very reduced, but also very luminous. It will have seen with a superior clarity what mathematical procedures borrow from concrete reality, and it will continue in the direction of concrete reality, not of mathematical methods. Let us say, then, with all due qualifications to what might seem either too modest or too ambitious in this formula, that *one of the objects of metaphysics is to operate differentiations and qualitative integrations*.

VIII. What has caused this object to be lost sight of, and misled science itself about the origin of certain methods it employs, is that intuition once grasped must find a mode of expression and application which conforms to our habits of thought and which furnishes us, in well-defined concepts, the solid basis [*points d'appui solides*] we so greatly need. That is the condition of what we call strictness, precision, and indefinite extension of a general method to particular cases. Now this extension and this work of logical perfectioning can be carried on for centuries, while the generative act of the method lasts only an instant. That is why we so often take the logical apparatus of science for science itself,[14] forgetting the intuition from which the rest was able to ensue.[15]

All that has been said by the philosophers and by scientists themselves about the 'relativity' of scientific knowledge is due to forgetting this intuition. *Relative is symbolic knowledge through pre-existing concepts, which goes from the fixed to the moving, but not so intuitive knowledge which establishes itself in the moving reality and adopts the life itself of things*. This intuition attains the absolute.

Science and metaphysics then meet in intuition. A truly intuitive philosophy would realize the union so greatly desired, of metaphysics and science.

At the same time that it constituted metaphysics in positive science – I mean progressive and indefinitely perfectible – it would lead the positive sciences, properly speaking, to become conscious of their true bearing, which is often very superior to what they suppose. It would put more of science into metaphysics and more of metaphysics into science. Its result would be to reestablish the continuity between the intuitions which the various positive sciences have obtained at intervals in the course of their history, and which they have obtained only by strokes of genius.

IX. That there are not two different ways of knowing things thoroughly, that the various sciences have their roots in metaphysics, is what the philosophers of antiquity, in general, believed. Not in that lay their error. It consisted in adopting the belief so natural to the human mind, that a variation can only express and develop invariabilities. The result of this was that Action was a weakened Contemplation, duration a false, deceptive and mobile image of immobile eternity, the Soul a fall of the Idea. The whole of that philosophy which begins with Plato and ends with Plotinus is the development of a principle that we should formulate thus: 'There is more in the immutable than in the moving, and one passes from the stable to the unstable by a simple diminution.' Now the contrary is the truth.

Modern science dates from the day when mobility was set up as an independent reality. It dates from the day when Galileo, rolling a ball down an inclined plane, made the firm resolution to study this movement from high to low for itself, in itself, instead of seeking its principle in the concepts of the *high* and the *low*, two immobilities by which Aristotle thought he sufficiently explained its mobility. And that is not an isolated fact in the history of science. I take the view that several of the great discoveries, of those at least which have transformed the positive sciences or created new ones, have been so many soundings made in pure duration. The more living was the reality touched, the more profound had been the sounding.

But the sounding made on the sea floor brings up a fluid mass which the sun very quickly dries into solid and discontinuous grains of sand. And the intuition of duration, when exposed to the rays of the understanding, also quickly congeals into fixed, distinct and immobile concepts. In the living mobility of things, the understanding undertakes to mark out real or virtual stations, it notes arrivals and departures; that is all that is important to the thought of man in its natural exercise. But philosophy should be an effort to go beyond the human state.

On the concepts with which they have blazed the trail of intuition scholars have preferred to fix their glance. The more they considered these residua which have reached the state of symbols, the more they attributed to all science a symbolic character.[16] And the more they believed in the symbolic character of science, the more they effected it and emphasized it. It was not long before they noticed no difference, in positive science, between the data of immediate intuition and the immense work of analysis that the understanding pursues around intuition. Thus they prepared the way for a doctrine which affirms the relativity of all our forms of knowledge. But metaphysics has also worked toward that.

Why did the masters of modern philosophy, who were renovators of science in addition to being metaphysicians, not have the feeling of the mobile continuity of the real? Why did they not place themselves in what we call concrete duration? They did so more than they thought, and much more than they said they did. If any attempt is made to connect by continuous links the intuitions around which systems are organized, one finds, along with several other convergent or divergent lines, a well-determined direction of thought and feeling. What is this latent thought? How is this feeling to be expressed? To borrow once more the language of the Platonists, and stripping the words of their psychological meaning, by calling Idea a certain *assurance of easy intelligibility* and Soul a certain *preoccupation* with life, we shall say that an invisible current makes modern philosophy tend to lift the Soul above the Idea. In this, as in modern science and even more so, it tends to move in the opposite direction from ancient thought.

But this metaphysics, like this science, has deployed around its inner life a rich tissue of symbols, occasionally forgetting that if science needs symbols in its analytical development, the principal justification for metaphysics is a break with symbols. Here again the understanding has pursued its work of fixing, dividing, reconstructing. True, it has pursued it under a somewhat different form. Without emphasizing a point I propose to develop elsewhere, let me confine myself to saying that the understanding, whose role is to operate on stable elements, can seek stability either in *relations* or in *things*. In so far as it works on relational concepts, it ends in *scientific* symbolism. In so far as it operates on concepts of things, it ends in *metaphysical* symbolism. But in either case the arrangement comes from it. It would willingly believe itself independent. Rather than recognizing at once what it owes to the deep intuition of reality, it is exposed to what is only seen in all its work, to an artificial arrangement of symbols. With the result that if one keeps to the letter of what metaphysicians and scholars say, as well as to the content of what they do, one might believe that the first have dug a deep tunnel under reality, while the others have thrown over it an elegant bridge, but that the moving river of things passes between these two works of art without touching them.

One of the principal tricks of Kantian criticism consisted in taking the metaphysician and the scholar at their word, in pushing metaphysics and science to the utmost possible limit of symbolism, where, in any case, they lead of their own accord the moment the understanding lays claim to an independence full of dangers. Once the relation of science and metaphysics with 'intellectual intuition' is misunderstood, Kant has no difficulty in showing that our science is entirely relative and our metaphysics wholly artificial. Because he strained the independence of the understanding in both cases, because he relieved metaphysics and science of the 'intellectual intuition' which gave them their inner weight, science with its relations presents to him only an outer wrapping of form, and metaphysics with its things, an outer wrapping of matter. Is it surprising, then, that the first shows him only frameworks within frameworks, and the second phantoms pursuing phantoms?

He struck our science and metaphysics such rude blows that they have not yet entirely recovered from their shock. Our mind would willingly resign itself to see in science a wholly relative knowledge and in metaphysics an empty speculation. It seems to us even today that Kantian criticism applies to all metaphysics and to all science. In reality it applies especially to the philosophy of the ancients, as well as to the form – still ancient – that the moderns have given most often to their thought. It is valid against a metaphysics which claims to give us a *unique* and ready-made system of things, against a science which would be a *unique* system of relations, finally against a science and a metaphysics which present themselves with the architectural simplicity of the Platonic theory of Ideas, or of a Greek temple. If metaphysics claims to be made up of concepts we possessed prior to it, if it consists in an ingenious arrangement of pre-existing ideas which we utilize like the materials of construction for a building, in short, if it is something other than the constant dilation of our mind, the constantly renewed effort to go beyond our actual ideas and perhaps our simple logic as well, it is too evident that it becomes artificial like all works of pure understanding. And if science is wholly the work of analysis or of conceptual representation, if experience is only to serve as the verification of 'clear ideas,' if instead of starting from multiple and varied intuitions inserted into the movement proper to each reality but not always fitting into one another, it claims to be an immense mathematics, a single system of relations which imprisons the totality of the real in a mesh prepared for it, it becomes a knowledge purely relative to the human understanding.

A close reading of the *Critique of Pure Reason* will show that for Kant this kind of *universal mathematics* is science, and this barely modified Platonism, metaphysics. To tell the truth, the dream of a universal mathematics is itself only a survival of Platonism. Universal mathematics is what the world of Ideas becomes when one assumes that the Idea consists in a relation or a law, and no longer in a thing. Kant took for a reality this dream of certain modern philosophers:[17] much more, he thought that all scientific knowledge was only a detached fragment, or rather a projecting stone of universal mathematics. The main task of the *Critique*, therefore, was to lay the foundations of this mathematics, that is, to determine what the intelligence should be and what should be the object in order that an unbroken mathematics might bind them together. And it follows that if all possible experience is thus assured of admittance into the rigid and already constituted frameworks of our understanding (unless we assume a pre-established harmony), our understanding itself organizes nature and finds itself reflected in it as in a mirror. Whence the possibility of science, which owes all its effectiveness to its relativity – and the impossibility of metaphysics, since the latter will find nothing more to do than to parody, on the phantoms of things, the work of conceptual arrangement which science pursues seriously on relations. In short, *the whole* Critique of Pure Reason *leads to establishing the fact that Platonism, illegitimate if Ideas are things, becomes legitimate if ideas are relations, and that the ready-made idea, once thus brought down from heaven to earth, is indeed as Plato wished, the common basis of thought and nature. But the whole* Critique of Pure Reason *rests also upon the postulate that our thought is incapable of anything but Platonising*, that is, of pouring the whole of possible experience into pre-existing moulds.

That is the whole question. If scientific knowledge is indeed what Kant insisted it was, there is a simple science pre-formed and even pre-formulated in nature, as Aristotle believed: from this logic immanent in things the great discoveries only illuminate point by point the line traced in advance, as, on a festival night, a string of bulbs flick on, one by one, to give the outline of a monument. And if metaphysical knowledge is indeed what Kant intended, it is reduced to the equal possibility of two opposed attitudes of mind toward all the great problems; its manifestations are so many arbitrary choices, always ephemeral, between two solutions virtually formulated from all eternity: it lives and dies from antinomies. But the truth is that neither does the science of modern times present this unilinear simplicity, nor the metaphysics of the moderns these irreducible oppositions.

Modern science is neither one nor simple. It rests, I readily agree, upon ideas one ultimately finds clear; but these ideas, when they are profound, become progressively clear by the use made of them; they owe then the best part of their luminosity to the light cast back upon them, through reflection, by the facts and applications to which they have led, the clarity of a concept being little else, accordingly, than the assurance, once it is acquired, of manipulating it to advantage. At the start, more than one of them must have appeared obscure, difficult to reconcile with the ideas already accepted by science, and bordering on the absurd. That is to say that science does not proceed by the regular nesting of concepts predestined to fit neatly inside one another. Profound and fruitful ideas are so many points of contact with currents of reality which do not necessarily converge on a same point. It is true that the concepts in which they lodge always manage somehow or other, in rounding off their corners by reciprocal friction, to make shift among themselves.

On the other hand, the metaphysics of the moderns is not made of solutions so radical that they can lead to irreducible oppositions. This would no doubt be so if there were no means of accepting at the same time and in the same field the thesis and antithesis of the antinomies. But to philosophise consists precisely in placing oneself, by an effort of intuition, inside this concrete reality on which from the outside the *Critique* takes the two opposing views, thesis and antithesis. I shall never imagine how black and white intermingle if I have not seen grey, but I have no difficulty in understanding, once I have seen grey, how one can envisage it from the double viewpoints of black and white. Doctrines which have a basis of intuition escape

Kantian criticism to the exact extent that they are intuitive; and these doctrines are the whole of metaphysics, provided one does not take the metaphysics congealed and dead in *theses*, but living in *philosophers*. To be sure, these divergences are striking between the schools, that is to say, in short, between the groups of disciples formed around certain of the great masters. But would one find them as clear-cut between the masters themselves? Something here dominates the diversity of systems, something, I repeat, simple and definite like a sounding of which one feels that it has more or less reached the bottom of a same ocean, even though it brings each time to the surface very different materials. It is on these materials that disciples normally work: in that is the role of analysis. And the master, in so far as he formulates, develops, translates into abstract ideas what he brings, is already, as it were, his own disciple. But the simple act which has set analysis in motion and which hides behind analysis, emanates from a faculty quite different from that of analysing. This is by very definition intuition.

Let it be said, in conclusion, that there is nothing mysterious about this faculty. Whoever has worked successfully at literary composition well knows that when the subject has been studied at great length, all the documents gathered together, all notes taken, something more is necessary to get down to the work of composition itself: an effort, often painful, immediately to place oneself in the very heart of the subject and to seek as deeply as possible an impulsion which, as soon as found, carries one forward of itself. This impulsion, once received, sets the mind off on a road where it finds both the information it had gathered and other details as well; it develops, analyses itself in terms whose enumeration follows on without limit; the farther one goes the more is disclosed about it; never will one manage to say everything: and yet, if one turns around suddenly to seize the impulsion felt, it slips away; for it was not a thing but an urge to movement, and although indefinitely extensible, it is simplicity itself. Metaphysical intuition seems to be something of the same kind. What in this case matches the notes and documents of the literary composition, is the collection of observations and experiences gathered by positive science and above all by a reflection of the mind on the mind. For one does not obtain from reality an intuition, that is to say, a spiritual harmony with its innermost quality if one has not gained its confidence by a long comradeship with its superficial manifestations. And it is not a question simply of assimilating the outstanding facts; it is necessary to accumulate and fuse such an enormous mass of them that one may be assured, in this fusion, of neutralizing by one another all the preconceived and premature ideas observers may have deposited unknowingly in their observations. Only thus does the raw material of the known facts emerge. Even in the simple and privileged case which served us as an example, even for the direct contact of the self with the self, the definitive effort of distinct intuition would be impossible for anyone who had not gathered and collated a very great number of psychological analyses. The masters of modern philosophy have been men who had assimilated all the material of the science of their time. And the partial eclipse of metaphysics since the last half century has been caused more than anything else by the extraordinary difficulty the philosopher experiences today in making contact with a science already much too scattered. But metaphysical intuition, although one can achieve it only by means of material knowledge, is an entirely different thing from the summary or synthesis of this knowledge. It is as distinct from it as the motor impulsion is distinct from the path traced by the moving object, as the tension of the spring is distinct from the visible movements in the clock. In this sense, metaphysics has nothing in common with a generalization of experience, and yet it could be defined as the whole of experience (*l'expérience intégrale*).

Bergson and Kant

Beyond the Noumenal[1]

What the *Transcendental Aesthetic* of Kant appears to have established once for all is that extension is not a material attribute of the same kind as others. We cannot reason indefinitely on the notions of heat, colour, or weight: in order to know the modalities of weight or of heat, we must have recourse to experience. Not so of the notion of space. Supposing even that it is given empirically by sight and touch (and Kant has not questioned the fact) there is this about it that is remarkable: that our mind, speculating on it with its own powers alone, cuts out in it, *a priori*, figures whose properties we determine *a priori*: experience, with which we have not kept in touch, yet follows us through the infinite complications of our reasonings and invariably justifies them. That is the fact. Kant has set it in clear light. But the explanation of the fact, we believe, must be sought in a different direction to that which Kant followed.

Intelligence, as Kant represents it to us, is bathed in an atmosphere of spatiality to which it is as inseparably united as the living body to the air it breathes. Our perceptions reach us only after having passed through this atmosphere. They have been impregnated in advance by our geometry, so that our faculty of thinking only finds again in matter the mathematical properties which our faculty of perceiving has already deposed there. We are assured, therefore, of seeing matter yield itself with docility to our reasonings; but this matter, in all that it has that is intelligible, is our own work; of the reality 'in itself we know nothing and never shall know anything, since we only get its refraction through the forms of our faculty of perceiving. So that if we claim to affirm something of it, at once there rises the contrary affirmation, equally demonstrable, equally plausible. The ideality of space is proved directly by the analysis of knowledge, indirectly by the antinomies to which the opposite theory leads. Such is the governing idea of the Kantian criticism. It has inspired Kant with a peremptory refutation of 'empiricist' theories of knowledge. It is, in our opinion, definitive in what it denies. But, in what it affirms, does it give us the solution of the problem?

With Kant, space is given as a ready-made form of our perceptive faculty – a veritable *deus ex machina*, of which we see neither how it arises, nor why it is what it is rather than anything else. 'Things-in-themselves' are also given, of which he claims that we can know nothing: by what right, then, can he affirm their existence, even as 'problematic'? if the unknowable reality projects into our perceptive faculty a 'sensuous manifold' capable of fitting into it exactly, is it not, by that very fact, in part known? And when we examine this exact fitting, shall we not be led, in one point at least, to suppose a pre-established harmony between things and our mind – an idle hypothesis, which Kant was right in wishing to avoid? At bottom, it is for not having distinguished degrees in spatiality that he has had to take space ready-made as given – whence the question how the 'sensuous manifold' is adapted to it. It is for the same reason that he has supposed matter wholly developed into parts absolutely external to one another; – whence antinomies, of which we may plainly see that the thesis and antithesis suppose the perfect coincidence of matter with geometrical space, but which vanish the moment we cease to extend to matter what is true only of pure space. Whence, finally, the conclusion that there are three alternatives, and three only, among which to choose a theory of knowledge: either the mind is determined by things, or things are determined by the mind, or between mind and things we must suppose a mysterious agreement.

But the truth is that there is a fourth, which does not seem to have occurred to Kant – in the first place because he did not think that the mind overflowed the intellect, and in the second place (and this is at bottom the same thing) because he did not attribute to duration an absolute existence, having put time, *a priori*, on the same plane as space. This alternative consists, first of all, in regarding the intellect as a special function of the mind, essentially turned toward inert matter; then in saying that neither does matter determine the form of the intellect, nor does the intellect impose its form on matter, nor have matter and intellect been regulated in regard to one another by we know not what pre-established harmony, but that intellect and matter have progressively adapted themselves one to the other in order to attain at last a common form. *This adaptation has, moreover, been brought about quite naturally, because it is the same inversion of the same movement which creates at once the intellectuality of mind and the materiality of things.*

From this point of view the knowledge of matter that our perception on the one hand and science on the other give to us appears, no doubt, as approximative, but not as relative. Our perception, whose role it is to hold up a light to our actions, works a dividing up of matter that is always too sharply defined, always subordinated to practical needs, consequently always requiring revision. Our science, which aspires to the mathematical form, over-accentuates the spatiality of matter; its formulae are, in general, too precise, and ever need remaking. For a scientific theory to be final, the mind would have to embrace the totality of things in block and place each thing in its exact relation to every other thing; but in reality we are obliged to consider problems one by one, in terms which are, for that very reason, provisional, so that the solution of each problem will have to be corrected indefinitely by the solution that will be given to the problems that will follow, thus, science as a whole is relative to the particular order in which the problems happen to have been put. It is in this meaning, and to this degree, that science must be regarded as conventional. But it is a conventionality of fact so to speak, and not of right. In principle, positive science bears on reality itself, provided it does not overstep the limits of its own domain, which is inert matter.

[. . .]

Certainly, the philosophy of Kant is also imbued with the belief in a science single and complete, embracing the whole of the real. Indeed, looked at from one aspect, it is only a continuation of the metaphysics of the moderns and a transposition of the ancient metaphysics. Spinoza and Leibniz had, following Aristotle, hypostatised in God the unity of knowledge. The Kantian criticism, on one side at least, consists in asking whether the whole of this hypothesis is necessary to modern science as it was to ancient science, or if part of the hypothesis is not sufficient. For the ancients, science applied to *concepts*, that is to say, to kinds of *things*. In compressing all concepts into one, they therefore necessarily arrived at a *being*, which we may call Thought, but which was rather thought-object than thought-subject. When Aristotle defined God the νοήσεως νόησις it is probably on νοήσεως and not on νόησις that he put the emphasis. God was the synthesis of all concepts, the idea of ideas. But modern science turns on laws, that is, on relations. Now, a relation is a bond established by a mind between two or more terms. A relation is nothing outside of the intellect that relates. The universe, therefore, can only be a system of laws if phenomena have passed beforehand through the filter of an intellect. Of course, this intellect might be that of a being infinitely superior to man, who would found the materiality of things at the same time that he bound them together: such was the hypothesis of Leibniz and of Spinoza. But it is not necessary to go so far, and, for the effect we have here to obtain, the human intellect is enough: such is precisely the Kantian solution. Between the dogmatism of a Spinoza or a Leibniz and the criticism of Kant there is just the same distance as between 'it may be maintained that –' and 'it suffices that –'. Kant stops this dogmatism on the incline that was making it slip too far toward the Greek metaphysics; he reduces to the strict minimum the hypothesis which is necessary in order to suppose the physics of Galileo indefinitely extensible. True, when he speaks of the human intellect, he means neither yours nor mine: the unity of nature comes indeed from the human understanding that unifies, but the unifying function that operates here is impersonal. It imparts itself to our individual consciousnesses, but it transcends them. It is much less than a substantial God; it is, however, a little more than the isolated work of a man or even than the collective work of humanity. It does not exactly lie within man; rather, man lies within it, as in an atmosphere of intellectuality which his consciousness breathes. It is, if we will, a *formal* God, something that in Kant is not yet divine, but which tends to become so. It became so, indeed, with Fichte. With Kant, however, its principal role was to give to the whole of our science a relative and *human* character, although of a humanity already somewhat deified. From this point of view, the criticism of Kant consisted chiefly in limiting the dogmatism of his predecessors, accepting their conception of science and reducing to a minimum the metaphysic it implied.

But it is otherwise with the Kantian distinction between the matter of knowledge and its form. By regarding intelligence as pre-eminently a faculty of establishing relations, Kant attributed an extra-intellectual origin to the terms between which the relations are established. He affirmed, against his immediate predecessors, that knowledge is not entirely resolvable into terms of intelligence. He brought back into philosophy – while modifying it and carrying it on to another plane – that essential element of the philosophy of Descartes which had been abandoned by the Cartesians.

Thereby he prepared the way for a new philosophy, which might have established itself in the extra-intellectual matter of knowledge by a higher effort of intuition. Coinciding with this matter, adopting the same rhythm and the same movement, might not consciousness, by two efforts of opposite direction, raising itself and lowering itself by turns, become able to grasp from within, and no longer perceive only from without, the two forms of reality, body and mind? Would not this twofold effort make us, as far as that is possible, re-live the absolute? Moreover, as, in the course of this operation, we should see intellect spring up of itself, cut itself out in the whole of mind, intellectual knowledge would then appear as it is, limited, but not relative.

Such was the direction that Kantianism might have pointed out to a revivified Cartesianism. But in this direction Kant himself did not go.

He *would* not, because, while assigning to knowledge an extra-intellectual matter, he believed this matter to be either coextensive with intellect or less extensive than intellect. Therefore he could not dream of cutting out intellect in it, nor, consequently, of tracing the genesis of the understanding and its categories. The moulds of the understanding and the understanding itself had to be accepted as they are, already made. Between the matter presented to our intellect and this intellect itself there was no relationship. The agreement between the two was due to the fact that intellect imposed its form on matter. So that not only was it necessary to posit the intellectual form of knowledge as a kind of absolute and give up the quest of its genesis, but the very matter of this knowledge seemed too ground down by the intellect for us to be able to hope to get it back in its original purity. It was not the 'thing-in-itself,' it was only the refraction of it through our atmosphere.

If now we inquire why Kant did not believe that the matter of our knowledge extends beyond its form, this is what we find. The criticism of our knowledge of nature that was instituted by Kant consisted in ascertaining what our mind must be and what Nature must be *if* the claims of our science are justified; but of these claims themselves Kant has not made the criticism. I mean that he took for granted the idea of a science that is one, capable of binding with the same force all the parts of what is given, and of co-ordinating them into a system presenting on all sides an equal solidity. He did not consider, in his *Critique of Pure Reason*, that science became less and less objective, more and more symbolical, to the extent that it went from the physical to the vital, from the vital to the psychical. Experience does not move, to his view, in two different and perhaps opposite ways, the one conformable to the direction of the intellect, the other contrary to it. There is, for him, only *one* experience, and the intellect covers its whole ground. This is what Kant expresses by saying that all our intuitions are sensuous, or, in other words, infra-intellectual. And this would have to be admitted, indeed, if our science presented in all its parts an equal objectivity. But suppose, on the contrary, that science is less and less objective, more and more symbolical, as it goes from the physical to the psychical, passing through the vital: then, as it is indeed necessary to perceive a thing somehow in order to symbolize it, there would be an intuition of the psychical, and more generally of the vital, which the intellect would transpose and translate, no doubt, but which would none the less transcend the intellect. There would be, in other words, a supra-intellectual intuition. If this intuition exist, a taking possession of the spirit by itself is possible, and no longer only a knowledge that is external and phenomenal. What is more, if we have an intuition of this kind (I mean an ultra-intellectual intuition) then sensuous intuition is likely to be in continuity with it through certain intermediaries, as the infra-red is continuous with the ultraviolet. Sensuous intuition itself, therefore, is promoted. It will no longer attain only the phantom of an unattainable thing-in-itself. It is (provided we bring to it certain indispensable corrections) into the absolute itself that it will introduce us. So long as it was regarded as the only material of our science, it reflected back on all science something of the relativity which strikes a scientific knowledge of spirit; and thus the perception of bodies, which is the beginning of the science of bodies, seemed itself to be relative. Relative, therefore, seemed to be sensuous intuition. But this is not the case if distinctions are made between the different sciences, and if the scientific knowledge of the spiritual (and also, consequently, of the vital) be regarded as the more or less artificial extension of a certain manner of knowing which, applied to bodies, is not at all symbolical. Let us go further: if there are thus two intuitions of different order (the second being obtained by a reversal of the direction of the first), and if it is toward the second that the intellect naturally inclines, there is no essential difference between the intellect and this intuition itself. The barriers between the matter of sensible knowledge and its form are lowered, as also between the 'pure forms' of sensibility and the categories of the understanding. The matter and form of intellectual knowledge (restricted to its own object) are seen to be engendering each other by a reciprocal adaptation, intellect modelling itself on corporeity, and corporeity on intellect.

But this duality of intuition Kant neither would nor could admit. It would have been necessary, in order to admit it, to regard duration as the very stuff of reality, and consequently to distinguish between the substantial duration of things and time spread out in space. It would have been necessary to regard space itself, and the geometry which is immanent in space, as an ideal limit in the direction of which material things develop, but which they do not actually attain. Nothing could be more contrary to the letter, and perhaps also to the spirit, of the *Critique of Pure Reason*. No doubt, knowledge is presented to us in it as an ever-open roll, experience as a push of facts that is for ever going on. But, according to Kant, these facts are spread out on one plane as fast as they arise; they are external to each other and external to the mind. Of a knowledge from within, that could grasp them in their springing forth instead of taking them already sprung, that would dig beneath space and spatialised time, there is never any question. Yet it is indeed beneath this plane that our consciousness places us; there flows true duration.

In this respect, also, Kant is very near his predecessors. Between the non-temporal, and the time that is spread out in distinct moments, he admits no mean. And as there is indeed no intuition that carries us into the non-temporal, all intuition is thus found to be sensuous, by definition. But between physical existence, which is spread out in space, and non-temporal existence, which can only be a conceptual and logical existence like that of which metaphysical dogmatism speaks, is there not room for consciousness and for life? There is, unquestionably. We perceive it when we place ourselves in duration in order to go from that duration to moments, instead of starting from moments in order to bind them again and to construct duration.

Yet it was to a non-temporal intuition that the immediate successors of Kant turned, in order to escape from the Kantian relativism. Certainly, the ideas of becoming, of progress, of evolution, seem to occupy a large place in their philosophy. But does duration really play a part in it? Real duration is that in which each form flows out of previous forms, while adding to them something new, and is explained by them as much as it explains them; but to deduce this form directly from one complete Being which it is supposed to manifest, is to return to Spinozism. It is, like Leibniz and Spinoza, to deny to duration all efficient action. The post-Kantian philosophy, severe as it may have been on the mechanistic theories, accepts from mechanism the idea of a science that is one and the same for all kinds of reality. And it is nearer to mechanism than it imagines; for though, in the consideration of matter, of life and of thought, it replaces the successive degrees of complexity that mechanism supposed, by degrees of the realization of an Idea or by degrees of the objectification of a Will, it still speaks of degrees, and these degrees are those of a scale which Being traverses in a single direction. In short, it makes out the same articulations in nature that mechanism does.

Of mechanism it retains the whole design; it merely gives it a different colouring. But it is the design itself, or at least one half of the design, that needs to be re-made.

If we are to do that, we must give up the method of *construction*, which was that of Kant's successors. We must appeal to experience – an experience purified, or, in other words, released, where necessary, from the moulds that our intellect has formed in the degree and proportion of the progress of our action on things. An experience of this kind is not a non-temporal experience. It only seeks, beyond the spatialised time in which we believe we see continual rearrangements between the parts, that concrete duration in which a radical recasting of the whole is always going on. It follows the real in all its sinuosities. It does not lead us, like the method of construction, to higher and higher generalities – piled-up stories of a magnificent building. But then it leaves no play between the explanations it suggests and the objects it has to explain. It is the detail of the real, and no longer only the whole in a lump, that it claims to illumine.

The Two Sources of Morality and Religion

Morality, Obligation and the Open Soul[1]

The remembrance of forbidden fruit is the earliest thing in the memory of each of us, as it is in that of mankind. We should notice this, were not this recollection overlaid by others which we are more inclined to dwell upon. What a childhood we should have had if only we had been left to do as we pleased! We should have flitted from pleasure to pleasure. But all of a sudden an obstacle arose, neither visible nor tangible: a prohibition. Why did we obey? The question hardly occurred to us. We had formed the habit of deferring to our parents and teachers. All the same we knew very well that it was because they were our parents, because they were our teachers. Therefore, in our eyes, their authority came less from themselves than from their status in relation to us. They occupied a certain station; that was the source of the command which, had it issued from some other quarter, would not have possessed the same weight. In other words, parents and teachers seemed to act by proxy. We did not fully realize this, but behind our parents and our teachers we had an inkling of some enormous, or rather some shadowy, thing that exerted pressure on us through them. Later we would say it was society. And speculating upon it, we should compare it to an organism whose cells, united by imperceptible links, fall into their respective places in a highly developed hierarchy, and for the greatest good of the whole naturally submit to a discipline that may demand the sacrifice of the part. This, however, can only be a comparison, for an organism subject to inexorable laws is one thing, and a society composed of free wills another. But, once these wills are organized, they assume the guise of an organism; and in this more or less artificial organism habit plays the same role as necessity in the works of nature. From this first standpoint, social life appears to us a system of more or less deeply rooted habits, corresponding to the needs of the community. Some of them are habits of command, most of them are habits of obedience, whether we obey a person commanding by virtue of a mandate from society, or whether from society itself, vaguely perceived or felt, there emanates an impersonal imperative. Each of these habits of obedience exerts a pressure on our will. We can evade it, but then we are attracted towards it, drawn back to it, like a pendulum which has swung away from the vertical. A certain order of things has been upset, it *must be* restored. In a word, as with all habits, we feel a sense of obligation.

But in this case the obligation is immeasurably stronger. When a certain magnitude is so much greater than another that the latter is negligible in comparison, mathematicians say that it belongs to another order. So it is with social obligation. The pressure of it, compared to that of other habits, is such that the difference in degree amounts to a difference in kind. It should be noted that all habits of this nature lend one another mutual support. Although we may not speculate on their essence and on their origin, we feel that they are interrelated, being demanded of us by our immediate surroundings, or by the surroundings of those surroundings, and so on to the uttermost limit, which would be society. Each one corresponds, directly or indirectly, to a social necessity; and so they all hang together, they form a solid block. Many of them would be trivial obligations if they appeared singly. But they are an integral part of obligation in general, and this whole, which is what it is owing to the contributions of its parts, in its turn confers upon each one the undivided authority of the totality. Thus the sum-total comes to the aid of each of its parts, and the general sentence 'do what duty bids' triumphs over the hesitations we might feel in the presence of a single duty. As a matter of fact, we do not explicitly think of a mass of partial duties added together and constituting a single total obligation. Perhaps there is really not an aggregation of parts. The strength which one obligation derives from all the others is rather to be compared to the breath of life drawn, complete and invisible, by each of the cells from the depths of the organism of which it is an element. Society, present within each of its members, has claims which, whether great or small, each express the sum-total of its vitality. But let us again repeat that this is only a comparison. A human community is a collectivity of free beings. The obligations which it lays down, and which enable it to subsist, introduce into it a regularity which has merely some analogy to the inflexible order of the phenomena of life.

And yet everything conspires to make us believe that this regularity is comparable with that of nature. I do not allude merely to the unanimity of mankind in praising certain acts and blaming others. I mean that, even in those cases where moral precepts implied in judgments of values are not observed, we contrive that they should appear so. Just as we do not notice disease when walking along the street, so we do not gauge the degree of possible immorality behind the exterior which humanity presents to the world. It would take a good deal of time to become a misanthrope if we confined ourselves to the observation of others. It is when we detect our own weaknesses that we come to pity or despise mankind. The human nature from which we then turn away is the human nature we have discovered in the depths of our own being. The evil is so well screened, the secret so universally kept, that in this case each individual is the dupe of all: however severely we may profess to judge other men, at bottom we think them better than ourselves. On this happy illusion much of our social life is grounded.

It is natural that society should do everything to encourage this idea. The laws which it promulgates and which maintain the social order resemble, moreover, in certain aspects, the laws of nature. I admit that the difference is a radical one in the eyes of the philosopher. To him the law which enunciates facts is one thing, the law which commands, another. It is possible to evade the latter; here we have obligation, not necessity. The former is, on the contrary, inescapable, for if any fact diverged from it we should be wrong in having assumed it to be a law; there would exist another one, the true one, formulated in such a way as to express everything we observe and to which the recalcitrant fact would then conform like the rest. True enough; but to the majority of people the distinction is far from being so clear. A law, be it physical, social or moral – every law – is in their eyes a command. There is a certain order of nature which finds expression in laws: the facts are presumed to 'obey' these laws so as to conform with that order. The scientist himself can hardly help believing that the law 'governs' facts and consequently is prior to them, like the Platonic Idea on which all things had to model themselves. The higher he rises in the scale of generalizations the more he tends, willy-nilly, to endow the law with this imperative character; it requires a very real struggle against our own prepossessions to imagine the principles of mechanics otherwise than as inscribed from all eternity on the transcendent tables that modern science has apparently fetched down from another Sinai. But if physical law tends to assume in our imagination the form of a command when it attains to a certain degree of generality, in its turn an imperative which applies to everybody appears to us somewhat like a law of nature. The two ideas, coming against each other in our minds, effect an exchange. The law borrows from the command its prerogative of compulsion; the command receives from the law its inevitability. Thus a breach of the social order assumes an anti-natural character; even when frequently repeated, it strikes us as an exception, being to society what a freak creation is to nature.

And suppose we discern behind the social imperative a religious command? No matter the relation between the two terms: whether religion be interpreted in one way or another, whether it be social in essence or by accident, one thing is certain, that it has always played a social role. This part, indeed, is a complex one: it varies with time and place; but in societies such as our own the first effect of religion is to sustain and reinforce the claims of society. It may go much further. It goes at least thus far. Society institutes punishments which may strike the innocent and spare the guilty; its rewards are few and far between; it takes broad views and is easily satisfied; what human scales could weigh, as they should be weighed, rewards and punishments? But, just as the Platonic Ideas reveal to us, in its perfection and fullness, that reality which we see only in crude imitations, so religion admits us to a city whose most prominent features are here and there roughly typified by our institutions, our laws and our customs. Here below, order is merely approximate, being more or less artificially obtained by man; above, it is perfect and self-creative. Religion therefore, in our eyes, succeeds in filling in the gap, already narrowed by our habitual way of looking at things, between a command of society and a law of nature.

We are thus being perpetually brought back to the same comparison, defective though it be in many ways, yet appropriate enough to the point with which we are dealing. The members of a civic community hold together like the cells of an organism. Habit, served by intelligence and imagination, introduces among them a discipline resembling, in the interdependence it establishes between separate individuals, the unity of an organism of anastomotic cells.

Everything, yet again, conspires to make social order an imitation of the order observed in nature. It is evident that each of us, thinking of himself alone, feels at liberty to follow his bent, his desire or his fancy, and not consider his fellow-men. But this inclination has no sooner taken shape than it comes up against a force composed of the accumulation of all social forces: unlike individual motives, each pulling its own way, this force would result in an order not without analogy to that of natural phenomena. The component cell of an organism, on becoming momentarily conscious, would barely have outlived the wish to emancipate itself when it would be recaptured by necessity. An individual forming part of a community may bend or even break a necessity of the same kind, which to some extent he has helped to create, but to which, still more, he has to yield; the sense of this necessity, together with the consciousness of being able to evade it, is none the less what he calls an obligation. From this point of view, and taken in its most usual meaning, obligation is to necessity what habit is to nature.

It does not come then exactly from without. Each of us belongs as much to society as to himself. While his consciousness, delving downwards, reveals to him, the deeper he goes, an ever more original personality, incommensurable with the others and indeed undefinable in words, on the surface of life we are in continuous contact with other men whom we resemble, and united to them by a discipline which creates between them and us a relation of interdependence. Has the self no other means of clinging to something solid than by taking up its position in that part of us which is socialized? That would be so if there were no other way of escape from a life of impulse, caprice and regret. But in our innermost selves, if we know how to look for it, we may perhaps discover another sort of equilibrium, still more desirable than the one on the surface. Certain aquatic plants as they rise to the surface are ceaselessly jostled by the current: their leaves, meeting above the water, interlace, thus imparting to them stability above. But still more stable are the roots, which, firmly planted in the earth, support them from below. However, we shall not dwell for the present on the effort to delve down to the depths of our being. If possible at all, it is exceptional:

and it is on the surface, at the point where it inserts itself into the close-woven tissue of other exteriorised personalities, that our ego generally finds its point of attachment; its solidity lies in this solidarity. But, at the point where it is attached, it is itself socialized. Obligation, which we look upon as a bond between men, first binds us to ourselves.

It would therefore be a mistake to reproach a purely social morality with neglecting individual duties. Even if we were only in theory under a state of obligation towards other men, we should be so in fact towards ourselves, since social solidarity exists only in so far as a social ego is superadded, in each of us, to the individual self. To cultivate this social ego is the essence of our obligation to society. Were there not some part of society in us, it would have no hold on us; and we scarcely need seek it out, we are self-sufficient, if we find it present within us. Its presence is more or less marked in different men; but no one could cut himself off from it completely. Nor would he wish to do so, for he is perfectly aware that the greater part of his strength comes from this source, and that he owes to the ever-recurring demands of social life that unbroken tension of energy, that steadiness of aim in effort, which ensures the greatest return for his activity. But he could not do so, even if he wished to, because his memory and his imagination live on what society has implanted in them, because the soul of society is inherent in the language he speaks, and because even if there is no one present, even if he is merely thinking, he is still talking to himself. Vainly do we try to imagine an individual cut off from all social life. Even materially, Robinson Crusoe on his island remains in contact with other men, for the manufactured objects he saved from the wreck, and without which he could not get along, keep him within the bounds of civilization, and consequently within those of society. But a moral contact is still more necessary to him, for he would be soon discouraged if he had nothing else to cope with his incessant difficulties except an individual strength of which he knows the limitations. He draws energy from the society to which he remains attached in spirit; he may not perceive it, still it is there, watching him: if the individual ego maintains alive and present the social ego, he will effect, even in isolation, what he would with the encouragement and even the support of the whole of society. Those whom circumstances condemn for a time to solitude, and who cannot find within themselves the resources of a deep inner life, know the penalty of 'giving way,' that is to say of not stabilising the individual ego at the level prescribed by the social ego. They will therefore be careful to maintain the latter, so that it shall not relax for one moment its strictness towards the former. If necessary, they will seek for some material or artificial support for it. You remember Kipling's Forest Officer, alone in his bungalow in the heart of the Indian rukh? He dresses every evening for dinner, so as to preserve his self-respect in his isolation.[2]

We shall not go so far as to say that this social ego is Adam Smith's 'impartial spectator,' or that it must necessarily be identified with moral conscience, or that we feel pleased or displeased with ourselves according as it is favourably or unfavourably affected. We shall discover deeper sources for our moral feelings. Language here groups under one name very different things: what is there in common between the remorse of a murderer and that racking, haunting pain, also a remorse, which we may feel at having wounded someone's pride or been unjust to a child? To betray the confidence of an innocent soul opening out to life is one of the most heinous offences for a certain type of conscience, which is apparently lacking in a sense of proportion, precisely because it does not borrow from society its standards, its gauges, its system of measurement. This type of conscience is not the one that is most often at work. At any rate it is more or less sensitive in different people. Generally the verdict of conscience is the verdict which would be given by the social self.

And also, generally speaking, moral distress is a throwing out of gear of the relations between the social and the individual self. Analyse the feeling of remorse in the soul of a desperate criminal. You might mistake it at first for the dread of punishment, and indeed you find most minute precautions, perpetually supplemented and renewed, to conceal the crime and avoid being found out; at every moment comes the awful thought that some detail has been overlooked and that the authorities will get hold of the tell-tale clue. But look closer: what the fellow wants is not so much to evade punishment as to wipe out the past, to arrange things just as though the crime had never been committed at all. When nobody knows that a thing exists, it is almost as if it were non-existent. Thus it is the crime itself that the criminal wants to erase, by suppressing any knowledge of it that might come to the human ken. But his own knowledge persists, and note how it drives him more and more out of that society within which he hoped to remain by obliterating the traces of his crime. For the same esteem for the man he was is still shown to the man he is no longer; therefore society is not addressing him; it is speaking to someone else. He, knowing what he is, feels more isolated among his fellow-men than he would on a desert island; for in his solitude he would carry with him, enveloping him and supporting him, the image of society; but now he is cut off from the image as well as the thing. He could reinstate himself in society by confessing his crime: he would then be treated according to his deserts, but society would then be speaking to his real self. He would resume his collaboration with other men. He would be punished by them, but, having made himself one of them, he would be in a small degree the author of his own condemnation; and a part of himself, the best part, would thus escape the penalty. Such is the force which will drive a criminal to give himself up. Sometimes, without going so far, he will confess to a friend, or to any decent fellow. By thus putting himself right, if not in the eyes of all, at least in somebody's eyes, he re-attaches himself to society at a single point, by a thread: even if he does not reinstate himself in it, at least he is near it, close to it; he no longer remains alienated from it; in any case he is no longer in complete rupture with it, nor with that element of it which is part of himself.

It takes this violent break to reveal clearly the nexus of the individual to society. In the ordinary way we conform to our obligations rather than think of them. If we had every time to evoke the idea, enunciate the formula, it would be much more tiring to do our duty. But habit is enough, and in most cases we have only to leave well alone in order to accord to society what it expects from us. Moreover, society has made matters very much easier for us by interpolating intermediaries between itself and us: we have a family; we follow a trade or a profession; we belong to our parish, to our district, to our country; and, in cases where the insertion of the group into society is complete, we may content ourselves, if need be, with fulfilling our obligations towards the group and so paying our debts to society. Society occupies the circumference; the individual is at the centre: from the centre to the circumference are arranged, like so many ever-widening concentric circles, the various groups to which the individual belongs. From the circumference to the centre, as the circles grow smaller, obligations are added to obligations, and the individual ends by finding himself confronted with all of them together. Thus obligation increases as it advances; but, if it is more complicated, it is less abstract, and the more easily accepted. When it has become fully concrete, it coincides with a tendency, so habitual that we find it natural, to play in society the part which our station assigns to us. So long as we yield to this tendency, we scarcely feel it. It assumes a peremptory aspect, like all deep-seated habits, only if we depart from it.

It is society that draws up for the individual the programme of his daily routine. It is impossible to live a family life, follow a profession, attend to the thousand and one cares of the day, do one's shopping, go for a stroll, or even stay at home, without obeying rules and submitting to obligations. Every instant we have to choose, and we naturally decide on what is in keeping with the rule. We are hardly conscious of this; there is no effort. A road has been marked out by society; it lies open before us, and we follow it; it would take more initiative to cut across country. Duty, in this sense, is almost always done automatically; and obedience to duty, if we restrict ourselves to the most usual case, might be defined as a form of non-exertion, passive acquiescence. How comes it, then, that on the contrary this obedience appears as a state of strain, and duty itself as something harsh and unbending? Obviously because there occur cases where obedience implies an overcoming of self. These cases are exceptions; but we notice them because they are accompanied by acute consciousness, as happens with all forms of hesitation – in fact consciousness is this hesitation itself; for an action which is started automatically passes almost unperceived. Thus, owing to the interdependence of our duties, and because the obligation as a whole is immanent in each of its parts, all duties are tinged with the hue taken on exceptionally by one or the other of them. From the practical point of view this presents no inconvenience, there are even certain advantages in looking at things in this way. For, however naturally we do our duty, we may meet with resistance within ourselves; it is wise to expect it, and not take for granted that it is easy to remain a good husband, a decent citizen, a conscientious worker, in a word an honest fellow. Besides, there is a considerable amount of truth in this opinion; for if it is relatively easy to keep within the social order, yet we have had to enrol in it, and this enrolment demands an effort. The natural disobedience of the child, the necessity of education, are proof of this. It is but just to credit the individual with the consent virtually given to the totality of his obligations, even if he no longer needs to take counsel with himself on each one of them. The rider need only allow himself to be borne along; still he has had to get into the saddle. So it is with the individual in relation to society. In one sense it would be untrue, and in every sense it would be dangerous, to say that duty can be done automatically. Let us then set up as a practical maxim that obedience to duty means resistance to self.

But a maxim is one thing, an explanation another. When, in order to define obligation, its essence and its origin, we lay down that obedience is primarily a struggle with self, a state of tension or contraction, we make a psychological error which has vitiated many theories of ethics. Thus artificial difficulties have arisen, problems which set philosophers at variance and which will be found to vanish when we analyse the terms in which they are expressed. Obligation is in no sense a unique fact, incommensurate with others, looming above them like a mysterious apparition. If a considerable number of philosophers, especially those who follow Kant, have taken this view, it is because they have confused the sense of obligation, a tranquil state akin to inclination, with the violent effort we now and again exert on ourselves to break down a possible obstacle to obligation.

After an attack of rheumatism, we may feel some discomfort and even pain in moving our muscles and joints. It is the general sensation of a resistance set up by all our organs together. Little by little it decreases and ends by being lost in the consciousness we have of our movements when we are well. Now, we are at liberty to fancy that it is still there, in an incipient, or rather a subsiding, condition, that it is only on the look-out for a chance to become more acute; we must indeed expect attacks of rheumatism if we are rheumatic. Yet what should we say of a philosopher who saw in our habitual sensations, when moving our arms and legs, a mere diminution of pain, and who then defined our motory faculty as an effort to resist rheumatic discomfort? To begin with, he would thus be giving up the attempt to account for motory habits, since each of these implies a particular combination of movements, and can be explained only by that combination. The general faculty of walking, running, moving the body, is but an aggregation of these elementary habits, each of them finding its own explanation in the special movements it involves. But having only considered the faculty as a whole, and having then defined it as a force opposed to a resistance, it is natural enough to set up rheumatism beside it as an independent entity. It would seem as though some such error had been made by many of those who have speculated on obligation. We have any number of particular obligations, each calling for a separate explanation. It is natural, or, more strictly speaking, it is a matter of habit to obey them all. Suppose that exceptionally we deviate from one of them, there would be resistance; if we resist this resistance, a state of tension or contraction is likely to result. It is this rigidity which we objectify when we attribute so stern an aspect to duty.

It is also what the philosophers have in mind, when they see fit to resolve obligation into rational elements. In order to resist resistance, to keep to the right paths, when desire, passion or interest tempt us aside, we must necessarily give ourselves reasons. Even if we have opposed the unlawful desire by another, the latter, conjured up by the will, could arise only at the call of an idea. In a word, an intelligent being generally exerts his influence on himself through the medium of intelligence. But from the fact that we get back to obligation by rational ways it does not follow that obligation was of a rational order. We shall dwell on this point later; we do not intend to discuss ethical theories for the present. Let us merely say that a tendency, natural or acquired, is one thing, another thing the necessarily rational method which a reasonable being will use to restore to it its force and to combat what is opposing it. In the latter case the tendency which has been obscured may reappear; and then everything doubtless happens as though we had succeeded by this method in re-establishing the tendency anew. In reality we have merely swept aside something that hampered or checked it. It comes to the same thing, I grant you, in practice: explain the fact in one way or another, the fact is there, we have achieved success. And in order to succeed it is perhaps better to imagine that things did happen in the former way. But to state that this is actually the case would be to vitiate the whole theory of obligation. Has not this been the case with most philosophers?

Let there be no misunderstanding. Even if we confine ourselves to a certain aspect of morality, as we have done up to now, we shall find many different attitudes towards duty. They line the intervening space between the extremes of two attitudes, or rather two habits: that of moving so naturally along the ways laid down by society as barely to notice them; or on the contrary hesitating and deliberating on which way to take, how far to go, the distances out and back we shall have to cover if we try several paths one after another. In the second case new problems arise with more or less frequency; and even in those instances where our duty is fully mapped out, we make all sorts of distinctions in fulfilling it. But, in the first place, the former attitude is that of the immense majority of men; it is probably general in backward communities. And, after all, however much we may reason in each particular case, formulate the maxim, enunciate the principle, deduce the consequences: if desire and passion join in the discussion, if temptation is strong, if we are on the point of falling, if suddenly we recover ourselves, what was it that pulled us up? A force asserts itself which we have called the 'totality of obligation': the concentrated extract, the quintessence of innumerable specific habits of obedience to the countless particular requirements of social life. This force is no one particular thing and, if it could speak (whereas it prefers to act), it would say: 'You must because you must.' Hence the work done by intelligence in weighing reasons, comparing maxims, going back to first principles, was to introduce more logical consistency into a line of conduct subordinated by its very nature to the claims of society; but this social claim was the real root of obligation. Never, in our hours of temptation, should we sacrifice to the mere need for logical consistency our interest, our passion, our vanity. Because in a reasonable being reason does indeed intervene as a regulator to assure this consistency between obligatory rules or maxims, philosophy has been led to look upon it as a principle of obligation. We might as well believe that the fly-wheel drives the machinery.

Besides, the demands of a society dovetail into one another. Even the individual whose decent behaviour is the least based on reasoning and, if I may put it so, the most conventional, introduces a rational order into his conduct by the mere fact of obeying rules which are logically connected together. I freely admit that such logic has been late in taking possession of society. Logical co-ordination is essentially economy. From a whole it first roughly extracts certain principles and then excludes everything which is not in accordance with them. Nature, by contrast, is lavish. The closer a community is to nature, the greater the proportion of unaccountable and inconsistent rules it lays down. We find in primitive races many prohibitions and prescriptions explicable at most by vague associations of ideas, by superstition, by automatism. Nor are they without their use, since the obedience of everyone to laws, even absurd ones, assures greater cohesion to the community. But in that case the usefulness of the rule accrues, by a kind of reverse action, solely from the fact of our submission to it. Prescriptions or prohibitions which are intrinsically useful are those that are explicitly designed for the preservation or well-being of society. No doubt they have gradually detached themselves from the others and survived them. Social demands have therefore been co-ordinated with each other and subordinated to principles. But no matter. Logic permeates indeed present-day communities, and even the man who does not reason out his conduct will live reasonably if he conforms to these principles.

But the essence of obligation is a different thing from a requirement of reason. This is all we have tried to suggest so far. Our description would, we think, correspond more and more to reality as one came to deal with less developed communities and more rudimentary stages of consciousness. It remains a bare outline so long as we confine ourselves to the normal conscience, such as is found today in the ordinary decent person. But precisely because we are in this case dealing with a strange complex of feelings, of ideas and tendencies all interpenetrating each other, we shall avoid artificial analyses and arbitrary syntheses only if we have at hand an outline which gives the essential. Such is the outline we have attempted to trace. Conceive obligation as weighing on the will like a habit, each obligation dragging behind it the accumulated mass of the others, and utilising thus for the pressure it is exerting the weight of the whole: here you have the totality of obligation for a simple, elementary, moral conscience. That is the essential: that is what obligation could, if necessary, be reduced to, even in those cases where it attains its highest complexity.

This shows when and in what sense (how slightly Kantian!) obligation in its elementary state takes the form of a 'categorical imperative.' We should find it very difficult to discover examples of such an imperative in everyday life. A military order, which is a command that admits neither reason nor reply, does say in fact: 'You must because you must.' But, though you may give the soldier no reason, he will imagine one. If we want a pure case of the categorical imperative, we must construct one *a priori* or at least make an arbitrary abstraction of experience. So let us imagine an ant who is stirred by a gleam of reflection and thereupon judges she has been wrong to work unremittingly for others. Her inclination to laziness would indeed endure but a few moments, just as long as the ray of intelligence. In the last of these moments, when instinct regaining the mastery would drag her back by sheer force to her task, intelligence at the point of relapsing into instinct would say, as its parting word: 'You must because you must.' This 'must because you must' would only be the momentary feeling of awareness of a tug which the ant experiences – the tug which the string, momentarily relaxed, exerts as it drags her back. The same command would ring in the ear of a sleepwalker on the point of waking, or even actually beginning to wake, from the dream he is enacting: if he lapsed back at once into a hypnotic state, a categorical imperative would express in words, on behalf of the reflexion which had just been on the point of emerging and had instantly disappeared, the inevitableness of the relapse. In a word, an absolutely categorical imperative is instinctive or somnambulistic, enacted as such in a normal state, represented as such if reflexion is roused long enough to take form, not long enough to seek for reasons. But, then, is it not evident that, in a reasonable being, an imperative will tend to become categorical in proportion as the activity brought into play, although intelligent, will tend to become instinctive? But an activity which, starting as intelligent, progresses towards an imitation of instinct is exactly what we call, in man, a habit. And the most powerful habit, the habit whose strength is made up of the accumulated force of all the elementary social habits, is necessarily the one which best imitates instinct. Is it then surprising that, in the short moment which separates obligation merely experienced as a living force from obligation fully realized and justified by all sorts of reasons, obligation should indeed take the form of the categorical imperative: 'you must because you must'?

Let us consider two divergent lines of evolution with societies at the extremities of each. The type of society which will appear the more natural will obviously be the instinctive type; the link that unites the bees of a hive resembles far more the link which holds together the cells of an organism, co-ordinate and subordinate to one another. Let us suppose for an instant that nature has intended to produce at the extremity of the second line societies where a certain latitude was left to individual choice: she would have arranged that intelligence should achieve here results comparable, as regards their regularity, to those of instinct in the other; she would have had recourse to habit. Each of these habits, which may be called 'moral,' would be incidental. But the aggregate of them, I mean the habit of contracting these habits, being at the very basis of societies and a necessary condition of their existence, would have a force comparable to that of instinct in respect of both intensity and regularity. This is exactly what we have called the 'totality of obligation.' This, be it said, will apply only to human societies at the moment of emerging from the hands of nature. It will apply to primitive and to elementary societies. But, however much human society may progress, grow complicated and spiritualised, the original design, expressing the purpose of nature, will remain.

Now this is exactly what has happened. Without going deeply into a matter we have dealt with elsewhere, let us simply say that intelligence and instinct are forms of consciousness which must have interpenetrated each other in their rudimentary state and become dissociated as they grew. This development occurred on the two main lines of evolution of animal life, with the Arthropods and the Vertebrates. At the end of the former we have the instinct of insects, more especially the Hymenoptera; at the end of the second, human intelligence. Instinct and intelligence have each as their essential object the utilisation of implements: in the first case, organs supplied by nature and hence immutable; in the second, invented tools, and therefore varied and unforeseen. The implement is, moreover, designed for a certain type of work, and this work is all the more efficient the more it is specialized, the more it is divided up between diversely qualified workers who mutually supplement one another. Social life is thus immanent, like a vague ideal, in instinct as well as in intelligence: this ideal finds its most complete expression in the hive or the ant-hill on the one hand, in human societies on the other. Whether human or animal, a society is an organization; it implies a co-ordination and generally also a subordination of elements; it therefore exhibits, whether merely embodied in life or, in addition, specifically formulated, a collection of rules and laws. But in a hive or an ant-hill the individual is riveted to his task by his structure, and the organization is relatively invariable, whereas the human community is variable in form, open to every kind of progress. The result is that in the former each rule is laid down by nature, and is necessary: whereas in the latter only one thing is natural, the necessity of a rule. Thus the more, in human society, we delve down to the root of the various obligations to reach obligation in general, the more obligation will tend to become necessity, the nearer it will draw, in its peremptory aspect, to instinct. And yet we should make a great mistake if we tried to ascribe any particular obligation, whatever it might be, to instinct. What we must perpetually recall is that, no one obligation being instinctive, obligation as a whole *would have been* instinct if human societies were not, so to speak, ballasted with variability and intelligence. It is a virtual instinct, like that which lies behind the habit of speech. The morality of a human society may indeed be compared to its language. If ants exchange signs, which seems probable, those signs are provided by the very instinct that makes the ants communicate with one another. On the contrary, our languages are the product of custom. Nothing in the vocabulary, or even in the syntax, comes from nature. But speech is natural, and unvarying signs, natural in origin, which are presumably used in a community of insects, exhibit what our language would have been, if nature in bestowing on us the faculty of speech had not added that function which, since it makes and uses tools, is inventive and called intelligence. We must perpetually recur to what obligation *would have been* if human society had been instinctive instead of intelligent: this will not explain any particular obligation, we shall even give of obligation in general an idea which would be false, if we went no further; and yet we must think of this instinctive society as the counterpart of intelligent society, if we are not to start without any clue in quest of the foundations of morality.

From this point of view obligation loses its specific character. It ranks among the most general phenomena of life. When the elements which go to make up an organism submit to a rigid discipline, can we say that they feel themselves liable to obligation and that they are obeying a social instinct? Obviously not; but whereas such an organism is barely a community, the hive and the ant-hill are actual organisms, the elements of which are united by invisible ties, and the social instinct of an ant – I mean the force by virtue of which the worker, for example, performs the task to which she is predestined by her structure – cannot differ radically from the cause, whatever it be, by virtue of which every tissue, every cell of a living body, toils for the greatest good of the whole. Indeed it is, strictly speaking, no more a matter of obligation in the one case than in the other, but rather of necessity. It is just this necessity that we perceive, not actual but virtual, at the foundations of moral obligation, as through a more or less transparent veil. A human being feels an obligation only if he is free, and each obligation, considered separately, implies liberty. But it is necessary that there should be obligations; and the deeper we go, away from those particular obligations which are at the top, towards obligation in general, or, as we have said, towards obligation as a whole, which is at the bottom, the more obligation appears as the very form assumed by necessity in the realm of life, when it demands, for the accomplishment of certain ends, intelligence, choice, and therefore liberty.

Here again it may be alleged that this applies to very simple human societies, that is to say primitive or rudimentary societies. Certainly, but, as we shall have occasion to point out later, civilized man differs from primitive man above all by the enormous mass of knowledge and habits which he has absorbed, since the first awakening of his consciousness, from the social surroundings in which they were stored up. What is natural is in great measure overlaid by what is acquired; but it endures, almost unchangeable, throughout the centuries; habits and knowledge by no means impregnate the organism to the extent of being transmitted by heredity, as used to be supposed. It is true that we could consider what is natural as negligible in our analysis of obligation, if it had been crushed out by the acquired habits which have accumulated over it in the course of centuries of civilization. But it remains in excellent condition, very much alive, in the most civilized society. To it we must revert, not to account for this or that social obligation, but to explain what we have called obligation as a whole. Our civilized communities, however different they may be from the society to which we were primarily destined by nature, exhibit indeed, with respect to that society, a fundamental resemblance.

For they too are closed societies. They may be very extensive compared to the small agglomerations to which we were drawn by instinct and which the same instinct would probably tend to revive today if all the material and spiritual acquisitions of civilization were to disappear from the social environment in which we find them stored; their essential characteristic is none the less to include at any moment a certain number of individuals, and exclude others. We have said above, that underlying moral obligation there was a social demand. Of what society were we speaking? Was it of that open society represented by all mankind? We did not settle the matter, any more than one usually does when speaking of a man's duty to his fellows; one remains prudently vague; one refrains from making any assertion, but one would like to have it believed that 'human society' is already an accomplished fact. And it is well that we should like to have it believed, for if incontestably we have duties towards man as man (although these duties have an entirely different origin, as we shall see a little later) we should risk undermining them, were we to make a radical distinction between them and our duties to our fellow-citizens. This is right enough so far as action is concerned. But a moral philosophy which does not emphasize this distinction misses the truth; its analyses will thereby be inevitably distorted. In fact when we lay down that the duty of respecting the life and property of others is a fundamental demand of social life, what society do we mean? To find an answer we need only think what happens in time of war. Murder and pillage and perfidy, cheating and lying become not only lawful, they are actually praiseworthy. The warring nations can say, with Macbeth's witches: 'Fair is foul, and foul is fair.' Would this be possible, would the transformation take place so easily, generally and instantaneously, if it were really a certain attitude of man towards man that society had been enjoining on us up till then? Oh, I know what society says (it has, I repeat, its reasons for saying so); but to know what it thinks and what it wants, we must not listen too much to what it says, we must look at what it does. It says that the duties it defines are indeed, in principle, duties towards humanity, but that under exceptional circumstances, regrettably unavoidable, they are for the time being inapplicable. If society did not express itself thus, it would bar the road to progress for another morality, not derived from it, which it has every inducement to humour. On the other hand, it is consistent with our habits of mind to consider as abnormal anything relatively rare or exceptional, disease for instance. But disease is as normal as health, which, viewed from a certain standpoint, appears as a constant effort to prevent disease or to avoid it. In the same way, peace has always hitherto been a preparation for defence or even attack, at any rate for war. Our social duties aim at social cohesion; whether we will or no they compose for us an attitude which is that of discipline in the face of the enemy. This means that, however much society may endow man, whom it has trained to discipline, with all it has acquired during centuries of civilization, society still has need of that primitive instinct which it coats with so thick a varnish. In a word, the social instinct which we have detected at the basis of social obligation always has in view – instinct being relatively unchangeable – a closed society, however large. It is doubtless overlaid by another morality which for that very reason it supports and to which it lends something of its force, I mean of its imperative character. But it is not itself concerned with humanity. For between the nation, however big, and humanity there lies the whole distance from the finite to the indefinite, from the closed to the open. We are fond of saying that the apprenticeship to civic virtue is served in the family, and that in the same way, from holding our country dear, we learn to love mankind. Our sympathies are supposed to broaden out in an unbroken progression, to expand while remaining identical, and to end by embracing all humanity. This is *a priori* reasoning, the result of a purely intellectualist conception of the soul. We observe that the three groups to which we can attach ourselves comprise an increasing number of people, and we conclude that a progressive expansion of feeling keeps pace with the increasing size of the object we love. And what encourages the illusion is that, by a fortunate coincidence, the first part of the argument chances to fit in with the facts; domestic virtues are indeed bound up with civic virtues, for the very simple reason that family and society, originally undifferentiated, have remained closely connected. But between the society in which we live and humanity in general there is, we repeat, the same contrast as between the closed and the open; the difference between the two objects is one of kind and not simply one of degree. How much greater it would be if, passing to the realm of feeling, we compared with each other the two sentiments, love of country and love of mankind! Who can help seeing that social cohesion is largely due to the necessity for a community to protect itself against others, and that it is primarily as against all other men that we love the men with whom we live? Such is the primitive instinct. It is still there, though fortunately hidden under the accretions of civilization; but even today we still love naturally and directly our parents and our fellow-countrymen, whereas love of mankind is indirect and acquired. We go straight to the former, to the latter we come only by roundabout ways; for it is only through God, in God, that religion bids man love mankind; and likewise it is through reason alone, that Reason in whose communion we are all partakers, that philosophers make us look at humanity in order to show us the pre-eminent dignity of the human being, the right of all to command respect. Neither in the one case nor the other do we come to humanity by degrees, through the stages of the family and the nation. We must, in a single bound, be carried far beyond it, and, without having made it our goal, reach it by outstripping it. Besides, whether we speak the language of religion or the language of philosophy, whether it be a question of love or respect, a different morality, another kind of obligation supervenes, above and beyond the social pressure. So far we have only dealt with the latter. The time has come to pass to the other.

We have been searching for pure obligation. To find it we have had to reduce morality to its simplest expression. The advantage of this has been to indicate in what obligation consisted; the disadvantage, to narrow down morality enormously. Not indeed because that part of it which we have left on one side is not obligatory: is there such a thing as a duty which is not compulsory? But it is conceivable that, starting from a primitive basis of obligation pure and simple, such as we have just defined, this obligation should radiate, expand, and even come to be absorbed into something that transfigures it. Let us now see what complete morality would be like. We shall use the same method and once more proceed, not downwards as up to now but upwards, to the extreme limit.

In all times there have arisen exceptional men, incarnating this morality. Before the saints of Christianity, mankind had known the sages of Greece, the prophets of Israel, the Arahants of Buddhism, and others besides. It is to them that men have always turned for that complete morality which we had best call absolute morality. And this very fact is at once characteristic and instructive; this very fact suggests to us the existence of a difference of kind and not merely one of degree between the morality with which we have been dealing up to now and that we are about to study, between the minimum and the maximum, between the two extremes. Whereas the former is all the more unalloyed and perfect precisely in proportion as it is the more readily reduced to impersonal formulae, the second, in order to be fully itself, must be incarnate in a privileged person who becomes an example. The generality of the one consists in the universal acceptance of a law, that of the other in a common imitation of a model.

Why is it, then, that saints have their imitators, and why do the great moral leaders draw the masses after them? They ask nothing, and yet they receive. They have no need to exhort; their mere existence suffices. For such is precisely the nature of this other morality. Whereas natural obligation is a pressure or a propulsive force, complete and perfect morality has the effect of an appeal.

Only those who have come into touch with a great moral personality have fully realized the nature of this appeal. But we all, at those momentous hours when our usual maxims of conduct strike us as inadequate, have wondered what such or such a one would have expected of us under the circumstances. It might have been a relation or a friend whom we thus evoked in thought. But it might quite as well have been a man we had never met, whose life-story had merely been told us, and to whose judgment we in imagination submitted our conduct, fearful of his censure, proud of his approval. It might even be a personality brought up from the depths of the soul into the light of consciousness, stirring into life within us, which we felt might completely pervade us later, and to which we wished to attach ourselves for the time being, as the disciple to his teacher. As a matter of fact this personality takes shape as soon as we adopt a model; the longing to resemble, which ideally generates the form, is an incipient resemblance; the word which we shall make our own is the word whose echo we have heard within ourselves. But the person matters little. Let us merely make the point that, whereas the first morality was the more potent the more distinctly it broke up into impersonal obligation, on the contrary the latter morality, at first dispersed among general precepts to which our intelligence gave its allegiance, but which did not go so far as to set our will in motion, becomes more and more cogent in proportion as the multiplicity and generality of its maxims merge more completely into a man's unity and individuality.

Whence does it derive its strength? What is the principle of action which here takes the place of the natural obligation, or rather which ends by absorbing it? To discover this, let us first see what is tacitly demanded of us. The duties dealt with so far are those imposed on us by social life; they are binding in respect of the city more than in respect of humanity. You might say that the second morality – if we *do* distinguish two – differs from the first in that it is human instead of being merely social. And you would not be entirely wrong. For we have seen that it is not by widening the bounds of the city that you reach humanity; between a social morality and a human morality the difference is not one of degree but of kind. The former is the one of which we are generally thinking when we feel a natural obligation. Superimposed upon these clearly defined duties we like to imagine others, the lines of which are perhaps a little blurred. Loyalty, sacrifice of self, the spirit of renunciation, charity, such are the words we use when we think of these things. But have we, generally speaking, in mind at such times anything more than words? Probably not, and we fully realize this. It is sufficient, we say, that the formula is there; it will take on its full meaning, the idea which is to fill it out will become operative, when the occasion arises. It is true that for many people the occasion will never arise or the action will be put off till later. With certain people the will does make a feeble start, but so feeble that the slight shock they feel can in fact be attributed to no more than the expansion of social duty broadened and weakened into human duty. But only let these formulae be invested with substance, and that substance become animate, lo and behold! a new life is proclaimed; we understand, we feel the advent of a new morality. Consequently, in speaking here of love of humanity we should doubtless be denoting this morality. And yet we should not be expressing the essence of it, for the love of humanity is not a self-sufficient force or one which has a direct efficacy. The teachers of the young know full well that you cannot prevail over egoism by recommending 'altruism.' It even happens that a generous nature, eager to sacrifice itself, experiences a sudden chill at the idea that it is working 'for mankind.' The object is too vast, the effect too diffuse. We may therefore conjecture that if a love of humanity constitutes this morality, it constitutes it in much the same way as the intention of reaching a certain point implies the necessity of crossing an intervening space. In one sense it is the same thing; in another sense it is something entirely different. If we think only of the interval and the various points, infinite in number, which we still have to pass one by one, we shall be discouraged from starting, like Zeno's arrow, and besides there would be no object, no inducement. But if we step across the intervening space, thinking only of the goal or looking even beyond it, we shall easily accomplish a simple act, and at the same time overcome the infinite multiplicity of which this simplicity is the equivalent. What then, in this case, is the goal, what the direction of the effort? What exactly, in a word, is required of us?

Let us first define the moral attitude of the man we have been considering up to now. He is part and parcel of society; he and it are absorbed together in the same task of individual and social preservation. Both are self-centred. True, it is doubtful whether private interest invariably agrees with public interest: we know against what insurmountable difficulties utilitarian ethics has always come up when it laid down the principle that the individual could seek only his own good, while maintaining that this would lead him to desire the good of others. An intelligent being, pursuing his personal advantage, will often do something quite different from what the general interest demands. Yet, if utilitarian ethics persists in recurring in one form or another, this means that it is not untenable, and if it is tenable the reason is precisely because, beneath the intelligent activity, forced in fact to choose between its own interests and those of others, there lies a substratum of instinctive activity, originally implanted there by nature, where the individual and the social are well-nigh indistinguishable. The cell lives for itself and also for the organism, imparting to it vitality and borrowing vitality from it; it will sacrifice itself to the whole, if need be; and it would doubtless then say, if it were conscious, that it made this sacrifice in its own interest. Such would probably be the state of mind of an ant reflecting on her conduct. She would feel that her activity hinges on something intermediate between the good of the ant and the good of the ant-hill. Now it is just with this fundamental instinct that we have associated obligation as such: it implies at the beginning a state of things in which the individual and society are not distinguishable. This is what enables us to say that the attitude to which it corresponds is that of an individual and a community concentrated on themselves. At once individual and social, the soul here moves round in a circle. It is closed.

The other attitude is that of the open soul. What, in that case, is allowed in? Suppose we say that it embraces all humanity: we should not be going too far, we should hardly be going far enough, since its love may extend to animals, to plants, to all nature. And yet no one of these things which would thus fill it would suffice to define the attitude taken by the soul, for it could, strictly speaking, do without all of them. Its form is not dependent on its content. We have just filled it; we could as easily empty it again. 'Charity' would persist in him who possesses 'charity,' though there be no other living creature on earth.

Once again, it is not by a process of expansion of the self that we can pass from the first state to the second. A psychology which is too purely intellectualist, following the indications of speech, will doubtless define feelings by the things with which they are associated; love for one's family, love for one's country, love of mankind, it will see in these three inclinations one single feeling, growing ever larger, to embrace an increasing number of persons. The fact that these feelings are outwardly expressed by the same attitude or the same sort of motion, that all three *incline* us to something, enables us to group them under the concept 'love,' and to express them by one and the same word; we then distinguish them by naming three objects, each larger than the other, to which they are supposed to apply. This does in fact suffice to distinguish them. But does it describe them? Or analyse them? At a glance, consciousness perceives between the two first feelings and the third a difference of kind. The first imply a choice, therefore an exclusion; they may act as incentives to strife, they do not exclude hatred. The latter is all love. The former alight directly on an object which attracts them. The latter does not yield to the attraction of its object; it has not aimed at this object; it has shot beyond and reached humanity only by passing through humanity. Has it, strictly speaking, an object? We shall ask this question. But for the present we shall confine ourselves to noting that this psychic attitude, or rather psychic motion, is self-sufficient.

Nevertheless there arises in regard to it a problem which stands ready solved in the case of the other. For that other was ordained by nature; we have just seen how and why we feel bound to adopt it. But the second attitude is acquired; it calls for, has always called for, an effort. How comes it that the men who have set the example have found other men to follow them? And what is the power that is in this case the counterpart of social pressure? We have no choice. Beyond instinct and habit there is no direct action on the will except feeling. The impulse given by feeling can indeed closely resemble obligation. Analyse the passion of love, particularly in its early stages; is pleasure its aim? Could we not as well say it is pain? Perhaps a tragedy lies ahead, a whole life wrecked, wasted, ruined, we know it, we feel it, no matter, we must because we must. Indeed the worst perfidy of a nascent passion is that it counterfeits duty. But we need not go as far as passion. Into the most peaceful emotion there may enter a certain demand for action, which differs from obligation as described above in that it will meet with no resistance, in that it imposes only what has already been acquiesced in, but which none the less resembles obligation in that it does impose something. Nowhere do we see this more clearly than in those cases where the demand ceases to have any practical consequence, thus leaving us the leisure to reflect upon it and analyse what we feel. This is what occurs in musical emotion, for example. We feel, while we listen, as though we could not desire anything else but what the music is suggesting to us, and that that is just as we should naturally and necessarily act did we not refrain from action to listen. Let the music express joy or grief, pity or love, every moment we are what it expresses. Not only ourselves, but many others, nay, all the others, too. When music weeps, all humanity, all nature, weeps with it. In point of fact it does not introduce these feelings into us; it introduces us into them, as passers-by are forced into a street dance. Thus do pioneers in morality proceed. Life holds for them unsuspected tones of feeling like those of some new symphony, and they draw us after them into this music that we may express it in action.

It is through excess of intellectualism that feeling is made to hinge on an object and that all emotion is held to be the reaction of our sensory faculties to an intellectual representation. Taking again the example of music, we all know that it arouses in us well-defined emotions, joy, sorrow, pity, love, that these emotions may be intense and that to us they are complete, though not attached to anything in particular. Are you going to say that we are here in the realm of art and not among real things, that therefore we are playing at emotion, that our feeling is purely imaginative, and that, anyway, the musician could not produce this emotion in us, suggest it without causing it, if we had not already experienced it in real life, where it was caused by an object from which art had merely to detach it? That would be to forget that joy and sorrow, pity and love, are words expressing generalities, words which we must call upon to express what music makes us feel, whereas each new musical work brings with it new feelings, which are created by that music and within that music, are defined and delimited by the lines, unique of their kind, of the melody or symphony. They have therefore not been extracted from life by art; it is we who, in order to express them in words, are driven to compare the feeling created by the artist with the feeling most resembling it in life. But let us then take states of emotion caused in effect by certain things and, as it were, prefigured in them. Those ordained by nature are finite, that is to say limited in number. They are recognizable because they are destined to spur us on to acts answering to needs. The others, on the contrary, are real inventions, comparable to those of the musician, at the origin of which there has always been a man. Thus mountains may, since the beginning of time, have had the faculty of rousing in those who looked upon them certain feelings comparable with sensations, and indeed inseparable from mountains. But Rousseau created in connection with them a new and original emotion. This emotion has become current coin, Rousseau having put it into circulation. And even today it is Rousseau who makes us feel it, as much and more than the mountains. True, there are reasons why this emotion, sprung from the heart of Jean-Jacques, should fasten on to mountains rather than any other object; the elementary feelings, akin to sensations, which were directly aroused by mountains must have been able to harmonize with the new emotion. But Rousseau gathered them together, gave them their places, henceforth as mere harmonics in a sound for which he provided, by a true creation, the principal tone. It is the same with love of nature in general. Nature has ever aroused feelings which are almost sensations; people have always enjoyed the pleasant shade, the cool waters, etc., in fine all those things suggested in the word 'amoenus' by which the Romans described the charm of the country. But a fresh emotion, surely the creation of some person or persons, has arisen and used these pre-existing notes as harmonics, and produced in this way something to be compared with the fresh tones of a new instrument, what we call in our respective countries the sentiment of nature. The fundamental tone thus introduced might have been different, as is the case in the East, in Japan especially: the *timbre* would then have been different. Feelings akin to sensation, closely bound up with the objects which give rise to them, are indeed just as likely to attract a previously created emotion as they are to connect with an entirely new one. This is what happened with love. From time immemorial woman must have inspired man with an inclination distinct from desire, but in immediate contact, as though welded to it, and pertaining both to feeling and to sensation. But romantic love has a definite date: it sprang up during the Middle Ages on the day when some person or persons conceived the idea of absorbing love into a kind of supernatural feeling, into religious emotion as created by Christianity and launched by the new religion into the world. When critics reproach mysticism with expressing itself in the same terms as passionate love, they forget that it was love which began by plagiarizing mysticism, borrowing from it its fervour, its raptures, its ecstasies: in using the language of a passion it had transfigured, mysticism has only resumed possession of its own. We may add that the nearer love is to adoration, the greater the disproportion between the emotion and the object, the deeper therefore the disappointment to which the lover is exposed unless he decides that he will ever look at the object through the mist of the emotion and never touch it, that he will, in a word, treat it religiously. Note that the ancients had already spoken of the illusions of love, but these were errors akin to those of the senses, and they concerned the face of the beloved, her figure, her bearing, her character. Think of Lucretius' description: the illusion here applies only to the qualities of the loved one, and not, as with the modern illusion, to what we can expect of love. Between the old illusion and the illusion we have superadded to it there is the same difference as between the primitive feeling, emanating from the object itself, and the religious emotion summoned from without by which it has been pervaded and eventually submerged. The margin left for disappointment is now enormous, for it is the gap between the divine and the human.

That a new emotion is the source of the great creations of art, of science and of civilization in general there seems to be no doubt. Not only because emotion is a stimulus, because it incites the intelligence to undertake ventures and the will to persevere with them. We must go much further. There are emotions which beget thought; and invention, though it belongs to the category of the intellect, may partake of sensibility in its substance. For we must agree upon the meaning of the words 'emotion,' 'feeling' and 'sensibility.' An emotion is an affective stirring of the soul, but a surface agitation is one thing, an upheaval of the depths another. The effect is in the first case diffused, in the second it remains undivided. In the one it is an oscillation of the parts without any displacement of the whole; in the other the whole is driven forward. Let us, however, get away from metaphors. We must distinguish between two kinds of emotion, two varieties of feeling, two manifestations of sensibility which have this one feature in common, that they are emotional states distinct from sensation, and cannot be reduced, like the latter, to the psychical transposition of a physical stimulus. In the first case the emotion is the consequence of an idea, or of a mental picture; the 'feeling' is indeed the result of an intellectual state which owes nothing to it, which is self-sufficient, and which, if it does experience a certain reaction from the feeling, loses more than it gains. It is the stirring of sensibility by a representation, as it were, dropped into it. But the other kind of emotion is not produced by a representation which it follows and from which it remains distinct. Rather is it, in relation to the intellectual states which are to supervene, a cause and not an effect; it is pregnant with representations, not one of which is actually formed, but which it draws or might draw from its own substance by an organic development. The first is infra-intellectual; that is the one with which the psychologist is generally concerned, and it is this we have in mind when we contrast sensibility with intelligence, and when we make of emotions a vague reflection of the representation. But of the other we should be inclined to say that it is supra-intellectual, if the word did not immediately and exclusively evoke the idea of superiority of value: it is just as much a question of priority in time, and of the relation between that which generates and that which is generated. Indeed, the second kind of emotion can alone be productive of ideas.

This is just what the critic overlooks when he qualifies as 'feminine,' with a touch of contempt, a psychology which accords so extensive and so handsome a place to sensibility. First of all he should be blamed for abiding by the current commonplaces about women, when it is so easy to use one's eyes. I do not intend, for the mere sake of correcting an inappropriate word, to enter upon a comparative study of the two sexes. Suffice it to say that woman is as intelligent as man, but that she is less capable of emotion, and that if there is any faculty or power of the soul which seems to attain less development in woman than in man, it is not intelligence, but sensibility. I mean of course sensibility in the depths, not agitation at the surface.[3] But no matter. When the critic fancies that he would do injustice to man if he related to sensibility the highest faculties of the mind, he is still more to be blamed for not seeing precisely where the difference lies between that intelligence which understands, discusses, accepts or rejects – which in a word limits itself to criticism – and the intelligence which invents.

Creation signifies, above all, emotion, and that not in literature or art alone. We all know the concentration and effort implied in scientific discovery. Genius has been defined as 'an infinite capacity for taking pains.' True, we think of intelligence as something apart, and, too, as something equally apart a general faculty of attention which, when more or less developed, is supposed to produce a greater or lesser concentration of intelligence. But how could this indeterminate attention, extraneous to intelligence, bring out of intelligence something which is not there? We cannot help feeling that psychology is once more the dupe of language when, having used the same word to denote all efforts of attention made in all possible cases, and having thus been deceived into assuming them to be all of the same quality, it perceives between them only differences of degree. The truth is that in each case attention takes on a distinctive colouring, as though individualized by the object to which it applies: this is why psychology has already a tendency to use the term 'interest' as much as 'attention,' thus implicitly introducing sensibility, as being capable of more extensive variation according to particular cases. But then this diversity is not sufficiently insisted upon; a general faculty of being interested is posited, which, while always the same faculty, once again affords variety only through a greater or lesser application to its object. So do not let us speak of interest in general. Let us rather say that the problem which has aroused interest is a representation duplicated by an emotion, and that the emotion, being at one and the same time curiosity, desire and the anticipated joy of solving a stated problem, is, like the representation, unique. It is the emotion which drives the intelligence forward in spite of obstacles. It is the emotion above all which vivifies, or rather vitalizes, the intellectual elements with which it is destined to unite, constantly collecting everything that can be worked in with them and finally compelling the enunciation of the problem to expand into its solution. And what about literature and art? A work of genius is in most cases the outcome of an emotion, unique of its kind, which seemed to baffle expression, and yet which *had* to express itself. But is not this so of all work, however imperfect, into which there enters some degree of creativeness? Anyone engaged in writing has been in a position to feel the difference between an intelligence left to itself and that which burns with the fire of an original and unique emotion, born of the identification of the author with his subject, that is to say of intuition. In the first case the mind cold-hammers the materials, combining together ideas long since cast into words and which society supplies in a solid form. In the second, it would seem that the solid materials supplied by intelligence first melt and mix, then solidify again into fresh ideas now shaped by the creative mind itself. If these ideas find words already existing which can express them, for each of them this seems a piece of unexpected good luck; and, in truth, it has often been necessary to assist fortune, and strain the meaning of a word, to mould it to the thought. In that event the effort is painful and the result problematical. But it is in such a case only that the mind feels itself, or believes itself, to be creative. It no longer starts from a multiplicity of ready-made elements to arrive at a composite unity made up of a new arrangement of the old. It has been transported at a bound to something which seems both one and unique, and which will contrive later to express itself, more or less satisfactorily, in concepts both multiple and common, previously provided by language.

To sum up, alongside of the emotion which is a result of the representation and which is added to it, there is the emotion which precedes the image, which virtually contains it, and is to a certain extent its cause. A play may be scarcely a work of literature and yet it may rack our nerves and cause an emotion of the first kind, intense, no doubt, but commonplace, culled from those we experience in the course of daily life, and in any case devoid of mental content. But the emotion excited within us by a great dramatic work is of quite a distinct character. Unique of its kind, it has sprung up in the soul of the poet and there alone, before stirring our own; from this emotion the work has sprung, to this emotion the author was continually harking back throughout the composition of the work. It was no more than a creative exigency, but it was a specific one, now satisfied once the work is finished, which would not have been satisfied by some other work unless that other had possessed an inward and profound resemblance with the former, such as that which exists between two equally satisfactory renderings, in terms of ideas or images, of one and the same melody.

Which amounts to saying that, in attributing to emotion a large share in the genesis of the moral disposition, we are not by any means enunciating a 'moral philosophy of sentiment.' For we are dealing with an emotion capable of crystallising into representations and even into an ethical doctrine. From this particular doctrine we could never have elicited the moral disposition any more than from any other; no amount of speculation will create an obligation or anything like it: the theory may be all very fine, I shall always be able to say that I will not accept it; and even if I do accept it, I shall claim to be free and do as I please. But if the atmosphere of the emotion is there, if I have breathed it in, if it has entered my being, I shall act in accordance with it, uplifted by it; not from constraint or necessity, but by virtue of an inclination which I should not want to resist. And instead of explaining my act by emotion itself, I might in this case just as well deduce it from the theory built up by the transposition of that emotion into ideas. We here get a glimpse of the possible reply to a weighty question which we have just touched on incidentally and with which we shall be confronted later. People are fond of saying that if a religion brings us a new morality, it imposes that morality by means of the metaphysics which it disposes us to accept, by its ideas on God, the universe, the relation of the one to the other. To which the answer has been made that it is, on the contrary, by the superiority of its morality that a religion wins over souls and reveals to them a certain conception of things. But would intelligence recognize the superiority of the proposed morality, since it can appreciate differences of value only by comparing them with a rule or an ideal, and this ideal and this rule are perforce supplied by the morality which is already in occupation? On the other hand, how could a new conception of the universal order of things be anything but yet another philosophy to set alongside of those we know? Even if our intelligence is won over, we shall never see in it anything but an explanation, theoretically preferable to the others. Even if it seems to enjoin on us, as more in harmony with itself, certain rules of conduct, there will be a wide gap between this assent of the intellect and a conversion of the will. But the truth is that the doctrine cannot, as a purely intellectual representation, ensure the adoption and, above all, the practice of the corresponding morality, any more than the particular morality, considered by intelligence as a system of rules of conduct, can render the doctrine intellectually preferable. Antecedent to the new morality, and also the new metaphysics, there is the emotion, which develops as an impetus in the realm of the will, and as an explicative representation in that of intelligence. Take, for example, the emotion introduced by Christianity under the name of charity: if it wins over souls, a certain behaviour ensues and a certain doctrine is disseminated. But neither has its metaphysics enforced the moral practice, nor the moral practice induced a disposition to its metaphysics. Metaphysics and morality express here the selfsame thing, one in terms of intelligence, the other in terms of will; and the two expressions of the thing are accepted together, as soon as the thing is there to be expressed.

That a substantial half of our morality includes duties whose obligatory character is to be explained fundamentally by the pressure of society on the individual will be readily granted, because these duties are a matter of current practice, because they have a clear precise formula, and it is therefore easy for us, by grasping them where they are entirely visible, and then going down to the roots, to discover the social requirements from which they sprang. But that the rest of morality expresses a certain emotional state, that actually we yield not to a pressure but to an attraction, many people will hesitate to acknowledge. The reason is that here we cannot, generally speaking, get back to the original emotion in the depths of our hearts. There exist formulae which are the residue of this emotion, and which have settled in what we may call the social conscience according as, within that emotion, a new conception of life took form – or rather a certain attitude towards life. Precisely because we find ourselves in the presence of the ashes of an extinct emotion, and because the driving power of that emotion came from the fire within it, the formulae which have remained would generally be incapable of rousing our will, if older formulae, expressing the fundamental requirements of social life, did not by contagious influence communicate to them something of their own obligatory character. These two moralities, placed side by side, appear now to be only one, the first having lent to the second something of its imperative character and having, on the other hand, received from it in exchange a connotation less strictly social, more broadly human. But let us stir the ashes, we shall find some of them still warm, and at length the sparks will kindle into flame; the fire may blaze up again; and, if it does, it will gradually spread. I mean that the maxims of the second morality do not work singly, like those of the first: as soon as one of them, ceasing to be abstract, becomes filled with significance and acquires the capacity to act, the others tend to do the same: at last they will fuse in the warm emotion which left them behind long ago, and in the men, now come to life again, who experienced it. Founders and reformers of religions, mystics and saints, obscure heroes of moral life whom we have met on our way and who are in our eyes the equals of the greatest, they are all there: inspired by their example, we follow them, as if we were joining an army of conquerors. They are indeed conquerors: they have broken down natural resistance and raised humanity to a new destiny. Thus, when we dispel appearances to get at reality, when we set aside the common form assumed, thanks to mutual exchanges, by the two moralities in conceptual thought and in speech, then, at the two extremes of the single morality we find pressure and aspiration: the former the more perfect as it becomes more impersonal, closer to those natural forces which we call habit or even instinct, the latter the more powerful according as it is more obviously aroused in us by definite persons, and the more it apparently triumphs over nature. True, if we went down to the roots of nature itself we should perhaps find that the same force which manifests itself directly, rotating on its own axis, in the human species once constituted, also acts later and indirectly, through the medium of privileged persons, in order to drive humanity forward. [. . .]

But antecedent to this metaphysical theory, and far nearer to what we have directly experienced, are the simpler representations which in this case spring from the emotion in proportion as we dwell on it. We were speaking of the founders and reformers of religion, the mystics and the saints. Let us hearken to their language; it merely expresses in representations the emotions peculiar to a soul opening out, breaking with nature, which enclosed it both within itself and within the city.

They begin by saying that what they experience is a feeling of liberation. Well-being, pleasures, riches, all those things that mean so much to the common run of men, leave them indifferent. In breaking away from them they feel relief, and then exhilaration. Not that nature was wrong in attaching us by strong ties to the life she had ordained for us. But we must go further, and the amenities which are real comforts at home would become hindrances, burdensome impedimenta, if we had to take them on our travels. That a soul thus equipped for action would be more drawn to sympathize with other souls, and even with the whole of nature, might surprise us, if the relative immobility of the soul, revolving in a circle in an enclosed society, was not due precisely to the fact that nature has split humanity into a variety of individuals by the very act which constituted the human species. Like all acts creative of a species, this was a halt on the road. By a resumption of the forward movement, the decision to halt is broken. True, to obtain a complete effect, the privileged soul would have to carry the rest of humanity with it. But if a few follow, and if the others imagine they would do likewise on occasion, this already means a great deal; henceforth, with the beginning of accomplishment, there will be the hope that the circle may be broken in the end. In any case, we cannot repeat too often that it is not by preaching the love of our neighbour that we can obtain it. It is not by expanding our narrower feelings that we can embrace humanity. However much our intelligence may convince itself that this is the line of advance, things behave differently. What is simple for our understanding is not necessarily so for our will. In cases where logic affirms that a certain road should be the shortest, experience intervenes, and finds that in that direction there is no road. The truth is that heroism may be the only way to love. Now, heroism cannot be preached, it has only to show itself, and its mere presence may stir others to action. For heroism itself is a return to movement, and emanates from an emotion – infectious like all emotions – akin to the creative act. Religion expresses this truth in its own way by saying that it is in God that we love all other men. And all great mystics declare that they have the impression of a current passing from their soul to God, and flowing back again from God to mankind.

Let no one speak of material obstacles to a soul thus freed! It will not answer that we can get round the obstacle, or that we can break it; it will declare that there is no obstacle. We cannot even say of this moral conviction that it moves mountains, for it sees no mountains to move. So long as you argue about the obstacle, it will stay where it is; and so long as you look at it, you will divide it into parts which will have to be overcome one by one; there may be no limit to their number; perhaps you will never exhaust them. But you can do away with the whole, at a stroke, if you deny its existence. That is what the philosopher did who proved movement by walking: his act was the negation pure and simple of the effort, perpetually to be renewed, and therefore fruitless, which Zeno judged indispensable to cover, one by one, the stages of the intervening space. By going deeply into this new aspect of morality, we should find an impression of coincidence, real or imaginary, with the generative effort of life. If seen from outside, the activity of life lends itself, in each of its works, to an analysis which might be carried on indefinitely; there is no end to a description of the structure of an eye such as ours. But what we call a series of means employed is, in reality, but a number of obstacles overcome; the action of nature is simple, and the infinite complexity of the mechanism which it seems to have built up piece by piece to achieve the power of vision is but the endless network of opposing forces which have cancelled one another out to secure an uninterrupted channel for the functioning of the faculty. So, if we took into account only what we saw, the simple act of an invisible hand plunged into iron filings would seem like an inexhaustible interplay of actions and reactions among the filings themselves in order that they might effect an equilibrium. If such is the contrast between the real working of life and the aspect it presents to the senses and the intelligence which analyse it, is it surprising that a soul which no more recognizes any material obstacle should feel itself, rightly or wrongly, at one with the principle of life?

Whatever heterogeneity we may at first find between the effect and the cause, and though the distance is great from a rule of conduct to a power of nature, it has always been from the contact with the generative principle of the human species that a man has felt he drew the strength to love mankind. By this I mean, of course, a love which absorbs and kindles the whole soul. But a more lukewarm love, faint and fleeting, can only be a radiation of the former, if not a still paler and colder image of it, left behind in the mind or deposited in speech. Thus, morality comprises two different parts, one of which follows from the original structure of human society, while the other finds its explanation in the principle which explains this structure. In the former, obligation stands for the pressure exerted by the elements of society on one another in order to maintain the shape of the whole; a pressure whose effect is prefigured in each of us by a system of habits which, so to speak, go to meet it: this mechanism, of which each separate part is a habit, but whose whole is comparable to an instinct, has been prepared by nature. In the second, there is still obligation, if you will, but that obligation is the force of an aspiration or an impetus, of the very impetus which culminated in the human species, in social life, in a system of habits which bears a resemblance more or less to instinct: the primitive impetus here comes into play directly, and no longer through the medium of the mechanisms it had set up, and at which it had provisionally halted. In short, to sum up what has gone before, we should say that nature, setting down the human species along the line of evolution, intended it to be sociable, in the same way as it did the communities of ants and bees; but since intelligence was there, the maintenance of social life had to be entrusted to an all but intelligent mechanism: intelligent in that each piece could be remodelled by human intelligence, yet instinctive in that man could not, without ceasing to be a man, reject all the pieces together and cease to accept a mechanism of preservation. Instinct gave place temporarily to a system of habits, each one of which became contingent, their convergence towards the preservation of society being alone necessary, and this necessity bringing back instinct with it. The necessity of the whole, felt behind the contingency of the parts, is what we call moral obligation in general – it being understood that the parts are contingent in the eyes of society only; to the individual, into whom society inculcates its habits, the part is as necessary as the whole. Now the mechanism designed by nature was simple, like the societies originally constituted by her. Did she foresee the immense development and the endless complexities of societies such as ours? Let us first agree as to the meaning of this question. We do not assert that nature has, strictly speaking, designed or foreseen anything whatever. But we have the right to proceed like a biologist, who speaks of nature's intentions every time he assigns a function to an organ: he merely expresses thus the adequateness of the organ to the function. In spite of humanity's having become civilized, in spite of the transformation of society, we maintain that the tendencies which are, as it were, organic in social life have remained what they were in the beginning. We can trace them back and study them. The result of this investigation is clear; it is for closed, simple societies that the moral structure, original and fundamental in man, is made. I grant that the organic tendencies do not stand out clearly to our consciousness. They constitute, nevertheless, the strongest element of obligation. However complex our morality has grown and though it has become coupled with tendencies which are not mere modifications of natural tendencies, and whose trend is not in the direction of nature, it is to these natural tendencies that we come in the end, when we want to obtain a precipitate of the pure obligation contained in this fluid mass. Such then is the first half of morality. The other had no place in nature's plan. We mean that nature foresaw a certain expansion of social life through intelligence, but it was to be a limited expansion. She could not have intended that this should go on so far as to endanger the original structure. Numerous indeed are the instances where man has thus outwitted nature, so knowing and wise, yet so simple-minded. Nature surely intended that men should beget men endlessly, according to the rule followed by all other living creatures; she took the most minute precautions to ensure the preservation of the species by the multiplication of individuals; hence she had not foreseen, when bestowing on us intelligence, that intelligence would at once find a way of divorcing the sexual act from its consequences, and that man might refrain from reaping without forgoing the pleasure of sowing. It is in quite another sense that man outwits nature when he extends social solidarity into the brotherhood of man; but he is deceiving her nevertheless, for those societies whose design was prefigured in the original structure of the human soul, and of which we can still perceive the plan in the innate and fundamental tendencies of modern man, required that the group be closely united, but that between group and group there should be virtual hostility; we were always to be prepared for attack or defence. Not, of course, that nature designed war for war's sake. Those leaders of humanity drawing men after them, who have broken down the gates of the city, seem indeed thereby to have placed themselves again in the current of the vital impetus. But this impetus inherent in life is, like life, finite. Its path is strewn with obstacles, and the species which have appeared, one after the other, are so many combinations of this force with opposing forces: the former urging us forward, the others making us turn in a circle. Man, fresh from the hands of nature, was a being both intelligent and social, his sociability being devised to find its scope in small communities, his intelligence being designed to further individual and group life. But intelligence, expanding through its own efforts, has developed unexpectedly. It has freed men from restrictions to which they were condemned by the limitations of their nature. This being so, it was not impossible that some of them, specially gifted, should reopen that which was closed and do, at least for themselves, what nature could not possibly have done for mankind. Their example has ended in leading others forward, in imagination at least. There is a genius of the will as there is a genius of the mind, and genius defies all anticipation. Through those geniuses of the will, the impetus of life, traversing matter, wrests from it, for the future of the species, promises such as were out of the question when the species was being constituted. Hence in passing from social solidarity to the brotherhood of man, we break with one particular nature, but not with all nature. It might be said, by slightly distorting the terms of Spinoza, that it is to get back to *natura naturans* that we break away from *natura naturata*.

Hence, between the first morality and the second, lies the whole distance between repose and movement. The first is supposed to be immutable. If it changes, it immediately forgets that it has changed, or it acknowledges no change. The shape it assumes at any given time claims to be the final shape. But the second is a forward thrust, a demand for movement; it is the very essence of mobility. Thus would it prove, thus alone, indeed, would it be able at first to define, its superiority. Postulate the first, you cannot bring the second out of it, any more than you can from one or several positions of a moveable body derive motion. But, on the contrary, movement includes immobility, each position traversed by the moving object being conceived and even perceived as a virtual stop. But a detailed demonstration is unnecessary: the superiority is experienced before ever it is represented, and furthermore could not be demonstrated afterwards if it had not first been felt. There is a difference of vital tone. Those who regularly put into practice the morality of the city know this feeling of well-being, common to the individual and to society, which is the outward sign of the interplay of material resistances neutralizing each other. But the soul that is opening, and before whose eyes material objects vanish, is lost in sheer joy. Pleasure and well-being are something, joy is more. For it is not contained in these, whereas they are virtually contained in joy. They mean, indeed, a halt or a marking time, while joy is a step forward.

That is why the first morality is comparatively easy to formulate, but not the second. For our intelligence and our language deal in fact with things; they are less at home in representing transitions or progress. The morality of the Gospels is essentially that of the open soul: are we not justified in pointing out that it borders upon paradox, and even upon contradiction, in its more definite admonitions? If riches are an evil, should we not be injuring the poor in giving them what we possess? If he who has been smitten on the one cheek is to offer the other also, what becomes of justice, without which, after all, there can be no 'charity'? But the paradox disappears, the contradiction vanishes, if we consider the intent of these maxims, which is to create a certain disposition of the soul. It is not for the sake of the poor, but for his own sake, that the rich man should give up his riches: blessed are the poor 'in spirit'! The beauty lies, not in being deprived, not even in depriving oneself, but in not feeling the deprivation. The act by which the soul opens out broadens and raises to pure spirituality a morality enclosed and materialized in ready-made rules: the latter then becomes, in comparison with the other, something like a snapshot view of movement. Such is the inner meaning of the antitheses that occur one after the other in the Sermon on the Mount: 'Ye have heard that it was said . . . I say unto you . . .' On the one hand the closed, on the other the open. Current morality is not abolished; but it appears like a virtual stop in the course of actual progression. The old method is not given up; but it is fitted into a more general method, as is the case when the dynamic reabsorbs the static, the latter then becoming a mere particular instance of the former. We should need then, strictly speaking, a means of expressing directly the movement and the tendency; but if we still want – and we cannot avoid it – to translate them into the language of the static and the motionless, we shall be confronted with formulae that border on contradiction. So we might compare what is impracticable in certain precepts of the Gospels to what was illogical in the first explanations of the differential calculus. Indeed, between the morality of the ancients and Christianity we should find much the same relation as that between the mathematics of antiquity and our own.

The geometry of the ancients may have provided particular solutions which were, so to say, an anticipated application of our general methods; but it never brought out these methods; the impetus was not there which would have made them spring from the static to the dynamic. But at any rate it carried as far as possible the imitation of the dynamic by the static. Now, we have just the same impression when we compare, for example, the doctrine of the Stoics with Christian morality. The Stoics proclaimed themselves citizens of the world, and added that all men were brothers, having come from the same God. The words were almost the same; but they did not find the same echo, because they were not spoken with the same accent. The Stoics provided some very fine examples. If they did not succeed in drawing humanity after them, it is because Stoicism is essentially a philosophy. The philosopher who is so enamoured of this noble doctrine as to become wrapped up in it doubtless vitalizes it by translating it into practice; just so did Pygmalion's love breathe life into the statue once it was carven. But it is a far cry from that to the enthusiasm which spreads from soul to soul, unceasingly, like a conflagration. Such an emotion may indeed develop into ideas which make up a doctrine, or even several different doctrines having no other resemblance between them than a kinship of the spirit; but it precedes the idea instead of following it. To find something of the kind in classical antiquity, we must go not to the Stoics, but rather to the man who inspired all the great philosophers of Greece without contributing any system, without having written anything, Socrates. Socrates indeed exalts the exercise of reason, and particularly the logical function of the mind, above everything else. The irony he parades is meant to dispose of opinions which have not undergone the test of reflection, to put them to shame, so to speak, by setting them in contradiction with themselves. Dialogue, as he understands it, has given birth to the Platonic dialectics and consequently to the philosophical method, essentially rational, which we still practise. The object of such a dialogue is to arrive at concepts that may be circumscribed by definitions; these concepts will become the Platonic Ideas; and the theory of Ideas, in its turn, will serve as a model for the systems, also essentially rational, of traditional metaphysics. Socrates goes further still; virtue itself he holds to be a science, he identifies the practice of good with our knowledge of it; he thus paves the way for the doctrine which will absorb all moral life in the rational function of thought. Reason has never been set so high. At least that is what strikes us at first. But let us look closer. Socrates teaches because the oracle of Delphi has spoken. He has received a mission. He is poor, and poor he must remain. He must mix with the common folk, he must become one of them, his speech must get back to their speech. He will write nothing, so that his thought shall be communicated, a living thing, to minds who shall convey it to other minds. He is indifferent to cold and hunger, though in no way an ascetic; he is merely delivered from material needs, and emancipated from his body. A 'daemon' accompanies him, which makes its voice heard when a warning is necessary. He so thoroughly believes in this 'daemonic voice' that he dies rather than not follow it; if he refuses to defend himself before the popular tribunal, if he goes to meet his condemnation, it is because the 'daemon' has said nothing to dissuade him. In a word, his mission is of a religious and mystic order, in the present-day meaning of the words; his teaching, so perfectly rational, hinges on something that seems to transcend pure reason. But do we not detect this in his teaching itself? If the inspired, or at all events lyrical sayings, which occur throughout the dialogues of Plato, were not those of Socrates, but those of Plato himself, if the master's language had always been such as Xenophon attributes to him, could we understand the enthusiasm which fired his disciples, and which has come down the ages? Stoics, Epicureans, Cynics, all the Greek moralists spring from Socrates – not only, as has always been said, because they develop the teaching of the Master in its various directions, but also, and, above all, because they borrow from him the attitude which is so little in keeping with the Greek spirit and which he created, the attitude of the Sage. Whenever the philosopher, closeted with his wisdom, stands apart from the common rule of mankind – be it to teach them, to serve as a model, or simply to go about his work of perfecting his inner self – Socrates is there, Socrates alive, working through the incomparable prestige of his person. Let us go further. It has been said that he brought philosophy down from heaven to earth. But could we understand his life, and above all his death, if the conception of the soul which Plato attributes to him in the *Phaedo* had not been his? More generally speaking, do the myths we find in the dialogues of Plato, touching the soul, its origin, its entrance into the body, do anything more than set down in Platonic terms a creative emotion, the emotion present in the moral teaching of Socrates? The myths, and the Socratic conception of the soul to which they stand in the same relationship as the explanatory programme to a symphony, have been preserved along with the Platonic dialectics. They pursue their subterranean way through Greek metaphysics, and rise to the open air again with the Alexandrine philosophers, with Ammonius perhaps, in any case with Plotinus, who claims to be the successor of Socrates. They have provided the Socratic soul with a body of doctrine similar to that into which was to be breathed the spirit of the Gospels. The two metaphysics, in spite, perhaps because, of their resemblance, gave battle to each other, before the one absorbed the best that was in the other; for a while the world may well have wondered whether it was to become Christian or Neo-Platonic. It was Socrates against Jesus. To confine ourselves to Socrates, the question is: what would this very practical genius have done in another society and in other circumstances; if he had not been struck, above all, by the danger of the moral empiricism of his time, and the mental anarchy of Athenian democracy; if he had not had to deal with the most crying need first, by establishing the rights of reason; if he had not therefore thrust intuition and inspiration into the background, and if the Greek he was had not mastered in him the Oriental who sought to come into being? We have made the distinction between the closed and the open: would anyone place Socrates among the closed souls? There was irony running through Socratic teaching, and outbursts of lyricism were probably rare; but in the measure in which these outbursts cleared the road for a new spirit, they have been decisive for the future of humanity.

Between the closed soul and the open soul there is the soul in process of opening. Between the immobility of a man seated and the motion of the same man running there is the act of getting up, the attitude he assumes when he rises. In a word, between the static and the dynamic there is to be observed, in morality too, a transition stage. This intermediate state would pass unnoticed if, when at rest, we could develop the necessary impetus to spring straight into action. But it attracts our attention when we stop short – the usual sign of insufficient impetus. Let us put the same thing in a different way. We have seen that the purely static morality might be called infra-intellectual, and the purely dynamic, supra-intellectual. Nature intended the one, and the other is a contribution of man's genius. The former is characteristic of a whole group of habits which are, in man, the counterpart of certain instincts in animals; it is something less than intelligence. The latter is inspiration, intuition, emotion, susceptible of analysis into ideas which furnish intellectual notations of it and branch out into infinite detail; thus, like a unity which encompasses and transcends a plurality incapable of ever equalling it, it contains any amount of intellectuality; it is more than intelligence. Between the two lies intelligence itself. It is at this point that the human soul would have settled down, had it sprung forward from the one without reaching the other. It would have dominated the morality of the closed soul; it would not have attained to, or rather it would have not have created, that of the open soul. Its attitude, the result of getting up, would have lifted it to the plane of intellectuality. Compared with the position it had just left – described negatively – such a soul would be manifesting indifference or insensibility, it would be in the 'ataraxy' or the 'apathy' of the Epicureans and the Stoics. Considered in what it positively is, if its detachment from the old sought to be an attachment to something new, its life would be contemplation; it would conform to the Platonic and the Aristotelian ideal. From whatever angle we look at it, its attitude would be upright, noble, truly worthy of admiration and reserved for the chosen few. Philosophies which start from very different principles may find in it a common goal. The reason is that there is only one road leading from action confined in a circle to action developing in the freedom of space, from repetition to creation, from the infra-intellectual to the supra-intellectual. Anyone halting between the two is inevitably in the zone of pure contemplation, and in any case, no longer holding to the one but without having yet reached the other, naturally practises that half-virtue, detachment.

Frenzy, Mechanism, Mysticism[4]

The alterations of ebb and flow in history have often been discussed. All prolonged action, it would seem, brings about a reaction in the opposite direction. Then it starts anew, and the pendulum swings on indefinitely. True, in this case the pendulum is endowed with memory, and is not the same when it swings back as on the outward swing, since it is then richer by all the intermediate experience. This is why the image of a spiral movement, which has sometimes been used, is perhaps more correct than that of the oscillations of a pendulum. As a matter of fact, there are psychological and social causes which we might *a priori* predict will be productive of such effects. The uninterrupted enjoyment of an eagerly-sought advantage engenders weariness or indifference; it seldom fulfils completely its promise; it brings with it unforeseen drawbacks; it ends by making conspicuous the good side of what has been given up and arousing a desire to get it back. The desire will be found principally in the rising generations, who have not experienced the ills of the past, and have not had to extricate themselves from them. Whereas the parents congratulate themselves on the present state of things as an acquisition for which they remember paying dearly, the children give it no more thought than the air they breathe; on the other hand, they are alive to disadvantages which are nothing but the reverse side of the advantages so painfully won for them. Thus may arise a wish to put the clock back. Such actions and reactions are characteristic of the modern State, not by reason of any historical fatality, but because parliamentary government was conceived in part with the very object of providing a channel for discontent. The powers that be receive but moderate praise for the good they do; they are there to do it: but their slightest mistake is scored; and all mistakes are stored up until their accumulated weight causes the government to fall. If there are two opposing parties and two only, the game will go on with perfect regularity. Each team will come back into power, bringing with it the prestige of principles which have apparently remained intact during the period in which it had no responsibility to bear: principles sit with the Opposition. In reality the Opposition will have profited, if it is intelligent, by the experience it has left the party in power to work out; it will have more or less modified the content of its ideas and hence the significance of its principles. Thus progress becomes possible, in spite of the swing of the pendulum, or rather because of it, if only men care about it. But, in such cases, the oscillation between the two opposite extremes is the result of certain very simple contrivances set up by society, or certain very obvious tendencies of the individual. It is not the effect of a paramount necessity towering above the particular causes of alternation and dominating human events in general. Does such a necessity exist?

We do not believe in the fatality of history. There is no obstacle which cannot be broken down by wills sufficiently keyed up, if they deal with it in time. There is thus no inescapable historical law. But there are biological laws; and the human societies, in so far as they are partly willed by nature, pertain to biology on this particular point. If the evolution of the organized world takes place according to certain laws, I mean by virtue of certain forces, it is impossible that the psychological evolution of individual and social man should entirely renounce these habits of life. Now we have shown elsewhere that the essence of a vital tendency is to develop fan-wise, creating, by the mere fact of its growth, divergent directions, each of which will receive a certain portion of the impetus. We added that there was nothing mysterious about this law. It simply expresses the fact that a tendency is the forward thrust of an indistinct multiplicity, which is, moreover, indistinct, and multiplicity, only if we consider it in retrospect, when the multitudinous views taken of its past undivided character allow us to see it composed of elements which were actually created by its development. Let us imagine that orange is the only colour that has as yet made its appearance in the world. Would it be already a composite of yellow and red? Obviously not. But it *will have been* composed of yellow and red when these two colours are born in their turn; from that hour the original orange colour can be looked at from the twofold point of view of red and yellow; and if we supposed, by a trick of fancy, that yellow and red appeared through an intensification of orange, we should have a very simple example of what we call fan-wise growth. But there is no real necessity for fancy and comparisons. All we need is to look at life without letting any idea of artificial synthesis supervene. Some psychologists hold the act of volition to be a composite reflex, others are inclined to see in the reflex activity a curtailment of volition. The truth is that the reflex and the voluntary actions embody two views, now rendered possible, of a primordial, indivisible activity, which was neither the one nor the other, but which becomes retroactively, through them, both at once. We could say the same of instinct and intelligence, of animal life and vegetable life, of many other pairs of divergent and complementary tendencies. Only, in the general evolution of life, the tendencies thus created by a process of dichotomy are to be found in species different from one another; they have set forth, each independently, to seek their fortunes in the world; and the material form they have assumed prevents them from reuniting to bring back again, stronger than it was, more complex, more fully evolved, the original tendency. Not so in the evolution of the psychical and social life. Here the tendencies, born of the process of splitting, develop in the same individual, or in the same society. As a rule, they can be developed only in succession. If there are two of them, as is generally the case, one of them will be clung to first; with this one we shall move more or less forward, generally as far as possible; then, with what we have acquired in the course of this evolution, we shall come back to take up the one we left behind. That one will then be developed in its turn, the former being neglected, and our new effort will be continued until, reinforced by new acquisitions, we can take up the first one again and push it further forward still. Since, during the operation, we are entirely given up to one of the two tendencies, since it alone counts, we are apt to say that it alone is positive and that the other was only its negation; if we like to put things in this way, the other is, as a matter of fact, its opposite. It will then be said – and this will be more or less true according to circumstances – that the progress was due to an oscillation between the two opposites, the situation moreover not being the same and a gain having been realized by the time the pendulum has swung back to its original position. But it does sometimes happen that the expression is entirely accurate, and that there is really oscillation between two opposites. This is when a tendency, advantageous in itself, cannot be moderated otherwise than by the action of a counter-tendency, which hence becomes advantageous also. It would seem as though the wise course, then, would be a co-operation of the two tendencies, the first intervening when circumstances require, the other restraining it when it threatens to go too far. Unfortunately, it is difficult to say where exaggeration and danger begin. Sometimes the mere fact of going further than appeared reasonable leads to new surroundings, creates a new situation which removes the danger, at the same time emphasizing the advantage. This is especially the case with the very general tendencies which determine the trend of a society, and whose development necessarily extends over a more or less considerable number of generations. An intelligence, even a superhuman one, cannot say where this will lead to, since action on the move creates its own route, creates to a very great extent the conditions under which it is to be fulfilled, and thus baffles all calculation. In such a case, one pushes further and further afield, often stopping only on the very brink of disaster. The counter-tendency then steps into the place that has been vacated; alone, in its turn, it will go as far as it can go. If the other was called action, then this will be reaction. As the two tendencies, if they had journeyed together, would have moderated each other, as their interpenetration in an undivided primitive tendency is the very definition of moderation, the mere fact of taking up all the room imparts to each of them such an impetus that it bolts ahead as the barriers collapse one by one; there is something frenzied about it. Now we must not make exaggerated use of the word 'law' in a field which is that of liberty, but we may use this convenient term when we are confronted with important facts which show sufficient regularity. So we will call *law of dichotomy* that law which apparently brings about a materialization, by a mere splitting up, of tendencies which began by being two photographic views, so to speak, of one and the same tendency. And we propose to designate *law of twofold frenzy* the imperative demand, forthcoming from each of the two tendencies as soon as it is materialized by the splitting, to be pursued to the very end – as if there was an end! Once more, it is difficult not to wonder whether the simple tendency would not have done better to grow without dividing in two, thus being kept within bounds by the very coincidence of its propulsive force with the power of stopping, which would then have been virtually, but not actually, a distinct and contrary force of impulsion. There would have been, then, no risk of stumbling into absurdity; there would have been an insurance against disaster. Yes, but this would not have given the maximum of creation, in quantity and in quality. It is necessary to keep on to the bitter end in one direction, to find out what it will yield: when we can go no further, we turn back, with all we have acquired, to set off in the direction from which we had turned aside. Doubtless, looking from the outside at these comings and goings we see only the antagonism of the two tendencies, the futile attempt of the one to thwart the other, the ultimate defeat of the second and the revenge of the first: man loves the dramatic; he is strongly inclined to pick out from a whole more or less extended period of history those characteristics which make of it a struggle between two parties, two societies or two principles, each of them in turn coming off victorious. But the struggle is here only the superficial aspect of an advance. The truth is that a tendency on which two different views are possible can put forth its maximum, in quantity or quality, only if it materializes these two possibilities into moving realities, each one of which leaps forward and monopolizes the available space, while the other is on the watch unceasingly for its own turn to come. Only thus will the content of the original tendency develop, if indeed we can speak of a content when no one, not even the tendency itself if it achieved consciousness, could tell what will issue from it. It supplies the effort, and the result is a surprise. Such are the workings of nature; the struggles which she stages for us do not indicate pugnacity so much as curiosity. And it is precisely when it imitates nature, when it yields to the original impulsion, that the progress of humanity assumes a certain regularity and conforms – though very imperfectly, be it said – to such laws as those we have stated. But the time has come to close this all too long parenthesis. Let us merely show how our two laws would apply in the case which led us to open it.

We were dealing with the concern for comfort and luxury which has apparently become the main preoccupation of humanity. In considering how it has developed the spirit of invention, how so many inventions are the application of science, and how science is destined to extend its scope indefinitely, we should be tempted to believe in indefinite progress in the same direction. Never, indeed, do the satisfactions with which new inventions meet old needs induce humanity to leave things at that; new needs arise, just as imperious and increasingly numerous. We have seen the race for comfort proceeding faster and faster, on a track along which are surging ever denser crowds. Today it is a stampede. But should not this very frenzy open our eyes? Was there not some other frenzy to which it has succeeded, and which developed in the opposite direction an activity of which the present frenzy is the complement? In point of fact, it is from the fifteenth or sixteenth century onward that men seemed to aspire to easier material conditions. Throughout the Middle Ages, an ascetic ideal had predominated. There is no need to recall the exaggerations to which it led; here already you had frenzy. It may be alleged that asceticism was confined to a very small minority, and this is true. But just as mysticism, the privilege of a few, was popularised by religion, so concentrated asceticism, which was doubtless exceptional, became diluted for the rank and file of mankind into a general indifference to the conditions of daily existence. There was for one and all an absence of comfort which to us is astonishing. Rich and poor did without superfluities which we consider as necessities. It has been pointed out that if the lord lived better than the peasant, we must understand by this that he had more abundant food.[5] Otherwise, the difference was slight. Here we are, then, in the presence of two divergent tendencies which have succeeded each other and have behaved, both of them, frantically. So, we may presume that they correspond to two opposing manifestations of one primordial tendency, which in this way contrived to evolve from itself, in quantity and quality, everything that it was capable of, even more than it had to give, proceeding along each of the two roads, one after the other, getting back into one direction with everything that had been picked up by the way in the other. That signifies oscillation and progress, progress by oscillation. And we should expect, after the ever-increasing complexity of life, a return to simplicity. This return is obviously not a certainty; the future of humanity remains indeterminate, precisely because it is on humanity that it depends. But if, ahead of us, lie only possibilities or probabilities, which we shall examine presently, we cannot say the same for the past: the two opposite developments which we have just indicated are indeed those of a single original tendency.

And indeed the history of ideas bears witness to it. Out of Socratic thought, pursued in two different directions which in Socrates were complementary, came the Cyrenaic and the Cynic doctrines: the one insisted that we should demand from life the greatest possible number of satisfactions, the other that we should learn to do without them. They developed into Epicureanism and Stoicism with their two opposing tendencies, laxity and tension. If there were the least doubt about the common essence of the two mental attitudes to which these principles correspond, it would suffice to note that, in the Epicurean school itself, along with popular Epicureanism which was at times the unbridled pursuit of pleasure, there was the Epicureanism of Epicurus, according to which the supreme pleasure was to need no pleasures. The truth is that the two principles are at the heart of the traditional conception of happiness. Here is a word which is commonly used to designate something intricate and ambiguous, one of those ideas which humanity has intentionally left vague, so that each individual might interpret it after his own fashion. But in whatever sense it is understood, there is no happiness without security – I mean without the prospect of being able to rely on the permanence of a state into which one has settled oneself. This assurance is to be found either in the mastering of things, or in the mastering of self which makes one independent of things. In both cases there is delight in one's strength, whether inwardly perceived or outwardly manifested: the one may lead to pride, the other to vanity. But the simplification and complication of life do indeed follow from a 'dichotomy,' are indeed apt to develop into 'double frenzy,' in fact have all that is required to alternate periodically.

This being so, as we have said above, there is nothing improbable in the return to a simpler life. Science itself might show us the way. Whereas physics and chemistry help us to satisfy and encourage us to multiply our needs, it is conceivable that physiology and medical science may reveal more and more clearly to us all the dangers of this multiplication, all the disappointments which accompany the majority of our satisfactions. I enjoy a well-prepared dish of meat; to a vegetarian, who used to like it as much as I do, the mere sight of meat is sickening. It may be alleged that we are both right, and that there is no more arguing about taste than about colour. Perhaps: but I cannot help noting that my vegetarian is thoroughly convinced he will never revert to his old inclinations, whereas I am not nearly so sure that I shall always stick to mine. He has been through both experiments; I have only tried one. His repulsion grows stronger as he fixes his attention on it, whereas my satisfaction is largely a matter of inattention and tends to pale in a strong light. I do believe it would fade away altogether, if decisive experiments came to prove, as it is not impossible they will, that I am directly and slowly poisoning myself by eating meat.[6] I was taught in my school days that the composition of foodstuffs was known, the requirements of our organs also, that it was possible to deduce from this the necessary and sufficient ration to maintain life. The master would have been very much surprised to hear that chemical analysis did not take into account 'vitamins' whose presence in food is indispensable to health. It will probably be found that more than one malady, for which medical science has no cure, takes its remote origin from 'deficiencies' of which we have no inkling. The only sure means of absorbing all we need would be to have our food subjected to no preparation, perhaps even (who knows) not cooked at all. Here again the belief in the heredity of acquired habits has done great harm. It is commonly said that the human stomach has lost the habit, that we could not feed ourselves nowadays like primitive man. This is true, if taken as meaning that we have left certain natural tendencies lie dormant from our infancy, and that it would be difficult to reawaken them in middle age. But that we are born modified is hardly probable: even if our stomach is different from that of our prehistoric ancestors, the difference is not due to mere habit contracted down the ages. It will not be long before science enlightens us on all these points. Let us suppose that it does so in the sense we foresee: the mere reform of our food supply would have immeasurable reactions on our industry, our trade, our agriculture, all of which it would considerably simplify. What about our other needs? The demands of the procreative senses are imperious, but they would be quickly settled if we hearkened to nature alone. The trouble is that around a violent but paltry sensation, taken as the fundamental, humanity has made rise an endlessly increasing number of overtones: so rich a variety of timbres that almost any object struck on some particular point now gives out the sound that has become an obsession. Thus the senses are constantly being roused by the imagination. Sex-appeal is the keynote of our whole civilization. Here again science has something to say, and it will say it one day so clearly that all must listen: there will no longer be pleasure in so much love of pleasure. Woman will hasten the coming of this time according as she really and sincerely strives to become man's equal, instead of remaining the instrument she still is, waiting to vibrate under the musician's bow. Let the transformation take place: our life will be both more purposeful and more simple. What woman demands in the way of luxuries in order to please man, and, at the rebound, to please herself, will become to a great extent unnecessary. There will be less waste, and less enviousness. Luxury, pleasure and comfort are indeed closely akin, though the connexion between them is not what it is generally supposed to be. It is our way to arrange them in a certain gradation, we are supposed to move up the scale from comfort to luxury: when we have made sure of our comfort we want to cap it with pleasures, then comes love of luxury on top of all. But this is a purely intellectualist psychology, which imagines that our feelings can be measured exactly by their objects. Because luxuries cost more than mere conveniences, and pleasure more than comfort, they are supposed to be keeping pace with goodness knows what corresponding desire. The truth is that it is generally for the sake of our luxuries that we want our comforts, because the comforts we lack look to us like luxuries, and because we want to imitate and equal those people who can afford them. In the beginning was vanity. How many delicacies are sought after solely because they are expensive! For years civilized people spent a great part of their efforts abroad in procuring spices. It is amazing to think that this was the supreme object of navigation, so perilous in those days; that for this thousands of men risked their lives; that the courage, the energy and the spirit of adventure, of which the discovery of America was a mere incident, were mainly employed in the search for ginger, cloves, pepper and cinnamon. Who troubles about these flavourings which so long tasted delicious, now that they can be had for a few pence from the grocer round the corner? Such facts as these are sad reading for the moralist. But reflect a moment, they contain cause for hope as well. The continual craving for creature comforts, the pursuit of pleasure, the unbridled love of luxury, all these things which fill us with so much anxiety for the future of humanity, because it seems to find in them solid satisfactions, all this will appear as a balloon which man has madly inflated, and which will deflate just as suddenly. We know that one frenzy brings on the counter-frenzy. More particularly, the comparison of present-day facts with those of the past is a warning to us to regard as transient tastes which appear to be permanent. Since today the supreme ambition for so many men is to have a car, let us recognize the incomparable services rendered by motor-cars, admire the mechanical marvel they are, hope that they will multiply and spread wherever they are needed, but let us say to ourselves that a short time hence they may not be so greatly in demand just as an amenity or 'for swank,' though the chances are that they may not be quite so neglected, and we hope not, as cloves and cinnamon are today.

Here we come to the essential point of our discussion. We have just cited an example of the craving for luxuries arising from a mechanical invention. Many are of the opinion that it is mechanical invention in general which has developed the taste for luxuries, and indeed for mere comfort. Nay, if it is generally admitted that our material needs will go on indefinitely growing more numerous and more imperious, this is because there seems to be no reason why humanity should abandon the path of mechanical invention, once it has started on it. Let us add that, the more science advances, the more inventions are suggested by its discoveries; in many cases from theory to application is but a step; and since science cannot stop, it really does look indeed as though there could be no end to the satisfying of our old needs and the creation of new ones. But we must first ascertain whether the spirit of invention necessarily creates artificial needs, or whether in this case it is not the artificial need which has guided the spirit of invention.

The second hypothesis is by far the more probable. It is confirmed by recent research on the origin of mechanization.[7] The fact has been recalled that man has always invented machines, that antiquity has remarkable ones to show, that many a clever mechanical device was thought of long before the development of modern science, and, at a later stage, independently of it: even today a mere workman, without scientific culture, will hit on improvements which have never occurred to skilled engineers. Mechanical invention is a natural gift. Doubtless its effects were limited so long as it was confined to utilizing actual, and as it were visible, forces: muscular effort, wind or water power. The machine developed its full efficiency only from the day when it became possible to place at its service, by a simple process of releasing, the potential energies stored up for millions of years, borrowed from the sun, deposited in coal, oil, etc. But that was the day when the steam-engine was invented, and we know that this invention was not the outcome of theoretical considerations. Let us hasten to add that the progress made, slow enough at first, assumed giant proportions as soon as science took a hand. It is none the less true that the spirit of mechanical invention, which runs between narrow banks so long as it is left to itself, but expands indefinitely after its conjunction with science, remains distinct from it, and could, if need be, do without it. Similarly we have the Rhône entering the Lake of Geneva, apparently mingling with its waters, but showing, when it leaves it again, that it has preserved its independence.

There has not been then, as some people are inclined to believe, a demand on the part of science, imposing on men, by the mere fact of its development, increasingly artificial needs. If that were so, humanity would be doomed to a growing materiality, for the progress of science will never cease. But the truth is that science has given what was asked of it, and has not in this case taken the initiative; it is the spirit of invention which has not always operated in the best interests of humanity. It has created a mass of new needs; it has not taken the trouble to ensure for the majority of men, for all if that were possible, the satisfaction of old needs. To put it more clearly; though not neglecting the necessary, it has thought too much about the superfluous. It may be said that these two terms are hard to define, and that what are luxuries to some people are necessities to others. True, and it would be easy enough here to lose one's way amid subtle and fine distinctions. But there are cases where subtlety should be cast aside and a broad view taken. Millions of men never get enough to eat. There are some who starve to death. If the land produced much more, there would be far fewer chances of not getting enough to eat,[8] or of starving to death. Over-production here is but a *deceptio visus*. If mechanization is in any way to blame, it is for not having sufficiently devoted itself to helping man in his agricultural labour. It will be said that agricultural implements exist and are now widely used. I grant it, but all that mechanization has done here to lighten man's burden, all that science has done on its side to increase the yield of the soil, amounts to comparatively little. We feel strongly that agriculture, which nourishes man, should dominate all else, in any case be the first concern of industry itself. Generally speaking, industry has not troubled enough about the greater or lesser importance of needs to be satisfied. It simply complied with public taste, and manufactured with no other thought than that of selling. Here as elsewhere, we should like to see a central, organizing intelligence, which would co-ordinate industry and agriculture and allot to the machine its proper place, I mean the place where it can best serve humanity. Thus, when the case against mechanization is stated, the main grievance is often left out. The charge is first that it converts the workman into a mere machine, and then that it leads to a uniformity of production which shocks the aesthetic sense. But if the machine procures for the workman more free time, and if the workman uses this increase of leisure for something else than the so-called pleasures which an ill-directed industry has put within the reach of all, he will develop his intelligence as he chooses, instead of remaining content with the development which would have been imposed upon him, and necessarily maintained within very narrow limits, by a return (impossible in fact) to tools, were machines abolished. As regards uniformity of products, the disadvantage would be negligible, if the economy of time and labour thus realized by the mass of the nation permitted the furtherance of intellectual culture and the development of true originality. An author, writing about the Americans, criticizes them for all wearing the same hat. But the head should come before the hat. Allow me to furnish the interior of my head as I please, and I shall put up with a hat like everybody else's. Such is not our grievance against mechanization. Without disputing the services it has rendered to man by greatly developing the means of satisfying real needs, we reproach it with having too strongly encouraged artificial ones, with having fostered luxury, with having favoured the towns to the detriment of the countryside, lastly with having widened the gap and revolutionized the relations between employer and employed, between capital and labour. These effects, indeed, can all be corrected, and then the machine would be nothing but a great benefactor. But then, humanity must set about simplifying its existence with as much frenzy as it devoted to complicating it. The initiative can come from humanity alone, for it is humanity and not the alleged force of circumstances, still less a fatality inherent in the machine, which has started the spirit of invention along a certain track.

But did humanity wholly intend this? Was the impulsion it gave at the beginning exactly in the same direction that industrialism has actually taken? What is at the outset only an imperceptible deviation becomes in the end a considerable divergence, if the road has been straight and the journey long. Now, there is no doubt that the earliest features of what was destined later to become mechanization were sketched out at the same time as the first yearnings after democracy. The connexion between the two tendencies becomes plainly visible in the eighteenth century. It is a striking feature of the 'Encyclopaedists.' Should we not, then, suppose that it was a breath of democracy which urged the spirit of invention onward, that spirit as old as humanity, but insufficiently active so long as it was not given the necessary scope? There was surely no thought then of luxuries for all, or even of comforts for all. But there might have been the desire of an assured material existence, of dignity in security for all. Was this a conscious wish? We do not believe in the unconscious in history: the great undercurrents of thought of which so much has been written are due to the fact that masses of men have been carried along by one or several individuals. These individuals knew what they were doing, but did not foresee all the consequences. We, who know what followed, cannot help transferring back the image of it to the beginning: the present, reflected back into the past and perceived inside it as though in a mirror, is then what we call the unconscious of the past. The retroactivity of the present is at the origin of many philosophical delusions. We shall be careful, then, not to attribute to the fifteenth, sixteenth and eighteenth centuries (and still less the seventeenth, which is so different and has been considered as a sublime parenthesis) a concern for democratic ideas comparable to our own. Neither shall we attribute to them the vision of the power which lay hidden in the spirit of invention. It is none the less true that the Reformation, the Renaissance and the first symptoms or precursory signs of the great inventive impetus date from the same period. It is not impossible that there were here three reactions, interrelated, against the form taken until then by the Christian ideal. This ideal subsisted just the same, but it appeared like a heavenly body that had up to then always turned the same face towards man: people now began to catch a glimpse of the other side, though they did not always realize that it was the same body. That mysticism evokes asceticism there is no doubt. Both the one and the other will ever be peculiar to the few. But that true, complete, active mysticism aspires to radiate, by virtue of the charity which is its essence, is none the less certain. How could it spread, even diluted and enfeebled as it must necessarily be, in a humanity obsessed by the fear of hunger? Man will rise above earthly things only if a powerful equipment supplies him with the requisite fulcrum. He must use matter as a support if he wants to get away from matter. In other words, the mystical summons up the mechanical. This has not been sufficiently realized, because machinery, through a mistake at the points, has been switched off on to a track at the end of which lies exaggerated comfort and luxury for the few, rather than liberation for all. We are struck by the accidental result, we do not see mechanization as it should be, as what it is in essence. Let us go further still. If our organs are natural instruments, our instruments must then be artificial organs. The workman's tool is the continuation of his arm, the tool-equipment of humanity is therefore a continuation of its body. Nature, in endowing us with an essentially tool-making intelligence, prepared for us in this way a certain expansion. But machines which run on oil or coal or 'white coal,' and which convert into motion a potential energy stored up for millions of years, have actually imparted to our organism an extension so vast, have endowed it with a power so mighty, so out of proportion to the size and strength of that organism, that surely none of all this was foreseen in this structural plan of our species: here was a unique stroke of luck, the greatest material success of man on the planet. A spiritual impulsion had been given, perhaps, at the beginning: the extension took place automatically, helped as it were by a chance blow of the pick-axe which struck against a miraculous treasure underground.[9] Now, in this body, distended out of all proportion, the soul remains what it was, too small to fill it, too weak to guide it. Hence the gap between the two. Hence the tremendous social, political and international problems which are just so many definitions of this gap, and which provoke so many chaotic and ineffectual efforts to fill it. What we need are new reserves of potential energy – moral energy this time. So let us not merely say, as we did above, that the mystical summons up the mechanical. We must add that the body, now larger, calls for a bigger soul, and that mechanism should mean mysticism. The origins of the process of mechanization are indeed more mystical than we might imagine. Machinery will find its true vocation again, it will render services in proportion to its power, only if mankind, which it has bowed still lower to the earth, can succeed, through it, in standing erect and looking heavenwards.

In a long series of writings, which for depth and forcefulness are beyond praise, M. Ernest Seillière shows how national ambitions claim for themselves divine missions: 'imperialism' naturally becomes 'mysticism.' If we give to this latter word the sense M. Ernest Seillière[10] attributes to it, and which his many books have made abundantly clear, the fact is undeniable; by noting it, by linking it up with its causes and following it in its effects, the author makes an invaluable contribution to the philosophy of history. But he himself would probably be of the opinion that mysticism taken in this sense, and indeed understood in this way by 'imperialism' such as he exhibits it, is but a counterfeit of true mysticism, the mysticism of 'dynamic religion' which we studied in the last chapter. We believe the counterfeiting to have taken place in the following way. It was a borrowing from the 'static religion' of the ancients, stripped of its old tags and left in its static form with the new label supplied by dynamic religion. There was indeed nothing fraudulent in this imitation; it was almost unintentional. For we must remember that 'static religion' is natural to man, and that nature does not alter. The innate beliefs of our ancestors subsist in the depths of our inner selves; they reappear as soon as they are no longer inhibited by opposing forces. Now, one of the essential characteristics of ancient religions was the idea of a link between the human groups and the deities attached to them. The gods of the city fought with and for the city. This belief is incompatible with true mysticism, I mean with the feeling which certain souls have that they are the instruments of God who loves all men with an equal love, and who bids them to love each other. But, rising from the darkest depths of the soul to the surface of consciousness, and meeting there with the image of true mysticism as the modern mystics have revealed it to the world, it instinctively decks itself out in this garb; it endows the God of the modern mystic with the nationalism of the ancient gods. It is in this sense that imperialism becomes mysticism. So that if we keep to true mysticism, we shall judge it incompatible with imperialism. At the most it will be admitted, as we have just put it, that mysticism cannot be disseminated without encouraging a very special 'will to power.' This will be a sovereignty, not over men, but over things, precisely in order that man shall no longer have so much sovereignty over man.

Let a mystic genius but appear, he will draw after him a humanity already vastly grown in body, and whose soul he has transfigured. He will yearn to make of it a new species, or rather deliver it from the necessity of being a species; for every species means a collective halt, and complete existence is mobility in individuality. The great breath of life which swept our planet had carried organization as far along as nature, alike docile and recalcitrant, permitted. Nature – let us repeat it – is the name we give to the totality of compliances and resistances which life encounters in raw matter – a totality which we treat, just as the biologist does, *as though* intentions could be attributed to it. A body compact of creative intelligence, and, round about that intelligence, a fringe of intuition, was the most complete thing nature had found it possible to produce. Such was the human body. There the evolution of life stopped. But now intelligence, raising the construction of instruments to a degree of complexity and perfection which nature (so incapable of mechanical construction) had not even foreseen, pouring into these machines reserves of energy which nature (so heedless of economy) had never even thought of, has endowed us with powers beside which those of our body barely count: they will be altogether limitless when science is able to liberate the force which is enclosed, or rather condensed, in the slightest particle of ponderable matter. The material barrier then has well nigh vanished. Tomorrow the way will be clear, in the very direction of the breath which had carried life to the point where it had to stop. Let once the summons of the hero come, we shall not all follow it, but we shall all feel that we ought to, and we shall see the path before us, which will become a highway if we pass along it. At the same time, for each and every philosophy the mystery of the supreme obligation will be a mystery no longer: a journey had been begun, it had had to be interrupted; by setting out once more we are merely willing again what we had willed at the start. It is always the stop which requires explanation, and not the movement.

[. . .]

Joy indeed would be that simplicity of life diffused throughout the world by an ever-spreading mystic intuition; joy, too, that which would automatically follow a vision of the life beyond attained through the furtherance of scientific experiment. Failing so thoroughgoing a spiritual reform, we must be content with shifts and submit to more and more numerous and vexatious regulations, intended to provide a means of circumventing each successive obstacle that our nature sets up against our civilization. But, whether we go bail for small measures or great, a decision is imperative. Mankind lies groaning, half crushed beneath the weight of its own progress. Men do not sufficiently realize that their future is in their own hands. Theirs is the task of determining first of all whether they want to go on living or not. Theirs the responsibility, then, for deciding if they want merely to live, or intend to make just the extra effort required for fulfilling, even on their refractory planet, the essential function of the universe, which is a machine for the making of gods.

Mélanges

Translations by Melissa McMahon

Good Sense and Classical Studies[1]

Speech given at the award ceremony for the concours général,[2] *held in the Great Ampitheatre of the Sorbonne, July 30, 1895.*

It has always been a great honour and a difficult task to speak in this imposing atmosphere of academic solemnity; but it seems to me that the responsibility becomes heavier each year, because the problem of education, which we would rather not go over for ever, takes on an ever more grave appearance and poses itself in ever more urgent terms. Everyone accepts that classical studies should do more than embellish the mind, that it is incumbent upon us to produce citizens who are aware of their duty and capable of carrying it out: what society gives by way of education, it expects to get back in wisdom. We question, however, with growing concern, whether disinterested study has this practical efficacy, and in particular whether good sense, which is a civic virtue in the free nations, varies according to intellectual cultivation. Whichever way the question is decided, moreover, whether in the affirmative or the negative, nobody can consider themselves satisfied; for if good sense does not depend on education, society would have to declare itself powerless with regard to what it needs most; and if it above all depends on education, if wisdom increases in proportion with this higher cultivation of the mind, which will always remain a privilege, we would have to be saddened at the sight of the irresistible trend which places power into the hands of the majority. Very fortunately, it is in no way necessary to settle on either of these extremes. I would like to show that good sense partly consists in an active disposition of the intellect, but also partly in a certain and quite particular distrust on the part of the intellect with regard to itself; that education provides it with a support, but that its roots reach depths hardly penetrated by education; that classical studies are very useful to it, but through exercises common to all types of studies and which can be practised without a teacher; that thus the task of the educator consists above all, in such a matter, in leading some through the use of artifice where others are directly placed by nature. But what exactly is good sense, and with what forces, what general dispositions of the soul is this intellectual attitude connected?

The role of our senses, in general, is not so much to give us knowledge of material objects as to signal their utility to us. We taste flavours, we breathe odours, we distinguish hot and cold, darkness and light. But science tells us that none of these qualities belong to objects in the form that we apprehend them; they only tell us in their picturesque language the inconvenience or advantage that things have for us, the services they could render us, the dangers they could lead us into. Our senses thus serve us, above all, to orient us in space; they are not turned towards science, but towards life. But we do not only live in a material milieu, but also in a social milieu. If all of our movements are transmitted in space and thus disturb part of the physical universe, by contrast most of our actions have their immediate or far-reaching consequences, good or bad, first of all for us, then for the society that surrounds us. Foreseeing [*prévoir*] these consequences, or rather having a presentiment of them [*pressentir*]; distinguishing the essential from the inessential or indifferent in matters of behaviour; choosing from the various possible courses of action the one which will produce the greatest amount of attainable rather than imaginable good: this is, it seems to me, the role of good sense. It is thus indeed a sense in its own way; but while the other senses place us in relation to things, good sense presides over our relations with persons.

There is a subtle presentiment of true and false, which is able to discover secret incompatibilities or unsuspected affinities between things well before any rigorous proof or decisive experiment. We call this higher-order intuition genius, an intuition which is necessarily rare, since strictly speaking humanity could do without it. But everyday life demands of each one of us just such clear-cut solutions and rapid decisions. Every serious action closes a long series of reasons and conditions, and then spreads out in consequences which mean that, if the action depended on us, we in turn depend on it. And yet usually it makes no allowance for either experiment or delay: a course of action must be chosen, and we must comprehend the whole without anticipating all the details. The authority that we call upon in these cases, the one which dispels our hesitations and resolves the difficulty, is good sense. It thus seems that good sense is in practical life what genius is in the arts and sciences.

But let us take a closer look: good sense is no more a passive attitude of the mind than genius is – waiting, in the middle of the night, for the ray of brilliance and the dawning of the light. If genius divines nature, it is because it has lived in close camaraderie with it. And good sense also requires a constant wakefulness, an ever-renewed adjustment to ever-new situations. It dreads nothing more than the ready-made idea, a ripe fruit perhaps of the mind, but detached from the tree, soon withered, and representing nothing more, in its rigidity, than the inert residue of intellectual work. Good sense is this work itself. It wants us to take each problem as new and do it the honour of a new effort. It requires us to make the sometimes painful sacrifice of the opinions we had made for ourselves and the solutions we had at the ready. And in the end it seems to have less in common with a superficially encyclopaedic knowledge than with a self-aware ignorance, accompanied by the courage to learn.[3]

If it can be likened to instinct in the speed of its decisions and the spontaneity of its nature, it is deeply opposed to it in the variety of its means, the suppleness of its form, and the jealous guard it sets up around us to preserve us from intellectual automatism. If it resembles science in its concern for the real and its obstinate determination to stay in touch with the facts, it is distinguished by the kind of truth it seeks, for it does not aim, like science, for universal truth, but that truth of the present hour, and is not so much concerned with being right once and for all, but with always renewing the task of being right [*toujours recommencer d'avoir raison*]. Science moreover neglects no empirical fact, no consequence of its reasoning: it calculates the role of all the influences and takes the deduction of its principles to their end. Good sense chooses. It holds certain consequences to be practically negligible, and stops the development of a principle at the precise point that an excessively brutal logic would ruffle the delicacy of the real. A selection must be made between the facts and reasons which struggle, push and jostle with each other. In the end, good sense is more than instinct and less than science; it should be seen rather as a certain bent [*pli*] of the mind, a certain inclination of attention. We could almost say that good sense is attention itself, oriented in the direction of life.

It thus has no greater enemies in the city than the spirit of routine and the spirit of fantasy [*chimére*]. To cling stubbornly to habits that are raised to the status of laws, to repudiate change, is to let one's eyes be distracted from the movement that is the condition of life. But is it not also through weakness of will or mental distraction that we abandon ourselves to the hope for miraculous transformations? There is less distance between these two types of mind than one would first think: equally removed from effective action, their difference is above all that one claims simply to sleep, while the other wants in addition to dream. But good sense neither sleeps nor dreams. Like the principle of life, it is constantly watchful and at work, weighed down no doubt by the matter that it animates, but made aware of the reality of its action by the very materiality of its effort. Its moderation is not like that of timid people who consider action to be dangerous and seek to insure themselves against it; on the contrary, it loves action – it advances by degrees only in order to achieve a transformation at a more natural pace, and is again in this way like life, in respect of which it is hard to know what is more admirable: the harmoniously blended nuances of its transitions or the explosive contrast of its metamorphoses. The closer one comes to good sense, the more it seems to merge with the spirit of progress, provided that by this expression we understand both an energetic aspiration for improvement and a precise appreciation of the degree of elasticity of human things.

What is thus the principle of good sense? How can its essence be grasped? Where is its soul to be found? Does it derive, as has been said, from experience?[4] Does it represent the combined and condensed results of past observations? But as time advances, it unfolds ever-new situations, which demand of us an ever-original effort. Is it, on the other hand, only a greater sureness of reasoning, deployed in a logical process to deduce ever more far-reaching consequences from a general principle? But our deduction is quite rigid, and life is very supple. However strong a grip we have on our reasonings, they will have trouble following the delicate and elusive contours of moving reality. I freely admit that good sense reasons, and sometimes using general principles; but it begins by orienting them towards the present reality; and is not this work of adaptation, which is no longer a matter of pure reasoning, precisely the specific function of good sense? No, good sense lies neither in a greater experience, nor in better-organized memories, nor in a more accurate deduction, nor even, more generally, in a more rigorous logic. Above all an instrument of social progress, it can only draw its strength from the very principle of social life, the spirit of justice.

Oh, I don't mean the theoretical and abstract justice which, without regard for the real, traces a geometrical map in empty space and posits the form without giving itself the matter. Most often, it remains incapable of finding a point of contact with facts, or, if it succeeds, it is led by their resistance, which it had not taken into account in its calculations, into doubting its own virtue and despairing of itself. I am talking about justice embodied in the just man, living and acting justice, attentive to its insertion into events, but weighing up the act and the consequence on its scales, and fearing nothing so much as achieving the good at the price of a greater evil. Justice, when it is realized in this way in a man of good, becomes a delicate sense, a vision or rather a tact of practical truth. It gives him the exact measure of what he must ask of himself and what he can expect of others. It guides him straight ahead, like the surest instinct, to what is desirable and attainable. It shows him the injustices to correct, and consequently the good to be done, the arrangements to keep, which is to say the injustice not to commit. It protects him against error and awkwardness, through the rectitude of judgement that comes from the uprightness of the soul. Simple and clear, it is to chains of reasoning and multiplied experiments what pure gold is to money. If it carries the intelligence of life with it in this way, it is no doubt because it has touched its principle; and, although it shines in all its splendour only in the best of us, it no less shows what is most essential and intimate in humanity. Thus it is that in order to discover the deepest layers of the earth's crust, those that great upheavals have drawn from the very soul of the earth, one must climb to the summits.

I thus see in good sense the inner energy of an intelligence which is constantly winning itself back, eliminating ready-made ideas in order to free up space for the ideas in the process of being made, and modelling itself on the real through the continuous effort of a persistent attention. And I also see in it the intellectual radiance of an intense moral centre, the justness of ideas following the feeling of justice, ultimately the mind tempered by character. Our philosophy, infatuated with absolute distinctions, traces a very clear line of demarcation between intelligence and will, between morality and knowledge, between thought and action. And these are in effect two different directions which the development of human nature follows. But action and thought seem to me to have a common source, which is neither pure will nor pure intelligence, and this source is good sense. Is not good sense in effect what gives action its reasonable character, and thought its practical character?

Examine, in the great philosophical problems, the solution of good sense: you will find, I think, that it is the socially useful solution, the one that facilitates language and favours action. Study, on the other hand, the behaviours and acts advised by good sense: you will see that it has spoken, without any deep reflection, as would perfect reason. It thus seems that good sense proceeds in speculative matters via an appeal to the will, and in practical matters by recourse to reason. In such a way that one could be tempted to see in it the effect of a blend, an intimate accord between the requirements of thought and those of action. And we must indeed speak in this way for clarity's sake, but I would be inclined, to get to the heart of the matter, to envisage things in a quite different way, to see in good sense the original disposition and to see in the habits of thought and the laws of the will, by contrast two emanations, two divergent orientations of this basic faculty of orientation. For I can imagine neither the play of associated wills without an ultimately reasonable goal, nor the natural functioning of thought without a practical destination. We must thus be able to derive these two forms of activity from one and the same force, which corresponds to the fundamental necessities of social life; and this sort of social sense is precisely what is called good sense. If it is thus the ground, the very essence of the mind, should we not find it, as Descartes said, 'complete in each individual',[5] innate and universal, independent of education? This would be the case, I believe, if there was nothing but what was living in the soul and in society, if we were not condemned to drag along with us the dead weight of vices and prejudices, if also we did not sometimes, distracted momentarily or at length, live and think outside of ourselves, finally, if we did not let our intelligence make decisions that are, so to speak, abstract, instead of keeping it firmly in contact with the keen energy of the will. But it is rare that nature spontaneously produces an emancipated soul that is master of itself, a soul tuned in accord with life. Most often education must intervene, not so much to communicate an *élan* as to remove obstacles, rather, then, to lift a veil than to shed light.

How far does this influence of education go, and of classical studies in particular? What can they do, and what should we ask of them? They are far from having the same sway over the diverse forces that I have just listed which would all tend to lead good sense astray. One of the greatest obstacles, we were saying, to the freedom of the mind, are the ideas that language gives to us ready-made, and that we breathe, so to speak, in the environment which surrounds us. They are never assimilated with our substance: incapable of participating in the life of the mind, they persevere, as truly dead ideas, in their stiffness and immobility. Why then do we so often prefer them to those which are living and vibrant? Why does our thought, instead of working to become master of itself, prefer to exile itself from itself? It is firstly through distraction, and by dint of amusing ourselves along the road, we no longer know where we wanted to go.

Perhaps you have noticed, in front of our monuments and in our museums, foreigners who hold an open book in their hand, a book where they no doubt find described the marvels surrounding them. Absorbed in this reading, do they not sometimes seem to forget for its sake the beautiful things they came to see? It is in this way that many of us travel through existence, our eyes fixed on formulas which are read in a sort of internal guide book, neglecting to look at life in order simply to refer oneself to what is said about it, and tending to think of words rather than things. But perhaps there is something more and better here than an accidental distraction of the mind. Perhaps there is a natural and necessary law which intends for our mind to begin by accepting ready-made ideas and live in a sort of tutelage, while waiting for the act of will, for some forever postponed, by which the mind will take hold of itself again. The child only sees in the external world the crude and conventional forms which he sketches on paper as soon as he has a pencil in hand: for him they come between the eye and the object; they provide for him a convenient simplification, and for many of us they continue to interpose themselves in this way, until the day that art comes to open our eyes to nature.

I would readily compare the ideas that we find enclosed within words to these children's drawings. Each word indeed represents a portion of reality, but a portion crudely cut out, as if humanity had carved reality according to its convenience and needs, instead of following the articulations of the real. We are indeed obliged to adopt provisionally this ready-made philosophy and science; but they are only footholds in order to go higher. Beyond the ideas which are chilled and congealed in language, we must seek the warmth and mobility of life.

I precisely see, above all, in a classical education, an effort to break the ice of words and to find beneath it the free flow of thought. When you make the effort, young pupils, to translate ideas from one language to another, you become accustomed to crystallizing them, so to speak, in several different systems; in this way they are released from any definitively set verbal form, and you are invited to think the ideas themselves, independently of words. In the preference that a classical education gave to antiquity, there was not only a very great admiration for pure models; it was also no doubt considered that the ancient languages, carving the continuity of things along lines that are very different to ours, would lead to the liberation of the idea through a more violent and more quickly effective exercise. And then, was any effort ever attempted comparable to that of the ancient Greeks to give speech the fluidity of thought? But whatever the language they express themselves in, the great writers can render the same service to our intelligence; for they have all had and have all sought to give us a direct vision of the real, in cases where we perceived things only through our conventions, habits and symbols. In this sense, a classical education, even when it seems to attach the most importance to words, teaches us above all not to be taken in by them. While its particular object may change, it will always keep the same general aim, which is to remove our thought from automatism, release it from forms and formulas, and ultimately to re-establish the free circulation of life within it. Philosophy continues this work already begun along the same lines. It submits the ultimate principles of thought and action to criticism. It ascribes no value to passively received truth: it wants each of us to reconquer the truth through reflection, to become deserving of it through effort, and by making it deeply penetrate each one of us, animating truth with its life, it gives it enough force to enrich thought and direct the will. No doubt good sense can do without philosophy, but if good sense resides in effort and tends in the first place to freedom, I do not see where it would have a better apprenticeship.

But it is not enough to put aside symbols and get used to seeing. We must also, we were saying, rid ourselves of the habit of a certain over-abstract way of judging, and cultivate a quite particular mode of attention. Certain disciplines have the advantage of bringing us close up against life. It is thus that the thorough study of the past will help us to understand the present, on the condition however that we remain on guard against misleading analogies, and that we seek in history, according to the profound words of a contemporary historian, causes rather than laws.[6] The physical and mathematical sciences have a less concrete object; but they are excellent for making us understand the specific virtue and the special aim of methods that we employ somewhat thoughtlessly every day. As these sciences only generalize where there are stable laws, and only deduce when we can create our definitions, they clearly reveal to us, by a veritable 'passage to the limit', the ideal conditions of rigorous deduction and legitimate generalization. As a consequence, the further one goes into them, the less one is tempted to transpose their methods, wholesale, to the things of practical life. It is not only because the excessive precision of these methods would translate, at the moment of action, into excessively lengthy vacillations – a little as if one wanted to use a laboratory scale in the kitchen – it is rather and above all because good sense would, I think, run some very great risks in this transportation. There exists a serious error, which consists in reasoning about society in the same way as about nature, in discovering there some bizarre mechanism of ineluctable laws, finally in misjudging the efficacy of the will and the creative force of liberty. There is another error, made by minds given to fantasy, which posits the formula of a simple ideal, and geometrically deduces the consequences for the organization of society, as if definitions depended on us in this domain, as if our liberty did not encounter a limit, in the very conditions of human nature and social life. Good sense holds the middle ground between these two clumsy imitations of physics and geometry. Perhaps it has no method, strictly speaking, but rather a certain manner of doing things. At the risk of disturbing a widely held opinion, I will say that the manner of philosophers is that which seems closest to me to that of good sense; for every great philosophical doctrine is linked to principles and rests on facts, without either being able to be rigorously inferred from these facts, because it exceeds them, or being able to be entirely deduced from these principles, because it has known how to bend them. You will sometimes find, in the best disciple of a great master, a more systematic exposition of the doctrine as well as an apparently superior clarity. It is precisely because he has followed the dominant ideas of the system, with his simpler and more abstract logic, to their end. But one must go back to the work of the master to enter into communication with its personal and profound logic, one modelled on the real, supple like life, and capable, like nature, of presenting ever-new elements to our thought which in vain would seek to exhaust its analysis. This faculty seems indeed to me to be, in speculative matters, what good sense is in practical life.

The education of good sense will thus not only consist in rescuing intelligence from ready-made ideas, but also in turning it away from excessively simple ideas, stopping it on the slippery slope of deductions and generalizations, and finally, preserving it from excessive self-confidence. Let us go further: the greatest risk that education could represent to good sense would be to encourage our tendency to judge men and things from a purely intellectual point of view, to measure our value and that of others according to mental merit alone, to extend this principle to societies themselves, to only approve institutions, laws and customs which bear the outward and superficial mark of logical clarity and simple organization. This standard would perhaps be appropriate for a society of pure minds, devoted to an entirely speculative existence; but real life is turned towards action. I certainly grant that intelligence is one of its forces, and even the most obvious one, since its role is to shed light; but it is not the only one. Why are intellectual gifts less useful to us in life than qualities of character? Why is it that so many brilliant and insightful minds remain incapable, despite the greatest efforts, of producing a work or carrying out an action? And why do the most beautiful words remain without an echo if they are said without intonation? Is it not because intelligence acts by a strange hidden power whose effort it symbolizes, and that where this force is lacking, the mind has neither enough momentum [*élan*] to go far by itself, nor enough weight to leave any deep mark on what it touches? Here we have seen the function create the organ, and unexpected intellectual faculties burst forth under the pressure of an intense moral force. And history also tells us that the greatness of a nation lies less in its apparent intellectual development than in certain invisible reserves of energy which nourish the intelligence, by which I mean the force of the will and the passion for great things. Well now, this is the idea that education can deeply impress upon us – not by a special demonstration, but by a thousand lessons drawn from history and from life. In this way it will not only save us from many disappointments and many surprises; it will send out, through the intermediary of this intelligence which it necessarily addresses, a forceful appeal to the power of feeling and willing. And in this it will set the soul back on its natural course, which is precisely good sense.

These, it seems to me, are the different points on which good sense offers a grasp to education in general, and to classical studies in particular. In fixing your attention, *Messieurs*, on the last and most important of these, what have I done but commentate the words that you will not have forgotten, those pronounced in this very place, two years ago, by the head of the University:[7] 'I would like', he said, 'for us to undertake to seek the just and to propagate it, a little flame and imagination. Keep in mind that, even in a century of science and thought, the future will above all smile upon and favour those who have been careful to keep intact their ability to feel.'[8]

It is this strength of feeling that I believe can be seen in good sense.

Without this strict lineage, without this harmony between the sense of the real and the faculty to be profoundly moved for the good, we could not understand how France, this classical land of good sense, has felt itself uplifted throughout the whole course of its history, by the internal thrust of great enthusiasms and generous passions. It is to a young and ardent faith that it owes the revelation of the tolerance that it has inscribed in its laws and taught to other nations; it is in a moment of enthusiasm that the wisest, most balanced and most reasonable expressions of law and equality have risen from its heart to its lips. In those of its writers who are most enamoured of good sense, even in those who have sharpened their good sense on the intellect [*en esprit*], one can see, behind the qualities of order, method and clarity, an intense warmth that has become light. And does not the very transparency of its language, the winged lightness of its phrases, made to carry general ideas far, correspond to the *élan* of a soul which seeks free air and large spaces for the powerful feelings which run through it? Be in no doubt, young pupils: clarity of ideas, strength of attention, freedom and moderation in judgement, all this forms the material envelope of good sense; but it is the passion for justice that is its soul.

Letter to G. Lechalas[9]

End of 1897

Let us look for the reasons which lead philosophers (in contrast, as it happens, with common opinion) to suppose that the image of P is formed in a consciousness exterior to point P, then projected in P. In other words, what are the reasons that lead me to believe that I am situated elsewhere than in P? I doubt that you could first of all find any reason apart from this: 'In order to touch P, I would have to move my body.' I am outside P in the sense that I would have to move in order to touch it. In other words, my possible action on P is not immediate, and my body could not touch, modify or move P, except on the condition of traversing intermediary bodies. My belief in a real interval, and hence in a distinction between P and myself, is thus first of all only at bottom a distinction between this body and my body, a distinction uniquely related to tactile perception. Let us suppose for a moment that tactile sensibility is abolished (along with the motor functions attached to it), suppose a being which had only ever known visual perceptions (and who moreover would be condemned to immobility); would he not perceive himself as being in P as much and in the same way as at the point occupied by his body? In my opinion, we are in a real sense in each point that our perception covers. This, at least, would be the most natural way of expressing ourselves: it is the needs of action that have led us to adopt another mode of expression, giving tactile perception a privileged rank, and restricting our real presence to this very limited part of space where our tactile influence is exercised. This is the sense in which I have been able to say that our perception (putting aside affect, and above all memory, whose role is considerable) is above all in the 'collection [*ensemble*] of images', or, if you prefer, in things in general, whereas our sensory-motor, or rather tactile, experience, restricts our presence to that organized portion of matter by which we act upon all the others.

I believe that if we study all the realist and idealist doctrines since Descartes, we will find that they always begin – consciously or unconsciously – with this radical distinction between our body and the rest of matter. My body, being separate from the other bodies that I perceive, we imagine to be sufficient unto itself with its own concept, attached to the soul and detached from everything else: it thus becomes necessary to assume the existence somewhere, inside this body, or intimately connected with it, of more or less faithful *reproductions* or duplications of the rest of matter. We seek the materials for these representations in the peripheral sensations of the body; and, as these sensations are evidently insufficient for what we need from them, we have them converge toward the cerebral centres, which themselves become more and more contracted, until finally we cast the whole representation outside of space in an unextended consciousness, from which point it would be projected into space in order to cover the external bodies from which it emanated. I tried to show, in my first chapter,[10] that this conception raises insurmountable difficulties at every point. The truth is that my body is made of an analogous matter to other bodies, that my consciousness is no more attached to my body than to other bodies, and that it initially coincides (at least in part) with the totality of what it perceives and is able to perceive.

I believe I have established a radical distinction between *sensation*, properly speaking, or affect, which is internal to my body, and the image, which is external to it. The sensations of hot and cold, and more generally *all sensations that I localize in my body*, depend above all on the state of the part in which they are produced; they take on quite different aspects according to whether my body is disposed to welcome or reject them, etc. I am thus quite willing to grant that the sensations of hot, cold, and many others, are for the most part relative to the state of my body, and express above all the particular and variable requirements of that state. But it is a quite different matter when we come to *perceptions*, properly speaking, which is to say, images which are situated outside of my body.

I intentionally left this question in suspense.[11] In effect, in the case of memory [*souvenir*], I have positive reasons for affirming that recalled memories are chosen in the totality of past states, which are conserved in an unconscious form. By contrast, in the case of perception, I can see and I try to show how the perceived image is taken from a wider field than that of actual perception, but I have no means of determining how far this virtual perception extends. The very fact that you cite in your letter (i.e. that sound is abolished below a certain number of vibrations per second) and all other facts of this kind, is sufficient proof that our actual perception is a selection, just as the impossibility for us to conceive that the universe stops at the horizon of our actual perception further proves that we perceive virtually many more things than we perceive materially and actually: indeed, conscious perception seems unintelligible to me under any other hypothesis. But, I repeat, how far does the virtual extend? Does our mind virtually perceive the whole of matter, as Leibniz would have it? Or else does the universal perception from which our senses make a selection only include the things and elements which form an undivided system in relation to what we actually perceive (the material universe perhaps not forming a single and unique system)? Above all, would this virtual perception (which is to say independent of bodies) be comparable to our actual perception, which distinguishes *objects*; or else would it, while still remaining concrete, be closer to scientific knowledge, which deals with properties, qualities and forms? So many questions to which I could only respond with unproven hypotheses. I wanted, however, to follow as closely as possible the contours of facts, to refrain from all metaphysical construction, in short come back to intuition. Where intuition no longer spoke, I had to stop.

Bergson–James Correspondence[12]

Villa Montmorency, 6th January 1903.[13]

Mon cher Confrère,

I have just finished reading the book which you so kindly sent to me – *The Varieties of Religious Experience* – and I must tell you the profound impression that this reading has had on me. I began it at least ten days ago, and since that moment I cannot think of anything else, so captivating is the book and, if I may say, enthralling from one end to the other. It seems to me that you have managed to extract the very quintessence of religious emotion. We were already aware, no doubt, that this emotion is both a spontaneous [*sui generis*] joy and the awareness of a union with a superior power; but the nature of this joy and this union is what seemed neither analysable nor expressible, and yet this is what you have been able to analyse and express, thanks to a very novel procedure which consists in giving the reader an alternating series of *overall impressions* which play against each other and at the same time fuse together in his mind. In that respect you have opened up a path on which you will certainly be followed by many others, but on which you have so quickly gone so far that it will be a real struggle to overtake you and even catch up.

If you have had the chance, over the last ten or twelve years, to chat with French students passing through Cambridge, they must have told you that I was one of your earliest admirers, and that I have never passed up an opportunity to express the great sympathy I have for your ideas to my listeners. When I wrote my essay on *Les Données de la conscience* [*Time and Free Will*], I still only knew your essay on *Effort*,[14] but I was led, through an analysis of the idea of time and reflecting on its role in mechanics, to a certain conception of psychological life which is entirely compatible with the one in your psychology (except perhaps that I see *places of flight in the resting-places*[15] themselves, rendered apparently immobile by the fixed gaze of consciousness). This is another way of telling you that no approval could be more precious to me than that which you have so kindly given to the conclusions of my book *Matter and Memory*.[16]

In this book I sought to show – without sacrificing any of the results of cerebral physiology – how the relationship of consciousness to cerebral activity is something else entirely than what is supposed by physiologists and philosophers: and I see that, on this point as well, we are following two very close and probably converging paths. This at least is what I take from reading the very interesting paper on *Human Immortality* that you were so kind as to send to me.[17] The more I reflect on this question, the more I am convinced that life is, through and through, a phenomenon of attention. The brain is the very direction of this attention: it marks, delimits and measures the *psychological contraction* that is necessary for action; in the end it is neither the duplicate nor the instrument of conscious life, it is its extreme point, the part which inserts itself into events – something like the prow where the ship becomes narrow in order to cleave the ocean. But, as you so rightly say, this conception of the relationship of the brain to the mind requires us to maintain the distinction between the soul and the body, and hence to shatter many of the frameworks in which we are accustomed to think.

I very much hope that the occasion will present itself where I can talk about all of this with you. Might I ask you, in case of your coming to France, to be so good as to drop a small line letting me know in advance, so that we might arrange a meeting?

H. Bergson

Villa Montmorency, 25th March 1903.[18]

Mon cher Confrère,

I was greatly disappointed to hear that you will probably not be coming to Europe, and my regret would have been still more keen had I not known that it is the improvement of your health that has led you to abandon this trip. I hope that you recover promptly and completely from the tiredness that you mention, and which is easily explained when one thinks of the amount of effort and thought that this last book, *The Varieties of Religious Experience*, must have cost you.

The difficulties that you point out in certain passages of *Matter and Memory* are only too real to me, and I am far from having managed to completely overcome them.[19] I believe nevertheless that some of these difficulties are simply a result of the obstinate habits of our mind, habits which have an entirely practical origin and from which we must liberate ourselves for speculation. Such is, for example, the difficulty of admitting memories which are present and unconscious. If we assimilate memories to *things*, there is clearly no middle ground for them between presence and absence: they are either entirely present to our mind and, in this sense, conscious, or else, if they are unconscious, they are absent from our mind and must no longer count as actual psychological realities.

But in the world of psychological realities, I do not think there is any need to posit the alternative of *to be or not to be*[20] with such strictness. The more I try to grasp myself through consciousness, the more I apprehend myself as the totalization or the *Inbegriff*[21] of my past, this past being contracted with a view to action. 'The unity of the self' which philosophers speak of seems to me to be the unity of an extremity [*pointe*] or a summit in which I contract myself through an effort of attention, an effort which lasts over a whole lifetime and which, it seems to me, is the essence of life. But I certainly feel that in order to pass from this extremity of consciousness or summit to the base, which is to say to a state where every memory of every moment would be scattered and distinct, one would have to go from the normal state of concentration to a state of dispersion like that of certain dreams; there would thus be nothing positive to do, but simply something to undo; nothing to gain, or add, rather something to lose; it is in this sense that all my memories are there when I don't perceive them, and that nothing truly new is produced when they reappear in my consciousness.

I was deeply interested by the summary you kindly sent me of the course that you are giving at the moment. It contains so many new and original ideas that I have not yet managed to sufficiently grasp the whole, but one key idea strikes me at this point; that of the necessity to transcend concepts, simplistic logic, in short, the methods of an over-systematic philosophy which postulates the unity of the whole. This is a direction analogous to the one I am engaged on, and I am quite convinced that if a truly *positive* philosophy is possible, it can only be found there.

15th February 1905.[22]

Mon cher Confrère,
I beg you to forgive my delay in thanking you for sending me your last articles:[23] I don't need to tell you that I read them – and reread them – as soon as I received them; but I have been very overworked these past weeks and it has been impossible for me to write to you earlier. In these five articles there is the outline of a whole philosophy, and I await with some impatience the work which will present its complete development. But even now you indicate a certain number of applications, all extremely interesting. I think that on many essential points I would agree with you, but perhaps I would not go quite as far as you down the path of 'radical empiricism'. The main difference probably (I am still not quite sure about it) concerns the role of the *unconscious*.[24] I cannot help but provide a large place for the unconscious, not only in psychological life, but also in the universe in general, as the existence of unperceived matter seems to me to be something of the same kind as that of a non-conscious psychological state. This existence of some reality outside of all actual consciousness is no doubt not the existence *in itself* spoken of by the old substantialism; and yet it is not part of what is *actually presented*

to a consciousness, it is something between the two, always on the point of becoming or re-becoming conscious, something intimately mingled with conscious life, *interwoven with it, and not underlying it*,[25] as substantialism would have it. But it is possible that even on this point I am closer to you than I think.

I am very grateful for the friendly allusions you make to my work in several of your articles. They will call attention to the shared direction between the considerable movement of ideas that you have created in America and the one which makes more and more headway here. I hope that these converging efforts will lead to the constitution of a *positive* metaphysics, which is to say, one that is susceptible of progressing indefinitely, instead of being entirely taken or left, like the old systems.

Villa Montmorency, 20th July 1905.[26]

Mon cher Confrère,

To my great regret, I had to write to Abauzit that I couldn't take on the task of doing the preface that he kindly requested for his translation. For two or three weeks I have been suffering from a general nervous fatigue, caused by a very persistent case of insomnia: I have no doubt aggravated this state by insisting nevertheless on staying on in Paris to work. So now I am obliged to interrupt all work and go away, if I want to be able to resume my lectures at the return of classes. I am very sorry not to be able to make this sympathetic gesture to Abauzit, and, if I may say, this testimony of my great admiration for your book. But there was never a foreign work which less needed to be 'introduced' to the French public than yours.

I read the articles that you kindly sent me as soon as I received them, and I must tell you how much they interested me.[27] They clarify your doctrine and reply, it seems to me, to the objections that have been raised against it. The essential point seems to me to be the one you address in the second article: *How two minds can know one thing*.[28] The more I think about it, the more I think that philosophy must come to a solution close to the one you suggest: there is pure experience, which is neither subjective nor objective (I use the word *image* to designate a reality of this kind), and there is what you call the *appropriation* of this experience by one consciousness or another, an appropriation which seems to me to consist in a diminution of the image *sui generis*, but which you see rather, if I have understood you correctly, as consisting in the affective states which proceed after [*font cortége á*] the pure image. In any case, I do not think that these last two points of view are irreconcilable, for the diminution that I describe is always carried out to a practical end; it involves our body and must, as a consequence, be translated in an attitude of the body which embraces or repudiates the exterior image.[29] But this attitude of the body is perceived at the points where it is produced, which is to say *inside* the body-image. And a perception internal to our body is precisely, it seems to me, what is called an affective state.

I don't know if you have read an article in the last issue of the *Revue Philosophique* about the Congress of Rome.[30] In this article it is said that the conception of 'real duration' that I presented in my first work (*Time and Free Will*) was inspired by the ideas of Ward,[31] and also a little by yours, and that, reciprocally, the philosophy that you now espouse is inspired by my work. I wrote a letter straightaway to the *Revue Philosophique* in response to this article which will appear in the next issue,[32] in which I state: 1. That my *Essai* was written in all ignorance of both your and Ward's ideas, and that it is in any case evident that the theories developed in this *Essai* have a very different origin and significance; 2. That on the other hand you have not been able to be any more inspired by 'Bergsonism', for the very simple reason that you had set out on the path that you follow today well before *Matter and Memory*.

I felt I had to nip this emergent myth in the bud, because, in my opinion, one of the most striking arguments that one can invoke (from the outside) in favour of American 'pragmatism' and the French 'new philosophy' is precisely that these two doctrines were established independently of each other, with different points of departure and different methods. When, in such conditions, two doctrines tend to agree, there is every chance that they are both in the vicinity of the truth.

I very much hope that you follow up your project to spend a few months in France. And have no doubt that I am not the only one with these hopes.

Villa Montmorency, 27th June 1907.[33]

Cher Professor James,

Your letter gives me very great joy, and I must thank you for it straightaway. You are right to say that the philosopher loves praise and that in this he resembles the common run of mortals; but permit me to tell you that the approval I particularly cared about was that of the thinker who has so greatly contributed to remodelling the soul of new generations and whose work has always inspired such a deep admiration in me. Thus the letter where you declare your readiness to enter into the essential ideas of my work, and where you defend them in advance against the attacks they will surely provoke, touches me at the highest level. I am keeping it as sufficient reward for the ten years of work that this book [*Creative Evolution*] has cost me.

I began to read your *Pragmatism* the moment I received it by post and I have not been able to put it down before finishing it. It is the admirably drawn programme of the philosophy of the future. Through a very diverse series of considerations, which you always manage to make converge towards the same centre, through suggestions as much as explicit reasons, you give us the idea, and above all the feeling, of the supple and flexible philosophy which is destined to take the place of intellectualism. I have never been so conscious of the analogy between our two points of view as when reading your chapter 'Pragmatism and humanism'.[34] When you say that '*for rationalism reality is ready-made and complete from all eternity, while for pragmatism it is still in the making*',[35] you give the very formula of the metaphysics which I am convinced we will come to, which we would have come to long ago if we had not remained under the charm of Platonic idealism. Would I go so far as to affirm with you that '*truth is mutable*'?[36] I believe in the mutability of *reality* rather than that of truth. If we can make our intuition accord with the mobility of the real, would not this accord be something stable, and would not truth – which can only be this accord itself – participate in this stability? But much trial and error would be necessary before reaching this point. Thank you once again, dear Professor James; all my compliments on this new work, destined to be of considerable influence.

Villa Montmorency, 9th May 1908.[37]

Cher Professor James,
I cannot tell you what pleasure I had, yesterday, in recognizing your writing on an envelope bearing an English stamp. Here finally, I hope, is an opportunity to speak with you.

You do me a very great honour in dedicating one of your lectures to me at Oxford.[38] How happy I would have been to hear you, both in this lecture and in the others! I hope at least that you will not delay bringing them together in a book.

Here is the information that you were kind enough to ask of me. First my *curriculum vitae*. Born in Paris in 1859. Pupil at the Lycée Cordorcet, from 1868 to 1878. Student at the Ecole Normale Supérieure (an establishment where we train those who will become university teachers) from 1878 to 1881. Aggregated in philosophy in 1881, doctor of philosophy in 1889. Philosophy teacher in various provincial and Parisian schools, from 1881 to 1898. Lecturer at the Ecole Normale Supérieure from 1898 to 1900. Lecturer at the Collège de France since 1900. Member of the Institute since 1901.

Now, as for notable events, there haven't been any in the course of my career, at least nothing *objectively* notable. But, subjectively, I cannot avoid attributing a great importance to the change that came about in my way of thinking during the two years after leaving the Ecole Normale, from 1881 to 1883. Until that point I had remained completely steeped in the mechanistic theories to which I had been introduced very early on by reading Herbert Spencer, the philosopher to whom I adhered more or less unreservedly. My intention was to devote myself to what was then called 'the philosophy of sciences' and it was to this end that I had undertaken, upon leaving the Ecole Normale, the examination of several basic scientific notions. It was the analysis of the notion of time, such as it appears in mechanics or physics, which revolutionized all of my ideas. I realized, to my great amazement, that scientific time has no *duration*, that nothing would have to be changed in our scientific ideas of things if the totality of the real was deployed all at once and instantaneously, and that positive science essentially consists in the elimination of duration. This was the starting point of a series of reflections which led me, step by step, to reject almost all that I had previously accepted, and to completely change my point of view. In *Time and Free Will* (pages 116–20, 194–97, etc.), I have summarized these considerations on scientific time, which were to determine my philosophical orientation and which form the basis of all the reflections I have been able to make since . . .

Chalet Ferdinand de Reynier, Chaumont-Sur-Neuchatel (Switzerland), 23rd July 1908.[39]

Dear Professor James,

I must tell you straightaway the great joy I experienced reading you.[40] Never have I been examined, understood, penetrated in such a manner. Never, moreover, have I been so conscious of the sympathy and the sort of 'pre-established harmony' which attunes your thought and mine. Let me tell you, moreover, that you have not limited yourself to analysing my ideas; you have transfigured them, without ever disfiguring them in any way. In reading your exposition of my theses, I thought of those superb reproductions that the great engraving masters made of sometimes quite ordinary paintings.

From your fifth lesson and the beginning of the seventh, as also in the last pages of the chapter that you devote to me, I think I can see the essential idea of your book – the idea that is important above all others, which will dissipate the difficulties that have been accumulated by philosophers around the whole question. I hope I will soon be able to read this book,[41] which will form the link between the *Principles of Psychology* and the *Varieties of Religious Experience*, at the same time as defining the philosophy which pragmatism leads us to – a philosophy without any doubt destined to replace the old metaphysical dogmatism . . .

Villa Montmorency, 21st January 1909.[42]

Cher William James,

I have been so busy since the beginning of the academic year that I have not yet been able to read Fechner's *Zend-Avesta* that you spoke to me about in London;[43] I will set about studying it as soon as I have a bit more free time. But I had a foretaste of it recently reading your lovely article in the *Hibbert Journal*.[44] This hypothesis of an *earth-soul*,[45] which will perhaps seem arbitrary to many people, is in reality the one which most closely fits the facts, because it puts no more in the cause than precisely what is required to produce the effects that we observe. What is truly arbitrary is the immediate passage from these effects to an infinite cause which has neither a common measure nor point of contact with them. You have pointed this out so well in your article and enveloped all of it in such a beautiful poetry, that I now fear I will be disappointed when I read Fechner himself. – Your conception of intermediary beings between man and God seems to me to be one which will become increasingly necessary to philosophy.

9th April 1909.[46]

Cher William James,

I am writing you a couple of hasty words (as the post for America is leaving in a moment), simply to tell you the great pleasure I just had in reading your article in the *Hibbert Journal*, which arrived this very moment.[47] I was already familiar with it from the proofs which you kindly passed on to me; but I experienced a keen joy in rereading this truly masterly exposition of the leading ideas of my works. My thought is certainly there – but how I would have liked to have said it that way! and how much the idea gains from drawing on the original reflections that you surround it with!

Once again, thank you.

30th April 1909.[48]

Cher William James,

I waited impatiently for your new work and I thank you for sending it to me.[49] It is an admirable book, which I will only reproach for being too modest and for highlighting the names of Fechner and Bergson, when from one end to the other it is William James – his words, his thought, his very soul – that we are dealing with. The book says many things, and yet it suggests even more than it says. It defines and justifies pluralism, it places our finger on the concrete relation between beings, it definitively lays the foundations of 'radical empiricism': that is what it says. But it suggests something which goes beyond all of that – a certain *consoling emotion* drawn from the very heart of reality. You talk, in your conclusion, of those *saving experiences*[50] which have been the privilege of certain souls: either I am very much mistaken, or your book, combined with the *Varieties of Religious Experience*, will make widespread experiences of this kind, by inspiring them in those who had no *idea* of them, or developing them where they only existed in a nascent state . . .

There are many other points in your book which gave me cause for reflection. I will speak to you of them another time. I will limit myself for the moment to telling you the impression that this work has had on me. I look forward to having several days free in order to reread your last three books all in one session, one after the other. I would then no doubt be more able to put my impression *into words*. But it could not be more profound.

Rest assured, *cher William James*, of my feelings of great admiration as well as affectionate devotion.

Villa Montmorency, 31st March 1910.[51]

Mon cher James,

I hope that you have accepted the invitation that Boutroux[52] has issued to you on behalf of the Université de Paris, and that we will soon see you in France. If, as I hope, it is for this Spring or Summer, would you oblige me by letting me know the – at least approximate – date of your arrival? I absolutely count on being in Paris at that moment.

I have not yet told you the pleasure I had in reading your two articles 'The moral equivalent of war' and 'A suggestion about mysticism'.[53] The first is certainly the most beautiful and persuasive thing that has been written on the subject of the non-necessity of war, and the conditions under which we could eliminate it without thereby diminishing human energy. As for your article on mysticism, it will be, I am sure, the point of departure for many new observations and studies. I am not sure I have ever myself experienced an *uncovering*,[54] but perhaps there was something of the sort in the following fact which has sometimes (rarely, as it happens) occurred in me while dreaming. I believed myself to be present before a superb spectacle – generally the sight of a landscape of intense colours, through which I was travelling at high speed and which gave me such a profound impression of reality that I could not believe, during the first moments of waking up, that it was a simple dream. But during the quite short time that the dream seemed to last (two or three seconds at most), I have each time had the very clear feeling that I was in the process of having a *dangerous* experience, that it was up to me to prolong it and experience the outcome, but that something was stretching or swelling more and more within me and would end up bursting if I did not fix matters by waking up. And upon waking, I had at the same time the regret at having interrupted such a dream and the quite clear impression that it was me who had *wanted* to interrupt it. I give you this experience for what it is worth: perhaps it has some relationship with yours, in that it suggests the idea of a momentary extension of the field of consciousness, but due to an intense effort.

How I would like you to pursue this study of 'the *noetic* value of abnormal mental states'![55] Your article, combined with what you have said in the *Varieties of Religious Experience*, opens up great perspectives for us in this direction.

Letter to Harald Höffding[56]

15 March 1915

. . . First I must tell you how grateful I am to you for having discussed my works in such an attentive and insightful manner. No greater honour could be given me. Even where you criticize my views, one feels that your primary aim is to present them with absolute impartiality. Your method of discussion has nothing in common with the kind that is so often applied to me, which consists in ascribing me some strange and false idea, which is then easily refuted.

Even so, it is impossible for an original thinker to inhabit *entirely* the perspective of another. You will thus not be surprised if I tell you that, in your overall exposition of my ideas, there is no chapter that I can completely subscribe to, – consequently, no criticism which seems to me to pertain exactly to what I have said, or at the very least to what I have thought (for we are never sure that what we think has truly been communicated in what we have said). I cannot go into details; I leave aside certain criticisms that I consider to be of lesser importance – for example concerning the relationship of consciousness to the body (I also think that each state of consciousness has a motor accompaniment, and that one whole aspect of memory, that of motor habits, is embedded in the body); also as an example, concerning the problem of God (I have not really addressed this problem in my writings; I consider it inseparable from the moral problems whose study I have been absorbed in for several years; and the few lines in *Creative*

Evolution that you allude to were only put there as placeholders in anticipation of this work [*comme une pierre d'attente*]); – still another example is the identification of art with philosophy that you ascribe to me, an identification which I cannot subscribe to, because: 1. Art is only concerned with the living and appeals to intuition alone, whereas philosophy is necessarily concerned with matter at the same time as it explores the mind, and consequently appeals to the intellect as well as intuition (even though intuition is its specific instrument); 2. Philosophical intuition, having taken the same direction as artistic intuition, then goes much further: it captures the vital before its dispersal into images, whereas art is concerned with the images. But I will leave all of that aside and come to the important point.

In my opinion, any summary of my views will produce an overall distortion and, in virtue of this very fact, expose them to a mass of objections, if it is not first situated at and does not ceaselessly return to what I consider the very centre of the doctrine: the intuition of duration. The representation of a multiplicity of 'reciprocal penetration', quite different from numerical multiplicity – the representation of a heterogeneous, qualitative, creative duration – was my point of departure and the point to which I have constantly returned. It requires a very great mental effort, the rupture of many frameworks, something like a new method of thought (for the immediate is far from being the easiest thing to apprehend); but, once one has reached this representation and possesses it in its *simple* form (which must not be confused with a conceptual reconstruction), one feels obliged to displace one's point of view on reality; one sees that the greatest difficulties come from the fact that philosophers have always put time and space on the same level: most of these difficulties are diminished or fade away. The theory of intuition, to which you give much greater weight than that of duration, only emerged for me quite a long time after the latter: it is derived from it and can only be understood through it. This is why this intuition would not fit any of the four definitions that you enumerate. No doubt it allows of a series of successive *planes*; but on the last plane, which is the principal one, it is the intuition of duration.

There would in any case be a great deal to say, in relation to your book, on this intuition and this duration. I think that if you take my understanding of duration into account, you will see something more precise and also more persuasive in the 'vitalism' of *Creative Evolution*, than your account suggests. The essential argument that I oppose to mechanism in biology is that it does not explain how life unfolds a *story*, which is to say a succession where there is no repetition, where every moment is *unique* and carries within it the representation of the whole of the past. This idea is beginning to find some favour among certain biologists, as poorly inclined towards vitalism as biologists are in general: they thus see in it something other than 'the expression of admiration and wonder'. In a general sense, whoever has reclaimed their grasp on the intuition of duration can never again believe in universal mechanism; for, in the mechanistic hypothesis, real time becomes useless and even impossible. But duration is the most indisputable of facts for someone who has situated themselves within it. This is why I have said that it provides us with a definitive, *empirical* refutation of mechanistic philosophy.

Moreover, your remark on intuition, instinct and intelligence misses the fact that, for me, *practical* knowledge is truly a knowledge of reality *in itself*, absolute reality, when it remains in its proper domain. Intelligence, whose role is to master unorganized matter, is thus capable of knowing this matter absolutely (although incompletely). In the same way, instinct, which is made to use life, knows life absolutely and from the inside, although incompletely and in a barely conscious way. Thus human intuition, which prolongs, develops and makes reflective what remains of instinct in man, is capable of embracing life more and more completely. Knowledge, whether intellectual or intuitive, only becomes relative when the faculty of knowledge is applied to what it was not made for. Such is the knowledge of life which claims to give us conceptual intelligence (mechanism); and such also was, in former times, the representation of matter given using images drawn from the life world (hylozoism).

My letter is already long; and yet I would have to further lengthen it enormously if I wanted to write to you everything that your book suggests to me. I think that if I could speak with you and remove all the misunderstandings, I would also by the same stroke remove most of the criticisms and objections. I hope that you will give me the opportunity to do so. I cannot tell you what a good and vivid memory I have of the conversation we once had together. We must find a way to continue it one day. You must return to France, when we have recovered the necessary calm for philosophical speculation. At the moment France is fighting for justice, for the respect of the rights of individuals and peoples, large or small. She thus serves again, in this war, in which she has no selfish, ambitious or material interest, the cause of Ideas, to which she has always been devoted and which constitutes her greatness.

I thank you once again, and I beg you accept, Monsieur and very honoured Colleague, the expression of my most distinguished and devoted feelings.

H. Bergson

Letter to Floris Delattre[57]

24th December 1935.

. . . It is easy to see that Butler only uses images, comparisons, etc. to supplement or even simply to decorate the expression of his thought: he could, strictly speaking, do without it. By contrast, in a book like *Creative Evolution* or *The Two Sources*, images are most often introduced because they are indispensable, as none of the existing concepts are able to express the thought of the author, and the author is thus obliged to *suggest* it. This suggestion can only be made by an image, but by an image which has not been chosen by the philosopher, which presents itself independently as the sole means of communication, and imposes itself with absolute necessity.

To take only one example: when I relate the phenomena of life and evolution to an *élan vital*, it is not for the stylistic flourish, nor moreover is it in order to mask our ignorance of the deep cause with an image, as when the vitalist generally invokes a 'vital principal' or when Butler speaks to us of a 'life-force'. The truth is that in this area philosophy only provides philosophers with two explanatory principles: mechanism and finality (the latter characterizing the 'vital principle' of the vitalists and consequently the 'life-force' of Butler). Now, for reasons whose detail it is not useful to go into here, I accept neither the one nor the other of these two points of view, which correspond to concepts formed by the human mind for a completely different purpose than the explanation of life. It is somewhere *between* these two concepts that we have to place ourselves. How do we determine this place? I can only indicate it by hand since there is no intermediary concept between '*mechanism*' and '*finality*'. The image of an *élan* is nothing other than this indication. By itself it has no value. But it will acquire value if the reader is willing to place himself with me at this point, so that we can observe from this position what can be perceived of life and also what is not perceived. I have enumerated, in pages 111–116 of my book *The Two Sources*, the knowledges and *the ignorances* which make up a certain quite special vision of evolution and life, when one places oneself, between mechanism and finality, at the point that I mark by writing the word *élan*. I even amused myself, in this passage in my book, by counting them. I found precisely nine. My so-called metaphor is thus, in reality, the precise and at the same time global notation of possible observations. And this is why it is radically distinct from sterile images such as Schopenhauer's 'will-to-live' or the 'life-force' of vitalists such as Butler. This is also why we could have predicted that sooner or later biology would have to adopt something like it. It is starting to do this – not, I admit, without hesitation and repugnance. But I am digressing from what was asked of me. It was a matter of knowing whether there is something in common between the two doctrines.[58] I once again reply: 'No, I see nothing in common.' But I would like, this time, to go a bit further, and indicate why, *a priori*, it was very unlikely that they would have something in common.

It is not, to be sure, that I lay claim to some sort of deep originality. Quite the contrary, I have always preached modesty in philosophy, and I have done what I could to give the example. But precisely for this reason, precisely because it seems to me that the time of great original hypotheses serving a philosopher's vanity has passed, I recommend and have practised for some fifty years a method which essentially consists in envisaging special problems in philosophy, as it is done in the positive sciences. Each one of these problems could require lengthy investigations of the philosopher; often his whole life will not be too long to carry them out; and yet this will only be a beginning: the principal difficulty is not there. The true difficulty is to *pose* the problem, to abstract oneself to this end from language (which was made for conversation, not for philosophy), to carve reality along its natural lines, whereas language and common sense have tailored and distributed it with a view to the convenience of our actions. In this way the problem will be limited, but the effort to resolve it, and above all to pose it, will become unlimited. At bottom, resolving and posing amount to the same thing. The problem, such as I conceive it, is only posed once it is resolved.

Understanding philosophy in this way, what chances are there that a philosopher would find in advance or have a premonition of what another philosopher will find? This is not at all impossible, if this philosopher has a similar understanding of philosophical method and possesses the same determination to obtain a result. It is impossible if the first philosopher intends to remain an amateur. I can now moreover give a precise definition of the word that I have just uttered. I call an *amateur*, in philosophy, someone who accepts wholesale the terms of a common problem, considers it definitively posed, and limits himself to choosing from the apparent solutions to this problem, which necessarily pre-exist his choice. Such is Butler rejecting Darwin's solution and allying himself with Lamarck's. But in this matter really to do philosophy consists in *creating* the position of the problem and in *creating* the solution. How could it be otherwise? Is it not evident that if a problem has been posed for a long time and not yet been resolved, it is because it comprises, in the form it is posed, two or several equally possible solutions, which are mutually exclusive? The philosopher properly called cannot, must not, stop at this point. I thus call an *amateur* someone who chooses between ready-made solutions, like choosing which political party to join. And I call a *philosopher* someone who creates the solution, which is then necessarily unique, of the problem that he has newly posed, through the very fact of having made the effort to resolve it. Between these two there is a radical difference, but one which might escape readers of the one or the other if they themselves assume the attitude of the amateur, if they do not, through a study which necessarily requires an effort analogous to that of the philosopher, home in on the new sense which words assume in the new conception of the problem.

Message to the Descartes Congress, 1937: 'One Must Act like a Man of Thought and Think like a Man of Action'[59]

(Henri Bergson, honorary President of the International Congress of Philosophy, prevented from joining the members of this congress, but with them in spirit, has conveyed to M. Emile Bréhier, President of the Organizing Committee, this text, which places the Congress under the spiritual patronage of Descartes.)

I am old enough to have been able, when already no longer young, to be at the side of our dear and admirable Xavier Leon when he founded the Congress of Philosophy. It was also during an International Universal Exhibition, in 1900. Some were surprised at the idea of introducing among the tools, machines and other material products of civilization an exhibition of world thought in its highest and most abstract forms. In reality, Xavier Leon must have foreseen what subsequent events

have shown only too well: that our most marvellous discoveries and inventions will turn against us if we are not careful to dominate them, that the increasing size of the body of humanity will simply render it incapable of walking unless it is accompanied, for its direction and even support, by a surplus of moral energy. The political, economic, social and international problems that face us today only translate, each in their own way, this now monstrous disproportion between the body and soul of the human species, the soul tossing about inside a body that is too big for it, having been unable to expand in turn. Certainly our philosophy will not be sufficient to restore the balance: for this we will need a will stretched to the limit of its powers; we will also need the individual and collective experimentation which alone reveals the unforeseeable consequences of a decision, and thus separates the possible from the impossible. But a good and strong will fortunately exists in a great number of people; and as for experimentation, we see it practised in the form of political regimes and social organizations, whose antagonisms alone are visible to us now, but which we will find later to have collaborated in one and the same great experiment. If philosophy can then come forward to give all a full awareness of their movement, to help analyses and suggest syntheses, a new era could open up in the history of humanity. For my own part, I see the machine firstly worsening the inequality between men, but then settling for such a reduced level of human work in relation to such an abundant material production, that all would have the leisure to take up the most noble spiritual occupations: letters and science, arts, philosophy. The process of selection which produces elites will then bear as a matter of course on everyone, equally equipped from the start, and no longer only those chosen by circumstance. The elite will be reinforced, in number, and above all in value. It could change the face of humanity. The famous elegy of Thomas Gray, lamenting in a country cemetery the great man who is perhaps buried there,[60] will no longer correspond to anything. These are some of the thoughts – Utopian or paradoxical today, perhaps banal tomorrow – that the insertion of a philosophical Congress into a Universal Exhibition will incite in philosophers.

They will only be reinforced if we consider that our Congress is placed under the spiritual patronage of Descartes. It is true that Descartes was the very model of a speculative genius. A mind of universal scope, he remodelled human thought. He created from scratch, or almost, a mathematics to which a mathematician could apply, without too much exaggeration, the expression of the Latin poet: 'a child born without a mother', *proles sine matre creata*. The *Discourse on Method* is the analysis and commentary of this marvellous mathematics, or rather of a science of the same kind, made so as to be all-embracing. He created the ideal of physics, by tracing the broad outline of a universal mechanism. He created a spiritualism which was later to serve as a model, because he did not shrink from clear separations, because he boldly affirmed the coexistence of the soul with the body, of thought with extension, of freedom with necessity and of the world with God. He created modern metaphysics, by setting minds on the path of idealism, a path on which he himself decided to stop half-way, but where others have continued to the end. He created an ideal of education that we must never lose sight of, consisting in the complete substitution of reason for memory, with the implicit idea that true knowledge has less in common with a superficially encyclopaedic knowledge than with a self-aware ignorance accompanied by the resolution to know. He created, specially for the *Discourse on Method*, the form that French philosophy was subsequently to adopt, abandoning Latin speech in order to communicate generously to all: the virtue *par excellence*, in Descartes's eyes, was in effect generosity. By also avoiding, as much as possible, expressions which store ready-made ideas, and thus obliging ordinary words to assume enough flexibility, and to combine with one another in such a skilful way so as to present new thoughts, he encouraged invention, at the same time as suggesting that the philosopher become, by means of effort, a little of what he was himself by the grace of his genius: a writer. Above all, he created a mental attitude which was to set a standard in both philosophy and science: a proud, perhaps arrogant, posture of thought, standing against nature as well as tradition, an inflexible will to independence, an unlimited trust in the power of intelligence. Finally, he created the need to create in the speculative domain, in particular the need for thought to engender the object to be studied, instead of accepting it as already made (his analytic geometry is just this), and it is this which gives his doctrine, systematized in different ways by different historians, a unity which it would be difficult to specify further; for this doctrine, sometimes cited as the paradigm of deductive philosophy, is essentially intuitive. Intuitive in the Cartesian sense, which is close to the ordinary sense, but also intuitive in the sense in which it is sometimes used today, since Descartes spoke, without giving it a name, of a knowledge that is acquired 'by refraining from thinking about it', 'by drawing only on life'. Such would be, according to one of his letters to Princess Elizabeth, our knowledge of the union of the soul with the body.[61] Let us sum up then in a couple of words: all philosophy, directly or indirectly, can be traced back to Descartes. Those who have not read him closely might decide that this pure spirit (as Gassendi ironically called him) would only be moderately interested in, for example, an Exhibition like ours. I myself consider that he would have wandered through it with real delight. For the goal he set for both philosophy and science, which he merged together in a sort of universal knowledge, was to 'render us the masters and owners of nature', no doubt alluding to the study of life and in particular medicine, but imagining this study in such a way that it presupposed our physics and mechanics. Recent commentators have thus taken this very far and maintained that, for Descartes, theory was subordinate to its application. One of them has said: 'Aristotle's physics is the physics of an artist; Descartes's is the physics of an engineer.' Is this quite right? My answer would be yes, and yet no. Certainly not if the ultimate aim would be the comfort, well-being or even prolongation of life that philosophy would bring us, according to Descartes, via the intermediary of a physical and mechanical biology. Yes, on the other hand, if we consider that aside from their material utility, scientific applications are so many successes through which we demonstrate our force to ourselves, and affirm our independence, even our sovereignty. He made a clean sweep of Aristotelianism, and consequently of the method which proceeds by manipulating preexisting concepts: the new elements he will operate with must be 'clear and distinct ideas'. But by what criteria do we recognize a clarity that is not artificial or accidental, or a distinction that is not the result of an arbitrary division of experience? It can only be by its effectiveness, or rather, taking the French word in its English sense, by its 'efficiency' [*efficience*]. Such that philosophy, which includes science, will make us little by little masters of nature, and this mastery, as it progresses, will provide an ever more complete material for philosophical speculation. Theory and application would thus condition each other in what we could call, from a certain point of view and to a certain extent, a metaphysical pragmatism.

Let us then reflect on the modernity of Cartesianism, which was already striking well before the theory of relativity once again inflected our physics in a Cartesian direction, and which could become so again if some new kind of determinism comes along, as is probable, to translate the indetermination that a recent physics has discovered in the heart of things. Let us also reflect on the modernity of the author, who was so ahead of his time in his conception both of the philosopher and of philosophy. He put aside what was said about things in order to be concerned solely with things themselves. He practised tourism in the grand style, travelling, first as a soldier, then out of pleasure, through Germany, Hungary, Switzerland, Holland and other countries still. He had something of a premonition of the international intellectual cooperation which the League of Nations and the French government has installed in Geneva and Paris, when he made contact with scholars from various countries, corresponded with a Princess, instructed a Queen. He organized his life in such a way as to draw the maximum return, settling overseas, or travelling, for greater tranquillity and independence: it was, in his case, the best way of serving his country. He disdained the science of books. Although obliged to accept controversy, he never liked it. In the closed room and heavy atmosphere in which professional thinkers have their discussions, he was the genius amateur who comes uninvited, throws wide open all the doors and windows, calls for air and light, and invites and obliges others to breathe freely. The Lord Chancellor Francis Bacon had already done something of this kind. Descartes provides the great example. When I try to imagine him in person, I see him first in his heated room in Germany, 'conversing with his thoughts'; but I also see him in the boat where the boatmen were plotting to rob him and throw him overboard, guessing their plan, drawing his sword and keeping the robbers at bay. I know there is much to be said on the relations between thought and action. But the motto that I would suggest for the philosopher, and even for the ordinary man, is the simplest one of all and, in my opinion, the most Cartesian. I would say that one must act like a man of thought and think like a man of action.

Laughter

An Essay on the Meaning of the Comic

The first point to which attention should be called is that the comic does not exist outside the pale of what is strictly *human*. A landscape may be beautiful, charming and sublime, or insignificant and ugly; it will never be laughable. You may laugh at an animal, but only because you have detected in it some human attitude or expression. You may laugh at a hat, but what you are making fun of, in this case, is not the piece of felt or straw, but the shape that men have given it – the human caprice whose mold it has assumed. It is strange that so important a fact, and such a simple one too, has not attracted to a greater degree the attention of philosophers. Several have defined man as 'an animal which laughs.' They might equally well have defined him as an animal which is laughed at; for if any other animal, or some lifeless object, produces the same effect, it is always because of some resemblance to man, of the stamp he gives it or the use he puts it to.

Here I would point out, as a symptom equally worthy of notice, the *absence of feeling* which usually accompanies laughter. It seems as though the comic could not produce its disturbing effect unless it fell, so to say, on the surface of a soul that is thoroughly calm and unruffled. Indifference is its natural environment, for laughter has no greater foe than emotion. I do not mean that we could not laugh at a person who inspires us with pity, for instance, or even with affection, but in such a case we must, for the moment, put our affection out of court and impose silence upon our pity. In a society composed of pure intelligences there would probably be no more tears, though perhaps there would still be laughter; whereas highly emotional souls, in tune and unison with life, in whom every event would be sentimentally prolonged and re-echoed, would neither know nor understand laughter. Try, for a moment, to become interested in everything that is being said and done; act, in imagination, with those who act, and feel with those who feel; in a word, give your sympathy its widest expansion: as though at the touch of a fairy wand you will see the flimsiest of objects assume importance, and a gloomy hue spread over everything. Now step aside, look upon life as a disinterested spectator: many a drama will turn into a comedy. It is enough for us to stop our ears to the sound of music, in a room where dancing is going on, for the dancers at once to appear ridiculous. How many human actions would stand a similar test? Should we not see many of them suddenly pass from grave to gay, on isolating them from the accompanying music of sentiment? To produce the whole of its effect, then, the comic demands something like a momentary anesthesia of the heart. Its appeal is to intelligence, pure and simple.

This intelligence, however, must always remain in touch with other intelligences. And here is the third fact to which attention should be drawn. You would hardly appreciate the comic if you felt yourself isolated from others. Laughter appears to stand in need of an echo. Listen to it carefully: it is not an articulate, clear, well-defined sound; it is something which would fain be prolonged by reverberating from one to another, something beginning with a crash, to continue in successive rumblings, like thunder in a mountain. Still, this reverberation cannot go on forever. It can travel within as wide a circle as you please: the circle remains, nonetheless, a closed one. Our laughter is always the laughter of a group. It may, perchance, have happened to you, when seated in a railway carriage or at *table d'hôte,* to hear travelers relating to one another stories which must have been comic to them, for they laughed heartily. Had you been one of their company, you would have laughed like them; but, as you were not, you had no desire whatever to do so. A man who was once asked why he did not weep at a sermon, when everybody else was shedding tears, replied: 'I don't belong to the parish!' What that man thought of tears would be still more true of laughter. However spontaneous it seems, laughter always implies a kind of secret freemasonry, or even complicity, with other laughers, real or imaginary. How often has it been said that the fuller the theatre, the more uncontrolled the laughter of the audience! On the other hand, how often has the remark been made that many comic effects are incapable of translation from one language to another, because they refer to the customs and ideas of a particular social group! It is through not understanding the importance of this double fact that the comic has been looked upon as a mere curiosity in which the mind finds amusement, and laughter itself as a strange, isolated phenomenon, without any bearing on the rest of human activity. Hence those definitions which tend to make the comic into an abstract relation between ideas: 'an intellectual contrast,' 'a palpable absurdity,' etc. – definitions which, even were they really suitable to every form of the comic, would not in the least explain why the comic makes us laugh. How, indeed, should it come about that this particular logical relation, as soon as it is perceived, contracts, expands and shakes our limbs, whilst all other relations leave the body unaffected? It is not from this point of view that we shall approach the problem. To understand laughter, we must put it back into its natural environment, which is society, and above all must we determine the utility of its function, which is a social one. Such, let us say at once, will be the leading idea of all our investigations. Laughter must answer to certain requirements of life in common. It must have a *social* signification.

Let us clearly mark the point towards which our three preliminary observations are converging. The comic will come into being, it appears, whenever a group of men concentrate their attention on one of their number, imposing silence on their emotions and calling into play nothing but their intelligence. What, now, is the particular point on which their attention will have to be concentrated, and what will here be the function of intelligence? To reply to these questions will be at once to come to closer grips with the problem. But here a few examples have become indispensable.

A man, running along the street, stumbles and falls; the passers-by burst out laughing. They would not laugh at him, I imagine, could they suppose that the whim had suddenly seized him to sit down on the ground. They laugh because his sitting down is involuntary.

Consequently, it is not his sudden change of attitude that raises a laugh, but rather the involuntary element in this change – his clumsiness, in fact. Perhaps there was a stone on the road. He should have altered his pace or avoided the obstacle. Instead of that, through lack of elasticity, through absentmindedness and a kind of physical obstinacy, *as a result, in fact, of rigidity or of momentum*, the muscles continued to perform the same movement when the circumstances of the case called for something else. That is the reason for the man's fall, and also for the people's laughter.

Now, take the case of a person who attends to the petty occupations of his everyday life with mathematical precision. The objects around him, however, have all been tampered with by a mischievous wag, the result being that when he dips his pen into the inkstand he draws it out all covered with mud, when he fancies he is sitting down on a solid chair he finds himself sprawling on the floor, in a word his actions are all topsy-turvy or mere beating the air, while in every case the effect is invariably one of momentum. Habit has given the impulse: what was wanted was to check the movement or deflect it. He did nothing of the sort, but continued like a machine in the same straight line. The victim, then, of a practical joke is in a position similar to that of a runner who falls – he is comic for the same reason. The laughable element in both cases consists of a certain *mechanical inelasticity*, just where one would expect to find the wide-awake adaptability and the living pliableness of a human being. The only difference in the two cases is that the former happened of itself, whilst the latter was obtained artificially. In the first instance, the passer-by does nothing but look on, but in the second the mischievous wag intervenes.

All the same, in both cases the result has been brought about by an external circumstance. The comic is therefore accidental: it remains, so to speak, in superficial contact with the person. How is it to penetrate within? The necessary conditions will be fulfilled when mechanical rigidity no longer requires for its manifestation a stumbling-block which either the hazard of circumstance or human knavery has set in its way, but extracts by natural processes, from its own store, an inexhaustible series of opportunities for externally revealing its presence. Suppose, then, we imagine a mind always thinking of what it has just done and never of what it is doing, like a song which lags behind its accompaniment. Let us try to picture to ourselves a certain inborn lack of elasticity of both senses and intelligence, which brings it to pass that we continue to see what is no longer visible, to hear what is no longer audible, to say what is no longer to the point: in short, to adapt ourselves to a past and therefore imaginary situation, when we ought to be shaping our conduct in accordance with the reality which is present. This time the comic will take up its abode in the person himself; it is the person who will supply it with everything – matter and form, cause and opportunity. Is it then surprising that the absent-minded individual – for this is the character we have just been describing – has usually fired the imagination of comic authors? When La Bruyère came across this particular type, he realized, on analyzing it, that he had got hold of a recipe for the wholesale manufacture of comic effects. As a matter of fact he overdid it, and gave us far too lengthy and detailed a description of *Ménalque*, coming back to his subject, dwelling and expatiating on it beyond all bounds. The very facility of the subject fascinated him. Absentmindedness, indeed, is not perhaps the actual fountainhead of the comic, but surely it is contiguous to a certain stream of facts and fancies which flows straight from the fountainhead. It is situated, so to say, on one of the great natural watersheds of laughter.

Now, the effect of absentmindedness may gather strength in its turn. There is a general law, the first example of which we have just encountered, and which we will formulate in the following terms: when a certain comic effect has its origin in a certain cause, the more natural we regard the cause to be, the more comic shall we find the effect. Even now we laugh at absentmindedness when presented to us as a simple fact. Still more laughable will be the absentmindedness we have seen springing up and growing before our very eyes, with whose origin we are acquainted and whose life-history we can reconstruct. To choose a definite example: suppose a man has taken to reading nothing but romances of love and chivalry. Attracted and fascinated by his heroes, his thoughts and intentions gradually turn more and more towards them, till one fine day we find him walking among us like a somnambulist. His actions are distractions. But then his distractions can be traced back to a definite, positive cause. They are no longer cases of *absence* of mind, pure and simple; they find their explanation in the *presence* of the individual in quite definite, though imaginary, surroundings. Doubtless a fall is always a fall, but it is one thing to tumble into a well because you were looking anywhere but in front of you, it is quite another thing to fall into it because you were intent upon a star. It was certainly a star at which Don Quixote was gazing. How profound is the comic element in the overromantic, Utopian bent of mind! And yet, if you reintroduce the idea of absentmindedness, which acts as a go-between, you will see this profound comic element uniting with the most superficial type. Yes, indeed, these whimsical wild enthusiasts, these madmen who are yet so strangely reasonable, excite us to laughter by playing on the same chords within ourselves, by setting in motion the same inner mechanism, as does the victim of a practical joke or the passer-by who slips down in the street. They, too, are runners who fall and simple souls who are being hoaxed – runners after the ideal who stumble over realities, child-like dreamers for whom life delights to lie in wait. But, above all, they are past-masters in absentmindedness, with this superiority over their fellows that their absentmindedness is systematic and organized around one central idea, and that their mishaps are also quite coherent, thanks to the inexorable logic which reality applies to the correction of dreams, so that they kindle in those around them, by a series of cumulative effects, a hilarity capable of unlimited expansion.

Now, let us go a little further. Might not certain vices have the same relation to character that the rigidity of a fixed idea has to intellect? Whether as a moral kink or a crooked twist given to the will, vice has often the appearance of a curvature of the soul. Doubtless there are vices into which the soul plunges deeply with all its pregnant potency, which it rejuvenates and drags along with it into a moving circle of reincarnations. Those are tragic vices. But the vice capable of making us comic is, on the contrary, that which is brought from without, like a ready-made frame into which we are to step. It lends us its own rigidity instead of borrowing from us our flexibility. We do not render it more complicated; on the contrary, it simplifies us. Here, as we shall see later on in the concluding section of this study, lies the essential difference between comedy and drama. A drama, even when portraying passions or vices that bear a name, so completely incorporates them in the person that their names are forgotten, their general characteristics effaced, and we no longer think of them at all, but rather of the person in whom they are assimilated; hence, the title of a drama can seldom be anything else than a proper noun. On the other hand, many comedies have a common noun as their title: *l'Avare*, *le Joueur*, etc. Were you asked to think of a play capable of being called *le Jaloux*, for instance, you would find that *Sganarelle* or *George Dandin* would occur to your mind, but not *Othello*: *le Jaloux* could only be the title of a comedy. The reason is that, however intimately vice, when comic, is associated with persons, it none the less retains its simple, independent existence, it remains the central character, present though invisible, to which the characters in flesh and blood on the stage are attached. At times it delights in dragging them down with its own weight and making them share in its tumbles. More frequently, however, it plays on them as on an instrument or pulls the strings as though they were puppets. Look closely: you will find that the art of the comic poet consists in making us so well acquainted with the particular vice, in introducing us, the spectators, to such a degree of intimacy with it, that in the end we get hold of some of the strings of the marionette with which he is playing, and actually work them ourselves; this it is that explains part of the pleasure we feel. Here, too, it is really a kind of automatism that makes us laugh – an automatism, as we have already remarked, closely akin to mere absentmindedness. To realize this more fully, it need only be noted that a comic character is generally comic in proportion to his ignorance of himself. The comic person is unconscious. As though wearing the ring of Gyges with reverse effect, he becomes invisible to himself while remaining visible to all the world. A character in a tragedy will make no change in his conduct because he will know how it is judged by us; he may continue therein, even though fully conscious of what he is and feeling keenly the horror he inspires in us. But a defect that is ridiculous, as soon as it feels itself to be so, endeavors to modify itself, or at least to appear as though it did. Were Harpagon to see us laugh at his miserliness, I do not say that he would get rid of it, but he would either show it less or show it differently. Indeed, it is in this sense only that laughter 'corrects men's manners.' It makes us at once endeavor to appear what we ought to be, what some day we shall perhaps end in being.

It is unnecessary to carry this analysis any further. From the runner who falls to the simpleton who is hoaxed, from a state of being hoaxed to one of absentmindedness, from absentmindedness to wild enthusiasm, from wild enthusiasm to various distortions of character and will, we have followed the line of progress along which the comic becomes more and more deeply imbedded in the person, yet without ceasing, in its subtler manifestations, to recall to us some trace of what we noticed in its grosser forms, an effect of automatism and of inelasticity. Now we can obtain a first glimpse – a distant one, it is true, and still hazy and confused – of the laughable side of human nature and of the ordinary function of laughter.

What life and society require of each of us is a constantly alert attention that discerns the outlines of the present situation, together with a certain elasticity of mind and body to enable us to adapt ourselves in consequence. *Tension* and *elasticity* are two forces, mutually complementary, which life brings into play. If these two forces are lacking in the body to any considerable extent, we have sickness and infirmity and accidents of every kind. If they are lacking in the mind, we find every degree of mental deficiency, every variety of insanity. Finally, if they are lacking in the character, we have cases of the gravest inadaptability to social life, which are the sources of misery and at times the causes of crime. Once these elements of inferiority that affect the serious side of existence are removed – and they tend to eliminate themselves in what has been called the struggle for life – the person can live, and that in common with other persons. But society asks for something more; it is not satisfied with simply living, it insists on living well. What it now has to dread is that each one of us, content with paying attention to what affects the essentials of life, will, so far as the rest is concerned, give way to the easy automatism of acquired habits. Another thing it must fear is that the members of whom it is made up, instead of aiming after an increasingly delicate adjustment of wills which will fit more and more perfectly into one another, will confine themselves to respecting simply the fundamental conditions of this adjustment: a cut-and-dried agreement among the persons will not satisfy it, it insists on a constant striving after reciprocal adaptation. Society will therefore be suspicious of all *inelasticity* of character, of mind and even of body, because it is the possible sign of a slumbering activity as well as of an activity with separatist tendencies, that inclines to swerve from the common centre round which society gravitates: in short, because it is the sign of an eccentricity. And yet, society cannot intervene at this stage by material repression, since it is not affected in a material fashion. It is confronted with something that makes it uneasy, but only as a symptom – scarcely a threat, at the very most a gesture. A gesture, therefore, will be its reply. Laughter must be something of this kind, a sort of *social gesture*. By the fear which it inspires, it restrains eccentricity, keeps constantly awake and in mutual contact certain activities of a secondary order which might retire into their shell and go to sleep, and, in short, softens down whatever the surface of the social body may retain of mechanical inelasticity. Laughter, then, does not belong to the province of esthetics alone, since unconsciously (and even immorally in many particular instances) it pursues a utilitarian aim of general improvement. And yet there is something aesthetic about it, since the comic comes into being just when society and the individual, freed from the worry of self-preservation, begin to regard themselves as works of art. In a word, if a circle be drawn round those actions and dispositions – implied in individual or social life – to which their natural consequences bring their own penalties, there remains outside this sphere of emotion and struggle – and within a neutral zone in which man simply exposes himself to man's curiosity – a certain rigidity of body, mind and character, that society would still like to get rid of in order to obtain from its members the greatest possible degree of elasticity and sociability. This rigidity is the comic, and laughter is its corrective.

Still, we must not accept this formula as a definition of the comic. It is suitable only for cases that are elementary, theoretical and perfect, in which the comic is free from all adulteration. Nor do we offer it, either, as an explanation. We prefer to make it, if you will, the *leitmotif* which is to accompany all our explanations. We must ever keep it in mind, though without dwelling on it too much, somewhat as a skilful fencer must think of the discontinuous movements of the lesson whilst his body is given up to the continuity of the fencing match. We will now endeavor to reconstruct the sequence of comic forms, taking up again the thread that leads from the horseplay of a clown up to the most refined effects of comedy, following this thread in its often unforeseen windings, halting at intervals to look around, and finally getting back, if possible, to the point at which the thread is dangling and where we shall perhaps find – since the comic oscillates between life and art – the general relation that art bears to life.

We will now pass from the comic element in *forms* to that in *gestures* and *movements*. Let us at once state the law which seems to govern all the phenomena of this kind. It may indeed be deduced without any difficulty from the considerations stated above.

The attitudes, gestures and movements of the human body are laughable in exact proportion as that body reminds us of a mere machine.

There is no need to follow this law through the details of its immediate applications, which are innumerable. To verify it directly, it would be sufficient to study closely the work of comic artists, eliminating entirely the element of caricature, and omitting that portion of the comic which is not inherent in the drawing itself. For, obviously, the comic element in a drawing is often a borrowed one, for which the text supplies all the stock-in-trade. I mean that the artist may be his own understudy in the shape of a satirist, or even a playwright, and that then we laugh far less at the drawings themselves than at the satire or comic incident they represent. But if we devote our whole attention to the drawing with the firm resolve to think of nothing else, we shall probably find that it is generally comic in proportion to the clearness, as well as the subtleness, with which it enables us to see a man as a jointed puppet. The suggestion must be a clear one, for inside the person we must distinctly perceive, as though through a glass, a set-up mechanism. But the suggestion must also be a subtle one, for the general appearance of the person, whose every limb has been made rigid as a machine, must continue to give us the impression of a living being. The more exactly these two images, that of a person and that of a machine, fit into each other, the more striking is the comic effect, and the more consummate the art of the draughtsman. The originality of a comic artist is thus expressed in the special kind of life he imparts to a mere puppet.

We will, however, leave on one side the immediate application of the principle, and at this point insist only on the more remote consequences. The illusion of a machine working in the inside of the person is a thing that only crops up amid a host of amusing effects; but for the most part it is a fleeting glimpse, that is immediately lost in the laughter it provokes. To render it permanent, analysis and reflection must be called into play.

In a public speaker, for instance, we find that gesture vies with speech. Jealous of the latter, gesture closely dogs the speaker's thought, demanding also to act as interpreter. Well and good; but then it must pledge itself to follow thought through all the phases of its development. An idea is something that grows, buds, blossoms and ripens from the beginning to the end of a speech. It never halts, never repeats itself. It must be changing every moment, for to cease to change would be to cease to live. Then let gesture display a like animation! Let it accept the fundamental law of life, which is the complete negation of repetition! But I find that a certain movement of head or arm, a movement always the same, seems to return at regular intervals. If I notice it and it succeeds in diverting my attention, if I wait for it to occur and it occurs when I expect it, then involuntarily I laugh. Why? Because I now have before me a machine that works automatically. This is no longer life, it is automatism established in life and imitating it. It belongs to the comic.

This is also the reason why gestures, at which we never dreamt of laughing, become laughable when imitated by another individual. The most elaborate explanations have been offered for this extremely simple fact. A little reflection, however, will show that our mental state is ever changing, and that if our gestures faithfully followed these inner movements, if they were as fully alive as we, they would never repeat themselves, and so would keep imitation at bay. We begin, then, to become imitable only when we cease to be ourselves. I mean our gestures can only be imitated in their mechanical uniformity, and therefore exactly in what is alien to our living personality. To imitate any one is to bring out the element of automatism he has allowed to creep into his person. And as this is the very essence of the ludicrous, it is no wonder that imitation gives rise to laughter.

Still, if the imitation of gestures is intrinsically laughable, it will become even more so when it busies itself in deflecting them, though without altering their form, towards some mechanical occupation, such as sawing wood, striking on an anvil, or tugging away at an imaginary bellrope. Not that vulgarity is the essence of the comic – although certainly it is to some extent an ingredient – but rather that the incriminated gesture seems more frankly mechanical when it can be connected with a simple operation, as though it were intentionally mechanical. To suggest this mechanical interpretation ought to be one of the favorite devices of parody. We have reached this result through deduction, but I imagine clowns have long had an intuition of the fact.

This seems to me the solution of the little riddle propounded by Pascal in one passage of his *Thoughts*: 'Two faces that are alike, although neither of them excites laughter by itself, make us laugh when together, on account of their likeness.' It might just as well be said: 'The gestures of a public speaker, no one of which is laughable by itself, excite laughter by their repetition.' The truth is that a really living life should never repeat itself. Wherever there is repetition or complete similarity, we always suspect some mechanism at work behind the living. Analyze the impression you get from two faces that are too much alike, and you will find that you are thinking of two copies cast in the same mold, or two impressions of the same seal, or two reproductions of the same negative – in a word, of some manufacturing process or other. This deflection of life towards the mechanical is here the real cause of laughter.

And laughter will be more pronounced still, if we find on the stage not merely two characters, as in the example from Pascal, but several, nay, as great a number as possible, the image of one another, who come and go, dance and gesticulate together, simultaneously striking the same attitudes and tossing their arms about in the same manner. This time, we distinctly think of marionettes. Invisible threads seem to us to be joining arms to arms, legs to legs, each muscle in one face to its fellow-muscle in the other: by reason of the absolute uniformity which prevails, the very litheness of the bodies seems to stiffen as we gaze, and the actors themselves seem transformed into automata. Such, at least, appears to be the artifice underlying this somewhat obvious form of amusement. I daresay the performers have never read Pascal, but what they do is merely to realize to the full the suggestions contained in Pascal's words. If, as is undoubtedly the case, laughter is caused in the second instance by the hallucination of a mechanical effect, it must already have been so, though in more subtle fashion, in the first.

Continuing along this path, we dimly perceive the increasingly important and far-reaching consequences of the law we have just stated. We faintly catch still more fugitive glimpses of mechanical effects, glimpses suggested by man's complex actions, no longer merely by his gestures. We instinctively feel that the usual devices of comedy, the periodical repetition of a word or a scene, the systematic inversion of the parts, the geometrical development of a farcical misunderstanding, and many other stage contrivances, must derive their comic force from the same source – the art of the playwright probably consisting in setting before us an obvious clockwork arrangement of human events, while carefully preserving an outward aspect of probability and thereby retaining something of the suppleness of life. But we must not forestall results which will be duly disclosed in the course of our analysis.

Regarded from this latter point of view, the comic seems to show itself in a form somewhat different from the one we lately attributed to it. Up to this point, we have regarded laughter as first and foremost a means of correction. If you take the series of comic varieties and isolate the predominant types at long intervals, you will find that all the intervening varieties borrow their comic quality from their resemblance to these types, and that the types themselves are so many models of impertinence with regard to society. To these impertinences society retorts by laughter, an even greater impertinence. So evidently there is nothing very benevolent in laughter. It seems rather inclined to return evil for evil.

But this is not what we are immediately struck by in our first impression of the laughable. The comic character is often one with whom, to begin with, our mind, or rather our body, sympathizes. By this is meant that we put ourselves for a very short time in his place, adopt his gestures, words, and actions, and, if amused by anything laughable in him, invite him, in imagination, to share his amusement with us; in fact, we treat him first as a playmate. So, in the laugher we find a 'hail-fellow-well-met' spirit – as far, at least, as appearances go – which it would be wrong of us not to take into consideration. In particular, there is in laughter a movement of *relaxation* which has often been noticed, and the reason for which we must try to discover. Nowhere is this impression more noticeable than in the last few examples. In them, indeed, we shall find its explanation.

When the comic character automatically follows up his idea, he ultimately thinks, speaks and acts as though he were dreaming. Now, a dream is a relaxation. To remain in touch with things and men, to see nothing but what is existent and think nothing but what is consistent, demands a continuous effort of intellectual tension. This effort is common sense. And to remain sensible is, indeed, to remain at work. But to detach oneself from things and yet continue to perceive images, to break away from logic and yet continue to string together ideas, is to indulge in play or, if you prefer, in *dolce far niente*. So, comic absurdity gives us from the outset the impression of playing with ideas. Our first impulse is to join in the game. That relieves us from the strain of thinking.

Now, the same might be said of the other forms of the laughable. Deep-rooted in the comic, there is always a tendency, we said, to take the line of least resistance, generally that of habit. The comic character no longer tries to be ceaselessly adapting and readapting himself to the society of which he is a member. He slackens in the attention that is due to life. He more or less resembles the absentminded. Maybe his will is here even more concerned than his intellect, and there is not so much a want of attention as a lack of tension: still, in some way or another, he is *absent*, away from his work, taking it easy. He abandons social convention, as indeed – in the case we have just been considering – he abandoned logic. Here, too, our first impulse is to accept the invitation to take it easy. For a short time, at all events, we join in the game. And that relieves us from the strain of living.

But we rest only for a short time. The sympathy that is capable of entering into the impression of the comic is a very fleeting one. It also comes from a lapse in attention. Thus, a stern father may at times forget himself and join in some prank his child is playing, only to check himself at once in order to correct it.

Laughter is, above all, a corrective. Being intended to humiliate, it must make a painful impression on the person against whom it is directed. By laughter, society avenges itself for the liberties taken with it. It would fail in its object if it bore the stamp of sympathy or kindness.

Shall we be told that the motive, at all events, may be a good one, that we often punish because we love, and that laughter, by checking the outer manifestations of certain failings, thus causes the person laughed at to correct these failings and thereby improve himself inwardly?

Much might be said on this point. As a general rule, and speaking roughly, laughter doubtless exercises a useful function. Indeed, the whole of our analysis points to this fact. But it does not therefore follow that laughter always hits the mark or is invariably inspired by sentiments of kindness or even of justice.

To be certain of always hitting the mark, it would have to proceed from an act of reflection. Now, laughter is simply the result of a mechanism set up in us by nature or, what is almost the same thing, by our long acquaintance with social life. It goes off spontaneously and returns tit for tat. It has no time to look where it hits. Laughter punishes certain failings somewhat as disease punishes certain forms of excess, striking down some who are innocent and sparing some who are guilty, aiming at a general result and incapable of dealing separately with each individual case. And so it is with everything that comes to pass by natural means instead of happening by conscious reflection. An average of justice may show itself in the total result, though the details, taken separately, often point to anything but justice.

In this sense, laughter cannot be absolutely just. Nor should it be kind-hearted either. Its function is to intimidate by humiliating. Now, it would not succeed in doing this, had not nature implanted for that very purpose, even in the best of men, a spark of spitefulness or, at all events, of mischief. Perhaps we had better not investigate this point too closely, for we should not find anything very flattering to ourselves. We should see that this movement of relaxation or expansion is nothing but a prelude to laughter, that the laugher immediately retires within himself, more self-assertive and conceited than ever, and is evidently disposed to look upon another's personality as a marionette of which he pulls the strings. In this presumptuousness we speedily discern a degree of egoism and, behind this latter, something less spontaneous and more bitter, the beginnings of a curious pessimism which becomes the more pronounced as the laugher more closely analyses his laughter.

Here, as elsewhere, nature has utilized evil with a view to good. It is more especially the good that has engaged our attention throughout this work. We have seen that the more society improves, the more plastic is the adaptability it obtains from its members; while the greater the tendency towards increasing stability below, the more does it force to the surface the disturbing elements inseparable from so vast a bulk; and thus laughter performs a useful function by emphasizing the form of these significant undulations.

Such is also the truceless warfare of the waves on the surface of the sea, whilst profound peace reigns in the depths below. The billows clash and collide with each other, as they strive to find their level. A fringe of snow-white foam, feathery and frolicsome, follows their changing outlines. From time to time, the receding wave leaves behind a remnant of foam on the sandy beach. The child, who plays hard by, picks up a handful, and, the next moment, is astonished to find that nothing remains in his grasp but a few drops of water, water that is far more brackish, far more bitter than that of the wave which brought it. Laughter comes into being in the self-same fashion. It indicates a slight revolt on die surface of social life. It instantly adopts the changing forms of the disturbance. It, also, is a froth with a saline base. Like froth, it sparkles. It is gaiety itself. But the philosopher who gathers a handful to taste may find that the substance is scanty, and the after-taste bitter.

Notes

Chronology of Life and Works

1 See p. 444 above.

Introduction

1 This introduction draws on material first presented in John Ó Maoilearca *Bergson and Philosophy* (1999) and Keith Ansell Pearson's *Philosophy and the Adventure of the Virtual* (2001).

2 While the essays from *Mind-Energy* and which are included here do not receive any sustained individual treatment in this introduction, they are referred to when the themes being treated make it appropriate.

3 See Durie 1999, p. xix.

4 It is a similar conception of continuity that leads Richard Sorabji to the view that we can put to rest a bogey that has troubled commentators more than any other concerning Aristotle's definition of time as number in the *Physics*. This relates to the criticism made by Plotinus: how can the continuous nature of time be generated from number, which is discrete? In other words, how can time, qua continuity, be number? Sorabji argues that while the stages which we choose to count are discrete this does not make time something discontinuous: 'On the contrary, it is infinitely divisible, in the sense that we can divide it at stages as close together as we please, and its infinite divisibility is precisely a mark of its continuity' (Sorabji 1983, p. 89). But this laying to rest of a bogey is only possible by construing time solely and simply in terms of an actual or discrete multiplicity. No other conception of multiplicity is allowed for.

5 Given the tags of mysticism and spiritualism that Bergsonism has acquired over the years, we perhaps need to be reminded of the fact that in his own day Bergson was read primarily as an empiricist whose thinking amounted, in the words of his former pupil and later harsh critic, Jacques Maritain, to a 'wild experimentalism' (Maritain 1955, p. 66). Indeed, Maritain accused Bergson of realizing in metaphysics 'the very soul of empiricism' and of producing an ontology of becoming not 'after the fashion of Hegel's panlogism' but rather 'after the fashion of an integral empiricism' (1943, p. 65). As a rationalist Julien Benda vigorously protested against Bergson's demand for new ways of thinking and new methods in philosophy and called for a return to Spinoza (see Benda 1954 and the study by Niess, 1956, pp. 112–13). See also James on Bergson, 1909, pp. 237ff. and, more recently, the remarks in Maoilearca 1999a, pp. 158–9.

6 See Clark 1997.

7 Dorothea Olkowski identifies the work of Antonio Damasio as falling into the internalist trap Bergson identified. See Olkowski 1999, note 28, pp. 257–8; and see Damasio 1994 and especially the treatment of images in his recent study *The Feeling of What Happens*, 1999, including the appendix, pp. 317ff. The work of Daniel C. Dennett is well known for its critique of Cartesian materialism, the view arrived at in the philosophy of mind when Descartes's mind-body dualism is discarded but the imagery of a central (and material) 'theatre' representing the locus of consciousness is retained (see Dennett 1991, p. 107). Dennett replaces the idea of a Cartesian theatre with what he calls a 'Multiple Drafts model' (chapter 5, and p. 321). Dennett's position is materialist in the sense that it adheres to the view that 'the mind is the brain' (p. 33). In spite of the innovations it endeavours to make, however, it is not clear, for the Bergsonian at least, that Dennett completely escapes the predicaments of the Cartesian materialist. See also the remarks made in Dennett 1996, pp. 72–3, 155–6.

8 See the helpful discussion in Moore 1996, pp. 30–1.

9 As Moore notes, representation 'is a bad picture of perception', because a living body does not make a picture of an object but rather selects some of its properties in accordance with its needs and projects (its virtual actions) (Moore 1996, p. 27). If we suppose that it is necessary to ask after the conditions of image-perception (of picturability and perceptibility), we should not simply equate Bergson's position with that of either Kant or Wittgenstein, Moore argues. This is because on Bergson's model the conditions are '*shallower*', arising neither from logical requirements of sense or meaning, nor from *a priori* ones for the existence of a perceptible world, but rather 'from the (realized) possibility that the world contains objects which are capable of *action* like our own bodies' (p. 26).

10 See Moore 1996, p. 52.

11 It should be noted, however, that Russell had great problems trying to make sense of the notion of a pure past. His difficulties with the idea stem, we believe, from his failure to grasp the notion of the virtual at work in Bergson's thinking on memory. He mistakenly insists that whenever Bergson speaks of the past he can only mean *a present memory* of the past. See the discussion in Russell 1912, pp. 341ff. Deleuze's reading of the pure past, by contrast, makes the strong claim that the past exists in and for itself on its own plane and not simply relative to a present.

12 See *MM*, p. 168: 'There is not, in man at least, a purely sensori-motor state, any more than there is in him an imaginative life without some slight activity beneath it. Our psychical life . . . oscillates normally between these two extremes.'

13 Durie 1999, p. xxiii note 12.

14 For a critique of Bergson that takes up this point see Deleuze and Guattari 1994, p. 132: 'It is not enough to assimilate the scientific observer (for example, the cannonball traveller of relativity) to a simple *symbol* that would mark states of variables, as Bergson does, while the philosophical persona would have the privilege of the *lived* (a being that endures) because he will undergo the variations themselves. The philosophical persona is no more lived experience than the scientific observer is symbolic.'

15 Bergson lectured on all three of Kant's *Critiques*. His lessons on the *Critique of Pure Reason* provide a straightforward explication and can be found in *Bergson Cours III*, 1995, pp. 131–201. For further insight see de Gruson 1959, pp. 171–90, and Barthelmy-Madaule's study of 1966.

16 In *CE* intuition is, indeed, conceived in terms of instinct but one that has become disinterested and self-conscious, 'capable of reflecting upon its object and of enlarging it indefinitely' (*CE*, p. 176).

17 Compare *MM*, p. 185: 'the task of the philosopher . . . closely resembles that of the mathematician who determines a function by starting from the differential. The final effort of philosophical research is a true work of integration.'

18 Bergson's contention is that Kant's first Critique continues the old dream of approaching the real in terms of a universal mathematics: 'In short, *the whole* Critique of Pure Reason *leads to establishing the fact that Platonism, illegitimate if Ideas are things, becomes legitimate if ideas are relations, and that the ready-made idea, once thus brought down from heaven to earth, is indeed as Plato wished, the common basis of thought and nature. The whole* Critique of Pure Reason *rests also upon the postulate that our thought is incapable of anything but Platonising*, that is, of pouring the whole of possible experience into preexisting moulds' (*CM*, p. 197; see below, p. 344).

19 See Scharfstein 1943, pp. 104–5 note 10, 125–6; *TSMR*, pp. 104–5 (*OE*, pp. 1063–4).

20 Scharfstein 1943, pp. 125–6.

21 Hartshorne 1987, p. 379.

22 See *TSMR*, p. 100 (*OE*, p. 1060).

23 See *TSMR*, p. 117 (*OE*, p. 1074), which says that individuals may already be societies or 'aggregates of aggregates'.

24 *TSMR*, pp. 177, 116 (*OE*, pp. 1125, 1073).

25 *TSMR*, pp. 101, 91–2 (*OE*, pp. 1061, 1052–3).

26 *TSMR*, pp. 161, 81, 24 (*OE*, pp. 1112, 1043, 994).

27 See Jacques Chevalier, Entretiens avec Bergson, pp. 75, 154–5, 159, cited in Gallagher 1970, p. 98.

28 *TSMR*, pp. 269, 68, 85, 89 (*OE*, pp. 1204, 1033, 1047, 1050–1).

29 *TSMR*, p. 90 (*OE*, p. 1051).

30 *TSMR*, p. 47 (*OE*, pp. 1014–15); see below, p. 390.

31 *TSMR*, p. 96 (*OE*, p. 1057).

32 See *TSMR*, pp. 9, 13–14, 26–7 (*OE*, pp. 981, 984–6, 996–7). We ought to note here that such collectivist thinking as this has often been accused of a romantic organicism along with the dangerous political implications purportedly attendant on this. Yet the charge of a more literal organicism need be neither so unpalatable nor so unwelcome as most collectivists assume it is. The impasse between a cultural view of morality, a rationalist one and a sociobiological one is undone by Bergson's plea that biology be understood 'broadly'. In Bergson's sociobiology, organicism leads to political views exactly opposite to those often repudiated. He does not argue for a closed image of the social on the basis of a rigid biological essentialism: rather, because his so-called vitalism is embedded in a process metaphysics, the organic and the social are both left ideally open. Bergson does not believe that organic systems are wholes, rather, they are dynamic dissociating phenomena which are only relative unities. Political organicism need only be feared if one's picture of the organic, the biological or the vital is of a particular variety.

33 *TSMR*, pp. 27, 21 (*OE*, pp. 997, 992).

34 *TSMR*, pp. 32, 18–19, 30, 31 (*OE*, pp. 1001, 989–90, 1000, 1001, 1002).

35 *TSMR*, pp. 39, 205–7 (*OE*, pp. 1007, 1150–1).

36 *TSMR*, pp. 17, 33–4 (*OE*, pp. 988, 1003).

37 *TSMR*, p. 38 (*OE*, pp. 1006–7); see below, p. 383.

38 See *TSMR*, pp. 52, 39, 254–5 (*OE*, pp. 1019, 1007, 1191–2).

39 *TSMR*, pp. 51, 84 (*OE*, pp. 1018, 1046).

40 *TSMR*, p. 96 (*OE*, p. 1057) our italics.

41 See *TSMR*, pp. 84, 213 (*OE*, pp. 1046, 1156).

42 *TSMR*, pp. 34, 49, 68, 84, 278 (*OE*, pp. 1003, 1016, 1032, 1046, 1212).

43 Nonetheless, religious dynamism needs static religion for its expression and diffusion (*TSMR*, p. 179 (*OE*, p. 1127)), and the two are not at all opposed in their common origin, which Bergson alludes to mysteriously as 'some intermediare thing' (*TSMR*, p. 178 (*OE*, p. 1126)). The object of dynamic religion is also its source: the generative action of life, which Bergson periodically describes as 'God', though this is clearly an immanent and suprapersonal divinity; see *TSMR*, pp. 53, 252–62 (*OE*, pp. 1119–20, 1189–98).

44 *ME*, p. 32 (*OE*, p. 834).

45 See *TSMR*, pp. 220, 228ff. (*OE*, pp. 1162, ll69ff.).

46 See *ME*, pp. 153–5 (*OE*, pp. 910–11).

47 See *TSMR*, p. 228 (*OE*, p. 1169).

48 *TSMR*, p. 225 (*OE*, pp. 1166–7); Bergson is here quoting N. Soderblom.

49 *TSMR*, p. 309 (*OE*, p. 1138); see below, p. 415. Hude 1989–1990, vol. i, p. 149, cites a lecture course on ethics where Bergson advises that in the resolution of moral conflicts we should opt for that action which involves 'the greatest sacrifice, give that which costs you the most'.

50 *TSMR*, p. 53 (*OE*, p. 1119). In Bergson's *Laughter*, p. 141 (*OE*, p. 454), an emotion is said to be dramatic and contagious when all the harmonics in it are heard along with the fundamental note.

51 See *TSMR*, pp. 61–2 (*OE*, pp. 1026–7). Bergson sees Socratic rationalism as a reaction against the moral empiricism of his day.

52 *M*, pp. 361, 363, 364, 371, 362.

53 Gunter 1995, p. 393. It should be no surprise that later in *TSMR* Bergson will attribute '*un bon sens supérieur*' to the mystics (*OE*, p. 1183 – though it is translated as 'common sense' in the English at *TSMR*, p. 245).

54 See *M*, p. 362.

55 See letter of 31 March 1910 at *M*, p. 817; see below, p. 448.

56 *M*, pp. 726–7; see below, p. 444.

57 *M*, pp. 331, 477.

58 *M*, p. 1092.

59 *CM*, p. 22 (*OE*, p. 1263).

Time and Free Will

1 [Editors' note: We have included all of chapter 2 in this extract from *TFW*, pp. 75–139 (*OE*, pp. 51–92).]

2 I had already completed the present work when I read in the *Critique philosophique* (for 1883 and 1884) F. Pillon's very remarkable refutation of an interesting article by G. Noël on the interconnexion of the notions of number and space. But I have not found it necessary to make any alterations in the following pages, seeing that Pillon does not distinguish between time as quality and time as quantity, between the multiplicity of juxtaposition and that of interpenetration. Without this vital distinction, which it is the chief aim of the present chapter to establish, it would be possible to maintain, with Pillon, that number may be built up from the relation of co-existence. But what is here meant by co-existence? If the co-existing terms form an organic whole, they will never lead us to the notion of number; if they remain distinct, they are in juxtaposition and we are dealing with space. It is no use to quote the example of simultaneous impressions received by several senses. We either leave these sensations their specific differences, which amounts to saying that we do not count them; or else we eliminate their differences, and then how are we to distinguish them if not by their position or that of their symbols? We shall see that the verb 'to distinguish' has two meanings, the one qualitative, the other quantitative: these two meanings have been confused, in my opinion, by the philosophers who have dealt with the relations between number and space.

3 [Editors' note: Coming at this early stage in Bergson's work, this reference to intuition owes more to Kant than the peculiar and truly Bergsonian meaning that would not be introduced until 1903.]

4 [Editors' note: What is given in the French (*OE*, p. 59) as 'dissocie' and later 'dissociation' in the description of counting is misleadingly translated into English (p. 87) as 'separate' and then 'separation'.]

5 Evellin, *Infini et quantité*, Paris, 1881.

Matter and Memory

1 [Editors' note: This is the Introduction from the English translation of *MM*, pp. 9–16 (*OE*, pp. 161–82).]

2 We have laid stress on this particular point in an essay on 'Le paralogisme psycho-physiologique,' *Revue de Métaphysique et de Morale* (Nov., 1904).

3 F. Moutier, *L'Aphasie de Broca*, Paris, 1908; especially Chapter VII. See the work of Professor Pierre Marie.

4 P. Janet, *Les Obsessions et la psychasthénie*, Paris, 1903; in particular pp. 474–502.

5 [Editors' note: This section is from the whole of chapter 1 of *MM*, pp. 17–76 (*OE*, pp. 169–223).]

6 The word representation is used throughout this book in the French sense, as meaning a mental picture, which mental picture is very often perception. [Translators' note.]

7 Lotze, *Metaphysic*, Oxford, 1887, vol. ii, p. 206.

8 Schwarz, *Das Wahrnehmungsproblem*, Leipzig, 1892, pp. 313ff.

9 [Editors' note: Once again, this is not the full-blown intuition for which Bergson is famed, but rather a Kantian use of the term.]

10 The word 'spiritualism' is used throughout this work to signify any philosophy that claims for spirit an existence of its own. [Translators' note.]

11 [Editors' note: This section is from *Matter and Memory*, chapter 3, pp. 132–41, 148–55, 161–3 (*OE*, pp. 276–83, 289–96, 301–2).]

12 Kay, *Memory and How to Improve It*, New York, 1888, p. 18.

13 Mathias Duval, 'Theorie histologique du sommeil', *C.R. de la Soc. De Biologie* (1895), p. 74. Cf. Lépine, p. 85; and *Revue de Medicine* (Aug., 1894); and, especially Pupin, *Le Neurone et les hypothéses histologiques*, Paris, 1896.

14 Forbes Winslow, *Obscure Diseases of the Brain*, pp. 25ff.; Ribot, *Maladies de la mémoire*, pp. 139ff; Mauro, *Le Sommeil et les rêves*, Paris, 1878, p. 439; Egger, 'Le Moi des mourants,' *Revue philosophique* (Jan. and Oct., 1896). Cf. Ball's dictum: 'Memory is a faculty which loses nothing and records everything.' (Quoted by Rouillard, *Les Amnésies* [medical thesis], Paris, 1885, p. 25.)

15 [Editors' note: This section is from the Summary and Conclusion of *Matter and Memory*, pp. 241–3 (*OE*, pp. 370–3).]

Mind-Energy

1 [Editors' note: We have chosen to reproduce only the sections of this essay where Bergson explains his own theory (*ME*, pp. 151–85 (*OE*, pp. 908–30)) and have omitted the opening literature review.]

2 Cf. especially the cases collected by Bernard-Leroy, *L'Illusion de fausse reconnaissance*, 1898, pp. 176, 182, 185, 232.

3 Bernard-Leroy, *op. cit.*, p. 186.

4 Lalande, *Rev. Philos.* (1893), p. 487.

5 Jensen, *Allgemeine Zeitschrift für Psychiatric Suppl*. (1868), p. 57.

6 F. Gregh, quoted by Bernard-Leroy, p. 183.

7 Bernard-Leroy, op. cit., p. 169.

8 Cf. especially the analysis of Kräpelin, *Arch, für Psychiatrie* (1876), also that of Dromard and *Albés, Journal de Psychologie* (1905), pp. 216–28.

9 [Editors' note: This essay is from *ME*, pp. 231–57 (*OE*, pp. 959–74).]

Creative Evolution

1 [Editors' note: This section comes from pp. 1–23, 26–31 of chapter 1 of *CE* (*OE*, pp. 495–513, 516–21).]

2 *Matiére et mémoire*, Paris, 1896, chaps ii and iii.

3 Calkins, *Studies on the Life History of Protozoa* (*Archiv f. Entwicklungsmechanik*, vol. xv, 1903, pp. 139–86).

4 Sedgwick Minot, *On Certain Phenomena of Growing Old* (*Proc. Amer. Assoc. for the Advancement of Science*, 39th Meeting, Salem, 1891, pp. 271–88).

5 Le Dantec, *L'individualite et l'erreur individualiste*, Paris, 1905, pp. 84ff.

6 Metchnikoff, *La Dégénérescence sénile* (*Année biologique*, iii, 1897, pp. 249ff.). Cf. by the same author, *La Nature humaine*, Paris, 1903, pp. 312ff.

7 [Editors' note: August Weismann (1834–1914), founding figure in the rise of neo-Darwinism, who sought a scientifically accurate account of heredity and whose theory of the germ-plasm (the hereditary substance) established Darwinism's break with the doctrine of inheritance of acquired characteristics derived from Lamarck.]

8 Roule, *L'Embryologie générale*, Paris, 1893, p. 319.

9 The irreversibility of the series of living beings has been well set forth by Baldwin (*Development and Evolution*, New York, 1902; in particular p. 327).

10 We have dwelt on this point and tried to make it clear in *Time and Free Will*, pp. 184–99.

11 In his fine work on *Genius in Art* (*Le Genie dans l'art*), M. Séailles develops this twofold thesis, that art is a continuation of nature and that life is creation. We should willingly accept the second formula; but by creation must we understand, as the author does, a *synthesis* of elements? Where the elements pre-exist, the synthesis that will be made is virtually given, being only one of the possible arrangements. This arrangement a superhuman intellect could have perceived in advance among all the possible ones that surround it. We hold, on the contrary, that in the domain of life the elements have no real and separate existence. They are manifold mental views of an indivisible process. And for that reason there is radical contingency in progress, incommensurability between what goes before and what follows – in short, duration.

12   [Editors' note: This section is from pp. 37–43 of *CE* (*OE*, pp. 526–31).]

13   Laplace, *Introduction à la théorie analytique des probabilités* (*Oeuvres completes*, vol. vii., Paris, 1886, p. vi.).

14   Du Bois-Reymond, *Über die Grenzen des Naturerkennens*, Leipzig, 1892.

15   [Editors' note: Thomas Henry Huxley (1825–95), British biologist and popularizer of science, best known as an ardent defender and promoter of Darwin's ideas, which he publicly championed in the 1860 debate at Oxford University with Bishop Wilberforce; also founder of craniology and did important work reclassifying George Cuvier's system of classification.]

16   There are really two lines to follow in contemporary neo-vitalism: on the one hand, the assertion that pure mechanism is insufficient, which assumes great authority when made by such scientists as Driesch or Reinke, for example; and, on the other hand, the hypotheses which this vitalism superposes on mechanism (the 'entelechies' of Driesch, and the 'dominants' of Reinke, etc.). Of these two parts, the former is perhaps the more interesting. Cf. the admirable studies of Driesch – *Die Lokalisation morphogenetischer Vorgänge*, Leipzig, 1899; *Die organischen Regulationen*, Leipzig, 1901; *Naturbegriffe und Natururteile*, Leipzig, 1904; *Der Vitalismus als Geschichte und als Lehre*, Leipzig, 1905; and of Reinke –*Die Welt als Tat*, Berlin, 1899; *Einleitung in die theoretische Biologie*, Berlin, 1901; *Philosophie der Botanik*, Leipzig, 1905.

17   [Editors' note: This section of CE is from pp. 50–9, 87–96 (*OE*, pp. 537–45, 569–78).]

18   [Editors' note: Gustav Heinrich Theodor Eimer (1843–98): Swiss-German zoologist and neo-Lamarckian, an orthogeneticist along with Carl von Nageli and opponent of Weismann. As an advocate of orthogenesis, Eimet was committed to there being an immanent source of evolutionary change and trend towards diversification.]

19   Cf., on this subject, *Matiere et memoire*, chap. i.

Duration and Simultaneity

1   [Editors' note: This selection is from the whole of chapter 3, 'Concerning the nature of time'.]

2   For the development of the views presented here, see *Time and Free Will*, mainly Chaps II and III; *Matter and Memory*, Chaps I and IV; *Creative*

Evolution, passim. Cf. 'Introduction to metaphysics' and 'The perception of change' in *The Creative Mind*.

3 Cf. those of our works we have just cited.

4 See *Matter and Memory*, Chap. I.

5 See *Time and Free Will*, especially pp. 109ff.

6 [Editors' note: This is a clear step backwards from Bergson's position in *CE* which allowed matter a low level of duration.]

7 That the concept of the mathematical point is natural is well known to those who have taught geometry to children. Minds most refractory to the first elements imagine immediately and without difficulty lines without thickness and points without size.

8 It is obvious that our hypothesis would lose its meaning if we thought of consciousness as an 'epiphenomenon' added to cerebral phenomena of which it would be merely the result or expression. We cannot dwell here upon this theory of consciousness-as-epiphenomenon, which we rend more and more to consider arbitrary. We have discussed it in detail in several of our works, notably in the first three chapters of *Matter and Memory* and in different essays in *Mind-Energy*. Let us confine ourselves to recalling: (1) that this theory in no way stems from facrs, (2) that its metaphysical origins are easily made out, (3) that, taken literally, it would be self-contradictory. (Concerning this last point and the oscillation which the theory implies between two contrary assertions, see *Mind-Energy*, pp. 243–55.) In the present work, we take consciousness as experience gives it to us, without theorizing about its nature and origins.

9 *Time and Free Will*, p. 109.

10 Alfred North Whitehead, *The Concept of Nature* (Cambridge: Cambridge University Press, 1920). This work (which takes the theory of relativity into account) is certainly one of the most profound ever written on the philosophy of nature. [The relevant passage occurs on page 54 of Whitehead's work and reads as follows: 'It is an exhibition of the process of nature that each duration happens and passes. The process of nature can also be termed the "passage of nature." I definitely refrain at this stage from using the word "time," since the measurable time of science and of civilized life generally merely exhibits some aspects of the more fundamental fact of the passage of nature. I believe that in this doctrine I am in full accord with Bergson, though he uses "time" for the fundamental fact which I call the "passage of nature."']

The Creative Mind

1 [Editors' note: From *CM* we have selected all of the essays 'The possible and the real', 'Philosophical intuition', 'The perception of change' and 'On the pragmatism of William James: truth and reality', as well as the last section of 'Introduction to metaphysics' (*CM*, pp. 91–106, 107–29, 130–58, 188–200, 209–19; *OE,* pp. 1331–45, 1345–65, 1365–92, 1419–32, 1440–50).]

2 This article was the development of certain views presented at the opening of the 'philosophical meeting' at Oxford, September 24, 1920. In writing it for the Swedish review *Nordisk Tidskrift*, I wished to express my regret at being unable to go to Stockholm to give a lecture, as was the custom, on the occasion of the bestowal of the Nobel prize. Until it appeared in *The Creative Mind* the article existed only in the Swedish language.

3 In my *Time and Free Will*, p. 110, I did in fact show that measurable Time could be considered as 'a fourth dimension of Space'. It was, naturally, a question of pure Space, and not of the mixture Space–Time of the theory of Relativity, which is quite another thing.

4 Even then one must ask in certain cases, if the obstacles have not *become* surmountable thanks to the creative action which surmounted them: the action, unforeseeable in itself, would then have created the 'surmountability.' Before it, the obstacles were insurmountable, and without it, they would have remained so.

5 I reproduce these views in the form I gave them in my lecture, aware that they will probably cause the same misunderstanding as before, in spite of the applications and explanations I presented in subsequent works. From the fact that a being is action can one conclude that its existence is evanescent? What more does anyone say than I have said, in making it reside in a 'substratum,' which has nothing determined about it, since, by hypothesis, its determination, and consequently its essence, is this very action? Does an existence thus conceived ever cease to be present to itself, real duration implying the persistence of the past into the present and the indivisible continuity of an unfolding? All the misunderstandings derive from the fact that the applications of my conception of *real duration* have been approached through the usual notion of *spatialized time*.

6 This essay was written as the preface to William James's work on *Pragmatism*, translated by E. Le Brun (Paris, Flammarion, 1911).

7 *A Pluralistic Universe*, London, 1909. Translated into French in the 'Bibliothéque de philosophie scientifique,' under the title *Philosophie de l'Expérience*.

8 M. André Chaumeix has very ingeniously pointed out resemblances between the personality of James and that of Socrates (*Revue des Deux Mondes*, October 15, 1910). The effort of bringing man to a consideration of things human is in itself something Socratic.

9 In his study of William James (*Revue de metaphysique et de morale*, November 1910), M. Emile Bourroux has brought out the quite unique meaning of the English verb *to experience*, 'which means, not coldly to observe a thing happening outside us, but to undergo, to feel within oneself, to live oneself this or that manner of being. . . .'

10 I am not sure that James used the word 'invention' nor that he explicitly compared theoretical truth with a mechanical apparatus; but I believe that this comparison is in keeping with the spirit of the doctrine, and that it can help us to understand Pragmatism.

11 This essay appeared in the *Revue de métaphysique et de morale* in 1903. Since that period I have been led more accurately to define the meaning of the terms *metaphysics* and *science*. One is free to give words the meaning one wishes, when one is careful to define that meaning: nothing would hinder one from calling any kind of knowledge 'science' or 'philosophy,' as has long been done. As I have mentioned previously, one could even include everything in metaphysics. Nevertheless it is incontestable that knowledge bears in a well-defined direction when it arranges its object with measurement in view, and that it proceeds in a different, even opposite, direction when it frees itself of any thought of relation and comparison in order to be in *sympathy* with reality. I have shown that the first method was suited to the study of matter and the second to the study of mind, that there is, furthermore, reciprocal overlapping of the two objects and that the two methods should be mutually helpful. In the first case one is dealing with spatialized time and with space; in the second, with *real duration*. It has seemed to me more and more useful, for the clarity of ideas, to call the first form of knowledge 'scientific' and the second 'metaphysical.' It is then to the account of metaphysics that we shall put this 'philosophy of science' or 'metaphysics of science,' which inhabits the minds of great scholars, which is immanent in their science and which is often its invisible inspiration. In the present article I left it still to the account of science, because it was, in fact, practised by those searchers called, by general agreement, 'savants' rather than 'metaphysicians.'It must not be forgotten, on the other hand, that the present essay was written at a time when the criticism of Kant and the dogmatism of his successors were fairly generally accepted, if not as a conclusion, at least as point of departure for philosophical speculation.

12 Let me insist I am thereby in no way setting aside *substance*. On the contrary, I affirm the persistence of existences. And I believe I have facilitated their representation. How was it ever possible to compare this doctrine with the doctrine of Heraclitus?

13 Especially in Newton, in his consideration of *fluxions*.

14 On this point, as on several other questions dealt with in the present essay, consult the excellent works of Le Roy, Vincent and Wilbois, found in the *Revue de metaphysique et de morale*.

15 As I explain at the beginning of my second essay (Introduction II, p. 30 [*OE,* p. 1271]) I hesitated a long time before using the term 'intuition'; and when I finally decided to do so I designated by this word the metaphysical function of thought: principally the intimate knowledge of the mind by the mind, secondarily the knowledge by the mind of what there is essential in matter, intelligence being, no doubt, made above all to manipulate matter and consequently to know it, but not having as its especial destiny to touch the bottom of it. It is this meaning that I give to the word in the present essay (written in 1902), more especially in its last few pages. By all increasing care for precision I was later led to distinguish more clearly between intelligence and intuition, as well as between science and metaphysics. But in a general way the change of terminology has no serious disadvantage when one takes the trouble each time to define the term in its particular meaning, or even simply when the context makes the meaning sufficiently obvious.

16 In order to complete what I was saying in the previous note let me add that I have been led, since the time of writing these lines, to restrict the meaning of the word 'science,' and to call more particularly *scientific* the knowledge of inert matter by pure intelligence. That does not prevent me from saying that the knowledge of life and of the mind is scientific to a large extent – to the extent that it calls on the same methods of investigation as the knowledge of inert matter. Conversely, the knowledge of inert matter can be called *philosophical* to the extent that it utilizes, at a certain decisive moment in its history, the intuition of pure duration.

17 See a very interesting article on this subject, by Radulescu-Motru: *Zur Entwickelung von Kant's Theorie der Naturcausalität*, in the *Philosophische Studien* of Wundt (vol. IX, 1894).

Bergson and Kant: Beyond the Noumenal

1 [Editors' note: These extracts come from *CE*, pp. 203–7, 356–63 (*OE,* pp. 668–71, 795–801).]

The Two Sources of Morality and Religion

1 [Editors' note: This extract is taken from *TSMR*, pp. 3–51, 52–65 (*OE*, pp. 981–1017, 1018–29).]

2 Kipling, 'In the Rukh,' from *Many Inventions*.

3 We need hardly say that there are many exceptions. Religious fervour, for example, can attain, in women, to undreamt-of depths. But nature has probably ordained, as a general rule, that woman should concentrate on her child and confine within somewhat narrow bounds the best of her sensibility. In this department she is indeed incomparable; here the emotion is supra-intellectual in that it becomes divination. How many things rise up in the vision of a mother as she gazes in wonder upon her little one? Illusion perhaps! This is not certain. Let us rather say that reality is big with possibilities, and that the mother sees in the child not only what he will become, but also what he would become, if he were not obliged, at every step in his life, to choose and therefore to exclude.

4 [Editors' note: This section comes from *TSMR*, pp. 292–312, 317 (*OE*, pp. 1223–41, 1245).]

5 See Gina Lombroso's interesting work, *La Rangon du machinisme* (Paris, 1930).

6 We hasten to state that we have no particular knowledge of this subject. We have chosen the example of meat as we might have that of any other usual food.

7 We again refer the reader to Gina Lombroso's fine work. See also Mantoux, *La Revolution industrielle au dix-huitieme siecle*.

8 There are doubtless periods of 'over-production' which extend to agricultural products and may even start from these. But they are obviously not due to the fact that there is too much food for the consumption of mankind. The fact is simply that, production in general not being properly organized, there is no way of exchange.

9 We are speaking figuratively, of course. Coal was known long before the steam-engine turned it into a treasure.

10 A meaning only part of which we deal with here, as also in the case of the word 'imperialism.'

Mélanges

Except for the entries which are identified as translator's notes, all entries within
  square brackets are editors' notes.

1 [*M*, pp. 358–72. Text of lecture published in the *Concours général: Année*
    1895, Paris, Delalain, and by Editions de l'Epervier, Clermont-Ferrand,
    1947, also appearing in the journal *La Nef* 32 (July 1947), pp. 62–72, and
    in *Ecrits et Paroles*, vol. i, Paris, Presses Universitaires de France, 1957,
    pp. 84–94.]

2 [Translator's note: This was a competitive examination for French
    secondary school pupils.]

3 [See Descartes Address, p. 373 above.]

4 [Translator's note: *M* suggests that Bergson is thinking here of Auguste
    Comte; see *Discours sur l'esprit positif*, Paris, Schleicher, 1909, pp. 53–6.]

5 [Translator's note: Descartes, *Discourse on Method*, Part I, 11. 26–9: 'for
    as to the reason or sense, inasmuch as it is that alone which constitutes
    us men, and distinguishes us from the brutes, I am disposed to believe
    that it is to be found complete in each individual' (trans. J. Veitch, Chicago,
    Open Court, 1907).]

6 [Translator's note: *M* gives two references: Hippolyte Taine, 'To know an
    object is to know its cause and follow it through the whole order of its
    effects', 'De la méthode', in *Essais de critique et d'histoire*, 1858, p. iii,
    and Antoine Cournor, *Considérations*, ch. 1, 'L'étiologie historique' (no
    quote given).]

7 [Translator's note: Raymond Poincaré, subsequently president of the
    French republic (1913–20) and first cousin of the mathematician Henri
    Poincaré. He presided at this ceremony in his capacity at the time as
    Minister of Public Education.]

8 [Translator's note: Raymond Poincaré, *Concours général: Année 1893*,
    Paris, Delalain, p. 16.]

9 [*M*, pp. 410–13. Georges Lechalas, neo-Kantian author of *Etude
    sur l'espace et le temps*, Paris, Editions Alcan, 1896. This text from
    his '*Compte rendu de Matiére et memoire*', *Annales de philosophie
    chrétienne*, 36 (1897), pp. 154, 328, 333; also reproduced in *Ecrits et
    Paroles*, vol. i, pp. 95–7.]

10 [Of *Matter and Memory*.]

11 [The question of the extent of virtual perception.]

12 [The Bergson–James correspondence was reproduced in the *Revue des Deux Mondes* (*RDM*), 15 October 1933. Bergson's letters were also published in *Ecrits et Paroles* (*EP*).]

13 [*M*, pp. 579–81; *RDM*, pp. 793–4; *EP*, vol. i, pp. 192–3.]

14 [Translator's note: 'The feeling of effort', Anniversary Memoirs of the Boston Society of Natural History, Boston, 1880, also in *Mind*, 5 (1880). French translation 'Le Sentiment de l'effort', *Critique Philosophique*, 9:2 (1880), pp. 123–291.]

15 [Translator's note: Both expressions in English in the original.]

16 [Translator's note: The passage Bergson is referring to in James's letter of 14 December 1902 reads in the original: 'It is a work of exquisite genius. It makes a sort of Copernican revolution as much as Berkeley's 'Principles' or Kant's 'Critique' did, and will probably, as it gets better known, open a new era of philosophical discussions', *The Letters of William James*, edited by his son Henry James, vol. ii, London, Longmans, Green & Co., 1920, p. 179.]

17 [Translator's note: *Human Immortality: Two Supposed Objections to the Doctrine*, Ingersoll Lecture, Boston, 1898, published in Ingersoll Lecture Series, Westminster, 1899.]

18 [*M*, pp. 587–9; *RDM*, pp. 797–8; EP, vol. ii, pp. 197–8.]

19 [Translator's note: Regarding these 'difficulties', the passage from James's letter of 25 February 1903 reads: 'your unconscious or subconscious permanence of memories is . . . a notion that offers difficulties, seeming in fact to be the equivalent of the "soul" in another shape, and the manner in which these memories "insert" themselves into the brain action, and in fact the whole conception of the difference between the inner and outer worlds in your philosophy, still need to me a great deal of elucidation', *The Letters of William James*, edited by his son Henry James, vol. ii, London, Longmans, Green & Co., 1920, p. 184.]

20 [Translator's note: In English in the original.]

21 [Translator's note: German *Inbegriff* – (quint)essence, embodiment, paragon.]

22 [*M*, pp. 651–2; *RDM*, pp. 798–9; EP, vol. ii, pp. 235–6.]

23 [Translator's note: According to *Mélanges*, these would certainly include 'Is radical empiricism solipsistic?', *Journal of Philosophy*, 2 (1905), pp. 235–8, and most probably, 'Does consciousness exist?', ibid., 1 (1904), pp. 477–91; 'A world of pure experience', ibid., pp. 533–43; 'The pragmatic method', ibid., pp. 673–87; and 'Humanism and truth', *Mind*, 13 (1904), pp. 457–75.]

24 [Translator's note: See James's 'difficulties', n. 19 above. James does not treat the 'unconscious' as a special topic in, e.g., the *Essays in Radical Experience*, which reproduce much of the material Bergson is speaking of here. His non-position can be both explained by and extrapolated from the thesis he maintains in the essay 'Does consciousness exist?' (chapter 1 in the *Essays*), where he already contests the notion of *consciousness* as a separate entity or special property of the subject, arguing that it is rather a particular functional inflection of 'pure experience', which is neutral in itself and belongs to nobody in particular. In this sense the 'unconscious' for James would either also be a particular mode of pure experience, or be largely coextensive with the realm of 'pure experience' itself, if we understand Bergson to mean by the unconscious here what exists or subsists virtually beyond its particular 'actualization' (for James an appropriation) in, or as, a particular consciousness. Bergson later affirms James's notion of personal experience as simply an 'appropriation' of a generalized experience – see below, the letter of 20 July 1905, paragraph 2 – and specifies the differences in the details of their position.]

25 [Translator's note: Both italicized expressions in English in the original.]

26 [*M*, pp. 659–61; *RDM*, pp. 802–4; EP, vol. ii, pp. 241–2.]

27 [Translator's note: According to *Mélanges*, these would be the 1905 series of essays published in the *Journal of Philosophy* and gathered together in *Essays in Radical Empiricism*, New York/London, 1912.]

28 [Translator's note: *Essays in Radical Empiricism*, ch. 4.]

29 [Translator's note: See Letter to G. Lechalas, '*all sensations that I localize in my body*, depend above all on the state of the part in which they are produced; they take on quite different aspects according to whether my body is disposed to welcome or reject them'; see above, p. 355.]

30 [Translator's note: G. Rageot, '5th International Congress of Psychology', *Revue Philosophique de la France et de l'Etranger*, 60:1 (July 1905), pp. 84–5). Rageot is commentating on a paper given by James, 'La notion de conscience' (reproduced in the *Essays on Radical Empiricism*), and writes (p. 84): 'Nobody is unaware of – and he himself constantly proclaims – what our eminent philosopher, our master analyst, M. Bergson, owed, at the beginning of his career, to American works. It is firstly and above all from the inspiration of Ward, then a little under the influence of William James, that the author of the *Essay on the immediate data of consciousness* was led to his famous conception of an interior flow, the real duration of the deep and ineffable self. . . .']

31 [Translator's note: James Ward, 1843–1925.]

32 [Translator's note: *Revue Philosophique de la France et de l'Etranger*, 60:2 (August 1905), pp. 229–30.]

33 [*M*, pp. 726–7; *RDM*, pp. 808–9; EP, vol. ii, pp. 260–1.]

34 [Translator's note: In James, *Pragmatism: A New Name for Some Old Ways of Thinking*, London and New York, Longmans, Green, 1907.]

35 [Translator's note: *Pragmatism*, p. 257.]

36 [Translator's note: In English in the original.]

37 [*M*, pp. 765–6; *RDM*, pp. 810–11; EP, vol. ii, pp. 294–5.]

38 [Translator's note: James, 'The philosophy of Bergson', *Hibbert Journal*, 7 (1909), pp. 562–77.]

39 [*M*, pp. 775–7; RDM, pp. 813–14; EP, vol. ii, pp. 304–5.]

40 [Translator's note: Oxford lesson on Bergson sent as a proof to Bergson by James, 19 July 1908, published as 'The philosophy of Bergson', *Hibbert Journal*, 7 (1909).]

41 [Translator's note: *A Pluralistic Universe: Hibbert Lectures at Manchester College on the Present Situation in Philosophy*, London, Longmans, Green, 1909.]

42 [*M*, pp. 785–6; *RDM*, pp. 816–17; EP, vol. ii, p. 310.]

43 [Translator's note: Gustav Theodor Fechner, 1801–87, German physicist and philosopher, advocate of pan-psychism and founder of psychophysics, a science concerned with quantitative relations between sensations and the stimuli producing them.]

44 [Translator's note: 'The doctrine of the earth-soul and of being intermediate between man and God: an account of the philosophy of G. T. Fechner', *Hibbert Journal*, 7 (1909), pp. 278–94.]

45 [Translator's note: In English in the original.]

46 [*M*, p. 790; *RDM*, p. 817; EP, vol. ii, p. 315.]

47 [Translator's note: 'The philosophy of Bergson', *Hibbert Journal*, 7 (1909), see n. 40 above.]

48 [*M*, p. 791; *RDM*, pp. 817–18; *EP*, vol. ii, pp. 315–16.]

49 [Translator's note: *A Pluralistic Universe*, see n. 41 above.]

50 [Translator's note: In English in the original.]

51 [*M*, pp. 816–17; *RDM*, pp. 819–20; *EP*, vol. ii, pp. 335–6.]

52 [Translator's note: Emile Boutroux (1845–1921), French professor at the Sorbonne.]

53 [Translator's note: 'The moral equivalent of war' was based on a speech given at Stanford University in 1906, reproduced in *Memories and Studies*, London, 1911. 'A suggestion about mysticism', *Journal of Philosophy, Psychology and Scientific Methods*, 7:4 (1910), pp. 85–93, reproduced in James, *Collected Essays and Reviews*, London, Longmans, 1920.]

54 [Translator's note: In English in the original.]

55 [Translator's note: 'A suggestion about mysticism', p. 93, Bergson's italics.]

56 [*M*, pp. 1146–50, reproduced in *EP*, vol. iii, pp. 455–8.] [Translator's note: Originally a handwritten letter, the text was republished in Hoffding's second revised edition of *La Philosophic de Bergson*, Paris, Editions Alcan, 1917, pp. 157–65, with some slight corrections suggesting Bergson had access to the proof prior to its publication, this modified version being the text reproduced in *M*. The beginning of the letter reads:

15 March, 1915, Villa Montmorency

Monsieur et très honorè collègue,

I have been so occupied – and above all so preoccupied – recently that I have not yet been able to thank you for kindly sending me your work: *Modem Philosophers and Lectures on Bergson*. I don't need to tell you that I was quite familiar, already, with the first part of the book; I think I have already had the opportunity to tell you with what interest and benefit I had read these 1902 lectures which complete so well your 'History of Modern Philosophy'. It is thus more particularly on the second part of the work that I would like to speak today. First I must . . .]

57 [*M*, pp. 1526–28 (extract).] [Translator's note: Floris Delattre was Bergson's nephew by marriage, professor of English literature at the Sorbonne, and the founder and first president of the *Société des Amis de Bergson*. He also edited the three-volume collection of Bergson's *Ecrits et Paroles*, published between 1957 and 1959. This extract comes from a piece appearing in the *Revue Anglo-Americaine*, 13:5 (June 1936), pp. 395–401, reproduced in *EP*, vol. iii, pp. 600–5, in response to the suggestion that similarities existed between Bergson's doctrine and the neo-Lamarckian views of the English essayist and novelist Samuel Butler, expressed in non-fictional works of his such as *Life and Habit and Evolution Old and New*. Bergson begins his letter by claiming his complete ignorance of Butler prior to 1914, then gives his own account of Butler's position and finally underlines what he sees as their crucial differences, which form the substance of this extract.]

58 [Bergson's and Butler's.]

59 [*M*, pp. 1574–9.]

60 [Thomas Gray, 'Elegy written in a country churchyard'.]

61 [Translator's note: Descartes to Princess Elizabeth, 28 June 1643: 'et enfin, c'est en usant seulement de la vie et des conversations ordinaires, et en s'abstenant de mediter et d'étudier aux choses qui exercent l'imagination, qu'on apprend à concevoir l'union de l'âme et du corps.' English translation, Anthony Kenny, *Descartes: Philosophical Letters*, Oxford, Clarendon Press, 1970, p. 141: 'But it is the ordinary course of life and conversation, and abstention from meditation and from the study of things which exercise the imagination, that teaches us how to conceive the union of the soul and the body.']

Guide to Further Reading

Where two dates are given the one given in square brackets refers to the original date of publication. An asterisk indicates a text which is used in this book.

Texts by Henri Bergson
(1911) [1900], *Laughter: An Essay on the Meaning of the Comic*, trans. Cloudesley Brereton and Fred Rothwell, London, Macmillan.
*(1920), *Mind-Energy*, trans. H. Wildon Carr, New York, Henry Holt.
(1920) [1901], 'Dreams', in *Mind-Energy*, pp. 104–34.
*(1920) [1904], 'Brain and thought: a philosophical illusion', in *Mind-Energy*, pp. 231–57.
*(1920) [1908], 'Memory of the present and false recognition', in *Mind-Energy*, pp. 134–86.
(1920) [1911], 'Life and consciousness', in *Mind-Energy*, pp. 3–37.
(1959a) [1884], *The Philosophy of Poetry: The Genius of Lucretius*, trans. W. Baskin, New York, Philosophical Library.
(1959b), *Oeuvres*, Paris, PUF.
*(1960) [1889], *Time and Free Will*, trans. F. L. Pogson, New York, Harper & Row.
*(1965), *The Creative Mind*, trans. M. L. Andison, Totowa, Littlefield, Adams & Co.
*(1965) [1903], 'Introduction to metaphysics', in *The Creative Mind*, pp. 159–201.
(1965) [1904], 'The life and work of Ravaisson', in *The Creative Mind*, pp. 220–52.
*(1965) [1911], 'Philosophical intuition', in *The Creative Mind*, pp. 107–30.
*(1965) [1911], 'The perception of change', in *The Creative Mind*, pp. 130–59.
*(1965) [1911], 'On the pragmatism of William James: truth and morality', in *The Creative Mind*, pp. 188–200.
(1965) [1913], 'The philosophy of Claude Bernard', in *The Creative Mind*, pp. 201–9.
(1965) [1922], 'Introduction I and II', in *The Creative Mind*, pp. 11–30, 30–91.
*(1965) [1930], 'The possible and the real', in *The Creative Mind*, pp. 91–107.

(1970) [1889], *Aristotle's Concept of Place*, trans. J. K. Ryan, in *Studies in Philosophy and the History of Philosophy*, vol. v, pp. 13–72.

*(1972), *Mélanges*, Paris, PUF.

*(1977) [1932], *The Two Sources of Morality and Religion*, trans. R. Ashley Audra and C. Brereton, Notre Dame, IN, University of Notre Dame Press.

*(1983) [1907], *Creative Evolution*, trans. A. Mitchell, Lanham, MD, University Press of America.

(1990), *Cours I: Leçons de Psychologie et de Métaphysique* (Clermont-Ferrand 1887–8), Paris, PUF.

*(1991) [1896], *Matter and Memory*, trans. N. M. Paul and W. S. Palmer, New York, Zone Books.

(1992), *Cours II Leçons d'esthetique; leçons de morale, psychologie et metaphysique*, Paris, PUF.

(1995), *Cours III: Leçons d'histoire de la philosophic moderne & Theories de l'âme*, Paris, PUF.

*(2000) [1922], *Duration and Simultaneity*, trans. L. Jacobson and M. Lewis, Manchester, Clinamen Press.

(2007) [1907], *Creative Evolution*, trans. A. Mitchell, ed. Keith Ansell Pearson, Michael Kolkman and Michael Vaughan, Basingstoke, Palgrave Macmillan.

(2007) [1903], *Introduction to Metaphysics*, trans. T. E. Hulme, ed. John Ó Maoilearca and Michael Kolkman, Basingstoke, Palgrave Macmillan.

(2007) [1919], *Mind-Energy*, trans. H. Wildon Carr, ed. Keith Ansell Pearson and Michael Kolkman, Basingstoke, Palgrave Macmillan.

Recent texts on Bergson

Ardoin, Paul, S. E. Gontarski, and Mattison, Laci (eds) (2013), *Understanding Bergson, Understanding Modernism*, London, Bloomsbury Academic.

Barnard, G. William (2012), *Living Consciousness: The Metaphysical Vision of Henri Bergson*, Albany, NY, SUNY Press.

Cooper, S. (2013), *The Soul of Film Theory*, Basingstoke, Palgrave Macmillan.

Crocker, S. (2013), *Bergson and the Metaphysics of Media*, Basingstoke, Palgrave Macmillan.

Cronin, T. (2013), *Against Affective Formalism: Matisse, Bergson, Modernism*, Minneapolis, University of Minnesota Press.

Cull, L. (2012), *Theatres of Immanence: Deleuze and the Ethics of Performance*, Basingstoke, Palgrave Macmillan.

Fell, E. (2012), *Duration, Temporality, Self: Prospects for the Future of Bergsonism*, Bern, Peter Lang.

Goddard, J.-C. (2002), *Mysticisme et folie: Essai sur la simplicité*, Paris, Desclée de Brouwer.

Guerlac, S. (2006), *Thinking in Time: An Introduction to Henri Bergson*, Ithaca, NY, Cornell University Press.

Hansen, Mark B. N. (2004), *New Philosophy for New Media*, Cambridge, MA, MIT Press.

Hill, R. (2011), *The Interval: Relation and Becoming in Irigaray, Aristotle, and Bergson*, New York, Fordham University Press.

Kelly, M. (ed.) (2010), *Bergson and Phenomenology*, Basingstoke, Palgrave Macmillan.

Lawlor, L. (2003), *The Challenge of Bergson*, London, Continuum Press.

Lefebvre, A. (2008), *The Image of Law: Deleuze, Bergson, Spinoza*, Redwood, CA, Standford University Press.

Lefebvre, A. (2013), *Human Rights as a Way of Life: On Bergson's Political Philosophy*, Redwood, CA, Standford University Press.

Lefebvre, A. (ed.) (2012), *Bergson, Politics and Religion*, Durham, NC, Duke University Press.

Muldoon, Mark, S. (2006), *Tricks of Time: Bergson, Merleau-Ponty and Ricoeur in Search of Time, Self and Meaning*, Pittsburgh, PA, Duquesne University Press.

Maoilearca, J. (2007), 'The very life of things: reversing thought and thinking objects in Bergsonian metaphysics', in *Introduction to Metaphysics*, Basingstoke, Palgrave Macmillan, pp. ix–xxxii.

Maoilearca, J. (2010), *Philosophy and the Moving Image: Refractions of Reality*, Basingstoke, Palgrave Macmillan.

Maoilearca, J. and Charlotte De Mille (eds) (2013), *Bergson and the Art of Immanence: Painting, Photography, Film*, Edinburgh, Edinburgh University Press.

O'Sullivan, S. (2012), *On the Production of Subjectivity: Five Diagrams of the Finite-Infinite Relation*, Basingstoke, Palgrave Macmillan.

Riquier, C. (2009), *Archéologie de Bergson: Temps et métaphysique*, Paris, Presses Universitaires de France.

Robinson, K. (ed.) (2008), *Deleuze, Whitehead, Bergson: Rhizomatic Connections*, Basingstoke, Palgrave Macmillan.

Worms, F. (2013), *Bergson ou les deux sens de la vie*, Paris, Presses Universitaires de France.

For useful general introductions (mostly sympathetic but sometimes critical) to Bergson's work, consult the following:

Alexander, Ian W. (1957), *Bergson: Philosopher of Reflection*, London, Bowes & Bowes.

Béguin, A., and Thevanez, P. (eds) (1943), *Henri Bergson: Essais et témoignages*, Neuchâtel, Editions de la Baconniere.

Benda, J. (1954), *Sur le succès du Bergsonisme*, Paris, Mercure de France.

Chevalier, J. (1928), *Henri Bergson*, trans. L. A. Clare, London, Rider & Co.

Dale Adamson, G. (1999), 'Henri Bergson: time, evolution, and philosophy', *World Futures*, 54: 1, pp. 135–62.

Deleuze, G. (1991) [1966], *Bergsonism*, trans. H. Tomlinson and B. Habberjam, New York, Zone Books.

Deleuze, G. (1994) [1968], *Difference and Repetition*, trans. P. Patton, London, Athlone Press.

Delhomme, Jeanne (1960), *Vie et conscience de la Vie: Essais sur Bergson*, Paris, PUF.

Gunn, A. (1920), *Bergson and His Philosophy*, London, Methuen & Co.

Gunter, P. A. Y. (ed.) (1986), *Henri Bergson: A Bibliography*, Bowling Green, OH, Philosophy Documentation Center, Bowling Green State University.

Hanna, T. (ed.) (1962), *The Bergsonian Heritage*, New York and London, Columbia University Press.

Höffding, H. (1915), *Modern Philosophers and Lectures on Bergson*, trans. A. C. Mason, London, Macmillan.

Hude, H. (1989–90), *Bergson I et II*, Paris, Editions Universitaires.

Jankelevitch, V. (1959), *Henri Bergson*, Paris, PUF.

Kolakowski, L. (1985), *Bergson*, Oxford, Oxford University Press.

Lacey, A. R. (1989), *Bergson*, London, Routledge.

de Lattre, A. (1990), *Bergson: Une ontologie de la perplexité*, Paris, PUF.

Le Roy, E. (1913), *A New Philosophy: Henri Bergson*, London, Williams & Norgate; New York, Henry Holt.

Lindsay, A. D. (1911), *The Philosophy of Bergsonism*, London, J. M. Dent & Sons Ltd.

Maritain, J. (1943), *Redeeming the Time*, London, The Centenary Press.

Maritain, J. (1955), *Bergsonian Philosophy and Thomism*, trans. M. L. Andison, New York, Philosophical Library.

Moore, F. C. T. (1996), *Bergson: Thinking Backwards*, Cambridge, Cambridge University Press.

Mourelos, G. (1964), *Bergson et les niveaux de realité*, Paris, PUF.

Maoilearca, J. (1999a), *Bergson and Philosophy*, Edinburgh, Edinburgh University Press.

Maoilearca, J. (ed.) (1999b), *The New Bergson*, Manchester, Manchester University Press.

Papanicolaou, A. C. and Gunter, P. A. Y. (eds) (1987), *Bergson and Modern Thought: Towards a Unified Science*, Chur, Switzerland, Harwood Academic Press.

Robinet, A. (1965), *Bergson et les métamorphoses de la durée*, Paris, Editions Seghers.

Russell, B. (1912), 'The philosophy of Bergson', *The Monist*, 22: 3, pp. 321–47 (reprinted in *The Collected Papers of Bertrand Russell*, vol. vi, London, Routledge, 1992, pp. 313–38).

Santayana, G. (1940), *Winds of Doctrine: Studies in Contemporary Opinion*, London, Dent (first published 1913, new edition 1940).

Stephen, K. (1922), *The Misuse of Mind: A Study of Bergson's Attack on Intellectualism*, London, Kegan Paul, Trench, Trubner & Co.

Trotignon, P. (1968), *L'Idée de vie chez Bergson et la critique de la métaphysique*, Paris, PUF.

Wahl, J. (1965), *Bergson*, Cours de Sorbonne, Paris, Centre de
    Documentation Universitaire.
Worms, F. (2000), *Le Vocabulaire de Bergson*, Paris, Ellipses.

*For studies relating Bergsonism to other philosophers or taking a historical
    approach to his thought, consult:*
Alliez, E. (1998), 'On Deleuze's Bergsonism', *Discourse*, 20: 3, pp. 226–47.
Ansell Pearson, K. (2001), 'Thinking immanence: on the event of Deleuze's
    Bergsonism', in G. Genosko (ed.), *Deleuze and Guattari: Critical
    Assessments*, London and New York, Taylor & Francis, pp. 412–41.
Barrhelmy-Madaule, M. (1966), *Bergson, adversaire de Kant: Etude critique de
    la conception Bergsonienne du Kantisme*, Paris, PUF.
de Gruson, F. F. L. (1959), 'Bergson, lecteur de Kant', *Les Etudes
    Bergsoniennes*, 5, pp. 171–90.
Delattre, F. (1948), 'Bergson and Proust: accords et dissonances', *Les Etudes
    Bergsoniennes*, 1, pp. 13–127.
Gillies, M. A. (1996), *Henri Bergson and British Modernism*, Montreal, McGill-
    Queen's University Press.
Grogin, R. C. (1988), *The Bergsonian Controversy in France*, 1900–1914,
    Calgary, University of Calgary Press.
Gross, D. (1985), 'Bergson, Proust, and the revaluation of memory',
    International Philosophical Quarterly, 25: 4, pp. 369–80.
Pilkington, A. E. (1976), *Bergson and His Influence: A Reassessment*,
    Cambridge, Cambridge University Press.
Quirk, T. (1990), *Bergson and American Culture*, Chapel Hill, University of
    North Carolina Press.
Scharfstein, B.-A. (1943), *Roots of Bergson's Philosophy*, New York, Columbia
    University Press.
Sokal, A. and Bricmont, J. (1997), *Impostures Intellectuelles*, Paris, Editions
    Odile Jacob.
Soulez, P. (1989), *Bergson politique*, Paris, PUF.
Soulez, P. and Worms, F. (1997), *Bergson: Biographie*, Paris, Flammarion.
Zac, S. (1968), 'Les Themes Spinozistes dans la philosophie de Bergson', *Les
    Etudes Bergsoniennes*, 8, pp. 123–58.

For examinations of Bergsonian methodology, read:
Deleuze, G. (1995) [1990], *Negotiations*, trans. M. Joughin, New York,
    Columbia University Press.
Deleuze, G., and Guattari, F. (1994) [1991], *What Is Philosophy?*, trans. G.
    Burchill and H. Tomlinson, London, Verso.
Merleau-Ponty, M. (1964), 'Einstein and the crisis of reason', in M. Merleau-
    Ponty, *Signs*, trans. Richard C. McCleary, Evanston, Northwestern
    University Press, pp. 192–7.

Merleau-Ponty, M. (1988) [1953], *In Praise of Philosophy and Other Essays*, trans. J. Wild and J. Edie, Evanston, Northwestern University Press.

Maoilearca, J. (1995), 'Bergson's method of multiplicity', *Metaphilosophy*, 26: 3, pp. 230–59.

For discussions of ontological issues in relation to Bergsonism, read:

Ansell Pearson, K. (2001), *Philosophy and the Adventure of the Virtual*, London, Routledge.

Badiou, A. (2000), *Deleuze: The Clamor of Being*, trans. L. Burchill, Minneapolis, University of Minnesota Press.

Deleuze, G. (1996), 'L'actuel et le virtuel', in *Dialogues*, 2nd edn, Paris, Flammarion, pp. 179–85.

Deleuze, G. (1999) [1956], 'Bergson's conception of difference', trans. M. McMahon, in Maoilearca, J. (ed.), *The New Bergson*, Manchester, Manchester University Press, pp. 42–66.

Deleuze, G., and Guattari, F. (1988) [1980], *A Thousand Plateaus*, London, Athlone Press.

Gilson, Bernard (1978), *L'Individualité dans la philosophie de Bergson*, Paris, Librairie Philosophique J.Vrin.

James, W. (1909), *A Pluralistic Universe*, London, Longmans, Green & Co.

de Lattre, Alain (1990), *Bergson: Une ontologie de la perplexité*, Paris, Presses Universitaires de France.

Merleau-Ponty, M. (1964), 'Bergson in the making', in M. Merleau-Ponty, *Signs*, trans. by Richard C. McCleary, Evanston, Northwestern University Press, pp. 182–91.

Moore, A. W. (1990), *The Infinite*, London, Routledge.

Olkowski, D. (1999), *Gilles Deleuze and the Ruin of Representation*, Berkeley, University of California Press.

Paradis, B. (1991), 'Indétermination et mouvements de birfurcation chez Bergson', *Philosophie*, 32, pp. 11–40.

Rescher, N. (1996), *Process Metaphysics: An Introduction to Process Philosophy*, Albany, NY, SUNY Press.

For further information on duration and the philosophy of space and time (both Bergsonian and non-Bergsonian), consult:

Bachelard, G. (1999) [1950], *The Dialectic of Duration*, trans. M. MacAllister Jones, Manchester, Clinamen Press.

Bachelard, G. (2000), 'The instant', in R. Durie (ed.), *Time and the Instant*, Manchester, Clinamen Press, pp. 64–95.

Čapek, M. (1971), *Bergson and Modern Physics*, Dordrecht, Nijhoff.

Dale Adamson, G. (2000), 'Science and philosophy: two sides of the absolute', *Pli: The Warwick Journal of Philosophy*, 9, pp. 53–86.

Durie, R. (2000), 'Splitting time: Bergson's philosophical legacy', *Philosophy Today*, 44, pp. 152–68.

Game, A. (1991), *Undoing the Social: Towards a Deconstructive Sociology*, Milton Keynes, Open University Press.

Giroux, L. (1971), *Durée pure et temporalité: Bergson et Heidegger*, Montreal, Ballarmin.

Gunter, P. A. Y. (ed.) (1969), *Bergson and the Evolution of Physics*, Knoxville, University of Tennessee Press.

Gunter, P. A. Y. (1971), 'Bergson's theory of matter and modern cosmology', *Journal of the History of Ideas*, 32: 4, pp. 525–43.

Gunter, P. A. Y. (1991), 'Bergson and non-linear non-equilibrium thermodynamics: an application of method', *Revue Internationale de Philosophie*, 45: 2, pp. 108–22.

Heidsieck, François (1957), *Henri Bergson et la notion d'espace*, Paris, Le Circle du Livre.

Horkheimer, M. (1934), 'Zu Bergson Metaphysik der Zeit', *Zeitschrift fur Sozialforschung*, 3: 3, pp. 321–43.

Levinas, E. (1987), *Time and the Other*, trans. R. A. Cohen, Pittsburgh, Duquesne University Press.

Lewis, W. (1927), *Time and Western Man*, London, Chatto & Windus.

Murphy, T. S. (1999), 'Beneath relativity: Bergson and Bohm on absolute time', in J. Maoilearca (ed.), *The New Bergson*, Manchester, Manchester University Press, pp. 66–84.

Russell, B. (1915), 'On the experience of time', *The Monist*, 25, pp. 212–33.

Sorabji, R. (1983), *Time, Creation, and the Continuum*, London, Duckworth.

Turetzky, P. (1998), *Time*, London, Routledge.

Wiener, N. (1961) [1948], 'Newtonian and Bergsonian time', in *Cybernetics, or Control and Communication in the Animal and the Machine*, Cambridge, MA, MIT Press.

For reading in physics or the philosophy of physics that throws further light on Bergson's work, consult:

Čapek, M. (1971), *Bergson and Modern Physics*, Dordrecht, Nijhoff.

May, William E. (1970), 'The reality of matter in the metaphysics of Bergson', *International Philosophical Quarterly*, 10: 4, pp. 611–42.

Murphy, T. S. (1999), 'Beneath relativity: Bergson and Bohm on absolute time', in J. Maoilearca (ed.), *The New Bergson*, Manchester, Manchester University Press, pp. 66–84.

Serres, M. (1977), 'Boltzmann et Bergson' in *Hermes IV: Le Distribution*, Paris, Les Éditions de la Minuit.

For analyses of Bergson's approach to memory and psychology in general as well as contrasting views in the philosophy of mind, consult:

Benjamin, W. (1973), *Illuminations*, trans. H. Zohn, London, Collins.

Cariou, M. (1990), *Lectures Bergsoniennes*, Paris, PUF.

Clark, A. (1997), *Being There: Putting Brain, Body and World Together Again*, Cambridge, MA, MIT Press.

Crary, J. (1999), *Suspensions of Perception: Attention, Spectacle, and Modern Culture*, Cambridge, MA, MIT Press.

Damasio, A. (1994), *Descartes' Error: Emotion, Reason, and the Human Brain*, London, Macmillan.

Damasio, A. (1999), *The Feeling of What Happens: Body, Emotion, and the Making of Consciousness*, London, Heinemann.

Deleuze, G. (1986) [1983], *Cinema 1: The Movement-Image*, trans. H. Tomlinson and B. Habberjam, London, Athlone Press.

Deleuze, G. (1989) [1985], *Cinema 2: The Time-Image*, trans. H. Tomlinson and R. Galeta, London, Athlone Press.

Deleuze, G. (2000) [1972], *Proust and Signs: The Complete Text*, trans. R. Howard, London, Athlone Press.

Dewey, J. (1912), 'Perception and organic action', *The Journal of Philosophy, Psychology, and Scientific Methods*, 9: 24, pp. 645–68.

Elsasser, W. (1953), 'A reformulation of Bergson's theory of memory', *Philosophy of Science*, 20, pp. 7–21.

Gallois, P., and Forzy, G. (eds) (1997), *Bergson et les Neurosciences*, Le Plessis Robinson, Institut Synthelabo.

Game, A. (1991), *Undoing the Social: Towards a Deconstructive Sociology*, Milton Keynes, Open University Press.

Hyppolite, J. (1991), *Jean Hyppolite: Figures de la Pensee Philosophique*, 2 vols, Paris, Presses Universitaires de France.

Jay, M. (1993), *Downcast Eyes: The Denigration of Vision in Twentieth-Century French Thought*, Berkeley, University of California Press.

McNamara, P. (1999), *Mind and Variability: Mental Darwinism, Memory, and Self*, London, Praeger.

Meissner, W. W. (1967), 'The problem of psychophysics in Bergson's critique', *Journal of General Psychology*, 66, pp. 301–9.

Merleau-Ponty, M. (1968), *L'Union de l'âme et du corps chez Malebranche, Biran et Bergson: notes prises au cours de Maurice Merleau-Ponty a L'Ecole Normale Superieure 1947–1948*, recueillies et rédigées par Jean Deprun, Paris, Librairie Philosophique J. Vrin.

Minkowski, Eugène (1970) [1933], *Lived Time: Phenomenological and Psychopathological Studies*, trans. Nancy Metzel, Evanston, IL, Northwestern University Press.

Sartre, J.-P. (1962) [1936], *Imagination*, Ann Arbor, University of Michigan Press.

Sartre, J.-P. (1995) [1940], *The Psychology of the Imagination*, London, Routledge.

Wolff, E. (1957), 'La Théorie de la mémoire chez Bergson', *Archives de Philosophie*, 20, pp. 42–77.

Worms, F. (1997), *Introduction a 'Matèrie et mèmoire' de Bergson*, Paris, PUF.

For useful explorations of biology which either analyse or complement
  Bergson's theory of the élan vital, consult:
Adolphe, L. (1952), 'Bergson et L'Elan Vital', *Les Etudes Bergsoniennes*, 3,
  pp. 81–138.
Ansell Pearson, K. (1999), *Germinal Life: The Difference and Repetition of*
  Deleuze, London, Routledge.
Burwick, F., and Douglass, P. (eds) (1992), *The Crisis in Modernism:*
  Bergsonism and the Vitalist Controversy, Cambridge, Cambridge University
  Press.
Canguilhem, G. (1943), 'Commentaire au troisième chapitre de *L'Evolution*
  Creatrice, Bulletin de la Faculté Lettres de Strasbourg, 21, pp. 126–43.
Grasse, P. (1977), *Evolution of Living Organisms: Evidence for a New Theory of*
  Transformation, New York, Academic Press.
Kampis, G. (1993), 'Creative evolution', *World Futures*, 38, pp. 131–7.
Miquel, P. A. (1997), *Le Problème de la nouveauté dans l'évolution du vivant:*
  Dialogue entre Bergson et la biologie contemporaine, Villeneuve d'Ascq,
  Presses Universitaires du Septentrion.
Monod, J. (1971), *Chance and Necessity*, trans. A. Wainhouse, New York,
  Knopf.
Wolsky, M., and Wolsky, A. (1992), 'Bergson's vitalism in the light of modern
  biology', in F. Burwick and P. Douglass (eds), *The Crisis in Modernity:*
  Bergsonism and the Vitalist Controversy, Cambridge, Cambridge University
  Press, pp. 153–70.

For investigations of Bergsonian epistemology, especially the concept of
  intuition, consult:
Husson, L. (1947), *L'Intellectualisme de Bergson*, Paris, PUF.
Milet, J. (1974), *Bergson et le calcul infinitesimal*, Paris, PUF.
Olkowski, D. (1999), *Gilles Deleuze and the Ruin of Representation*, Berkeley,
  University of California Press.
Pariente, J. C. (1973), *Le Langage et l'individuel*, Paris, Armand Colin.

For works investigating Bergson's ideas in ethics and the philosophy of
  religion, consult:
Foubert, J. (1973), 'Mystique plotinienne. Mystique bergsonienne', *Les Etudes*
  Bergsoniennes, 10, pp. 7–73.
Gallagher, Idealla J. (1970), *Morality in Evolution: The Moral Philosophy of Henri*
  Bergson, The Hague, Martinus Nijhoff.
Gouhier, H. (1961), *Bergson et le Christ des évangiles*, Paris, Vrin.
Hude, H. (1989–90), *Bergson I et II*, Paris, Editions Universitaires.
Kennedy, E. (1987), *Freedom and the Open Society: Henri Bergson's*
  Contribution to Political Philosophy, New York and London, Garland.
Levinas, E. (1987), *Time and the Other*, trans. R. A. Cohen, Pittsburgh,
  Duquesne University Press.

Levinas, E. (1998), *Entre Nous*, trans. M. B. Smith and B. Harshav, London, Athlone Press.
Levinas, E. (1999), *Alterity and Transcendence*, trans. M. B. Smith, London, Athlone Press.

Other texts referred to in the Introduction
Davies, P. (1995), *About Time*, Harmondsworth, Penguin.
Deleuze, G. and Guattari, F. (1994) [1991], *What Is Philosophy?*, trans. Graham Burchill and Hugh Tomlinson, London, Verso.
Dennett, D. C. (1991), *Consciousness Explained*, London, Allen Lane.
Dennett, D. C. (1996), *Kinds of Minds: Towards an Understanding of Consciousness*, London, Weidenfeld & Nicolson.
Durie, R. (1999), 'Introduction' in Bergson (2000), pp. vii–xxiii.
Einstein, A. (1999), *Relativity: The Special Theory and General Theory*, London, Routledge.
Gunter, P. A. Y. (1995), 'Bergson's philosophy of education', *Educational Theory*, 45, pp. 379–94.
Hartshorne, C. (1987), 'Bergson's aesthetic creationism compared to Whitehead's', in A. C. Papanicolaou and P. A. Y. Gunter (eds), *Bergson and Modern Thought: Towards a Unified Science*, Chur, Switzerland, Harwood Academic Press, pp. 369–82.
Kant, I. (1952), *Critique of Pure Reason*, trans. Norman Kemp Smith, London, Macmillan.
Khandker, Wahida (ed.) (2004), *Lives of the Real: Bergsonian Perspectives*, special; edition of *Pli: The Warwick Journal of Philosophy*, Vol. 15.
Kolkman, Michael, and Michael Vaughan, (eds) (2007), *Henri Bergson's Creative Evolution 100 Years Later*, special issue of *Substance*, Vol. 36, No. 3.
Linstead, Stephen, and John Ó Maoilearca, (eds) (March 2003), *Bergson*, special issue of *Culture and Organization*, Vol. 9, No. 1.
Maoilearca, John, and Stephen Linstead (eds) (January 2004), Bergson Now, special issue of the *Journal of British Society for Phenomenology*, Vol. 35, No.1.
Niess, N. J. (1956), *Julien Benda*, Ann Arbor, University of Michigan Press.
Russell, B. (1922) [1914], *Our Knowledge of the External World*, London, Allen & Unwin.

Index

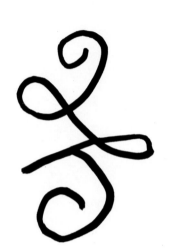